THE FLUME, BEFORE THE BOULDER FELL
The Boulder (shown lodged between the Walls) fell into the Stream during a Storm and Flood in June, 1883

CHRONICLES

— OF THE —

WHITE MOUNTAINS

BY

Frederick W. Kilbourne

HERITAGE BOOKS
2013

HERITAGE BOOKS
AN IMPRINT OF HERITAGE BOOKS, INC.

Books, CDs, and more—Worldwide

For our listing of thousands of titles see our website
at
www.HeritageBooks.com

A Facsimile Reprint
Published 2013 by
HERITAGE BOOKS, INC.
Publishing Division
100 Railroad Ave. #104
Westminster, Maryland 21157

Library of Congress Cataloging in Publication Data
Kilbourne, Frederick Wilkinson, 1872 –
  Chronicles of the White Mountains.
  Reprint of the 1916 ed. published by
Houghton-Mifflin, New York.
  1. White Mountains -- History. I. Title.
F41.3.K48   1978   974.2'2   78-15826

Front cover: Mount Washington from the Conway Road
Back cover: The Descent from Mt. Washington
Illustrations from *Picturesque America*, 1872

— Publisher's Notice —
In reprints such as this, it is often not possible to remove blemishes from the original. We feel the contents of this book warrant its reissue despite these blemishes and hope you will agree and read it with pleasure.

International Standard Book Numbers
Paperbound: 978-1-55613-053-3
Clothbound: 978-0-7884-6967-1

IN THE WHITE MOUNTAINS

Mountains in whose vast shadows live great names,
On whose firm pillars rest mysterious dawns,
And sunsets that redream the apocalypse;
A world of billowing green that, veil on veil,
Turns a blue mist and melts in lucent skies;
A silent world, save for slow waves of wind,
Or sudden, hollow clamor of huge rocks
Beaten by valleyed waters manifold; —
Airs that to breathe is life and joyousness;
Days dying into music; nights whose stars
Shine near, and large, and lustrous; these, O these,
These are for memory to life's ending hour.

RICHARD WATSON GILDER

PREFACE

ALLEN H. BENT, in the Introduction to his admirable *Bibliography of the White Mountains*, published in 1911, makes the doubtless somewhat surprising remark that "the White Mountains... have had more written about them, probably, than any other mountains, the Alps alone excepted." When one seeks an explanation for this circumstance, that a district of so limited area and mountains of such relatively low elevation have received an apparently disproportionate amount of literary attention, one may find it, in part at least, as pointed out by the author [1] of an article printed now nearly twenty-five years ago, in the facts that these mountains are the only considerable group worthy of the name of mountains in the northeastern United States and that they are, with the exception of the until recently almost unknown and comparatively inaccessible Southern Appalachians of North Carolina, the only highlands of scenic consequence in the eastern part of the country. The facts just named, coupled with that of the nearness of the White Mountains to the North Atlantic coast and their consequent accessibility to the people of the earliest settled portion of the United States and to European visitors to America as well, early rendered them

[1] William Howe Downes in "The Literature of the White Mountains," *New England Magazine*, August, 1891.

PREFACE

widely famed for their scenery and thus drew to them the attention of the makers of books.

If it should be inquired, further, why these hills, so insignificant as compared with the Rockies, for instance, should have been made so much of and should still retain so much of men's interest, it may be adduced that as respects mountains in general scenic attractiveness depends far more upon other considerations than that of altitude for its appeal and that the White Mountains are a striking case in support of this opinion, for it is the testimony of travelers that the relative inferiority in height of the New England hills does not detract from their grandeur and beauty or cause them to lose interest for those familiar with loftier peaks and ranges. Indeed, it is doubtful if any other mountains of anything like their altitude are more impressive or stupendous in aspect, and, as to the character of the landscape views they offer for the pleasure of the beholder, it is enough to say that they prove the truth of Humboldt's dictum — "The prospect from minor mountains is far more interesting than that from extreme elevations, where the scenery of the adjacent country is lost and confounded by the remoteness of its situation." At any rate, the appeal of the White Hills to the imagination of men has always been strong, and therein lies the chief reason for the existence of so many books about them.

In view of this fact of there being so voluminous a literature on the subject, the preparation of another volume to be added to such an apparent

PREFACE

plethora would seem at first blush to be, if not an absolutely gratuitous performance, at least a work of supererogation. The only circumstance that may be brought forward to justify the undertaking of such a project must be the notion that the book fills a gap — occupies, as it were, a field that is not now cultivated and that has been for a long time neglected — and thus supplies a need. Such, in any event, is my belief, and it is to the historical side of the subject that I allude.

Let me name and briefly characterize the principal books on the White Mountains and thereby achieve, if I can, the double purpose of demonstrating that there is such a lack in this literature as I have just maintained to exist, and of acknowledging some of the sources of the information I shall present later on.

The first extended and detailed descriptions of the scenery of the region are those which are to be found in volume II of President Dwight's *Travels in New England and New York*, published in 1821. The Mountains were first descriptively dealt with to such an extent as to be the exclusive subject of a separate volume, by the botanist William Oakes, whose *Scenery of the White Mountains*, with sixteen lithographic plates, appeared in 1848. The scenic beauties of the region were delineated and interpreted in poetry and poetic prose by the genius of Starr King, whose *The White Hills; their Legends, Landscape and Poetry*, originally published in 1859–60, is a classic of mountain literature and will doubtless ever remain the best book of its kind about the

PREFACE

Mountains. The Reverend Julius H. Ward's *The White Mountains; a Guide to their Interpretation* (1890[1]), is another work, to quote from the author's preface, "written in illustration of the modern interpretation of Nature which has been taught us by Emerson and Wordsworth and Ruskin." In this volume of Ward's, the scenery of different localities is described and the emotions evoked and thoughts suggested by mountain peaks or groups and other scenic features of the district are presented. Samuel Adams Drake, in his *The Heart of the White Mountains, their Legend and Scenery*, with illustrations by W. Hamilton Gibson (1881), not only describes the region, but gives a wealth of legendary, historical, and other information. Mr. Gibson's pictures are, it may be remarked in passing, of high merit, giving, as they do perhaps better than any others, an adequate idea of the height, massiveness, and precipitousness of the mountain walls, as well as of the beauties of landscape and of forest scenery.

The scientific aspects of the region have been thoroughly studied and extensively set forth in a multitude of books and articles written by a host of trained and competent scholars and observers, including Oakes, Tuckerman, Hitchcock, Huntington, Agassiz, Guyot, Scudder, Slosson, and Emerton, while the natural history has been amply and well taken care of in the books of the late Frank Bolles, the late Bradford Torrey, Winthrop Packard, and others.

The field of the guide-book is fairly well covered

[1] Third edition, 1896.

PREFACE

by Chisholm's *White Mountain Guide-Book*, prepared originally by the late M. F. Sweetser. The same writer's *The White Mountains; a Handbook for Travelers*, which embodies the results of thorough and extensive explorations made in 1875, was first published in 1876 and was last revised down to 1896, the year before its editor's death. It is the most complete local guide I have ever seen, and revision to date is all that is needed to make it still of exceptional value. Baedeker's *United States* contains an accurate and comprehensive section on the Mountains. The Appalachian Mountain Club published in 1907 the first part of a valuable *Guide to the Paths and Camps in the White Mountains*. Part II will be published this year.

The history of the White Mountains is literary ground that has been for the most part untilled for many years. Frank H. Burt, editor of *Among the Clouds* in succession to his father, prints regularly a valuable chronology (copyrighted) in his paper, and in his booklet *Mount Washington*, published in 1904, he has given a summary of the history of the chief peak and various items of historical information about the Mountains generally. Sweetser's *White Mountains* contains an abundance of historical material, mainly in the form of notes. The principal historical works on the Mountains are more than half a century old and are out of print. Lucy Crawford's *The History of the White Mountains from the First Settlement of Upper Coos and Pequaket* was first published in 1846; J. H. Spaulding's *Historical Relics of the White Mountains* appeared in 1855; and

PREFACE

Benjamin G. Willey's *Incidents in White Mountain History* dates also from 1855.[1]

None of these is a systematic chronicle of events. The first is not a history, as it purports to be, but is in reality mostly an autobiography of the pioneer Ethan Allen Crawford, apparently dictated in large part by him to his wife, the nominal author. It is full of interesting information, simply and often quaintly set down, about the early days. The second is a very miscellaneous collection of Indian legends, old traditions, and brief relations of early events and incidents, some of which were important and many trivial, with accounts of some later occurrences of which the author had personal knowledge. The last is the most serious attempt to write the history of the district. It presents, without much sense of proportion, a great body of information concerning the pioneer days in the region, much of it in the form of anecdotes illustrating backwoods life, and is especially full in its account of the destruction of the author's brother's family and in Indian history and traditions.

It is this last long unoccupied and never adequately cultivated field that I have attempted to till, with the result that follows and constitutes the body of this work.

The existence of Mr. Bent's *Bibliography*[2] renders

[1] The date of publication is 1856. It was reissued, with minor revisions and under the title, *History of the White Mountains*, by Frederick Thompson in 1870.

[2] The Society of American Foresters has published an extensive and valuable *Bibliography of the Southern Appalachian and White Mountain Regions*, compiled by Helen E. Stockbridge. It dates also from 1911.

PREFACE

superfluous the appending of any to this book. My indebtedness is to many writers. Much information was obtained also from correspondents. To all I make grateful acknowledgment. I have examined many guide-books, books of travel, newspapers (particularly *Among the Clouds* and the *White Mountain Echo*), and other sources. Specific obligations, not hereinbefore acknowledged by naming books, will appear in place. Pains have been taken to verify quotations and statements by going to the original sources whenever I could obtain access to them. I have purposely refrained from adding footnotes unless some additional information contributed or sidelight thrown thereby seemed to warrant them. Mere references to the places or authorities cited I have omitted, as interruptions to the reading and affectations of scholarliness.

A word, in conclusion, as to the guiding principle followed in selecting subjects for illustration. As this is a work dealing more especially with man's associations with the region and his modifications of the appearance of it, the pictures presented should have to do mostly with human works. Whenever a picture combining scenic with historical interest could be used, the idea of doing so was kept in mind, but, in general, in the presentation of illustrations, emphasis has been laid, properly, upon the historical side of this matter.

CONTENTS

INTRODUCTION xxiii

I. INDIAN LEGEND AND HISTORY 1

II. EARLY EXPLORERS 17

III. FIRST SETTLEMENTS AND SETTLERS: I. THE TOWNS 39

IV. FIRST SETTLEMENTS AND SETTLERS: II. THE SOLITARY PLACES — THE WILLEY DISASTER 70

V. FURTHER DISCOVERIES AND EXPLORATIONS — SOME NOTED AMERICAN VISITORS OF THE EARLY DAYS 101

VI. SOME FOREIGN VISITORS AND THEIR ACCOUNTS OF THEIR TOURS OF THE WHITE MOUNTAINS 139

VII. THE EARLY HOTELS AND THE BEGINNINGS OF THE REGION AS A SUMMER RESORT . . 154

VIII. THE POETS AND PAINTERS IN THE WHITE HILLS 175

IX. THE LATER SCIENTIFIC EXPLORATIONS OF THE MOUNTAINS 204

X. THE COMING OF THE RAILROADS — THEIR LATER EXTENSIONS 220

XI. THE HOTELS ON MOUNT WASHINGTON — THE CARRIAGE ROAD AND THE MOUNT WASHINGTON RAILWAY — HOTELS AND SHELTERS ON OTHER SUMMITS 229

CONTENTS

XII. SOME NOTEWORTHY WHITE MOUNTAIN "CHARACTERS" 259

XIII. CASUALTIES ON THE PRESIDENTIAL RANGE — THE TERRIBLE EXPERIENCE OF DR. BALL — SOME DESTRUCTIVE LANDSLIDES . . 267

XIV. WINTER ASCENTS OF MOUNT WASHINGTON — THE WINTER OCCUPATION OF MOUNT MOOSILAUKE AND OF MOUNT WASHINGTON — THE U.S. SIGNAL SERVICE ON MOUNT WASHINGTON 305

XV. LATER HOTELS 331

XVI. EARLY TRAILS AND PATH-BUILDERS — THE APPALACHIAN MOUNTAIN CLUB AND ITS WORK IN THE WHITE MOUNTAINS . . 345

XVII. THE GREAT FIRE ON MOUNT WASHINGTON — OTHER RECENT EVENTS OF INTEREST . 360

XVIII. THE LUMBER INDUSTRY IN THE WHITE MOUNTAINS — THE PERIL OF THE FORESTS — THE WHITE MOUNTAIN NATIONAL FOREST — OTHER RESERVATIONS 377

XIX. THE CHANGES IN THE CHARACTER OF WHITE MOUNTAIN TRAVEL AND BUSINESS IN RECENT YEARS 405

INDEX 411

ILLUSTRATIONS

THE FLUME BEFORE THE BOULDER FELL   *Frontispiece*
    From a photograph by F. G. Weller

THE DEATH OF CHOCORUA 12
    From an engraving by G. W. Hatch after the painting by Thomas Cole

THE NOTCH HOUSE 86
    From an engraving by J. Cousen in Willis's *American Scenery*, after a drawing by W. H. Bartlett

THE WILLEY HOUSE 90
    From an engraving by E. Benjamin in Willis's *American Scenery*, after a drawing by W. H. Bartlett

THE OLD MAN OF THE MOUNTAIN 102
    From a photograph by Blair, Bretton Woods, N. H.

THE OLD MOUNT CRAWFORD HOUSE AT BEMIS . 158
    From Starr King's *The White Hills*, Estes & Lauriat, Boston, 1887

THE FRANCONIA NOTCH, WITH THE LAFAYETTE HOUSE 166
    From a lithograph by J. H. Bufford, Boston, in Oakes's *White Mountain Scenery*, after a drawing by Isaac Sprague

THE OLD PROFILE HOUSE, OPENED 1853, CLOSED 1905 170
    From a photograph by F. G. Weller

THE FLUME HOUSE 170
    An old view showing the house when smaller than at present

A VIEW NEAR CONWAY 192
    From an engraving by Fenner, Sears & Co., after a painting by Thomas Cole

ILLUSTRATIONS

THE DOUBLE GATE OF CRAWFORD NOTCH . . 226
    From a photograph by Blair

HALFWAY HOUSE ON THE CARRIAGE ROAD . . 234
    From a photograph by the Shorey Studio, Gorham, N. H.

JACOB'S LADDER, MOUNT WASHINGTON RAILWAY . 240
    Showing the early type of locomotive with vertical boiler
    From a heliotype in M. F. Sweetser's *Views in the White Mountains*

SUMMIT HOUSE AND OBSERVATORY, MOUNT WASHINGTON, ABOUT 1895 250
    From a photograph by Peter Eddy, Fabyan, N. H.

THE NEW SUMMIT HOUSE ON MOUNT WASHINGTON, ERECTED AND OPENED IN 1915 250
    From a photograph by the Shorey Studio

SUMMIT OF MOUNT WASHINGTON IN 1854: TIP-TOP HOUSE, OLD SUMMIT HOUSE, AND FIRST OBSERVATORY 256
    From Willey's *Incidents in White Mountain History*

TIP-TOP HOUSE ON MOUNT MOOSILAUKE . . . 256
    From a copyright photograph by F. C. Jackson, Warren, N. H., 1912

THE HOUSE THAT JACK BUILT 264
    From a photograph by Peter Eddy

CURTIS MONUMENT, LAKE OF THE CLOUDS, AND A. M. C. HUT 278
    From a photograph by the Shorey Studio

CLIMBING MOUNT WASHINGTON IN WINTER . . 306
    From a photograph by the Shorey Studio

OBSERVER, SUMMIT OF MOUNT WASHINGTON, ABOUT 1875 316
    From a photograph by B. W. Kilburn

ILLUSTRATIONS

THE SUMMIT HOUSE IN WINTER, ABOUT 1875 . 316
    From a photograph by B. W. Kilburn

THE FIRST GLEN HOUSE 338
    From a heliotype in M. F. Sweetser's *Views in the White Mountains*

THE SECOND GLEN HOUSE, 1885–1893 . . . 338
    From the Glen House Book, 1889

THE MOUNT WASHINGTON HOTEL, BRETTON WOODS 342
    From a photograph by Blair

THE MOUNT PLEASANT TRAIL 350
    From a photograph by Blair

A. M. C. HUTS ON MOUNT MADISON 350
    From a photograph by the Shorey Studio

A. M. C. HUT ON MOUNT MONROE 354
    From a photograph by the Shorey Studio

MOUNT MONROE HUT INTERIOR 354
    From a photograph by the Shorey Studio

THE FIRE ON MOUNT WASHINGTON AS SEEN FROM
    GORHAM 364
    From a photograph by Guy L. Shorey

LOST RIVER 372
    From a photograph

MAP OF THE WHITE MOUNTAIN NATIONAL FOREST 398

ROAD AND TRAIL MAP OF THE WHITE MOUNTAIN
    REGION . . . . . 436 - 437

INTRODUCTION

SEVENTY miles in an air line from the Atlantic, northwesterly from Portland, Maine, lies the grand and beautiful group of stern and lofty hills, with rugged valleys and gentle intervales interspersed, which is called by the commonplace appellation of the "White Mountains," or, sometimes, especially in literary use, the "White Hills." This name is applied both to the entire group (made by some to include, besides the New Hampshire ranges and peaks, the neighboring hills in western Maine), and also, specifically, to the range containing the highest peaks, now commonly designated, for obvious reasons, the "Presidential Range."

In the nomenclature of physical geography these northern hills are termed monadnocks, a name given to more or less isolated residual elevations composed of rock which has resisted the general wearing-down of the former plateau, of which the heights formed a part, to the present peneplain. Geologically, the White Mountains belong to the older or crystalline belt of the Appalachian system and are made up of ancient metamorphic rocks, chiefly gneisses with a core of granite forming the highest portion. The area of the region is about 812,000 acres.

The epithet "White" alludes, of course, to the appearance of the summits and seems most appropriate in the six months, more or less, when they

INTRODUCTION

are covered with snow. The winter dress of the Mountains, which is often worn temporarily in other seasons, would seem to furnish the most probable explanation of the origin of their name, for which the early navigators along the coast, to whom they were a landmark, appear to be responsible. This very plausible supposition becomes, however, upon investigation more and more improbable, the preponderance of evidence in the end inclining the scale in favor of the view that the Mountains are so called from their white or whitish-gray aspect when seen from a distance,[1] which appearance is due partly to the bare grayish rocks of the treeless summits, but chiefly to atmospheric conditions. The question is not one, it would seem, that can be definitively settled. Indeed, it is not one of great moment; but, nevertheless, I have thought it a subject of sufficient interest to justify a bringing together of such references bearing on it as I have been able to collect. From these statements, the reader may, if he will, form his own conclusion, with the firm assurance that, whichever way his mental vote may be cast, no one can declare him to be absolutely wrong. The regrettable thing in connection with this matter of the name of the Mountains is not, in any case, the uncertainty as to its origin, but is, rather, the unpleasing certainty that a commonplace and undistinctive appellation has been fastened upon them for good and all.

[1] On the side of Samuel Lewis's map of 1794 in the following note: "N. B. The White Hills appear many leagues off at Sea like White Clouds; just rising above the Horizon."

INTRODUCTION

Just when the White Mountains received their present designation is another subject of inquiry that cannot be positively determined. The earliest name I have found is that of "the Christall hill," applied to the highest peak or to the main range. This occurs in a passage in Christopher Levett's *A Voyage into New-England*, published in 1628. Now, as the region had not then been visited by white men, this name must, it is evident, allude to the appearance of the summits as affected by distance and the atmosphere. The fact of the earlier occurrence, also, of this appellation negatives the explanation of the origin of it given in Belknap's *History of New Hampshire* on the authority of Hubbard's manuscript History of New England. The passage in Belknap's work refers to the explorers of 1642, the first white visitors, and runs as follows: "They had great expectation of finding precious stones on these mts.; and something resembling crystal being picked up, was sufficient to give them the name of the *crystal-hills*." Whatever the origin of this name, which appears to have been the common one in the earlier part of the seventeenth century, it antedates, as its occurrence in Levett's narrative testifies, the connection of Darby Field with the Mountains, and so cannot have been given to them by him, as some writers say. Governor Winthrop, recording in his journal Field's ascent of the future Mount Washington, speaks of it as "the white hill," and when again mentioning the event uses the plural of the same name.[1] The present designation first appears in

[1] The first passage is quoted in full on page 20. The second be-

INTRODUCTION

print as a distinctive name, it is believed, in Josselyn's *New England's Rarities Discovered*, a work published in 1672.[1]

Drake, who holds strongly to the opinion that the name of the Mountains does not allude to the presence of snow on them, declares that "the early writers succeed only imperfectly in accounting for this phenomenon [the white appearance of the summits], which for six months of the year at least," he says, "has no connection whatever with the snows that cover the highest peaks only from the middle of October to the middle of April, a period during which few navigators of the sixteenth and seventeenth centuries visited our shores, or, indeed, ventured to put to sea at all." He adduces quotations directly denying the theory he is opposing, from two eighteenth-century writers, one of whom, William Douglass, says [2] positively: "They ['the White Hills, or rather mountains'] are called White, not from their being continually covered with snow, but because they are bald a-top, producing no trees or brush, and covered with a whitish stone or shingle"; while the other, the celebrated ranger, Major Robert Rogers, states [3] that the Mountains are "so called from their

gins, "Mention is made before of the white hills, discovered by one Darby Field."

[1] The passage is quoted on page 23.
[2] In his *A Summary . . . of the First Planting, . . . and Present State of the British Settlements in North America* (1748–53).
[3] In his *A Concise Account of America* (1765). Rogers says further: "I cannot learn that any person was ever on the top of these mountains. I have been told by the Indians that they have often attempted it in vain, by reason of the change of air they met with, which I am inclined to believe, having ascended them myself till the alteration

INTRODUCTION

appearance, which is much like snow, consisting, as is generally supposed, of a white flint, from which the reflection of the sun is very brilliant and dazzling."

In support of the other view may be cited the statement of Josselyn [1] as to the presence of snow on the Mountains, which he evidently regards as the reason for their name, and the following remark of Belknap in this connection: "During this period, of nine or ten months [end of October or beginning of November to July] the mountains exhibit more or less of that bright appearance from which they are denominated white ... it may with certainty be concluded, that the whiteness of them is wholly caused by snow, and not by any other white substance, for in fact, there is none." [2]

The most extended discussion of the subject of the whiteness of these mountains and its cause that I have come across in my reading is in volume III of the English writer Edward Augustus Kendall's *Travels through the Northern Parts of the United States in the Years 1807 and 1808*, a work published in 1809. Of the twenty pages devoted to an account of his tour through the White Mountains, eight are entirely given up to this topic, of which he also speaks briefly in another, and earlier, chapter.

After quoting Belknap's conclusion, just given,

---

of air was very perceptible, and even then I had not advanced half-way up; the valleys below were then concealed from me by clouds."
[1] See page 23.
[2] Belknap says in another place: "Some writers, who have attempted to give an account of these mountains, have ascribed the whiteness of them to shining rocks, or a kind of white moss."

INTRODUCTION

and expressing the opinion that the historian relied "on the statements of persons very incompetent to make such as are to the purpose," he goes on to say that, while he saw the Mountains only when they were covered with snow, he was assured that they appear white at all seasons of the year, and he says further, that he had himself observed a similar phenomenon elsewhere. As authority for this fact of the perennial white appearance of the New Hampshire hills, he cites the result of the observations of "the younger Rosebrook, in Briton's Woods," who was frequently employed as a guide and invariably, when performing this service, questioned as to this matter by those whom he was conducting. Rosebrook's statement was that, when the snow is melted, the summits still appear white when seen from a considerable distance, but not when viewed from nearer points, and that he was puzzled to account for this, the explanation that it is due to moss not being satisfactory to him. That this condition must be true of the White Mountains and that it is not peculiar to them was shown, it seemed to the traveler, by the remark made to him by a Vermont farmer with respect to the mountains west of Lake Champlain as seen from his side of the lake: "Some of their tops were white all the year round, even when the snow was gone." Mr. Kendall was finally, when visiting the St. Lawrence country, enabled to settle the question to his own satisfaction, as by his own observations he made sure of the fact and discovered the explanation of it. He had opportunity, while traveling there, to pass over some of the sum-

INTRODUCTION

mits west of the river, which he observed to exhibit the same phenomenon and which he found to be composed of the same kind of rock as the White Mountains. His investigations in the Laurentians led him to the conclusion that the white appearance of these and other high mountains like them is due to the reflection of the sunlight from the rock when the atmosphere is rare and the distance is sufficiently great to permit of only the high bare portions being seen. In producing this effect, he affirms, the color of the rock is of minor importance, the chief requisite being that the rock should be bare and of a density of composition adapted for reflecting the rays of light. So much for the question as to why the White Mountains are "white" and have their name.

When we come to the perhaps more important, and doubtless more interesting, subject of Indian names of the Mountains, we are again on uncertain ground. Several of such designations of the principal range have come to us, vouched for by various authorities. Belknap speaks of the name "Agiocochook," which occurs in a reduced form as "Agiochook," as having been applied to what is now known as the "Presidential Range." This name Mr. Drake found in print as early as 1736 in the narrative [1] of John Gyles's captivity published in Boston in that year. It is also recorded by Schoolcraft, who says it is plural in form.

As to its meaning, which the Reverend Edward

---

[1] "These White Hills, at the head of the Penobscot River, are by the Indians said to be much higher than those called Agiockochook, above Saco," says Captain Gyles.

INTRODUCTION

Ballard thought to be "The Place of the Great Spirit of the Forest," Dr. J. Hammond Trumbull's opinion is that the word Captain Gyles imperfectly represented in English syllables is Algonquin for "at the mountains on that side" or "over yonder." As to the fanciful interpretations, such as that given above, or that of another writer, "The Place of the Storm Spirit," Dr. Trumbull affirms that there is no element of any Algonquin word meaning "great," "spirit," "forest," "storm," or "abode," or any combination of the meaning of any two of these words, in "Agiocochook." The shortened form of this name, which occurs in the early ballad on the death of Captain Lovewell, has been adopted by Whittier, Edna Dean Proctor, and other authors as a poetical name for Mount Washington.

Another Indian name was communicated to the Corresponding Secretary of the Massachusetts Historical Society by the Reverend Timothy Alden, afterwards founder and president of Allegheny College, in a letter dated 1806, which was published in the *Collections* of the Society in 1814. "I have lately been informed," he says, "that the *White Hills* were called by one of the eastern tribes, I cannot ascertain which, *Waumbekketmethna*. I have spelt it, as I think all aboriginal names ought to be, as pronounced. *Waumbekket* signifies *white*, and *methna*, mountains, as I am told." This name is the only Indian name for the White Hills that, according to Drake, bears internal evidence of genuineness. That writer says that it "easily resolves itself into the Kennebec-Abnaki waubeghiket-amadinar, 'white

INTRODUCTION

greatest mountain.'" "It is very probable, however," he says further, "that this synthesis is a mere translation, by an Indian, of the English 'White Mountains.' I have never, myself, succeeded in obtaining this name from the modern Abnakis." Schoolcraft, commenting on "Waumbek," says that it is "a word, which in some of the existing dialects of the Algonquin, is pronounced Waubik, that is, White Rock." In the form "Waumbek Methna," or sometimes still further shortened to "Waumbek," this name, which has been given the fanciful interpretation of "Mountains with Snowy Foreheads," or the like, has also been much used by the poets. Would that it might have been the geographical name also!

Still another alleged Indian appellation of the Mountains, which is mentioned by a number of writers, may be set down here for the sake of having the record complete. This is the harsh-sounding combination of words, "Kan Ran Vugarty," said to mean "The Continued Likeness of a Gull," and having, obviously, in common with the others, reference to the white appearance of the summits.

Among these hills rise four great New England rivers, the Connecticut, the Merrimac, the Androscoggin, and the Saco. As the source, then, of these very important elements in the existence and development of New England's industry and commerce, the White Mountains have a more than local significance, all of the States of this section, saving Rhode Island, being thus directly affected by them. As a summer playground and region of scenic beauty, they have acquired a reputation more than nation-

INTRODUCTION

wide. The district, indeed, was the first to receive that rather often applied sobriquet of American Mountain regions, "The Switzerland of America," Philip Carrigain, once secretary of state of New Hampshire, in his state map [1] of 1816, bestowing that, in this instance perhaps somewhat far-fetched, appellative upon the hills of his native State.

This northern upland, which it is my purpose to treat on the historical side only, has not, it must be admitted at the outset, been the theater of great events. No wars or battles have been fought there; no great political movements have been initiated or carried on there; indeed, the region is not a political entity and "White Mountains" is only a geographical expression. It has not even been to any great extent the scene of thrilling adventures with the Indians. Little, in fact, of a nature to make the region interesting historically, in the usual connotation of that term, has occurred during the nearly three centuries it has been known to us. And so the materials of the historian of the White Mountains are meager, especially as compared with the data available to the historian of a region that has an eventful history, such as, for instance, the Lake George and Lake Champlain locality, and this dearth is not altogether encouraging to one who would fain have an interesting story to tell.

---

[1] The text on the side of the map contained these words: "With regard to the face of the country, its features are striking and picturesque. The natural scenery of mountains of greater elevation than any others [!] in the UNITED STATES; of lakes, of cataracts, of vallies [sic] furnishes a profusion of the sublime and beautiful. It may be called the Switzerland of AMERICA."

INTRODUCTION

It must be, therefore, of peaceful and comparatively uneventful pioneer life in a district remote from the centers of population, industrial life, and civilization, and of the unsung heroisms of hardy men in contending with the forces of nature, that the first part of the story will largely consist.

There will be something of interest also, I venture to think, in such chronicles as I shall set down of the small beginnings of the region as a vacation playground and of its great growth as such when the beautiful scenery and health-giving air had become known to a nation in course of time sufficiently increased in population and possessed of leisure, wealth, and facilities to travel and to maintain summer resorts.

Besides these main events of exploration, settlement, and development as a district for summer rest and recreation, there have occurred in the region from time to time many minor incidents, as to which, as well as to the matters just mentioned, I have assumed frequenters of the Mountains and even occasional visitors to them may desire to inform themselves. Acting, at any rate, on this assumption, I have undertaken in the ensuing pages the pleasant task of culling out and recording the more important occurrences. These events and incidents, then, form the materials of this chronicle.

CHRONICLES OF THE WHITE MOUNTAINS

I

INDIAN LEGEND AND HISTORY

LITTLE can be told of the character and life of the Indians who inhabited or frequented this region during the prehistoric ages comprising the period before the coming of the white man. Investigators have not been able to ascertain much about them, and consequently the information that has been accumulated as compared with that gathered concerning the Indians of southern New England, who were, after the white man's advent, in close contact with the settlements, is comparatively meager and indefinite. Even the names and relationships of the northern Indians are by no means certain.

That powerful tribes once lived in and roamed over the valleys shadowed by these hills, not only does tradition tell us, but also remains bear witness. Of their encampments and favorite retreats, however, there is lack of adequate knowledge. By the time that the settlers had begun to penetrate to this region the aborigines had been so reduced by pestilences and wars that those who were then living were probably but a very small fraction of their former number. According to what seems to be the most reliable information, the tribes inhabiting the

THE WHITE MOUNTAINS

foothills and intervales of the White Mountains more especially were the Sokokis on the Saco and the Arosagunticooks, or Anasagunticooks, on the Androscoggin. The former were divided into numerous branches, of which the Ossipees and Pequawkets (or Pigwackets) — especially the latter, who by some are identified with the Sokokis as a whole — were the most prominent. To the south in the valley of the Merrimac was the country of the Pennacooks, under whose sachem were all the clans occupying the territory now constituting New Hampshire, while to the west at the junction of the Connecticut and Ammonoosuc Rivers were the Coosucs, a small band, probably a branch of the Pennacooks. These tribes all belonged to the Abnaki group of the great Algonquian family. They were savages of a not very high type of culture, who relied for their subsistence mainly on the results of their hunting and fishing, their agriculture being confined to the cultivation of maize on a limited scale. They built conical houses or wigwams and lived in villages, which were in some cases inclosed with palisades. Such remains, therefore, as we find of their occupancy of the region are of the most primitive kind. On the banks of the rivers and near the ponds or lakes traces of their encampments are frequently discovered. In some of the intervales corn hills [1] used to be seen, and there were also here and there evidences of the destruction of trees by girdling. In

---

[1] "The remains of their fields are still visible in many places; these are not extensive, and the hills which they made about their corn stalks were small." (Belknap.)

INDIAN LEGEND AND HISTORY

Conway, pipes and pieces of kettles made of a soft, easily cut earthenware have often been found.

In Ossipee, near the lake, is a large monumental mound about fifty feet in diameter and ten feet high, from which skeletons buried with the face downward, tomahawks, and other relics have been taken, and tomahawks and pieces of ancient earthenware have been found on the surrounding meadow. Here also corn hills were once discernible. "In their capital fishing places, particularly in great Ossapy & Winipiseogee rivers," says Belknap, "are the remains of their wears, constructed with very large stones."

Within the limits of the town of Fryeburg, Maine, there are many mounds, one of them sixty feet in circuit, and various other remains which indicate the sites of Indian encampments. Northwest of Fryeburg village, in a bend of the Saco and on its east bank, was situated Pequawket, a large village of the Indians of that name. Hither, after the English began to occupy the seacoast, retired the Sokokis, originally a large tribe, whose principal village had been upon Indian Island near the mouth of the Saco. Mounds believed to be of prehistoric origin are also extant in Woodstock, West Thornton, and other towns in the region.

Of Indian legend not much has come down to us, and most of that belongs to other parts of the Mountains than the main ranges. Says Starr King: —

The Indian names and legends are shorn from the upper mountain region. They have not been caught for our literature. The valleys are almost as bare of them as

THE WHITE MOUNTAINS

the White Mountain cones are of verdure. What a pity it is that our great hills

> Piled to the clouds, — our rivers overhung
> By forests which have known no other change
> For ages, than the budding and the fall
> Of leaves — our valleys lovelier than those
> Which the old poets sang of — should but figure
> On the apocryphal chart of speculation
> As pastures, wood-lots, mill-sites, with the privileges,
> Rights and appurtenances, which make up
> A Yankee Paradise — unsung, unknown
> To beautiful tradition; even their names
> Whose melody yet lingers like the last
> Vibration of the red man's requiem,
> Exchanged for syllables significant
> Of cotton mill and rail-car!

We can scarcely find a settler who can tell any story learned in childhood of Indian bravery, suffering, cruelty, or love.

Such a region in Europe would have a world of tradition and mythology associated with it — witness the wealth of legend possessed by the low hills of the Rhine Valley or by the Scottish Border.

The chief legends worthy of recording, of the few that there are, center about the names of the Indian chiefs Passaconaway and Chocorua. Of the former, a great New Hampshire chieftain, whose name means Child of the Bear and who was long the head of the Pennacook Confederation, his leadership probably antedating the landing of the Pilgrims, Indian tradition has it that he was carried to Mount Washington in a sleigh drawn by wolves, whence he rose toward Heaven in a chariot of fire, like Elijah. This legend of his apotheosis suggested

INDIAN LEGEND AND HISTORY

to Mr. Sweetser the mysterious story of St. Aspinquid, an Indian sage, who, it has been handed down, was converted to Christianity in 1628 and preached the Gospel widely for forty years. His death occurred more than fifty years later and his funeral on Mount Agamenticus in York County, Maine, is said to have been attended by many sachems and to have been marked by a great hunting feast. One antiquary believes Passaconaway and St. Aspinquid, because of the correspondences between their ages and reputations, to be the same person, and he advances the theory that Passaconaway retired to Mount Agamenticus during King Philip's War, received the other name from the seashore Indians, and died there some years afterward.

Passaconaway's life story is an interesting one and his character was of a remarkably high order. He became known to the white men soon after their coming, for Captain Levett reported having seen him in 1623. His confederation, which is estimated to have had at the beginning of the seventeenth century several thousand warriors, had, in less than twenty years, been almost exterminated by famine, pestilence, and pitiless warfare with other Indians. In 1629, Passaconaway and his subchiefs granted a considerable tract of land between the Piscataqua and Merrimac Rivers to the banished Antinomian, Rev. John Wheelwright, and others of the Massachusetts Bay Colony, in return for what the Indians deemed a valuable consideration in "coats, shirts, and kettles." Three years later, the sachem dispatched to Boston an Indian who had killed an

THE WHITE MOUNTAINS

English trader named Jenkins while the latter was asleep in a wigwam. When, in 1642, Massachusetts sent a force of forty armed men to disarm Passaconaway, he voluntarily delivered up his guns, after the General Court had sent an apology to him for some unwarranted proceedings on the part of the white men, which he, as the authorities to their credit admitted, rightfully resented.

Some two or three years later, Passaconaway and his sons put themselves, their people, and their lands under the jurisdiction and protection of Massachusetts, and from this time he was nominally a sort of Puritan magistrate, administering the colonial laws upon his subjects. John Eliot, the apostle to the Indians, visited the chieftain in 1647, and by his preaching so impressed him and his sons that the clergyman was entreated to live with them as their teacher. Eliot probably converted Passaconaway about this time.

In 1660, the great sachem, overcome with the burden of his years and weary of honors, abdicated his chieftainship at a solemn assembly of the mountain and river Indians held at Pawtucket Falls (Lowell). His farewell address was heard by two or three Englishmen, who reported it to be a fine piece of oratory. Various forms [1] of it have come down to

---

[1] There is one version in Hubbard's *Indian Wars*, another in Bouton's *History of Concord*, and another in Barstow's *History of New Hampshire*. In view of these, Little, in his *History of Warren*, facetiously remarks, "We come to the probably correct conclusion that Passaconaway said something very pretty and exceedingly eloquent sometime." One paragraph of the Potter version I have omitted.

INDIAN LEGEND AND HISTORY

us. A fanciful version, given by Hon. Chandler E. Potter in his "History of Manchester," runs as follows: —

Hearken to the words of your father. I am an old oak, that has withstood the storm of more than an hundred winters. Leaves and branches have been stripped from me by the winds and frosts — my eyes are dim.— my limbs totter — I must soon fall! But when young and sturdy, when my bow no young man of the Pennacooks could bend it — when my arrows would pierce a deer at an hundred yards — and I could bury my hatchet in a sapling to the eye — no wigwam had so many furs — no pole so many scalp locks, as Passaconaway's. Then I delighted in war. The whoop of the Pennacooks was heard on the Mohawk — and no voice so loud as Passaconaway's. The scalps upon the pole of my wigwam told the story of Mohawk suffering. . . .

The oak will soon break before the whirlwind — it shivers and shakes even now; soon its trunk will be prostrate — the ant and the worm will sport upon it! Then think, my children, of what I say; I commune with the Great Spirit. He whispers me now — "Tell your people, Peace, Peace, is the only hope of your race. I have given fire and thunder to the pale faces for weapons — I have made them plentier than the leaves of the forest, and still shall they *increase!* These meadows they shall turn with the plow — these forests shall fall by the axe — the pale faces shall live upon your hunting grounds, and make their villages upon your fishing places!" The Great Spirit says this, and it must be so! We are few and powerless before them! We must bend before the storm! The wind blows hard! The old oak trembles! Its branches are gone! Its sap is frozen! It bends! It falls! Peace, Peace, with the white man — is the command of the Great Spirit — and the wish — the last wish — of Passaconaway.

THE WHITE MOUNTAINS

After his abdication, the province of Massachusetts granted him a tract of land in Litchfield, where he lived for a time. Eliot and General Gookin saw him when he was in his one-hundred-and-twentieth year. When and how he died are unknown; the tradition of his departure from earth has been already given.

Many were the wild and fascinating stories about this great chief current among the Indians and the colonists. He seems to have been in early life a great warrior and later to have become a powwow, a sort of priest and necromancer combined. When the settlers came to Massachusetts, he used all his magic arts against them, but with such lack of success that he became convinced that they were protected by the Great Spirit, and so he avoided warfare with them. To the Puritans his actions in this instance suggested themselves as a parallel to those of a character in their favorite book, and one of the fathers gave him accordingly the name of the Indian Balaam. Some of the powers attributed to him are thus quaintly described in William Wood's "New England's Prospect" (1634):—

He can make the water burne, the rocks move, the trees dance, metamorphise himself into a flaming man. Hee will do more; for in winter, when there are no green leaves to be got, he will burne an old one to ashes, and putting those into the water, produce a new green leaf, which you shall not only see, but substantially handle and carrie away; and make of a dead snake's skin a living snake, both to be seen, felt, and heard. This I write but upon the report of the Indians, who confidently affirm stranger things.

INDIAN LEGEND AND HISTORY

Passaconaway's son Wonnalancet succeeded him as chief. He is said to have been "a sober and grave person, of years between fifty and sixty," and to have been "always loving and friendly to the English." He was converted to Christianity by the Apostle Eliot and lived a noble life, restraining his warriors from attacking the colonists, even during King Philip's War. Finding it impossible, at a later day, to prevent his people from engaging in open hostilities, he gave up the chieftaincy and with a few families who adhered to him, sought retreat at St. Francis[1] in Canada. He returned to the Merrimac valley in 1696, but after a short time finally retired to St. Francis, where he died.

His successor as chieftain, after his abdication in 1685, was his nephew, Passaconaway's "grantson," Kancamagus. This resolute warrior made several attempts to retain the friendship of the colonists, as is evident from his letters to Governor Crandall, but was unsuccessful and finally yielded, after many slights and much ill-treatment, to the solicitations of the warlike and patriotic party in the confederation. He organized and led the terrible attack on Dover in 1689, which was the death-throe of the Pennacooks. He was present at the signing of the truce of Sagadahoc, but after that disappears from history. He may have retired with the remainder of his people to St. Francis. Potter thus characterizes him: —

[1] The Indian town of St. François de Sales, near Becancour, opposite Three Rivers on the St. Lawrence, which had from the earliest times been inhabited by a clan of the Abnakis.

THE WHITE MOUNTAINS

Kancamagus was a brave and politic chief, and in view of what he accomplished at the head of a mere remnant of a once powerful tribe, it may be considered a most fortunate circumstance for the English colonists, that he was not at the head of the tribe at an earlier period, before it had been shorn of its strength, during the old age of Passaconaway, and the peaceful and inactive reign of Wonnalancet. And even could Kancamagus have succeeded to the sagamonship ten years earlier than he did, so that his acknowledged abilities for counsel and war could have been united with those of Philip, history might have chronicled another story than the inglorious death of the sagamon of Mount Hope in the swamp of Pokanoket.

After the powerful confederacy of the Pennacooks was broken up, the northern tribes remained in their ancestral home a few years longer, but were soon nearly annihilated by expeditions from the New England towns, the remnant finally migrating to Canada.

Perhaps the most celebrated Indian name associated with White Mountain legend is that of the chieftain Chocorua, whose name has been attached to the easternmost peak [1] of the Sandwich Range, a peak which Sweetser says "is probably the most picturesque and beautiful of the mountains of New England." Near its summit Chocorua was killed by white men.

One form of the legend concerning this Indian was narrated to Mr. Sweetser by an old inhabitant of

[1] The mountain was known and mapped as Chocorua decades before the legend ever appeared in print. On Belknap's map of New Hampshire, issued with the second volume of his history, in 1791, Chocorua appears, being the only mountain of the Sandwich Range to be located or named.

INDIAN LEGEND AND HISTORY

Tamworth, who had written it down many years before as he had received it from his ancestors. The story runs as follows: —

When the Pequawket Indians retreated to Canada, after Lovewell's battle [1725], Chocorua refused to leave the ancient home of his people and the graves of his forefathers. He remained behind, and was friendly to the incoming white settlers, and especially with one Campbell, who lived near what is now Tamworth. He had a son, in whom all his hopes and love were centered. On one occasion he was obliged to go to Canada to consult with his people at St. Francis, and, wishing to spare his son the labors of the long journey, he left him with Campbell until his return. The boy was welcomed to the hut of the pioneer, and tenderly cared for. One day, however, he found a small bottle of poison, which had been prepared for a mischievous fox, and, with the unsuspecting curiosity of the Indian, he drank a portion of it. Chocorua returned only to find his boy dead and buried. The improbable story of his fatality failed to satisfy the heartbroken chief, and his spirit demanded vengeance. Campbell went home from the fields one day, and saw the dead and mangled bodies of his wife and children on the floor of the hut. He tracked Chocorua and found him on the crest of the mountain, and shot him down, while the dying Indian invoked curses on the white men.

In another form of the legend,[1] Campbell was an active partisan of Cromwell, who, on the restoration of the Stuarts, fled to America with his beautiful and high-born wife and settled in this remote wilderness. The son of Chocorua, who was then prophet

---

[1] This is the form adopted by Mrs. Lydia Maria Child in her story of "Chocorua's Curse," printed in the 1830 issue of *The Token*, an annual published at Boston. The story is accompanied by a steel engraving, by George W. Hatch, of Thomas Cole's painting of "The Death of Chocorua."

THE WHITE MOUNTAINS

of the powerful Pequawkets, was a frequent visitor at Campbell's house and there met his death by accidental poisoning. The murder of the family and the death of the chief on the mountain are related to have occurred also substantially as narrated in the other form of the story.

Another account, which is probably nearer the truth, makes Chocorua an inoffensive Indian, a friend of the whites, who was shot by a party of hunters, at a time when Massachusetts was, during a campaign against the Indians, offering a bounty of £100 for every scalp brought to Boston.[1]

Legend represents the chieftain as raising himself upon his hands, when wounded to death by the bullet of Campbell, on the precipice of the mountain which has received his name, to utter an anathema upon his enemies, which Mrs. Child has put into this form: —

A curse upon ye, white men! May the Great Spirit curse ye when he speaks in the clouds, and his words are fire! Chocorua had a son — and ye killed him while the sky looked bright! Lightning blast your crops! Wind and fire destroy your dwellings! The Evil Spirit breathe death upon your cattle! Your graves lie in the war path of the Indian! Panthers howl, and wolves fatten over your bones! Chocorua goes to the Great Spirit — his curse stays with the white man!

Although tradition would have it that the curse was effectual, as a matter of fact the towns in this

---

[1] The Chocorua legend has been the subject of a number of poems, including a juvenile production of Longfellow's, mentioned elsewhere, a spirited lyric of forty lines by Charles J. Fox, and a 280-line poem by Mrs. V. G. Ranney.

THE DEATH OF CHOCORUA
After the Painting by Thomas Cole

INDIAN LEGEND AND HISTORY

vicinity were never molested by Indians, pestilence, or other severe troubles. Even such a calamity as the continued dying of cattle in the town of Albany, which was attributed to Chocorua's curse, was found after many years to be due to a natural cause, the presence of muriate of lime in the water they drank.

A fanciful legend purporting to give the Indians' idea of the origin of the White Mountains, or, rather, of the formation of the lofty Agiocochook, is thus set down in Spaulding and in Willey: —

Cold storms were in the northern wilderness, and a lone red hunter wandered without food, chilled by the frozen wind. He lost his strength and could find no game; and the dark cloud that covered his life-path made him weary of wandering. He fell down upon the snow, and a dream carried him to a wide, happy valley, filled with musical streams, where singing birds and game were plenty. His spirit cried aloud for joy; and the *"Great Master of Life"* waked him from his sleep, gave him a dry coal and a flint-pointed spear, telling him that by the shore of the lake he might live, and find fish with his spear, and fire from his dry coal. One night, when he had laid down his coal, and seen a warm fire spring up therefrom, with a blinding smoke, a loud voice came out of the flame, and a great noise, like thunder, filled the air; and there rose up a vast pile of broken rocks. Out of the cloud resting upon the top came numerous streams, dancing down, foaming cold; and the voice spake to the astonished red hunter, saying, *"Here the Great Spirit will dwell, and watch over his favorite children."*

The Indians who lived in the valleys of this region looked with awe upon the Mountains, or at least, the upper parts of the ranges. By them the highest

THE WHITE MOUNTAINS

summits, cloud-capped often in all seasons or dazzlingly white in winter, were thought to be the abodes of superior beings, who were invisible but who revealed their presence by the appalling tempests and by the deafening noises which we now know to be due to slides and falling rocks, and the ascent of the peaks was, therefore, regarded as not only perilous or impossible but sacrilegious. The terrible thunder and the blinding lightning seemed to them the voice of the Supreme Being and the sign of his wrath and omnipotence.

A deluge tradition similar to that held by so many savage tribes was current among them. A quaint account of this legend is given in Josselyn's "Account of Two Voyages to New England":—

Ask them whither they go when they dye, they will tell you pointing with their finger to Heaven beyond the white mountains, and do hint at *Noah's* Floud, as may be conceived by a story they have received from Father to Son, time out of mind, that a great while agon their Countrey was drowned, and all the People and other Creatures in it, only one *Powaw* and his *Webb* foreseeing the Floud fled to the white mountains carrying a hare along with them and so escaped; after a while the *Powaw* sent the *Hare* away, who not returning emboldned thereby they descended, and lived many years after, and had many Children, from whom the Countrie was filled again with *Indians*.

Another tradition of the early days is connected with the Giant's Grave, a mound of river gravel or sand on which was situated the first public house in the Fabyan region. It was affirmed that an Indian maniac once stood here and, waving a burning pitch-

INDIAN LEGEND AND HISTORY

pine torch kindled at a tree struck by lightning an instant before, cried out this prophecy, "No paleface shall take deep root here; this the Great Spirit whispered in my ear." Two inns on this site have been burned and considerable damage has been done by freshets. These facts very likely have given rise to the tradition.

One of the wildest and most beautiful of the Indian legends connected with the Crystal Hills is that of the mystery of the Great Carbuncle, which Hawthorne has immortalized in a characteristic twice-told tale, bearing this title and introducing eight adventurers of various degrees, conditions, and descriptions as seekers for the marvelous stone.

There are several forms of the tradition,[1] which was acquired from the aborigines by some of the early explorers and which was reported by them on their return to the settlements, a few even going so far as solemnly to affirm having seen the wondrous object. According to a generally received form of the legend, somewhere in the glen of the Dry, or Mount Washington, River, a tributary of the Saco which joins the latter nearly opposite the Frankenstein Cliff, was hidden, under a shelving rock, a glorious carbuncle. This gem, it was declared, had been placed there by the Indians, who killed one of their number so that an evil spirit might haunt the

[1] Says the matter-of-fact historian Belknap of this fancy: "From them [the Indians], and the captives whom they sometimes led to Canada through the passes of these mountains, many fictions have been propagated, which have given rise to marvelous and incredible stories; particularly, it has been reported, that at immense and inaccessible heights, there have been seen carbuncles, which are supposed to appear luminous in the night."

THE WHITE MOUNTAINS

place. The great stone ever and anon startled the rangers in their lonely night camps or the farmers in the log houses in the Saco lowlands by flashing its glittering light far out over the country. Led by the reports of the gem's existence and marvelous brilliancy, several parties of adventurers are said to have gone in quest of it, hoping in some way to obtain fabulous riches as the reward of their search. One expedition, it is recorded, even took along "a good man to lay the evil spirit," but all got nothing for their arduous toil but sore bruises and bitter disappointment.

There is a further tradition that one old Indian pronounced a curse upon the pale-faced seekers, and, as his dying wish, prayed that the Great Spirit by a black storm of fire and thunder would rend the cliff, roll the carbuncle down to the valley, and bury it deeply under the ruins of rocks and trees. So firm and persistent became belief in this mysterious jewel's existence that, even after the Revolution, as we are informed by the author of an early history of Maine, it had not been entirely given up by dwellers in the region.

II

EARLY EXPLORERS

PLAINLY visible from the sea as the summits of the White Mountains are in clear weather, they must have been seen by a number of the early explorers of northeastern America when cruising along the coast. Who was the first European to behold them cannot be told, but the Florentine navigator Verrazano is the first, it appears, who speaks of having seen them. In the year 1524, as he was skirting the coast of the future New England, he visited the site of Portsmouth, New Hampshire. His record of the progress of his voyage at this point says, "We departed from thence keeping our course Northeast along the coast, which we found more pleasant champion and without woods, with high mountains within the land." [1]

The Mountains appear, it is probable, vaguely lo-

[1] Letter of Giovanni da Verrazano to the King of France, July 8, 1524, of which three copies exist. The version given above is from the translation made for Hakluyt's *Voyages*, in 1583, of the copy printed by Ramusio in 1556. A second copy was found in the Strozzi Library in Florence. A third copy, which has the distinction of being contemporaneous, is now in Rome and was first printed in Italy in 1909. It was translated into English by Dr. Edward Hagaman Hall, Secretary of the American Scenic and Historic Preservation Society, and was published in the *Report* of that society for 1910. Our passage reads thus in Dr. Hall's translation: "We departed, skirting the coast between east and north, which we found very beautiful, open and bare of forests, with high mountains back inland, growing smaller toward the shore of the sea."

THE WHITE MOUNTAINS

cated, on a number of early maps. They are doubtless the *montañas* of Ribero's map of the Polus Mundi Arcticus (1529). They are shown as *Les Montaignes* on a map of the world painted on parchment by the Bishop of Viseu in 1542 under the orders of Francis I, and they appear also in Nicolo del Dolfinato's map in the "Navigationi del Mondo Nuovo," published at Venice in 1560. Probably the *Montes S. Johannis* of Michael Lok's map (1582) are the White Mountains. They are drawn on the "Mappemonde" of Mercator, published at Duisburg in 1569, as lying west of the great city of Norumbega. On Sebastian Cabot's map of the world, drawn in 1544, *montagnas* is found in the location, roughly, of this group. John Foster's map of New England, 1677, is the first in which the name of "White Hills" appears.[1] In Holland's map of 1784, which embodies the results of a survey made at public expense by Captain Samuel Holland in 1773-74 and which is entitled, "A Topographical Map of the State of New Hampshire," the names of individual peaks are given for the first time. Philip Carrigain, whose name is commemorated by that striking mountain of bold and massive form, which stands almost exactly in the center of the White Mountain region, published a map of New Hampshire in 1816. This well-known work was compiled by him from town surveys which the legislatures of 1803 and 1805 had ordered and which had been

[1] This map was printed in the Reverend William Hubbard's *Narrative of the Troubles with the Indians in New England*. In the first impression the name was printed "Wine Hills," obviously a misprint, but the map was recut the same year with the correct name substituted.

EARLY EXPLORERS

returned to the office of the secretary of state, a position held by Carrigain in the years just named. The first carefully prepared map of the Mountains was that published by Professor G. P. Bond of Harvard College in 1853. It was made from original triangulations.

To return to the subject of exploration. The great French explorer and founder of Canada, Samuel de Champlain, evidently descried these mountains during his expedition of 1605, for in his account of his voyage along the coast of Maine, when he must have reached the vicinity of Portland, he made this entry in his journal: "From here large mountains are seen to the west, in which is the dwelling place of a savage captain called Aneda, who encamps near the river Quinibequy." [1]

The Englishman Christopher Levett, the pioneer colonist in Casco Bay, in his account of his voyage to New England of 1623 and 1624, which was published in 1628, has this reference to the White Mountains: "This River [undoubtedly the Saco], as I am told by the *Salvages*, commeth from a great mountain called the Christall hill, being as they say 100 miles in the Country, yet it is to be seene at the sea side, and there is no ship arives in *New England*, either to the West so farre as *Cape Cod*, or to the East so farre as *Monhiggen*, but they see this mountaine the first land, if the weather be cleere." [2]

[1] The Kennebec.
[2] Apparently the voyagers of those early days were blessed with exceptionally good eyesight. President Dwight states that the sailors of his day averred that they could see Mount Washington from a point at sea 165 miles from it.

THE WHITE MOUNTAINS

It was not until some years after the coast was settled that any one could venture so far away from the security and supplies of the settlements as these remote hills, even for the purpose of exploration. But at length adventurous spirits undertook this arduous and dangerous exploit. Darby Field, whom recent researches recorded by Warren W. Hart in *Appalachia* show to have been probably a native of Boston, England, and therefore not of the nationality attributed to him in Winthrop's "Journal," is generally credited with being the first European to visit and explore the White Mountains.

It was in June, 1642,[1] that he made the first and probably also the second of his expeditions to this region, accounts of which are thus set down by Winthrop: —

One Darby Field, an Irishman, living about Pascataquack,[2] being accompanied with two Indians, went to the top of the white hill. He made his journey in 18 days. His relation — at his return was, that it was about one hundred miles from Saco, that after 40 miles travel he did, for the most part, ascend, and within 10 miles of the top was neither tree nor grass, but low savins, which they went upon the top of sometimes, but a continual ascent upon rocks, on a ridge between two valleys filled with snow, out of which came two branches of the Saco River, which meet at the foot of the hill, where was an Indian town of some 200 people. Some of them accompanied

[1] "1642, (4) [i. e., fourth month, or June]. The first discovery of the great mountaine (called the Christall Hills) to the N. W. by Darby Field." Quoted from the Reverend Samuel Danforth's *Almanac* for 1647, in Belknap and elsewhere.

[2] Pascataquack appears to have been a general name for the region along the Piscataqua River. Field was a resident of Exeter at this time.

EARLY EXPLORERS

him within 8 miles of the top, but durst go no further, telling him that no Indian ever dared go higher, and that he would die if he went. So they staid there till his return, but his two Indians took courage by his example and went with him. They went divers times through the thick clouds for a good space, and within 4 miles of the top they had no clouds, but very cold. By the way, among the rocks, there were two ponds, one a blackish water and the other reddish. The top of all was plain about 60 feet square. On the north side there was such a precipice, as they could scarcely discern to the bottom. They had neither cloud nor wind on the top, and moderate heat. All the country about him seemed a level, except here and there a hill rising above the rest, but far beneath them. He saw to the north a great water which he judged to be 100 miles broad, but could see no land beyond it. The sea by Saco seemed as if it had been within 20 miles. He saw also a sea to the eastward, which he judged to be the Gulf of Canada: He saw some great waters in parts to the westward which he judged to be the great lake which Canada River comes out of. He found there much Muscovy glass, they could rive out pieces of 40 feet long and 7 or 8 broad. When he came back to the Indians, he found them drying themselves by the fire, for they had had a great tempest of wind and rain. About a month after he went again, with five or six of his company, then they had some wind on the top, and some clouds above them which hid the sun. They brought some stones which they supposed had been diamonds, but they were most crystal.

Field was then, evidently, the first person to ascend Mount Washington, for the Indians of the region, if we may believe Field's statement given in the passage just quoted from Winthrop, and there is no reason to doubt its truth, had never dared to undertake the ascent to this supposed

THE WHITE MOUNTAINS

abode of the Great Spirit. He is thought to have gone up the ridge (Boott Spur) between Tuckerman's Ravine and the valley of the Dry, or Mount Washington, River.

The glowing account Field gave on his return of the riches he had found fired other daring men to undertake the exploration of the Mountains. Thomas Gorges, Deputy-Governor, and Richard Vines, Esq., Councillor, of the Province of Maine, started out later in the same year. Winthrop gives the following account of their journey and its results: —

The report he [Darby Field] brought of shining stones, etc., caused divers others to travel thither, but they found nothing worth their pains. Among others, Mr. Gorge [sic] and Mr. Vines, two of the magistrates of Sir Ferdinand Gorge his province, went thither about the end of this month [October]. They went up Saco river in birch canoes, and that way, they found it 90 miles to Pegwagget, an Indian town, but by land it is but 60. Upon Saco river they found many thousand acres of rich meadow, but there are ten falls, which hinder boats, etc. From the Indian town they went up hill (for the most part), about 30 miles in woody lands, then they went about 7 or 8 miles upon shattered rocks, without tree or grass, very steep all the way. At the top is a plain about three or four miles over, all shattered stones, and upon that is another rock or spire, about a mile in height, and about an acre of ground at the top. At the top of the plain arise four great rivers, each of them so much water, at the first issue, as would drive a mill; Connecticut river from two heads at the N. W., and S. W. which join in one about 60 miles off, Saco river on the S. E., Amascoggen which runs into Casco Bay at the N. E., and Kennebeck, at the N. by E. The mountain runs E. and W. 30 or

EARLY EXPLORERS

40 miles, but the peak is above all the rest. They went and returned in 15 days.

John Josselyn, traveler and writer, appears to have explored the White Hills during his second visit to New England, between 1663 and 1671. He gives a quaint and curious description of them in his "New England's Rarities Discovered" (1672):—

Four score miles (upon a direct line), to the Northwest of *Scarborow*, a ridge of Mountains run Northwest and Northeast an hundred Leagues, known by the name of the *White Mountains*, upon which lieth Snow all the year, and is a Landmark twenty miles off at Sea. It is a rising ground from the Sea shore to these Hills, and they are inaccessible, but by the Gullies which the dissolved Snow hath made; in these Gullies grow Saven Bushes, which being taken hold of are a good help to the climbing Discoverer; upon the top of the highest of these Mountains is a large Level or Plain of a day's journey over, whereon nothing grows but Moss; at the farther end of this Plain is another Hill called the *Sugar Loaf*, to outward appearance a rude heap of massie stones piled one upon another, and you may as you ascend step from one stone to another, as if you were going up a pair of stairs, but winding still about the Hill till you come to the top, which will require half a days time, and yet it is not above a Mile, where there is also a Level of about an Acre of ground, with a pond of clear water in the midst of it; which you may hear run down, but how it ascends is a mystery. From this rocky Hill you may see the whole Country round about; it is far above the lower Clouds, and from hence we beheld a Vapour (like a great Pillar), drawn up by the Sun Beams out of a great Lake or Pond into the Air, where it was formed into a Cloud. The Country beyond these Hills Northward is daunting terrible, being full of rocky Hills, as thick as Mole-hills in a Meadow, and cloathed with infinite thick Woods.

THE WHITE MOUNTAINS

In his "An Account of Two Voyages to New England" (1674), Josselyn gives further description of the country "as Rockie and Mountanious, full of tall wood." "One stately mountain there is surmounting the rest, about four score mile from the Sea," he says, and continues, "Between the mountains are many ample rich and pregnant valleys as ever eye beheld, beset on each side with variety of goodly Trees, the grass man-high unmowed, uneaten, and uselessly withering"; and "within these valleys are spacious lakes or ponds well stored with Fish and Beavers; the original of all the great Rivers in the Countrie." He corrects his previous statement as to the snow's lying upon the mountains the entire year by excepting the month of August; speaks of the black flies as "so numerous ... that a man cannot draw his breath, but he will suck of them in"; remarks that "some suppose the white mountains were first raised by earthquakes"; and adds, "they are hollow, as may be guessed by the resounding of the rain upon the level on the top."

Belknap records an ascent of Mount Washington made by "a ranging company," April 29, 1725, which found the snow four feet deep on the northwest side, the summit almost bare of snow though covered with white frost and ice, and the alpine pond frozen. A similar party, he relates, was "in the neighborhood of the White Mountains, on a warm day, in the month of March," in 1746, and was "alarmed with a repeated noise, which they supposed to be the firing of guns. On further

EARLY EXPLORERS

search," he continues, "they found it to be caused by rocks, falling from the south side of a steep mountain." The same authority tells also of an ascent to the summit made on the 6th of June, 1774, by Captain Evans and some other men who were making a road through the eastern pass of the mountains, and who found "on the south side, in one of the deep gullies, a body of snow thirteen feet deep, and so hard as to bear them." On the 19th of the same month, some of the same party ascended again, and in the same spot the snow, they found, was five feet deep. In the first week of September, 1783, two men who attempted to ascend the Mountain, found the bald top so covered with snow and ice that they could not reach the summit. "But this," says the historian, "does not happen every year so soon; for the mountain has been ascended as late as the first week in October, when no snow was upon it."

The pass now called Crawford Notch was known to the Indians, but was probably little used by them, because of their superstitious fear of the Mountains. It is maintained by some, however, that certain war parties of Canadian Indians used this passage in making raids upon the New England coast. Belknap says that the Indians formerly led their captives through it to Canada, and we are told that in the spring of 1746 a raiding party attacked Gorham, Maine, and carried off several prisoners, one of whom described the march to Canada as being through the Notch.

It was in 1771 that the pass was first made known

THE WHITE MOUNTAINS

to the New England colonists. Timothy Nash, a hunter, when in pursuit of a moose which had eluded him, climbed a tree on Cherry Mountain and, as he was looking about in the hope of espying his game, he saw to his surprise a deep depression in the mountain wall. As soon as possible he made his way thither and explored the defile, following the Saco down through. On his arrival at Portsmouth, he informed Governor Wentworth of his discovery, a most important one, as such a gap in the Mountains would save much in journeying between the seacoast and the upper Connecticut valley. The governor, wishing to test the value of the pass as a trade route, offered Nash a grant of the tract of land (known to-day as "Nash and Sawyer's Location") extending from the Notch to a point beyond the present Fabyan House, if he would bring a horse through from Lancaster. Enlisting the aid of a fellow hunter by the name of Benjamin Sawyer, Nash succeeded in performing the required task and in thus gaining the promised reward for himself and his partner.[1] The two worthies soon squandered, however, the proceeds of their grant. A road [2] was

---

[1] The story of the discovery as given in the *Crawford History* varies somewhat from the account I have followed, which is based on another and later source. According to the former record, the two hunters went out together for the express purpose of discovering such a means of communication and the tree-climbing was done after the discovery to obtain a better view and thus make sure of the fact. The condition upon which the grant was made by Governor Wentworth in 1773, according to this authority, was that they should make a good road through their tract and procure the settlement of five families on it within five years.

[2] This "never well-finished county road" was paid for out of the proceeds of a confiscated Tory estate. It is said to have been a singu-

EARLY EXPLORERS

shortly after built and thus a direct route between the seacoast and upper Coös was established. The first merchandise carried down from Lancaster was a barrel of tobacco and the first commodity transported in the opposite direction a barrel of whiskey, most of the contents of which are said to have been consumed on the way. On December 28, 1803, a turnpike, the tenth in New Hampshire, was incorporated and shortly afterwards [1] was constructed through the Notch at an expense of $40,000 for twenty miles, the money being raised by lottery. It occupied to some extent the site of the old road, was more skillfully built than its predecessor, and soon became one of the best-paying turnpikes in the northern part of the State.

In July, 1784, a journey to the Mountains was accomplished, which is noteworthy for the number and character of the members of the party who made it and because of the purpose for which it was undertaken. I refer to the expedition made by the Reverend Dr. Jeremy Belknap, the historian of New Hampshire, then a resident of Dover; the Reverend Daniel Little, of Wells, Maine; the Reverend

lar specimen of highway engineering, being laid out, in the main, fifty or sixty feet higher than the later turnpike, being so steep in places that it was necessary to draw horses and wagons up with ropes, and crossing the Saco, we are told, no less than thirty-two times in ascending the valley. Theodore Dwight, Jr., says the road was built in 1785. It was in part at least constructed in 1774, as the statement of Belknap given on page 25 bears witness.

[1] Dr. Shattuck, of Boston, in his account, published in the Philadelphia *Medical and Physical Journal* (1808), of his excursion to the White Hills in the preceding year, says, in speaking of the Notch, "A turnpike-road is now [August, 1807] building from Bath, through the Notch, to Portland."

THE WHITE MOUNTAINS

Manasseh Cutler, of Ipswich, Massachusetts; Dr. Joshua Fisher, of Beverly, Massachusetts; Mr. Heard, of Ipswich, and two young collegians, Hubbard and Bartlett, who set out to make a tour of the White Mountains "with a view to make particular observations on the several phenomena that might occur." For this purpose they were equipped with various instruments, including barometers, thermometers, a sextant, and surveying compasses. They were thus the first of a considerable line of scientific inquirers to visit these hills.

The historian has left several records [1] of the trip. Let me briefly advert to these, noting their character and provenience. In the first place, much of the Reverend Doctor's correspondence with his friend Ebenezer Hazard, of Philadelphia, has been preserved and printed in the "Collections" of the Massachusetts Historical Society.

Among these letters we find a record of Belknap's intention to make such a journey, for under date of July 4, 1784, he writes: "I expect, next week, to set out on a land tour to the White Mts., in company with several gentlemen of a scientific turn. I may write you again once before I go; but, if I live to come back, you may depend on such a description as I may be able to give." Dr. Belknap's letters to Mr. Hazard, giving an account of his tour are, un-

[1] Dr. Cutler also left an account of the journey, which is graphic and well written and which may be found in his *Life, Journals, and Correspondence*, published in 1888. Belknap was indebted to Cutler for his information about the ascent and descent of the chief peak. Cutler's manuscript breaks off before the description of the return is finished, but the remainder is covered in an account of the tour written by Mr. Little.

EARLY EXPLORERS

fortunately, not preserved among the Hazard letters. The want of such a narrative, however, is fully supplied, as has been intimated. There is extant, first, a memoir, "Description of the White Mountains," which was sent by him to the American Philosophical Society of Philadelphia, and to which "great attention was paid," writes Hazard. This was published in 1786, in the second volume of the Society's "Transactions," and in substance is similar to the account afterwards published in the third volume of Dr. Belknap's "History of New Hampshire." Both of these records are very different in form from the third account, which consists of the original notes kept by the doctor in the form of a diary. These have been printed with the correspondence above mentioned, and on them I shall largely rely for my summary of this notable trip. In the chapter on the White Mountains, given in the "History," the author refers to the visit to the Mountains made by a party of gentlemen in 1784, but gives no intimation that he was one of the company. A few additional particulars are, however, there given.

The historian's account of the trip recorded in his diary is so naïve and detailed that one may be pardoned for thinking that it may be of sufficient interest to give rather fully.

At Conway the travelers found Colonel Joseph Whipple, of Dartmouth (later Jefferson), and Captain Evans, who was to be their pilot, ready to go with them. Thence they journeyed through what is now Jackson and "along the Shelburne Road" to apparently about three fourths of a mile beyond the

THE WHITE MOUNTAINS

Glen Ellis Falls, where they encamped for the night. The next day, Saturday, July 24, the party undertook the ascent of "the Mountain" from the eastern side. Dr. Fisher soon gave out, owing to a pain in his side, and returned to the camp, where Colonel Whipple's negro man had been left in charge of the horses and baggage. After about two hours more of climbing, "having risen many very steep and extremely difficult precipices, I found my breath fail," says Dr. Belknap,[1] and in a consultation of the party it was decided that inasmuch as many stops had had to be made on his account and as the pilot supposed they were not more than halfway up to "the Plain," he should return. Refusing to deprive those who offered to go back with him of their expected pleasure, the good doctor came down safely alone in about an hour and a half and arrived "much fatigued," at the camp, "about 10 o'clock." It came on to rain toward night, so those at the camp repaired their tent with bark, took all the baggage into it, and anxiously awaited the return of their friends. The rain increased and continued all night, but although the tent leaked and the fire "decayed," they managed to keep the fire going and themselves dry.

It ceased raining at daylight on Sunday and soon thereafter the report of a gun partly relieved the anxiety of Drs. Belknap and Fisher. Shortly after the party of climbers arrived safely at the camp.

[1] "The spirit was willing but the flesh (i. e., the lungs) weak," he says in a letter to Hazard, and in the same letter, "You will not wonder that such a quantity of matter ('180 or 190 lbs. of mortality') could not ascend the White Mountains farther than it did."

EARLY EXPLORERS

They reported that they passed the night around a fire, which was their only defense against the rain, and that "they had ascended to the summit, but had not had so good a view as they wished, the Mountain being most of the time involved with clouds, which rolled up and down, in every direction, above, below, and around them." Their scientific observations were by "this unfortunate circumstance" for the most part prevented. They arrived at the pinnacle of the Sugar-Loaf at 1.06, their actual time of climbing from the tent being five hours and thirteen minutes. On the highest rock they found an old hat, which had been left there in June, 1774, by Captain Evans's party. They dined at 2 o'clock, we are told, on partridges and neat's tongue, cut the letters "N.H." on the uppermost rock and under a stone left a plate of lead [1] on which were engraved their names. The descent was a particularly difficult one, as, owing to the clouds, even the guide could not find the way down. Soon after their return to the camp they left for Dartmouth.

Their course in ascending the mountain was evidently through Tuckerman's Ravine, probably over Boott Spur, and up the east side of the cone, their route in the lower part being indicated by the stream which bears Dr. Cutler's name.[2] Dr. Cutler esti-

[1] The finding of this plate eighteen years later was "the source of great mystification to the villagers at Jackson." (Sweetser.)

[2] Given to the river, it is said, by Dr. Cutler's express desire. According to Belknap, another tributary of the Ellis River "falls from the same mountain," a short distance to the south, and is called New River. Belknap's map makes Cutler's River flow from the present Tuckerman's Ravine. The account of Dr. Bigelow, a later explorer, agrees with this. In later maps, however, the names of the

THE WHITE MOUNTAINS

mated the height of the "pinnacle" or "sugarloaf," as Belknap calls it, to be not less than three hundred feet. From some unsatisfactory observations with the barometer, the elevation of the principal summit above the sea was computed to be nearly ten thousand feet. The party were disappointed in their attempt to measure the altitude geometrically from the base, because "in the meadow they could not obtain a base of sufficient length, nor see the summit of the sugar-loaf; and in another place, where these inconveniences were removed, they were prevented by the almost continual obscuration of the mountains by clouds."

"It is likely," says Professor Tuckerman, "that the plants of the higher regions were observed,[1] and Mr. Oakes possessed fragments of such a collection made, either now or later, by Dr. Cutler, but the latter did not notice them in his memoir on the plants of New England published the next year in the transaction of the Academy,[2] nor is there any mention of them in the six small volumes of his botanical manuscripts which have come to my knowledge."

As the name of Mount Washington is found in Dr. Cutler's manuscript of 1784, it is probable that

streams were transposed, the error being noticed by Mr. Sweetser, who was confirmed in his decision in the matter by Professor Tuckerman. New River got its name from the fact of its recent origin, it having been formed in October, 1775, during a great flood.

Some general observations on the vegetation of the Mountains, set down by Dr. Cutler in a manuscript preserved by Belknap, are quoted in Belknap's *History* and Dwight's *Travels*.

[2] The American Academy of Arts and Sciences, of which Dr. Cutler was a member.

EARLY EXPLORERS

the appellation was given to the mountain by the party whose journey has just been described. The name first appears in print in Belknap's "History of New Hampshire," in the third volume, which was published in 1792.[1]

Dr. Cutler again visited the Mountains in July, 1804, this time chiefly to collect botanical specimens, in company with several friends, among whom were Dr. Nathaniel Bowditch and Dr. W. D. Peck, afterward professor of natural history at Cambridge. The party encamped on the side of Mount Washington on the night of the 27th, and on the next day Cutler, Peck, and one or two others made the ascent, arriving at 12.30. There were no clouds about the mountain, but the climbers were much chilled, and the descent was extremely fatiguing. Barometrical observations made at this time were computed by Dr. Bowditch to give an elevation of 7055 feet for the highest summit.

Dr. Peck made during the trip a collection of alpine plants, the citations of which in Pursh's "Flora of North America," published in 1814, "enable us," says Professor Tuckerman, "to determine the earliest recognition of several of the most interesting species."

Of early travelers to the Mountains one of the most distinguished was the Reverend Dr. Timothy Dwight, president of Yale College from 1794 to 1817. Dr. Dwight made two journeys on horseback to this region, the first in 1797 and the second in

---

[1] "It has lately been distinguished by the name of *Mount Washington*," is Belknap's statement.

THE WHITE MOUNTAINS

1803.[1] His companion on the first expedition ("Journey to the White Mountains") was a Mr. L., one of the tutors of Yale College, and their objects were to examine the Connecticut River and to visit the White Mountains. Their first objective point was Lancaster, whence they proposed to proceed through the Notch to their second, Portland. They reached Lancaster on the morning of September 30. They left there on October 2, stayed overnight at Rosebrook's, and on October 3 passed through the Notch, of which Dr. Dwight gives a vivid description. It is "a very narrow defile," he says, "extending two miles in length between two huge cliffs, apparently rent asunder by some vast convulsion of nature. This convulsion," he continues, "was, in my own view, unquestionably that of the deluge." He gives interesting information about the size and character of the mountain towns, describes Mount Washington and other features of the landscape graphically, and, altogether, has provided a very readable narrative of his tour. In his visit to the Mountains in 1803, President Dwight had as companion two graduates and a senior of Yale College, and their object was to ride up the Connecticut River as far as the Canadian boundary ("Journey to the Canada Line"). In the course of the tour, however, the party left the Connecticut, went up the Lower Ammonoosuc, turned aside from

---

[1] Dr. Dwight also made two horseback journeys to Lake Winnepesaukee. The first of these was made in the autumn of 1812 and the second in the same season of the next year. In both excursions he touched the fringe of the White Mountain region, passing through Plymouth in both and ascending Red Hill on the second.

EARLY EXPLORERS

the latter to visit Bethlehem, whence they returned to the Ammonoosuc, and then went on to the Notch, which they visited on September 30. "I renewed," says the traveler, "a prospect of all the delightful scenes, which I have mentioned in a former account." It was at this time that he gave to one of the waterfalls near the Gate of the Notch the name "Silver Cascade," which it still bears. He revisited Rosebrook's, and then went by way of Jefferson to Lancaster and thence onward to Canada.

Another early scientific explorer of the White Hills, who has left us an account of his excursion and a record of his observations, and who deserves a brief mention, was Dr. George Shattuck, of Boston. He was one of a party of six, which set out from Hanover, July 8, 1807, taking along various scientific instruments. On Saturday the 11th the members of the party started from Rosebrook's to ascend Mount Washington, at the summit of which they arrived the following day. Dr. Shattuck notes that the temperature there at noon was 66° and that the day was not very clear, the distant horizon being smoky. He describes briefly the plants, the character of the surface of the summit, the rareness of the atmosphere, and other phenomena. Unfortunately, his attempts to make barometrical observations for the purpose of estimating the height of the mountain were, he says, "defeated by an accident, the prevention of which was beyond my controul."

The next noteworthy American explorer of the White Hills was Dr. Jacob Bigelow. Botany was the

THE WHITE MOUNTAINS

particular interest of this famous Boston physician, who was born in 1797 and who lived to the ripe old age of ninety-two. His tour to the Mountains was made in 1816, in company with Francis C. Gray, Esq., Dr. Francis Boott, in whose honor a spur of Mount Washington has been named, Nathaniel Tucker, and Lemuel Shaw, Esq., afterward Chief Justice of Massachusetts. On their way they climbed Monadnock and Ascutney. The ascent of the White Mountains "was at that time," says the doctor,[1] "an arduous undertaking, owing to the rough state of the country and the want of roads or paths." "We were obliged," he says further, "to walk about fifteen miles and to encamp two nights in the brushwood on the side of the mountain." Each man of the party having carried up a stick, they were enabled to build a fire on the summit and to prepare a meal from such supplies as their guides had brought up. The day (July 2) was a fine one, but the atmosphere was hazy, so that their view of distant objects was very indistinct. The temperature at noon was 57° F. From the registration of a mountain barometer at that hour, calculations were made which gave the height within a few feet of the correct altitude. As a memorial of their achievement

[1] Dr. Bigelow published an account of the journey and a list of the plants collected in the *New England Journal of Medicine and Surgery*, for October, 1816. The quotations in the text are taken from some autobiographical notes, quoted in a *Memoir of Jacob Bigelow, M.D., LL.D.*, by George E. Ellis (1880). Writing these notes about fifty years after the event, Dr. Bigelow's memory must have played him false, for he gives the year of the journey as 1815 and states that it was the 4th of July when the party was on the summit and that in celebration of the day Mr. Gray was invited to deliver an impromptu address.

EARLY EXPLORERS

of the ascent they left their names and the date inclosed in a bottle cemented to the highest rock. In the afternoon they descended in about five hours to their camping place, and the following day they reached Conway.

This expedition, besides achieving the most satisfactory determination of the height of. Mount Washington that had been made, was noteworthy as a natural history survey. Dr. Bigelow's article "Some Account of the White Mountains of New Hampshire," provided a statement of all that was known of their mineralogy and zoölogy, but is especially important from a botanical standpoint, for his list of plants, or florula, "determined," says Professor Tuckerman, "in great measure the phænogamous botany of our Alps." Very appropriately Dr. Bigelow's name has been since given to a grassy plot (Bigelow's Lawn), rich in alpine plants, below the cone of Washington on Boott Spur. Dr. Boott returned to the Mountains in August of the same year, and as a result of his trip added a "considerable" number of species to the botanical collection.

Another noted botanist to explore the Mountains was William Oakes,[1] who visited them, in company

[1] There is a memoir of him in the *American Journal of Science and Arts* for January, 1849, by Asa Gray, who calls him "the most distinguished botanist of New England." Oakes was born at Danvers, July 1, 1799, and was drowned by falling overboard from a ferryboat between Boston and East Boston, July 31, 1848, it is supposed as a result of a sudden attack of faintness or vertigo. He graduated in 1820 from Harvard, where his previous fondness for natural history was developed under the instruction of Professor W. D. Peck. Oakes named Mounts Clay and Jackson, sending his guide to the summit of the latter to kindle a bonfire there to celebrate the event. His own

THE WHITE MOUNTAINS

with his friend Dr. Charles Pickering, in 1825, again in 1826, and from 1843 on, every summer. To him we are indebted for additions to our botanical knowledge, but especially for one of the classics of White Mountain literature, his "Scenery of the White Mountains," a book consisting of descriptive letterpress accompanying large lithographic plates from drawings by Isaac Sprague.[1] His purpose of publishing a smaller volume to be called "The Book of the White Mountains" and to consist of descriptions of things of interest, a flora of the alpine plants, with the mosses and lichens, and a complete guide for visitors, was frustrated by his tragic death the year (1848) of the publication of his "Scenery."

name is perpetuated in the Mountains by Oakes Gulf, the deep ravine to the east of Mounts Pleasant and Franklin.

[1] There are in all sixteen full folio pages of plates. The sixteenth plate and a part of the fourteenth are from paintings by G. N. Frankenstein, a well-known artist of Cincinnati, after whom a cliff and a railroad trestle in the Crawford Notch are named.

III

FIRST SETTLEMENTS AND SETTLERS

1. THE TOWNS

It was not until the latter part of the eighteenth century that the New England colonies were sufficiently established, and the country secure enough from Indian depredations, for the settlement of the remoter regions to be thought of and attempted. Fryeburg, just over the New Hampshire border in Maine, appears to be the first town in this region to have been chartered. The land there was granted, in March, 1762, to General Joseph Frye of Andover, Massachusetts, an officer in the king's army, in consideration of his gallant deeds on the frontier. The conditions of the grant were, according to Willey, —

That he should give bond to the province treasurer to have the township settled with sixty good families, each of which should have built, within the term of five years, a good house, twenty feet by eighteen, and seven feet stud, and have cleared seven acres for pasturage and tillage. He should reserve one sixty-fourth of the township for the first Protestant minister, one sixty-fourth for a parsonage forever, one sixty-fourth for a school fund forever, one sixty-fourth for Harvard College forever. A Protestant minister was to be settled in the township within ten years.

It was supposed that all of the land granted to General Frye was located in the province of Maine,

THE WHITE MOUNTAINS

but it was subsequently found that a considerable part of it was in New Hampshire. The readjustment of grants that was made after this became known is described farther on, where the settlement of Conway is narrated.

Nathaniel Smith made the first settlement on the west line of the town, on the same site as that of the ancient Indian village of Pequawket (or "Pegwagget," as Winthrop spelled it). Smith was, according to Willey, "a sort of *squatter*, led hither of his own free will and inclination." "His cabin was reared," the historian says further, "and his family moved into it the year succeeding the grant, in the summer of 1763." Among the other early settlers were Moses Ames, John and David Evans, Samuel Osgood, David Page, Nathaniel Frye, and Joseph Frye, Jr., who came chiefly from Concord, New Hampshire, and Andover, Massachusetts. To reach this point, they had to make their way through an unbroken wilderness for sixty or seventy miles. Their nearest white neighbors were, for a time, the inhabitants of Saco, and Sanford, nearly sixty miles distant, was their source of supplies. The only mode of conveyance was on horses and their only way thither was a blazed trail. Such were the hardships these first settlers had to encounter, and the willingness to endure them indicates of what stern stuff the pioneers were made! Fryeburg grew rapidly, in fact attained nearly its full size in a few years, and was for some time the chief village in the White Mountain region. It was incorporated in January, 1777. The locality had been a favorite

FIRST SETTLEMENTS AND SETTLERS

resort of the Indians, and for many years after the dispersion of the Pequawket tribe, solitary members of it continued to linger about their old home. Many of them fought on the American side in the Revolution and rendered good service, receiving testimonials for it from the Government.

The New England colonists had visited this region on several occasions long before its settlement was thought of, and for a very different purpose. In the early part of the eighteenth century, during Queen Anne's War, the savages, who were allies of the French, became very troublesome to the English settlements, keeping the colonists in a continual state of alarm by their attacks and depredations. At length, the authorities of Massachusetts, goaded to desperation by this condition and by fresh forays, determined upon punitive measures. Accordingly, in September, 1703, a force of three hundred and sixty soldiers was sent to invade the Pequawket country. But, on account of the obstacles they had to encounter in their journey and the ignorance of their guides, this incursion availed little. Another punitive expedition was undertaken in the autumn of the same year by Colonel March, of Casco, with very little success. He happened upon a party of Indians and twelve of them were either killed or captured. This partial success encouraged the General Court to offer a bounty of forty pounds for scalps, in the hope of inducing thereby more effective measures to be taken for preventing Indian raids on the settlements and for inflicting further punishment on the savages. One consequence of this offer

THE WHITE MOUNTAINS

was a snowshoe expedition, made in midwinter through the mountain passes and led by Colonel Tyng, of Tyngsboro, which brought back five of those repulsive trophies.

On May 8, 1725, O.S., occurred the foremost military event in the history of this entire region, the battle of Pequawket, or battle of Lovewell's Pond, as it is more usually called, the name of the brave commander of the white men having been later given to the pond on the border of which this engagement took place. This remote lakelet, situated in the midst of the woods and bordered by low hills, with its two islets and its placid waters, has to-day nothing about it suggestive of warfare, but rather everything suggestive of peace and quiet; but its north shore was once the scene of one of the bloodiest combats in the Indian history of New England.

During the year 1724 the Indians were uncommonly bold and savage and committed numerous depredations upon the more exposed settlements, such as Dunstable,[1] killing a considerable number of white men. In September of this year, the Indians carried away two men from the town just mentioned and killed eight or nine of the ten men sent in pursuit. The General Court of Massachusetts, aroused by the report of these forays and killings, passed a bill offering a bounty of a hundred pounds for every Indian scalp.

[1] Dunstable (later Nashua) was then a frontier town of Massachusetts, being south of the then recognized boundary between that colony and New Hampshire. The latter did not become an entirely separate colony until 1741.

FIRST SETTLEMENTS AND SETTLERS

Captain John Lovewell, Jr., son of an early settler in Dunstable, was an able colonial partisan, and his expeditions against the Indians were among the most successful of the retaliatory measures of the colonists. In December, 1724, with a few followers, he killed one Indian and took prisoner another, a boy, northeast of Lake Winnepesaukee. In February, 1725, he led a force of forty men to the head of Salmon Falls River, now in Wakefield, New Hampshire, where he came upon a party of ten Indians, who were asleep by their fires. Stationing his men advantageously, he killed the entire number. For the ten scalps his force received one thousand pounds when it reached Boston after a triumphal march there. We can realize to how desperate a pass the struggle between the settlers and the Indians had come, when we know that Lovewell's party did not wait to learn whether the Indians were friendly or not, but assumed, from their possession of new guns, much ammunition, and spare blankets and moccasins, that they were on a marauding excursion. That they had killed Indians was all the soldiers cared to know.

Lovewell's last and most memorable expedition, which resulted in the bloody encounter by the pond, left Dunstable on April 15, 1725, with the object of attacking the Indian village of Pequawket on the Saco. His force on this occasion consisted at the start of forty-six men, volunteers from Dunstable, Woburn, Concord, and other towns in the vicinity. It was an arduous and dangerous undertaking, a desperate adventure, to attempt to march more than

THE WHITE MOUNTAINS

a hundred miles into the wilderness, much of which was unbroken and all of which was without a friendly habitation or inhabitant. But Lovewell was a daring spirit and he had brave companions. By sickness, which compelled some to return and others to remain near Ossipee Pond, their ranks were reduced to thirty-four when they reached Saco (now Lovewell's) Pond on Thursday, May 6. Until Saturday morning they lay encamped on the west shore in the vicinity of the chief Indian village, preparing for the encounter, uncertain whether their presence had been detected, fearful of attack in the darkness of the night, and undecided as to what course were best to pursue. They were glad when Saturday morning dawned after a night of alarm, in which they had listened to the distant barking of dogs and the stealthy marching of Indians, as it seemed, in their near vicinity. After they had breakfasted and while they were at their devotions, a gunshot was heard and soon they caught sight of an Indian on a point of land on the opposite side of the pond. Concluding that the main body of the enemy was on the north side, the intrepid band marched thither. When they reached the slight elevation at the northeast point of the pond, they left their packs there. Freed from these impediments, they advanced cautiously and soon discovered an Indian, who had evidently been out hunting, and who, according to Belknap, was the Indian previously seen. They ambushed him, but missed him at the first fire, and he was not killed until after he had mortally wounded their leader

FIRST SETTLEMENTS AND SETTLERS

and also wounded another of their company. Then they started back for the place where the packs had been left.

Meanwhile the sachem Paugus, with forty-one warriors [1] in two companies, had discovered and counted the packs and had laid an ambuscade with the design of so surprising Lovewell's men as to cause them to surrender at once. When the white men came up and began searching for their packs, the Indians suddenly sprang up, with a terrible whoop, fired their guns directly over the heads of the whites and ran toward them with ropes demanding if they would have quarter. Replying that it would be "only at the muzzles of their guns," the brave captain and his band began the battle by rushing toward the Indians, firing as they advanced. Lovewell's men drove the Indians some distance by their charge, but were repulsed by a counter-charge in which the wounded Lovewell and eight of his men were killed. Then the intrepid band began a retreat, fighting step by step, until they reached a spot where a ridge of rocks was on their left, with the pond at their rear and the mouth of a brook on their right. Here they made a stand and continued to fight, maintaining their position until sundown, when the savages retreated, under the command of Wahwa. They left many dead and wounded, including Paugus, who was killed, late in the contest, prob-

[1] One account says seventy, another eighty, and another sixty-three. Belknap, however, declares that there were two companies and that their number was forty-one, and says in support of this statement that he had it from Evans, who had it from one of the Indians who was in the fight.

THE WHITE MOUNTAINS

ably by the fearless Ensign Seth Wyman, who had become the final leader of the white men. It had been a protracted and fierce fight at close quarters, the hideous yells of the Indians, the cheers of the whites, and the cracks of the muskets mingling in an indescribable hurly-burly. Chaplain Frye, after he was mortally wounded and could fight no longer, was often heard praying audibly for victory.

About midnight, when it became certain that the savages would not return to renew the contest, the remnant of the command, of whom only nine remained unwounded, began their memorable return. Thirteen or more of their number they left dead or dying on the field; four others, after they had gone but a mile and a half, found they could go no farther. The main party of eleven reached Dunstable on May 13 in the night. Several of those left behind managed after terrible sufferings to reach Dunstable or one or other of the coast settlements. Such is the story of the bloody battle [1] of Lovewell's Pond, which has been described at some length because of its intrinsic interest and because it was the only contest of this sort within the White Mountain region.

The Indians soon abandoned their village here and retired to St. Francis on the St. Lawrence. The bodies of the dead white men were buried a short time afterward by a party under Colonel Tyng, which went to the scene of the action for the pur-

[1] A number of ballads and poems have been composed on this historic encounter, including an early anonymous ballad and the first printed production of Longfellow.

FIRST SETTLEMENTS AND SETTLERS

poses of succoring the wounded and of attacking the Indians, if any were to be found.

Starr King has said of this historic pond that it is "more deeply dyed with tradition than any other sheet of water in New England." The village within whose limits the pond lies and whose settlement and growth have already been recorded is idyllic for its beauty and tranquillity and has a number of interesting associations. Here Daniel Webster taught in the noted academy for nine months in 1802, and often, it is said, he fished in Lovewell's Pond. Fryeburg was the old home of a number of prominent New England families, such as the Osgoods and the Danas; poets have made it a place of resort and have written of its beauties and noble views; and Howells has placed here the scene of the opening chapter of his "A Modern Instance."

The only notable happening in the latter-day history of this quiet White Mountain village occurred at the end of August, 1906, when the principal hotel, the Oxford, built about fifteen years before, was burned to the ground, together with many houses and stores. The fire started at 10.30 A.M., from some unknown cause, in the kitchen of the hotel and quickly spread, fanned by a high wind, to the neighboring houses. The whole business center was threatened and aid was summoned from Portland and elsewhere. Fortunately, the time of the occurrence of the fire enabled the guests all to get out in safety. From the village the fire spread to the woods in the direction of Lovewell's Pond, where it burned fiercely all night and for some time after. Between

THE WHITE MOUNTAINS

twenty-five and thirty buildings were destroyed, the total property loss being $100,000. The burning of the only large hotel in the village was a great blow to it as a summer resort, one, indeed, from which it has not as yet recovered.

Plymouth, beautiful for situation, on a terrace near the confluence of the Pemigewasset and Bakers Rivers, is on the border of the White Mountain region and has from early times been an important town. It was granted, July 15, 1763, to Joseph Blanchard and others, and the first settlement was made in the summer of the next year by Captain James Hobart and Lieutenant Zachariah Parker, of Hollis. Other settlers, with their families, joined them in the autumn. The intervales of Plymouth were doubtless favorite resorts of the Indians for hunting, and, according to tradition, they had a village or encampment near the mouth of Bakers River.[1] Indian remains of various kinds have been found in this vicinity.

In the year 1712, Captain Baker, of Newbury, led a force of Massachusetts rangers up the Pemigewasset Valley and surprised a body of Indians at this place, killing several of them and plundering their wigwams of a large quantity of furs the savages had collected. According to a story of doubtful authenticity, Baker's company was pursued by a larger band of Indians, but escaped through a stratagem, which is said to have been due to a friendly redskin who had accompanied them and

[1] Its beautiful Indian name was Asquamchemauke!

FIRST SETTLEMENTS AND SETTLERS

which deceived the pursuers as to the number of the pursued. After this foray into their ancestral domain, at any rate, the main body of the Pemigewassets retired to Canada.

A noted visitor to this particular region before the time of its settlement was the future hero of Bennington, who, in company with his brother William, David Stinson, and Amos Eastman, was trapping in April of the year 1752 within the limits of the present town of Rumney, north of Plymouth. When about to return home the party of trappers were surprised by a body of Indians. John Stark and Eastman were easily captured, as they were on the shore of a lake (afterward known as Lake Stinson) and had no chance to escape. The other two were in a canoe and attempted to get away, in which purpose William Stark alone was successful, Stinson being killed by a musket shot. The future general was taken to Canada, but was ransomed the next autumn.

Formerly a shire town of Grafton County, Plymouth has always had a goodly number of professional men among its permanent residents, and the beauty of its location and environment early attracted many summer visitors. The first county courthouse, which was raised before July, 1774, and which stood in the south part of the village until 1876, when it was removed to a new location, restored (it had been used as a wheelwright's shop), and presented to the Young Ladies' Library Association by a benefactor of the town, is historically interesting as the place where Daniel Webster made,

THE WHITE MOUNTAINS

in 1806, his first defense of a murderer and delivered his "only solitary" plea against capital punishment.[1] The chief business of the village was formerly the manufacture of gloves, begun in 1835. The "Plymouth buck gloves" were for years widely esteemed, but, following a number of years of prosperity, the business gradually declined. After the Boston, Concord, and Montreal Railroad reached Plymouth in 1850 and located its general offices there, the railroad and State business, combined with the fine natural advantages, soon rendered the town a rich and thriving one. When the lease of this railroad to the Boston and Lowell was made, in June, 1884, however, the business offices of the railroad were lost to Plymouth.

One of the next places to be settled in the White Hills was Conway,[2] the site of which was granted by Governor Benning Wentworth to Daniel Foster and others in October, 1765, on condition that each grantee should pay a rent, if it were demanded, of one ear of Indian corn annually for ten years, and, after the end of that period, of one shilling proclamation money for every one hundred acres. The

---

[1] This was not the first plea made by Webster, as is usually stated. The correct statement of the matter is to be found in E. S. Stearns's *History of Plymouth* (1906).

[2] I am indebted for some facts about the settlement of Conway to an article on "The Town of Conway," by Mrs. Ellen McRoberts Mason in the *Granite Monthly* for June, 1896. Conway gets its name, according to Sweetser, "from that gallant old English statesman, Henry Seymour Conway, Walpole's friend, commander in chief of the British army, and, at the time when this mountain glen was baptized, a prominent champion of the liberties of America."

FIRST SETTLEMENTS AND SETTLERS

charter was for 23,040 acres of land, with the addition of 1040 acres for roads, ponds, mountains, rocks, etc. This land was divided into sixty-nine equal shares, and each grantee, or his heirs and assigns, was required to plant and cultivate five acres of land within the term of five years, for each fifty acres contained in his share. Two shares, containing five hundred acres, were to be reserved for Governor Wentworth, one was to be reserved for the support of the gospel in heathen lands, one for the Church of England, one for the first settled minister, and one for the benefit of schools. Soon came an inflow of settlers from Concord, Pembroke, Exeter, Portsmouth, Durham, Lee, and other places, who had been led to remove to this locality by the glowing accounts they had heard of the fertility of the soil and of the abundance of game and fish. These settlers received their lands under the Maine grants to General Frye, whose territory, it was found on the subsequent adjustment of the boundary between the province of New Hampshire and the province of Maine, included more than four thousand acres in New Hampshire. Finally, the general relinquished his land in Conway and selected an equal number of acres in Maine. This addition of land to Conway caused the area of that town to exceed the number of acres granted, and so, to remedy this state of affairs, the area was reduced by moving the northern boundary line farther south. By this strange hap the first settlers on the intervale lands proved to be the first settlers of Conway, when they might have been expected to be the first of Fryeburg, and some

THE WHITE MOUNTAINS

of those early settlers who would have been otherwise citizens of Conway became citizens of the town of Bartlett.

Here on the intervales an Indian village or encampment had formerly been situated, — the relics found have been mentioned, — and the savages enviously witnessed the inroads of the white men upon their favorite haunt.

In 1766, Foster and several others built houses five miles farther north on the river bottoms and thus began the settlement of the village and future summer resort of North Conway.

As Conway was incorporated by its charter, held its first proprietary meeting in the town of Chester, December 2, 1765, elected its officers, and has ever since kept up its organization, it was the first White Mountain town, antedating Fryeburg by more than eleven years.

During the next thirty or forty years most of the other now well-known places were established. The site of the town of Jefferson was granted, under the name of Dartmouth, to Colonel Goffe, in 1765, and again, in 1772, to Theodore Atkinson, Mark H. Wentworth, and others. It was settled about 1773 by Colonel Joseph Whipple, who was the first settler to come through the Notch, and who owned a vast area and exercised for many years an almost feudal sway over the country in the vicinity of his home. The town was incorporated under its present name in 1796.

An adventure of Colonel Whipple's, related by

FIRST SETTLEMENTS AND SETTLERS

Willey and others, exhibits his bravery and resourcefulness. During the Revolutionary War, a party of Indians under the control of the English were admitted to his house, and, before he was aware of their purpose, the colonel was made prisoner. Being permitted to go to his bedroom to secure some clothes for his journey with the Indians, he managed, while his housekeeper was entertaining the Indians with some mechanical articles, to make his escape from the window. Going to a field where some of his men were at work, he ordered each of them to shoulder a stake from the fence as he would a gun. Thus reinforced the colonel again presented himself before the Indians, who were in pursuit of him. The enemy, seeing as they supposed a body of armed men approaching, hurriedly seized what plunder they could lay their hands upon and fled.

Among the defiles at the head of Israel's River [1] tradition locates the destruction of a detachment of Rogers's Rangers under horrible circumstances. In October, 1759, the famous colonial partisan, having led about one hundred and fifty of his veterans to the St. Lawrence, made a night attack on the Indian village of St. Francis, surprising the savages when they were sleeping after having spent most of the night in a grand dance. The village was plundered and burned, after its inhabitants had been killed or dispersed, and thus the errand on which

[1] This river, alas! is named after Israel Glines, a noted hunter and trapper of this region in the eighteenth century, whose brother John gave his name to a stream which runs through the neighboring village of Whitefield. Singrawack, said to mean "The Foaming Stream of the White Rock," is its Indian name!

THE WHITE MOUNTAINS

Rogers had been sent by General Amherst was accomplished. The victorious white men carried off the church plate, the candlesticks, and a large silver image. They kept together for about ten days, when, their provisions failing, the rangers broke up into small parties that they might the better procure subsistence by hunting. Two of these parties were overtaken by pursuing bodies of Indians, who captured or killed most of the unfortunate rangers. The main body, after enduring extreme suffering from hunger, finally reached Charlestown, or Number Four, the nearest place of relief. One party of nine, which had the silver image, attempted, so the story goes, to find a way of escape through the Notch, but was misled by a treacherous Indian guide, who piloted the unfortunate men into the gorges of Israel's River and fled after poisoning one of them with a rattlesnake's fang. Under terrible hardships all but one of the rangers, it is said, perished. The survivor eventually reached the settlements. The golden candlesticks of the church of St. Francis were found near Lake Memphremagog in 1816 and the early settlers of Coös came upon various relics of the rangers, but the silver image has not been recovered.

Numerous legends have grown up about this romantic episode, the most beautiful of which is that of a lonely hunter encamped one night up among the White Hills. The night mist rolled back and disclosed "a great stone church, and within this was an altar, where from a sparkling censer rose a curling wreath of incense-smoke, and around it lights dispersed a mellow glow, by which in groups before

FIRST SETTLEMENTS AND SETTLERS

that altar appeared a tribe of savages kneeling in profound silence. A change came in the wind; a song long and loud rose, as a voice-offering to the Great Spirit; then glittering church spire, church and altar, vanished, and down the steep rock trailed a long line of strange-looking men, in solemn silence. Before all, as borne by some airy sprite, sported a glittering image of silver, which in the deep shadows changed to fairy shape, and, with sparkling wings, disappeared in the rent rocks." This was followed by a loud laugh of triumph, whereupon the hunter awoke.

The pathetic story of Nancy,[1] who came up the Notch with Colonel Whipple and who lived with his family in Jefferson, may well be set down here. This poor girl, whose tragic fate is recalled by Nancy's Brook, Nancy's Bridge, and Mount Nancy, near Bemis Station in the Crawford Notch, was engaged to a farmhand of the Colonel's, who had completely won her affections. Her lover and she agreed to go to Portsmouth to be married. While she was at Lancaster, whither she had gone to make preparations for her journey through the wilderness, the prospective husband to whom she had entrusted her savings, the pay for two years' service, set out from Jefferson for Portsmouth, leaving no explanation or message for her. On her return at night she resolved to follow the recreant lover, in spite of all

[1] Her surname appears to be somewhat uncertain. Frank H. Burt's *Among the White Mountains* (1884) gives it as Barton. The same surname is given in an article on Jefferson by J. M. Cooper, in the *Granite Monthly* for August, 1898. The *White Mountain and Winnepissiogee Lake Guide Book* (1846), makes it Rogers and even gives the name of the treacherous lover as Jim Swindell (!).

THE WHITE MOUNTAINS

dissuasion, in the hope of overtaking him before dawn in his probable camp in the Notch. But she arrived there after an arduous journey through the snow and in the teeth of a northwest wind, only to find the camp abandoned. As the ashes of the campfire were still warm, the dauntless girl determined to push on, but she was soon compelled to give up and to sink down in utter exhaustion, near the brook which has been given her Christian name. There, at the foot of a tree, she was found curled up in the snow by a party of men from Colonel Whipple's, who, alarmed for her safety, had followed her trail. The perfidious lover is said to have become insane on learning of her fate. This episode of Nancy, which is recorded in many books and the truth of which is vouched for by Ethan Allen Crawford and by J. H. Spaulding, as told to them by persons who knew the facts, is assigned to the year 1778.

Another servant of Colonel Whipple's, who was said to be the first of her sex to come through the Notch, was a woman who in her old age was known as Granny Stalbird or Starbird. Having learned from the Indians the virtues of various roots and herbs, she became, after the death of her husband, a noted doctress, famous all through this region for her skill. A number of stories of her adventures and eccentricities have been handed down. Her memory was gratefully cherished by the early settlers for her many deeds of mercy. Among her patients was Ethan Allen Crawford, who was once treated by her for an injury to his foot.

Lancaster, named after Lancaster, Massachusetts,

FIRST SETTLEMENTS AND SETTLERS

whence several of its early settlers came, was granted in July, 1763, to Captain David Page and others and was occupied in the autumn of the same year by Captain Page, Edward Bucknam, and Emmons Stockwell and their families. The troubles of the Revolutionary War hindered the progress of the new settlement, all the inhabitants but Stockwell and his family leaving the new town for older and more secure settlements. Stockwell's brave determination to stay and abide the consequences induced some, emboldened by his example, to return.

Littleton was chartered in November, 1764, under the name of Chiswick. Among the grantees, who were mostly from southeastern Connecticut, was James Avery, who had associated with himself twelve others of the same name and many relatives and who thus controlled the franchise. This he disposed of to Colonel Moses Little and his associates in 1768. On account of non-compliance with the provisions of the charter, the town was rechartered in January, 1770, under the name of Apthorp. The first settlement was made shortly after by Captain Nathan Caswell, who was induced by the energetic proprietors of Apthorp to leave his home in Orford and make a hazard of new fortunes in the Ammonoosuc wilderness. Caswell reached his new home on the 11th of April, 1770. He found there only a barn, in which his son, Apthorp, was born that night, the first white child born within the limits of Littleton. In November, 1784, when Dalton[1]

[1] The name of the daughter town perpetuates that of the Honorable Tristram Dalton, another of the early proprietors of Apthorp.

THE WHITE MOUNTAINS

was separated from Apthorp and incorporated, the name of the mother town was changed to the present one, in honor of the principal proprietor.

Franconia was granted in 1764 under its present name to Jesse Searle and others. No move was made by them toward settlement, so a more extensive grant was made in 1772 to Sir Francis Bernard, Bart., His Excellency Thomas Hutchinson, the Honorable Corbyn Morris, Esq., and others, the tract being called Morristown in honor of the last-named gentleman. Franconia was settled permanently two years later by Captain Artemas Knight, Zebedee Applebee, and others. These conflicting grants later gave rise to much controversy, and it was not until nearly the beginning of the nineteenth century that the dispute was finally settled in favor of the original grantees. The name of Franconia was reassumed in 1782.

The town owed its early prosperity mainly to the discovery of iron ore in the vicinity. In December, 1805, a company was incorporated under the name of the New Hampshire Iron Factory Company. The principal works, which were owned by this company, were situated on the Gale River and consisted of a blast furnace, a cupola furnace, a forge, a machine shop, etc. About the middle of the last century from twenty to thirty men were constantly employed and two hundred and fifty tons of pig iron and from two to three hundred tons of bar iron were produced annually. The ore, which was said to be the richest up to then discovered in the United States, was obtained from a mountain in the east part of Lisbon,

FIRST SETTLEMENTS AND SETTLERS

about three miles from the furnace. The works have long since [1] been abandoned, but the remains of the furnace are plainly to be seen on the west bank of the river near the point where the road to Sugar Hill leaves the main thoroughfare of Franconia. Not far from this establishment were the upper works, called "The Haverhill and Franconia Iron works," which were incorporated in 1808 and which were built on the same plan as the other.

Jackson was first settled by Benjamin Copp in 1778.[2] Here he and his family lived alone until other settlers came in 1790. Among these latter was Captain Joseph Pinkham and his family (after whom the Pinkham Notch is named), who came when the snow was five feet deep on the level. Their handsled, it is said, was drawn by a pig which had been taught to work in harness. The settlement was first called New Madbury, but, on its incorporation in 1800, the name was changed to Adams. In 1829, to suit the prevailing political opinions, the name was again changed, to the present one.

Berlin was granted in 1771 to Sir William Mayne, Bart., his relatives, Thomas, Robert, and Edward Mayne, and several others from Barbados. Its original name was Maynesborough, which was changed to the present one in 1829, when the town was incorporated.

---

[1] About 1865, says a writer in the *Granite Monthly*, for August, 1881. According to another writer in the same periodical, operation was resumed in 1859 after some years of suspension and the buildings were burned in 1884.

[2] Some books say 1779. The centennial of the settlement was celebrated on July 4, 1878.

THE WHITE MOUNTAINS

Bartlett, named after the president of the State at the date of the town's incorporation (1790), was originally granted to William Stark and others for services during the French-and-Indian War. Two brothers by the name of Emery and a Mr. Harriman were among the first settlers there. A few years later, in 1777, Daniel Fox, Paul Jilly, and Captain Samuel Willey, from Lee, began a settlement in what is now known as Upper Bartlett.

Whitefield was granted, as Whitefields, to Josiah Moody and others in July, 1774, and was occupied soon after by Major Burns and other settlers. It was incorporated December 1, 1804.

The territory originally occupied by the town of Bethlehem was almost exactly that of the lost town of Lloyd Hills,[1] said to have been granted by Governor Wentworth in or about 1774. This town had only a paper existence, as the records of the grant are lost and the original grantees probably made no effort to settle it. In the silence of the charter records of New Hampshire as to the town, we know of it through its being given as a boundary in the grant of Whitefield in 1774 and from its name appearing on Holland's map (1784). The royal government having been overthrown, the territory became the property of the State and the earlier grant was ignored.

The first settlement in the limits of the town was made in 1790 by Jonas Warren, Nathaniel Snow, Amos Wheeler, and others. On December 27, 1799, the General Court of New Hampshire incorporated

---

[1] Various early histories say "Lord's Hill."

FIRST SETTLEMENTS AND SETTLERS

the town of Bethlehem and the first town meeting was held March 4, 1800. Additions of territory were made in 1848 and in 1873. The hamlet of Bethlehem led a precarious existence in its early days. Famine frequently frowned on the settlement and in 1799 the inhabitants were reduced to such straits that they were compelled to make a load of potash and to send it to Concord, Massachusetts, a distance of one hundred and seventy miles, for sale, subsisting on roots and plants until their envoys returned with provisions, four weeks later. President Dwight, in 1803, found chiefly log huts, the settlements being "recent, few, poor, and planted on a soil, singularly rough and rocky." "There is nothing in Bethlehem," he remarks, "which merits notice, except the patience, enterprise and hardihood, of the settlers, which have induced them to venture, and stay, upon so forbidding a spot; a magnificent prospect of the White Mountains; and a splendid collection of other mountains in their neighbourhood."

Lisbon, within whose limits is the summer resort of Sugar Hill, far-famed for the beauty of its views, was first granted to Joseph Burt and others on August 6, 1763, under the name later[1] given to the town which was to become the capital of the State. Much of the same territory was included in the grant bearing the name of Chiswick, made the following year. By the failure of the grantees to make the required settlements, however, both grants were forfeited, and in October, 1768, another charter was issued, to

[1] The future state capital received its present name in June, 1765. It had previously been called Penacook, and Rumford.

THE WHITE MOUNTAINS

Leonard Whiting and others, covering the territory now forming the town of Lisbon, the title of Gunthwaite being bestowed upon the grant. For some time the name of the town was evidently somewhat unsettled, for it appears in State documents of twenty years later as "Concord, *alias* Gunthwaite." In 1824, by act of legislature the town was given the name it now bears. The discovery of gold in the town in 1866 created great excitement and many mining operations were set in motion. Soon the business became of a highly speculative nature, and during ten years the sum of $1,500,000, it is estimated, was squandered in such operations in Lisbon and vicinity.

Woodstock, which received its present name in 1840 by act of legislature, was first granted in September, 1763, to Eli Demerit. On account of the indefiniteness or non-preservation of the records the course of events in the early history of the town is somewhat uncertain, but the charter appears to have been forfeited by non-settlement and the town to have been regranted, in 1771, to Nathaniel Cushman, Dr. Ebenezer Thompson, of Durham, and others, among whom was John Demerit, nephew of Eli, who had at least nine hundred acres. Most of the older authorities say that the town was originally granted under the name of Peeling, then for a time was called Fairfield, and subsequently bore again, by restoration, the name of Peeling, until 1840. They attribute the first settlement of the town to John Riant and others and make it date from about 1773.

FIRST SETTLEMENTS AND SETTLERS

A recent writer,[1] however, states that the town was originally granted under the name Fairfield and that in 1799 the legislature granted a town charter under the name of Peeling, the first town meeting of which any record is to be found being held in 1800. The same authority attributes the first settlement to one James McNorton, whose name does not appear in the early history of Peeling, but who is stated to have built a home, soon after the original grant, on the east bank of the Pemigewasset. At the outbreak of the Revolution, he joined the patriot army, leaving a wife and children in his newly made home and being destined never to return, perishing, it is said, at Valley Forge. In all, the infant town furnished four soldiers to the Continental army.

Randolph was granted in 1772 to John Durand and others, of London, and bore the name of its first proprietor until 1824, when it received the name of the famous Virginian. Its first settlers were Joseph Wilder and Stephen Jillson.

Carroll, originally called Bretton Woods, which name has recently been revived and applied to the locality and railroad stations of two large summer hotels in the limits of the township, was granted February 8, 1772, to Sir Thomas Wentworth, Bart., the Reverend Samuel Langdon, and eighty-one others. The town, whose permanent population has always been small, received its present name in 1832, the year of its incorporation.

[1] Justus Conrad, in his article "The Town of Woodstock," in the *Granite Monthly* for July, 1897.

THE WHITE MOUNTAINS

Warren[1] was granted to John Page, of Kingston, near Portsmouth, and others, July 14, 1763, and settlement was commenced in the autumn of 1767 by Joseph Patch, who came from Hollis, New Hampshire. The territory under the shadow of that outlying mountain, Moosilauke, one of the finest of viewpoints, was the special stamping-ground of the Pemigewassets, a local sub-tribe, or family, of Indians, whose retirement to Canada has been mentioned. The first settlers inherited the clearings in which these red men used to plant their maize and bury their dead. The region had been the scene of much Indian warfare, and even after the Indians' departure and the advent of the white men, the district was a thoroughfare for marauding bands from Canada, who used to sweep down upon the defenseless Massachusetts towns, and for their white enemies in pursuing or making counter-attacks. The first habitations built here by the colonists were two log huts for the temporary shelter of travelers journeying to the Coös country. Patch lived like a hunter with no companion but a faithful dog. The first family, that of John Mills, of Portsmouth, came in the spring of 1768. They were followed the next year by an Irishman by the name of James Aiken, who discovered after he had built his log house that he had neighbors. Joshua Copp was the fourth settler. The next family to come was that of a Mr.

[1] The history of this town has been fully dealt with by William Little, whose *History of Warren* was published in 1870. The town is said to take its name from Admiral Sir Peter Warren, who commanded the fleet in the attack on Louisburg in 1745; it may, however, have been named after a town of the same name in England.

FIRST SETTLEMENTS AND SETTLERS

True. Thus a hamlet was begun. The charter was renewed and a grant of additional territory made in 1770.

The town of Gorham, long a leading summer resort and now an important industrial community, formed until its corporation in 1836 a part of Shelburne, which was chartered as early as 1769 and rechartered in 1770, soon after which date it was settled.

An early incident in Shelburne's history has to do with an Indian raid. On August 3, 1781, a party of six of the savages who had visited Bethel and Gilead, Maine, capturing three men in the former and killing one in the latter, stopped at Shelburne on their way to Canada. At the house of Captain Rindge, they killed and scalped Peter Poor, and took Plato, a colored man, prisoner. The inhabitants, it is related, after spending the night on "Hark Hill" in full hearing of the whoops and cries of the Indians, fled in a body to Fryeburg, fifty-nine miles distant, where they remained until the danger was past.

The territory of the town of Campton, in the Pemigewasset Valley, formed, with that of the neighboring town of Rumney, a grant made, it appears, in 1761, just after the English conquest of Canada, to Jared Spencer of East Haddam, Connecticut, Christopher Holmes, and others. Campton took its name from the circumstance that the proprietors built their camp within its limit when they came up to survey this town and Rumney. Owing to the death of Spencer at East Windsor, Connecticut, on his way home from New Hamp-

THE WHITE MOUNTAINS

shire, in 1762, before any settlement was made, his heirs and others obtained a new charter in 1767. The town was settled in 1765 by two families by the name of Fox and Taylor. Joseph and Hobart Spencer, two of the early settlers, were very likely sons of the original grantee. Though but in its infancy, the town furnished nine or ten soldiers to the Revolutionary army, five of whom died in the service. Thirty of its citizens laid down their lives in the war for the Union. Campton Village and West Campton early became favorite resorts for artists, who are attracted by the rich bits of meadow and woodland scenery which abound there. Following the artists came literary people and families in search of the summer quiet and restfulness not to be found in the more fashionable mountain resorts. Campton was a favorite resort of James T. and Annie Fields, and of Miss Larcom. At West Campton was located, until its destruction a few years ago by fire, a famous inn, the Stag and Hounds, which was one of the most ancient among the Mountains and which in its early days was frequented by Durand, Gay, Gerry, Griggs, Richards, George L. Brown, and other landscape painters.

The neighboring town of Thornton was granted, in 1763, to the family from which it gets its name, and was settled in 1770 by Benjamin Hoit. There is no village, but there are several groups of farms, Thornton Street, Thornton Center, and West Thornton.

The southern outlying wall of the White Mountains is the picturesque and lofty Sandwich Range,

FIRST SETTLEMENTS AND SETTLERS

terminating on the east in the beautiful peak of Chocorua in Albany. The immense mass of Sandwich Dome, the slide-scarred Whiteface, and Passaconaway, loftiest of the summits of this group, are other notable features of the Range. On the southerly side of these mountains is the pleasant town of Sandwich, which has attained considerable reputation as a summer resort. It was granted originally in October, 1763, by Governor Benning Wentworth to Samuel Gilman, Jr., and others, of Exeter, and then contained an area of six miles square. Upon the representation of the grantees that the north and west sides of the tract were "so loaded with inaccessible mountains and shelves of rocks, as to be uninhabitable," an additional grant of territory on the east and south, called Sandwich Addition, was made by the governor in September of the following year, bringing the total area up to ten miles square. The town was settled soon after 1765, when Orlando Weed was granted by the proprietors at Exeter seven hundred acres, seventy pounds of lawful money, and seven cows, on condition that he would settle seven families in Sandwich, build seven substantial dwelling-houses, and clear forty acres of land within three years. Among the first settlers were Daniel Beede, John Prescott, David Bean, Jeremiah Page, and Richard Sinclair. Members of many noted New England families later settled in the new township. Soldiers were furnished to the Revolutionary army, a Sandwich regiment being honorably mentioned in the records of the battle of Bunker Hill. Many small industries were early

THE WHITE MOUNTAINS

established, but they declined after some years. Most of the descendants of the original settlers either were killed in the Civil War or moved away, the farms were taken possession of by strangers, and the town became mainly a summer resort. The picturesque village of Center Sandwich was another favorite haunt of the poet Lucy Larcom.

Situated east of Sandwich and between the Sandwich and Ossipee Ranges is the town of Tamworth, named after an English town on the river Tyne. The township was granted in October, 1766, to John Webster, Jonathan Moulton, and others, and was first settled in 1771 by Richard Jackman, Jonathan Choate, David Philbrick, and William Eastman.

The early settlers endured uncommon hardships on account of an early frost, which cut off nearly all their crops and reduced the families almost to utter starvation. The men were often obliged to go thirty or forty miles to Gilmanton or to Canterbury for grain, which they brought from thence on their backs or on hand-sleds. Amid all their discouragements the pioneers resolved not to abandon the settlement. Fortunately, they killed now and then a deer or other animal whose flesh was palatable, and thus managed to sustain themselves until they were able to secure permanent relief.

In the east part of the town, on the Chocorua River, is the small hamlet long known as Tamworth Iron Works, but now called Chocorua. An iron factory was established here before the Revolution, but was abandoned early in the nineteenth century. The metal was obtained from bog-iron ore in the bot-

FIRST SETTLEMENTS AND SETTLERS

tom of Ossipee Lake. Here, in 1775, the first American machine-made nails were turned out, and here also the first American screw-auger was made, in 1780, Mr. Weed, the maker, having seen an auger on a British prize frigate at Portsmouth. Many anchors were cast at Tamworth and were hauled thence to Portsmouth on sledges.

On account of the noble mountain scenery, the pleasant lowlands, and the beautiful lakes, Tamworth has been a favorite resort of nature-lovers. Near Chocorua Lake are the summer residences of the late Horace E. Scudder, the late Professor William James, the late Frank Bolles, Secretary of Harvard University, and others. In the closing years of his life ex-President Cleveland found a summer home in Tamworth.

Such are the facts, for the most part in brief statement, as to the settlement and early history of the principal towns in the Mountains. The later history of the towns is largely bound up with the story of the region's industrial development and so will be dealt with only as a part of this wider subject. In some cases, however, an event of recent occurrence, unrelated to any general movement, has for convenience been narrated, out of chronological order, in the foregoing pages.

IV

FIRST SETTLEMENTS AND SETTLERS

II. THE SOLITARY PLACES — THE WILLEY DISASTER

THE main interest of White Mountain settlement, however, lies aside from the history of the founding of the towns. It centers about the settlements made in the isolated places, such as Nash and Sawyer's Location and the Notch, where various individuals of hardy spirit established themselves; or, rather, the main interest lies in the settlers themselves of these localities and in the story of their hardships and of their perseverance. The names of Crawford, Rosebrook, and Willey are the most famous ones in this connection, and the days of the families of these names are the heroic days of White Mountain history.

In 1792, Eleazar Rosebrook, a native of Grafton, Massachusetts, settled with his family in Nash and Sawyer's Location, in a then remote and lonesome spot in the valley of the Ammonoosuc, near the site of the present Fabyan House, now such a busy railroad center in the summer. About 1775, he had come from Grafton with his wife and child into the remote district known as Upper Coös, making a temporary stay at Lancaster until he could look about and find such a place as he desired in which to settle. Pushing through the woods up the Connecticut River into what is now Colebrook (then known

FIRST SETTLEMENTS AND SETTLERS

as Monadnock), he built a log cabin to which he brought his wife and two small children — a second child, a daughter, had been born to them at Lancaster. Hannah Rosebrook was a true helpmate for such a sturdy pioneer, and she cheerfully endured the hardships and privations which their living in this solitary wilderness entailed. The narration of one or two homely incidents of their life here will show the mettle of this couple. They had taken with them a cow, and, as there were no fences, the animal was at liberty to go where she pleased. Many times Mrs. Rosebrook, when her husband was away, would shut her older child up in the house, and, taking her infant in her arms, would go in search of the animal, to which a bell was attached to enable her to be found. Expeditions of this nature would sometimes take the courageous woman far into the woods and force her to wade the river to get to the animal, but she never flinched from any hardship of this sort. Salt was an article much needed in this country and some families suffered considerably from lack of it. Once, when there was a shortage of this commodity, Rosebrook went on foot to Haverhill and returned, a distance of about eighty miles, with a bushel of it on his back. This was not regarded by this powerful and resolute man as any great feat.

Rosebrook served in the army during the Revolutionary War. Before he left to join his company, the pioneer took his family for safety to Northumberland, where a sort of fort had been built. Here a son was born. A man named White, who had an invalid wife, thereupon kindly took Mrs. Rose-

THE WHITE MOUNTAINS

brook and her children into his house, giving them their board for what household service Mrs. Rosebrook could give. During a leave of absence from the army, Rosebrook removed his family to Guildhall, Vermont. He rendered brave service in the army. On one occasion an officer and he had a narrow escape from capture when they were sent to Canada as spies, their pursuers being outwitted by a clever stratagem of Rosebrook's.

While her husband was in the army, Indians frequently came to the house where Mrs. Rosebrook was staying, and she had to tolerate their presence, as she feared to incur their displeasure when there was no man to resist them. On one occasion, however, when they had become intoxicated, she cleared her house of them, even dragging one drunken squaw out by the hair of the head, and narrowly escaping a tomahawk thrown by the angry female, who, when sober, came back next day, begged Mrs. Rosebrook's forgiveness, and promised amendment, which promise, it is said, was strictly kept.

At Guildhall the Rosebrooks remained for many years in comparative comfort, but at length, life having become too easy, the pioneer determined to move again, making in January, 1792, the change already mentioned. At the place to which he then came, his son-in-law, Abel Crawford, was living alone in a small hut, he having bought out three or four settlers who had decided to leave. Mr. Rosebrook in turn bought Crawford out, and, soon after, the latter, "rather than to be crowded by neighbors," moved twelve miles down the Saco River

FIRST SETTLEMENTS AND SETTLERS

into Hart's Location, near the present Bemis Station, where he lived to a great age, known and loved as the "Patriarch of the Mountains." Here he built, some time previous to 1820, the Mount Crawford House, which was kept for many years by his son-in-law, Nathaniel T. P. Davis, and whose site is east of the railroad track at Bemis.

Rosebrook lived in his new place of abode for a number of years in a small log cabin. At length, having sold his farm in Guildhall, he laid out the proceeds on his property here. The turnpike through the Notch was incorporated, as has been stated, in 1803. It was some time in that year that Rosebrook, as travel and business had increased, built a large and convenient two-story dwelling, with two rooms underground, on the high mound afterwards called the "Giant's Grave." He also built a large barn, stables, sheds, and mills. This house in the Ammonoosuc Valley, at the present Fabyan station, was the first house for the accommodation of travelers erected in the White Mountains. Here Rosebrook lived and prospered for the rest of his days. He died in 1817,[1] at seventy years of age, from a cancer, after patiently enduring great suffering.

[1] The inscription on his headstone in the little cemetery on the knoll near Fabyan reads as follows: —

"In memory of Cap. Eliezer Rosbrook [sic] who died Sept. 25, 1817 in the 70 year of his age.

"When I lie buried deep in dust,
My flesh shall be thy care,
These with'ring limbs with thee I trust
To raise them strong and fair."

The headstone to his wife's grave, on which the name is spelled correctly, states that she died May 4, 1829, aged 84.

THE WHITE MOUNTAINS

President Dwight, who, as we have seen, stayed overnight at Rosebrook's on his first journey to the Mountains, thus speaks of his host: —

This man, with a spirit of enterprise and industry, and perseverance, which has surmounted obstacles, demanding more patience and firmness, than are in many instances required for the acquisition of empire, planted himself in this spot, in the year 1788. . . . Here he stationed himself in an absolute wilderness; and was necessitated to look for everything which was either to comfort or support life, to those, who lived at least twenty miles from him, and to whom he must make his way without a road. By his industry he has subdued a farm of one hundred and fifty, or two hundred acres; and built two large barns, the very boards of which he must have transported from a great distance with such expense and difficulty, as the inhabitants of older settlements would think intolerable. . . . Hitherto he has lived in a log hut; in which he has entertained most of the persons traveling in this road during the last eight years. . . . For the usual inconveniences of a log house we were prepared; but we found comfortable beds, good food, and excellent fare for our horses; all furnished with as much good-will, as if we had been near friends of the family. Our entertainment would by most Englishmen, and not a small number of Americans, be regarded with disdain. To us it was not barely comfortable; it was, in the main, pleasant. . . . During twelve out of fourteen years, this honest, industrious man laboured on his farm without any legal title. The proprietor [1] was an inhabitant of New York; and sold him the land through the medium of an agent. When he bought it, the agent promised to procure a deed for him speedily. Throughout this period he alternately solicited, and was promised, the conveyance, which had been originally engaged. Nor

[1] This is different from what is given on a preceding page, which is taken from the *Crawford History*, the chief source for information about Rosebrook and Ethan Allen Crawford.

FIRST SETTLEMENTS AND SETTLERS

did he resolve, until he had by building and cultivation encreased the value of his farm twenty fold, to go in person to New York, and demand a deed of the proprietor himself. The truth is; he possesses the downright unsuspecting integrity, which, even in men of superior understanding often exposes them to imposition, from a confidence honourable to themselves, but, at times, unhappily misplaced. Here, however, the fact was otherwise: for the proprietor readily executed the conveyance, according to the terms of the original bargain. In my journey of 1803, I found Rosebrook in possession of a large, well-built farmer's house, mills and various other conveniences; and could not help feeling a very sensible pleasure at finding his industry, patience, and integrity thus rewarded.

Rosebrook left his property to his grandson, Ethan Allen Crawford, who, with his cousin and, later, wife, Lucy Howe, had tenderly cared for his grandfather in his last illness. Crawford, whose grave, situated in the little cemetery[1] not far from the Fabyan House and marked with a modest shaft, is seen yearly by thousands, was the most famous of the pioneers of the White Mountains. From his great strength and his stature — Starr King and others say "He grew to be nearly seven feet in height," but a daughter affirms that he stood just six feet two and one-half inches in his stockings — he was known as the "Giant of the Hills." He was born in 1792 in Guildhall, Vermont. When he was

[1] What more fitting resting-place for the remains of the pioneer could have been found! Here he lies near the site of his hotel and in view of the Notch named after his family and of the mountain up which so many times he guided persons. This is truly a hallowed spot, containing, as it does, the dust of four such noble men and women as Eleazar and Hannah Rosebrook and Ethan Allen and Lucy Crawford.

THE WHITE MOUNTAINS

an infant, his parents, as we have seen, moved to Hart's Location in New Hampshire and lived in a log house in the wilderness, twelve miles from neighbors in one direction and six miles in the other. Here he grew up in circumstances that made him tough and healthy. In 1811, he enlisted as a soldier for eighteen months. Soon he was taken sick with what he called "spotted fever," and, when he was recovering, he started for home on a furlough, reaching there, traveling mostly on foot, in fourteen days. After regaining his health, he returned to his duty. Upon the expiration of his term of service, he engaged in various occupations, such as making roads, working on a river, and farming. On the 8th and 9th of June, 1815, he records that the ground froze and snow fell to the depth of a foot or more, lasting for two days, during which he drew logs to a sawmill with four oxen. His extraordinary strength appears from his being able to lift a barrel of potash weighing five hundred pounds and to put it into a boat, hoisting it two feet. There was only one other man of those working with him who could do more than lift one end of the barrel. He had settled in Louisville, New York, near a brother, and had got a good start when, in 1816, a letter was received from his grandfather Rosebrook, telling of his illness and asking for one of them to come to live with him. Ethan went to visit his grandfather, not intending to stay permanently with him, but when the afflicted old man entreated him with tears to make his future home here, Ethan's determination to remain in Louisville was overcome. Returning to that

FIRST SETTLEMENTS AND SETTLERS

place, he sold his property there and came back to his grandparents, assuming the indebtedness on the farm and taking care of them, as has been noted. Then began his connection with the region in whose early annals he played so important a part.

In July, 1818, less than a year after his grandfather's death, while Crawford was absent, his house took fire and burned to the ground, causing him a loss from which he was never able to recover. With the help of his neighbors, a small house, twenty-four feet square, which belonged to him and was situated one and a half miles distant, was drawn by oxen to the site of the burned house. This was fitted up so as to be a comfortable home for the winter of 1819. In it he entertained individuals who came along, as best he could, but parties were compelled to go to his father's, eight miles from the Notch, for accommodation. From year to year he struggled along, working at various occupations, such as assisting travelers up and down the Notch, guiding people up Mount Washington, and building paths, endeavoring all the while to lighten the pecuniary burden which he was carrying.

In 1819, with his father, he opened the first path to Mount Washington, which started from the site of the present Crawford House, and which was improved into a bridle path by Thomas J. Crawford in 1840. This trail was advertised in the newspapers and soon visitors began to come. In the summer of 1820, a party consisting of Adino N. Brackett, John W. Weeks, General John Wilson, Charles J. Stuart, Noyes S. Dennison, Samuel A. Pearson,

THE WHITE MOUNTAINS

all of Lancaster, and Philip Carrigain, "the author of the New Hampshire Map" (as Mr. Crawford quaintly puts it), made the ascent of the chief peak of the Presidential Range and gave names to such peaks as were unnamed. These were Adams, Jefferson, Madison, Monroe, Franklin, and Pleasant. They engaged, as guide and baggage-carrier, Mr. Crawford, who has given a brief account of the expedition, which is enlivened by a quiet humor. He was, he says, "loaded equal to a pack horse," as the "party of distinguished characters" wished to be prepared to stay two nights. They reached the top of Washington via the Notch, where they stayed some hours enjoying the prospect and naming the peaks as aforesaid. Descending to a lower level, they spent one night. Mr. Crawford recorded that he was "tired to the very bone" that night through being compelled virtually to carry one member of the party, "a man of two hundred weight," who for some reason was not able to get along without his assistance. About a month later, Brackett, Weeks, and Stuart, accompanied by Richard Eastman, spent a week in leveling to the tops of all these mountains from Lancaster, camping on them four nights, one of which, that of August 31, was passed on the summit of Mount Washington. The height of the highest peak was computed by them to be 6428 feet.

The following summer, Crawford cut a new and shorter path [1] to the summit of Mount Washington,

---

[1] This path was made passable to horses by Horace Fabyan soon after 1840 and was known thereafter as the Fabyan Bridle Path.

FIRST SETTLEMENTS AND SETTLERS

which went directly up over a course nearly the same as that of the present railroad. On August 31 of the same year (1821), three young ladies, the Misses Austin, formerly of Portsmouth, came to Crawford's house to ascend the hills, as they wished to have the honor of being the first women to reach the top of Mount Washington. They were accompanied by their brother, a friend of the family, and a tenant on their farm in Jefferson. They went as far as Crawford's first camp that night, but, bad weather coming on, they could go no farther, and were compelled to stay there until a more favorable day should come. When their stock of provisions began to fail, Mr. Faulkner, the tenant, returned to Crawford's house and asked the pioneer to go to their relief. Mr. Crawford had severely injured himself with an axe when cutting the path, and was lame in consequence, but he nevertheless went to their assistance and accompanied them to the top, where they had the good fortune to have a splendid clear view. The ladies are said to have felt richly repaid for the discomfort and hardship entailed in a journey under such unfavorable conditions. They were out, all told, five days.

Mr. Crawford built in July, 1823, three small stone huts on Mount Washington, but, owing to the dampness of the place where they were located, they were little used. The ruined walls of one may still be seen near the Gulf Tank on the railroad.

In the spring of 1824, Mr. Crawford built and raised a frame, thirty-six by forty feet, the outside of which was in the autumn finished and painted. This

THE WHITE MOUNTAINS

addition, the interior work on which was completed in the winter and spring of 1825, was ready for the accommodation of the summer guests of the latter year. He thought his house with this enlargement would be sufficiently commodious to take care of all who would be likely to come, but in a few years, such was the increase in the number of visitors, another addition was imperatively demanded. Sometimes the guests were so numerous that they could be accommodated for the night only at great inconvenience to the family.

After considerable delay and much consideration, Mr. Crawford, although he was in debt, and would get, by such a step, more involved, finally decided to build again; so, having succeeded in getting a loan, in the winter and spring of 1832 he bought and drew the lumber and other materials for an addition. This was raised in May, and before the last of July the outside was finished and painted. It was sixty feet long and forty feet wide, consisted of two stories, and was provided with two verandas, that on the Mount Washington side being two-storied and extending the entire length of the building. The plastering and papering were postponed until the next year, in the summer of which the addition was first used.

About this time Mr. Crawford was much annoyed by the encroachment of the new proprietor of an establishment for the entertainment of travelers which had been erected three quarters of a mile below his house. This man, who bought the place in the autumn of 1831 and took possession of it the

FIRST SETTLEMENTS AND SETTLERS

following January, acted in such a clandestine manner toward Mr. Crawford in the matter of acquiring and occupying the property, that the latter, who was prepared to be neighborly, was much offended. Moreover, the rival landlord made use of the mountain road which Mr. Crawford had constructed at great expense of money and labor, and tried by false representations to the authorities at Washington to have the post-office taken away from Crawford's house and transferred to his own.

This rival hotel, which appears to have been on the site of the present White Mountain House,[1] did not, however, interfere with Crawford's summer business, and for a number of years the sturdy pioneer continued to entertain visitors and to conduct individuals or parties up the paths he had made.

At length, seriously involved in pecuniary difficulties and broken down in health, Crawford, on the advice of some friends and of members of his family, decided to give up his farm and to retire to a more secluded place, where health might be regained. Hard as it was for him to leave the spot where he had lived twenty years, had worked so

---

[1] The distance, as given in the text, and the additional statement of Mr. Crawford, that Mount Washington could not be seen from it on account of Mount Deception intervening, point to this conclusion. The English traveler Coke speaks of it as displaying a gayly painted sign of a lion and an eagle, "looking unutterable things at each other from opposite sides of the globe," and as having already attracted numerous guests. He declares that the spirit of rivalry had proved of some service to Mr. Crawford, as it had "incited him to make considerable additions to his own house, all of which were run up with true American expedition."

THE WHITE MOUNTAINS

hard, and, as he says, "had done everything to make the mountain scenery fashionable," and distressing as it was to let the property go into the possession of others, he bravely accepted his lot, and, having made an arrangement with his brother-in-law to change situations with him for a time, he moved to a farm at Guildhall, Vermont, his birthplace. This removal took place in 1837, the year which is signalized in White Mountain hotel history by the establishment in the landlordship of Crawford's old hostelry of the man who was to give his name to the railroad center that was to rise at this place, — Horace Fabyan, of Portland, of whom more will be said later.

After Crawford had remained on his brother-in-law's place ten months, where he raised barely enough to support his family, Mr. Howe was compelled to lease the Crawford farm at the Giant's Grave, which was put into other hands. As he wanted his own place at Guildhall to live on, Crawford again had to move. Fortunately, he was allowed to take the use of an unoccupied dwelling, one mile farther down the Connecticut River, and by various arrangements he was permitted to live for a number of years on this "beautiful farm," which included the site of his grandmother's home and the scene of her adventures with the Indians.

The fifth year a lawyer in Lancaster obtained a lease of the place and thereafter Crawford was obliged to give him half of what he raised. This condition not pleasing him and his family, he determined to make a change; so, in 1843, he hired the

FIRST SETTLEMENTS AND SETTLERS

large three-story dwelling,[1] then empty, which was in sight of where he had formerly lived at the Mountains. There he passed the remainder of his days.

In spite of his strength and wonderful endurance, Crawford was not destined to be long-lived. Worn out by the hardships of his early life and by the suffering caused by bodily ailments and by distress and anxiety due to the pecuniary embarrassments of his later life, he died prematurely on June 22, 1846, at the age of fifty-four.[2] He was a man of fine qualities — "one of nature's noblemen," says Willey. His wife, Lucy Crawford, was a fitting mate for such a hardy and brave man. Other members of the Crawford family were of the same sturdy type. Ethan's father, Abel, has already been mentioned. In his younger days he sometimes acted as guide to persons who wished to climb Mount Washington. In September, 1818, he performed this service for John Brazer, of Cambridge, and George Dawson, of Philadelphia, whose expedition deserves mention

[1] This building, the inn of his unneighborly rival of the early thirties, stood on the site of the present White Mountain House, a portion of which it still forms.

[2] Both the headstone and the granite shaft in the cemetery give his age at death as fifty-two. The *Crawford History* states, at the beginning of chapter II, that he was born in 1792, and on page 187, in giving the family genealogy, Crawford says, "Ethan Allen is my name, and I am fifty-three." The shaft of granite was erected in memory of Crawford and of his wife, who died February 17, 1869, aged seventy-six. Crawford's headstone bears the following interesting inscription: — "In Memory of Ethan Allen Crawford, who died June 22, A.D. 1846; aged 52.

"He built here the first Hotel at the White Mountains, of which he was for many years the owner and Landlord.

"He was of great native talent & sagacity, of noble, kind, and benevolent disposition, a beloved husband and father, and an honest & good man."

THE WHITE MOUNTAINS

because of the amusing fact that they nailed to a rock a brass plate[1] with a Latin inscription engraved on it as a record (of course, calmly prepared some time beforehand) of their ascent, the anticipated achievement and arduousness of which were evidently realized.

Another ascent under the guidance of the future "Patriarch" is pleasantly narrated by Grenville Mellen, the poet and miscellaneous writer, who was one of the participants in the excursion. This "pilgrimage" was made in August, 1819 (the year of the opening of the bridle path), and was from Portland through Fryeburg to the top of Mount Washington (the party camped out one night "in a rude-fashioned camp" part-way up the trail), and over the same route in returning. The chronicler portrays his guide and host, who, he says, "received us with a wintry smile (he never laughed, in the world!) and a sort of guttural welcome," in the following somewhat rhetorical paragraph: —

Crawford has no compeer. He stands alone; and we found him, in all the unapproachableness of his singularity. We defy Cruikshanks [sic] to hit him; and painting and poetry would despair, before such a subject. What we shall say, in downright prose, will be mere attempt. If you wish to unfold him, and his sons, go and hire him, or them, as guides; and let them act themselves out before you, on a pilgrimage to Mount Washington.

It was he, who in 1840, at seventy-five years of age, made the first ascent of Mount Washington on

[1] This brass plate remained intact on the summit until July, 1825, when it was carried off by some vandals from Jackson.

FIRST SETTLEMENTS AND SETTLERS

horseback. At eighty, he could, it is said, walk with ease five miles, before breakfast, to his son's house. He constantly attended the sessions of the New Hampshire Legislature, in which he was a representative of his district, when eighty-two years of age. A man of great good-humor, it was his pleasure, after he was confined to the house, to entertain visitors with amusing and interesting anecdotes. He died at eighty-five, having survived, it will be noted, his son Ethan by several years. His length of days is in striking contrast to the latter's short life.

His eight sons were all, it is affirmed, more than six feet tall, and Ethan was not alone in his endowment of unusual physical strength. Thomas J. Crawford, already spoken of as a pathbuilder, kept from 1829 to 1852 the Notch House, which was built in 1828 by Ethan and their father and which stood between the present Crawford House and the Gate of the Notch, its site being marked to-day by a signboard. About 1846 he constructed the carriage road up Mount Willard.

The tragic episode of the destruction of the household of Samuel Willey, Jr., in the Crawford Notch has been many times narrated — most fully by the householder's brother, the Reverend Benjamin G. Willey, who devotes two chapters of his "Incidents in White Mountain History" to this unhappy event. The lonely and awe-inspiring place of the disaster, and the fact that the slide caused the greatest loss of life of any accident or natural disturbance that has occurred in the White Mountain region, and the

THE WHITE MOUNTAINS

further fact that an entire household perished, have attached a melancholy interest to the event and its scene and have drawn to them an amount of attention which may seem disproportionate to the importance of the occurrence. However this may be, it is certain that the interest in the sad fate of the Willey family has been long-continued and general. One evidence which proves the existence of this interest comes to mind when one thinks of the great number of persons who, during all the years that have elapsed since the time of the disaster, have visited the scene from curiosity.[1]

Further witness to the generality of this interest is afforded by recalling the considerable literature which has grown up about the story of the catastrophe and which includes, besides numerous recountings of the circumstances, a romance[2] based in part upon this event and written by an author bearing the family name, one of Hawthorne's "Twice-Told Tales," and several poems. Hawthorne's allegory, "The Ambitious Guest," is the chief literary monument of the Willey disaster. Among the poems inspired by it the more notable are one by Mrs. Sigourney, the Connecticut poet,[3] and, particularly, a spirited narrative ballad by Dr.

---

[1] It was formerly the custom, one which was established early, for visitors to add a stone from the material of the slide to a memorial pile on the spot where the bodies of a number of the victims were found. In process of time this has accumulated into a natural monument of considerable size, but of late years it has become hidden because of the growth of vegetation about it.

[2] *Soltaire*, by George F. Willey.

[3] "The White Mountains after the Descent of the Avalanche in 1826," printed in the *Ladies' Magazine* (Boston), August, 1828.

THE NOTCH HOUSE

FIRST SETTLEMENTS AND SETTLERS

Thomas W. Parsons, the Dante translator and "the Poet" of Longfellow's "Tales of a Wayside Inn."

The sublimity of the scenery and the tragedy of the fate of an entire family made a profound impression upon travelers who passed that way in the score or so of years after the event, and those who published accounts of their tours in almost all cases devoted a goodly portion of the record of their trip to the White Mountains to a narration of the story of this sad occurrence. Especially is this true of the foreign travelers who traversed the Notch in these early days.

The facts about the terrible storm to which the avalanche was immediately due, and those relating to the disastrous effects of the heavy rain and of the landslide, which were learned or inferred by relatives and friends of the destroyed family as the result of visits to the scene a few days afterward, together with much conjecture as to the circumstances and course of events on the fatal Monday night, are set down in great detail by the historian brother, who was one of the searchers for the bodies of the victims. A few additional particulars may be gleaned from the narrative of Crawford and from the recollections of contemporaries recorded in the newspapers.

The highway, whose construction through the Notch shortly after the discovery of the pass has been already chronicled and which connected Upper Coös with the seaboard, soon became an important route of commerce. After the turnpike was built, early in the nineteenth century, long lines of wagons

THE WHITE MOUNTAINS

loaded down with merchandise of various descriptions passed through the gateway both summer and winter, and toward the end of the eighteenth century pleasure travelers — few in number, to be sure, when compared with the later travel of this character — had begun to find their way thither, mostly in private carriages. This increasing traffic made greatly felt the need of public houses as places of shelter, particularly in winter, when the northern winds are bitterly cold and the road is buried in snow, often deeply drifted, and the passage through the defile therefore extremely arduous and not a little hazardous. From soon after the beginning of the last decade of the eighteenth century, there had existed on this route simple taverns for the entertainment of the passing traveler who should be in need of a meal, or who, overtaken by night or storm, should require a lodging, in the house of the elder Crawford near the modern Bemis Station at the southern entrance of the Notch and in Eleazar Rosebrook's inn (near the present Fabyan House), thirteen miles distant from the other. In view of the circumstances just mentioned, it is evident that the opening of a public house somewhere on the road between these two places would be not only an act likely to be profitable to the innkeeper, but also one partaking of the nature of a benefaction to the traveler. Especially was such an establishment in the depths of the Notch itself a desideratum in those days.

There is a disagreement in the statements as to the time of building of the house which was to be-

FIRST SETTLEMENTS AND SETTLERS

come famous as the Willey House. Mr. Spaulding says it was erected by a Mr. Davis in 1793, which would make its building contemporaneous with the settlements of Rosebrook and Crawford. Mr. Willey is very indefinite as to the time when the house was constructed, his statement being that it "had been erected, some years previous to the time [1826] of which we write, by a Mr. Henry Hill." [1]

Be that as it may, this simple story-and-a-half dwelling, situated about midway between the two houses that have been mentioned, was doubtless a timely inn to many a weary teamster or "lated traveler" in its early days. The supervention of a tragedy was destined, however, to intermit its use as a place of shelter and to change the nature of the interest of visitors in the building and its environment.

After it had been kept by Mr. Hill and others for several years its occupancy was abandoned.[2] In

[1] Mr. Crawford says in the *History*, under 1845, "the Notch House, which place was settled, Uncle William [i.e., William Rosebrook, then seventy-two years old, who lived with the Crawfords] says, about fifty-three years ago, by one Mr. Davis, who first began there; since which period, others have lived there for a short time, until Samuel Willey bought the place, and repaired it." The signboard (missing in 1914) at the site states that the house was built by Davis in 1792, was repaired and occupied by Fabyan in 1844, and was burned in 1898. E. A. Kendall, who passed through the Notch in November, 1807, speaks of a house, twenty miles from Conway, evidently the old Mount Crawford House at Bemis, at which he ate a meal, and says that "at a distance of seven miles, there is another house, which second house is only three miles short of the Notch," the context showing that by the latter he means the Gate of the Notch.

[2] Ethan Allen Crawford engaged the house in the fall of 1823, "and agreed to furnish it with such things as are necessary for the comfort of travelers and their horses." He records the buying of hay at Jefferson in the winter of 1824 and the carrying of it sixteen miles to furnish the Notch place.

THE WHITE MOUNTAINS

the autumn of 1825, after the house had been for several months untenanted, Samuel Willey, Jr., a son of one [1] of the early settlers of Upper Bartlett, moved his family into it. As the house was much in need of repairs, he spent the autumn in making such as would render it comfortable during the winter, and he also enlarged the stable and made such other improvements as the time would permit. In the spring further improvements were planned and begun with the design of making the house more worthy of patronage, which had been good during the winter and was increasing.

Nothing unusual occurred during the winter and spring to arouse any apprehension as to the unsafeness of the situation of this lone abode, but one rainy afternoon in June Mr. and Mrs. Willey, when sitting by a window which looked out upon the mountain which now bears their name, saw, as the mist cleared up, a mass of earth begin to move, increase in volume and extent, and finally rush into the valley beneath. This was soon followed by another slide of lesser magnitude. Although these avalanches occurred near the house, they did no damage to the property, but they served to startle the occupants greatly, and Mr. Willey at first purposed to leave the place and, it is believed, even made ready to do so, under the impulse of the first panic. His decision against an immediate removal

[1] Samuel Willey, who came to Bartlett from Lee, later moved to North Conway and lived on what is known as the "Bigelow Farm" until his death, in 1844, when he was more than ninety years of age. His son, Benjamin G., the historian, was the second pastor of the Congregational Church in Conway. He died in 1867.

THE WILLEY HOUSE

FIRST SETTLEMENTS AND SETTLERS

was largely determined by the counsel of Abel Crawford, who with a force of men was at work the day of the storm repairing the turnpike near by.

After a short lapse of time, Mr. Willey, who had looked about in vain for a safer place in which to establish his home, became calmer and his apprehensions of danger were allayed, if not altogether removed. Would that he had heeded the warning! But he came to think that such an occurrence was unlikely to happen again, and so remained, little fearing danger and not presaging any evil, to fall a victim with all his family two months later.

The midsummer of 1826 was characterized in the White Mountain region by high temperatures and a long-continued drought. Under the hot sun the soil became dry to an unusual depth and so prepared to be acted upon powerfully by any heavy rain. The great heat and extreme drought continued until after the middle of August, when clouds began to gather and eventually to gain permanence and to give rain, at first but little in quantity. Finally on Monday, August 28, came a day of occasional showers, which were but a premonition of what was to follow, for toward evening the clouds began to gather in great volume. They were of dense blackness, which condition combined with their magnitude to make a sublime and awful aspect of the heavens. Just at nightfall it began to rain, and then ensued a storm which will be ever memorable for its violence and its disastrous consequences. Some time during this furious downpour, which lasted

THE WHITE MOUNTAINS

for several hours,[1] occurred the dreadful avalanche which buried the entire household of the little dwelling in the depths of the Notch.

The destructiveness of the storm began to be evident to the dwellers south of the Notch early the next morning when the intervales became so flooded that the cattle and horses had to be removed from them, and when daylight revealed the desolating effects of the copious rains on the summits and sides of the mountains. Many trees were seen to be destroyed, a vast amount of rocks and earth to be displaced, and many grooves and gorges to have been created on the slopes.

At first no fears were felt by the relatives and friends of the family in the solitary Notch House as to their safety and, indeed, so occupied were they with their own immediate concerns because of the floods, that they had little time to think of anything else. Not until Wednesday night, when unfavorable reports began to reach the southern settlements, did suspicions arise that all was not well with the household in the Notch. It seems that the first person to pass through the Notch after the storm was a man named John Barker. He left Ethan Allen Crawford's about four o'clock and reached the Notch House about sunset, on Tuesday. Finding it deserted except by the faithful dog,[2] he concluded that the

---

[1] "At eleven o'clock," says Ethan Allen Crawford, "we had a clearing-up shower, and it seemed as though the windows of heaven were opened and the rain came down almost in streams."

[2] This animal, it is recorded, did what he could to make the disaster known, for, before any news of it had reached Conway, he appeared at the home of Mr. Lovejoy, Mrs. Willey's father, and,

FIRST SETTLEMENTS AND SETTLERS

family had betaken themselves to Abel Crawford's, and he took up his lodging for the night in the vacated house. Evidences of a hasty departure were seen in the opened doors, the disarranged beds, the scattered clothes, and the Bible lying open on the table. When trying to compose himself to sleep he heard a low moaning. Unable, because of the dense darkness and of having no provision for striking a light, to do anything in the way of ascertaining the source of this or of rescuing the person or creature giving utterance to it, Barker lay terrified and sleepless until dawn, when he arose and, after a search, found the cause of his excitement. It was an ox, which had been crushed to the floor by the fallen timbers of the stable. After releasing the suffering animal, Barker proceeded on his way to Bartlett, and on arriving at Judge Hall's tavern told about the fearful slide at the Willey farm. That night a party of men from Bartlett started for the Notch. They arrived at their destination toward morning, on Thursday, after a difficult journey. As soon as day broke they began their search. The confirmed reports of the perishing of the family having reached the relatives, they too started for the scene of the disaster, which they reached about noon of that day. Many other people had come as the result of the spreading of the news.

by moanings and other expressions of anguish, tried to tell the members of the family that something dreadful had happened. But not succeeding in making himself understood, he left, and, although he was afterward frequently seen running at great speed, now up and now down the road between the Lovejoy home and the Notch House, he soon disappeared from the region, doubtless perishing through grief and loneliness.

THE WHITE MOUNTAINS

It was a vast scene of desolation and ruin that met the eyes of the searchers as they approached the spot. On a clearing perhaps a hundred rods below the house, one great slide had deposited its material, consisting of large rocks, trees, and sand. The sides of the mountain above the house, once green with woods, were lacerated and stripped bare for a vast extent, while the plain appeared one continuous bed of sand and rocks with broken trees and branches intermingled with them. Many separate scars and slide deposits were to be seen above and below the house, which stood unharmed amid the ruin all about it. The avalanche of greatest magnitude, which started far up on the mountain-side directly behind the house, would have overwhelmed it but for a curious circumstance arising from a peculiarity in the configuration of the ground. It so happened that the slide, when it had reached a point not far above the little dwelling, had to encounter in its course down the mountain a low ridge, or ledge of rock, which extended from this place to a more precipitous part of the mountain. This, when met, not only somewhat arrested the slide, but, what was yet more remarkable, served to divide it into two parts. One portion of the débris flowed to one side, carrying away the stable above the house, but avoiding the latter building, while the other passed by it on the other side. In front of the house the two divisions reunited and flowed on in the bed of the Saco. This strange circumstance in the action of the landslide, with its even more singular results, the sparing of the house and the destruction of its inmates, — for it

FIRST SETTLEMENTS AND SETTLERS

was doubtless this particular convulsion that was the occasion of the latter event, — lends to the story of the disaster, when one thinks of the perversity of fate in this instance and of what might have been, a peculiar pathos.

Just how the members of the household met their deaths will never be known. Whether, on hearing the frightful noise which must have accompanied the avalanche and have heralded its coming, they fled precipitately before it from the house and were overwhelmed by it when it reached the low ground, or whether they had already, for fear of being drowned by the rising waters above the habitation, betaken themselves to the foot of the mountain before the slide came down and there had been caught in its course and carried away with it, we cannot tell. However it may be, these alternative suppositions, at any rate, embody the principal theories that have been advanced as to the probable course of events, but, it must be admitted, they both rest upon inference and, largely, upon conjecture.

Such search[1] as had been made for the bodies up to noon on Thursday had been unavailing. Not long after, however, a man who was searching along the slide just below the house happened, through the accidental moving of a twig, to notice a number of flies about the entrance to a sort of cave formed by

[1] Among the searchers was Ethan Allen Crawford, who had been sent for by the friends of the Willey family. He tells of nailing to a dead tree, near the place where the bodies were found, a planed board on which he had written with a piece of red chalk, "The family found here," which "monument" was afterward taken away by some of the later occupants of the house and used for fuel.

THE WHITE MOUNTAINS

material of the slide, and as the result of a search which was immediately instituted about this spot the location of one of the bodies was disclosed. This body proved to be that of David Allen, one of the farmhands. Not long after, the eager searchers came upon the body of Mrs. Willey, even more terribly mangled than that of the farmhand. Further search soon revealed the body of Mr. Willey, not far away. These were all that were found that day, and, as it was decided to bury them near their habitation until they could be more conveniently moved to Conway the next winter, coffins were made of such materials as could be obtained there, and the bodies, after prayer by a Bartlett minister, were buried in a common grave.

Search was continued on the next day, and during its course the body of the youngest child was found and buried. On Saturday[1] the body of the eldest child, a girl of twelve years, and that of the other hired man, David Nickerson, were recovered and buried. The bodies of the three other children have never been found. They were covered so deeply beneath the sand and rocks that no search has ever been able to discover them. In view of the magnitude and extent of the avalanche and the quantity of materials deposited upon the valley, it is more remarkable that so many bodies were recovered than that these were not found.

The only living things about the premises to

[1] Mr. Crawford says Nickerson's body was recovered on Saturday and that of the eldest daughter on Sunday, the latter being found some distance from where the others were and across the river, she apparently having met death by drowning.

FIRST SETTLEMENTS AND SETTLERS

escape were the dog and two oxen. These latter were endangered by falling timbers, but suffered no serious injury. Two horses were, however, crushed to death by timbers of the stable.

The foregoing narrative embodies the main facts of this melancholy event. The story of the storm which was the proximate cause of the landslide would not, however, be complete without some mention of the disastrous work of this terrific downpour, not only in the region in the vicinity of the Willey House, but elsewhere, for it did great damage in other parts of the Mountains also.

The road through the Crawford Notch was in many places destroyed. All the bridges but two along the entire length of the turnpike, a distance of seventeen miles, were carried away. The directors, seeing it would take a great sum to repair the road, voted, after the good people of Portland had contributed fifteen hundred dollars to help and encourage them, to levy an assessment upon the shares. These sums, with some other assistance, provided means for accomplishing the work, which is said to have been carried on by the hardy natives by moonlight as well as in the daytime.

The storm utterly destroyed the road through the Franconia Notch also, and travel had to be suspended until after repairs were made by means of a state appropriation of thirteen hundred dollars.

The best part of Abel Crawford's farm was destroyed. A new sawmill, which had just been built by Crawford, who was away from home at the time of the flood, was swept away, together with a great

THE WHITE MOUNTAINS

number of logs and boards and all the fences on the intervale. Twenty-eight sheep were drowned and a great deal of standing grain was ruined. The water rose so high as to run through the entire house on the lower floors and sweep out the coals and ashes from the fireplace. Many other dwellers on the banks of the Saco and its tributaries suffered more or less damage.

At Ethan Crawford's on the Ammonoosuc much injury to property and live stock was occasioned by the flood. The whole intervale in the vicinity of the Giant's Grave was covered with water for a space of more than two hundred acres. The road was greatly damaged and in some places entirely demolished. The bridge was carried away, taking with it in its course down the river ninety feet of shed which had been attached to the barn that escaped the fire of 1818. Fourteen sheep were drowned and a large field of oats was destroyed. The flood came within a foot and a half of the door of the house, a strong stream ran between the house and the stable, and much wood was swept away. Mr. Crawford's camp at the foot of the mountain, with all its furnishings, which were enclosed in a sheet-iron chest, was carried away by the rising water. No part of the iron chest, or of its contents, which included eleven blankets and a supply of cooking-utensils, was ever found, except a few pieces of blanket that were caught on bushes at different places down the river.

An incident relating to a party of travelers, which occurred at the time of the storm, may well be narrated here. On the 26th of August, some gentlemen

FIRST SETTLEMENTS AND SETTLERS

from the West arrived at Crawford's for the purpose of ascending Mount Washington. Crawford, as the weather was threatening, advised them not to go that afternoon, but as their time was limited they said they must proceed, and so he guided them to the camp, where they arrived at ten o'clock at night. Early the next morning it began to rain, which took away all hope of ascending the mountain that day. Reluctant to abandon their excursion, now that they were so near the goal, it was decided that Crawford should go to his home for more provisions and return to the camp. Crawford arrived home tired from a slow and wearisome journey through the rain and mud. His brother Thomas, who happened to be at the house, cheerfully consented to take his place. When the latter arrived at the camp, he found that the rain had put out the fire and that the party were holding a council as to what was to be done. He told them that it would be very unpleasant, if not dangerous, to remain where they were, and that by rapid traveling it might be possible to reach the house. By fast walking, by wading, and by crossing the swollen streams on trees cut down and laid across to serve as bridges, they managed to reach the house safely about eight o'clock in the evening. Fortunately, they reached the bridge over the Ammonoosuc just in time to pass over it before it was swept away. Had they remained, they would have shared the same fate as the Willey family, or, at least, have suffered greatly from cold, hunger, and exposure. On the following Wednesday, the water having by that time suf-

THE WHITE MOUNTAINS

ficiently subsided to permit the fording of the Ammonoosuc, with Thomas Crawford for guide, some of the party, with the addition of another small party from the West, achieved the ascent of the mountain, although they had much difficulty in finding their way owing to the destructive effect of the rain on the path.

Farther down the Ammonoosuc, at Rosebrook's, and elsewhere in the valley, much damage was done, although conditions were not so bad as at Crawford's. Many other slides, also, besides the one at the Willey House, devastated great areas on the slopes of the Mountains, notably a very extensive one on the west side of Mount Pleasant.

Such, then, were some of the effects of this most remarkable storm in White Mountain history, which will be ever memorable for its destruction of property and human life.

The disaster at the Willey House did not deter others from occupying it, for, somewhat more than a year after, a man named Pendexter moved into it with the object chiefly of affording entertainment for travelers during the winter. Some time after his removal a storm, not so severe as that of 1826, but yet a very heavy one, took place. The impressive circumstances of this terrific storm of thunder, lightning, and rain, together with the remembrance of what had occurred there, so affected the family then residing there, that, it is said, not a word was spoken for nearly half an hour.

V

FURTHER DISCOVERIES AND EXPLORATIONS — SOME NOTED AMERICAN VISITORS OF THE EARLY DAYS

WHETHER or no the natural curiosity commonly called the "Old Man of the Mountain," or the "Profile," was known to the Indians cannot be determined with certainty; the tradition that it was worshiped by them, at any rate, is very doubtful, as they appear to have left us no legend concerning it. The story of the discovery of this the cardinal wonder of the New Hampshire highlands, and undoubtedly the most remarkable freak of nature of its kind in the world, is a prosaic one enough. According to Sweetser, the discovery was made in 1805 by Francis Whitcomb and Luke Brooks, two men who were working on the Notch Road, and who, happening to go to Profile Lake (then known as Ferrin's Pond) to wash their hands, were by this chance the first white men to behold the face.

Instead of exhibiting the nation-wide tendency to find in any such natural formation a fancied resemblance to the profile of the Father of his Country, one or other of them exclaimed, it is said, and perhaps thereby revealed his political affiliations, "That is Jefferson" (he was then President).

The late W. C. Prime, long a summer resident of the Franconia region, and, when occupying his cabin

THE WHITE MOUNTAINS

on Lonesome Lake,[1] a near neighbor, so to speak, of the Old Man, gives a different version of the finding. His account of it, which is based upon "Franconia tradition, tolerably well verified by my own investigations among old residents," bestows the honor of being the first white beholder of the Profile upon a Baptist clergyman from Lisbon, who, having occasion to see one of the men working on the new road, and having driven for this purpose up to this part of the Notch, happened, while talking to the man, to glance up through the trees in such a line of vision that he saw the face outlined against the sky. Exclaiming, "Look there!" he directed the attention of the men, who had been cutting out bushes on the knoll by the lake, to the startling object.

Mr. Justus Conrad has this to say of the matter in question in the *Granite Monthly* for July, 1897:—

It is claimed by some writers that the Old Man of the Mountain and the Flume were discovered in 1805, but these wonders were no doubt known to some long before this. The region was a favorite haunt of the red men, and it is stated, on reasonable authority, that the friends of Stark made the first discovery while searching for him after his capture by the Indians.

However this may be as to the finding of the Profile, it may be adduced in opposition to the view just

---

[1] This picturesque tarn is situated on the ridge, and under one of the high bluffs, of Mount Cannon, and is about one thousand feet above the road. The lake and the adjoining territory were for some years the property of this well-known New York journalist, author, and angler and his friend, W. F. Bridge. Here they used to stay for longer or shorter periods and to entertain their friends in their quaint woodland cottage on the shore of the lake. General McClellan spent many happy days in this secluded spot.

THE OLD MAN OF THE MOUNTAIN

FURTHER DISCOVERIES

put forward so far as it relates to the other Franconia curiosity, that, inasmuch as the Flume is situated off the main trail or road, it is not likely that it would be come upon by those passing through the Notch hurriedly. It seems more probable that its discovery came about in the manner that is related a little farther on.

The existence of the Profile was first made known to the world at large by General Martin Field, who, after visiting it in 1827, sent a brief description of it to Professor Silliman, editor of the *American Journal of Science and Arts*, who published the letter in the *Journal* for July, 1828, together with an engraving in which the figure is so curiously exaggerated as to be grotesque.

It remained, however, for Hawthorne to give the Profile literary immortality, which he did, by celebrating it in one of his most beautiful allegorical tales, "The Great Stone Face." It is introduced also into a later story, Professor Edward Roth's pleasing legendary tale of "Christus Judex." The theme of this is the search of an Italian painter, Casola, for a suitable model for the face of a figure of Christ sitting in judgment, which he had resolved to paint for the altar-piece of the church in his native town.[1]

[1] As the little book is probably known to but few, perhaps a brief summary of the story may be given here. Having failed, after much seeking, to find a satisfactory countenance or representation of one in the Old World, Casola is much discouraged until he hears from his mother that a dying missionary has told her of having seen a face in the wilderness of America such as might belong to a judging Christ. Acting upon this report, the painter immediately crosses the sea and has himself conducted to the region in the land of the Abnakis where

THE WHITE MOUNTAINS

Such is the fame of the Profile, that almost uncanny counterfeit presentment carved by Nature's hand, that perhaps a brief digression from the historical to the descriptive may be pardoned by the reader. This illusion, for, as Dr. Prime points out, "there is no rock-hewn face there," and "the profile, therefore, exists only in the eyes that see it," is produced by the accidental position of the edges and various projecting points of three disconnected ledges, which have different vertical axes and which form severally the forehead, the nose and upper lip, and the chin. These surfaces and projections form the outline of a profile when viewed in combination from a certain direction; but when the beholder moves a short distance from the proper line of vision the appearance vanishes and he finds himself looking only at a rough, jagged cliff.

Not content with the production of this startling optical effect, which alone would be a sufficient appeal to the vision of any traveler, Nature has lavishly provided a strikingly beautiful situation and most picturesque surroundings as a setting for this marvel. The combination of ledges which forms the material of this illusion is set on the southeast end of the long majestic ridge of Mount Cannon, or Profile, at an altitude of twelve hundred feet above Profile Lake, a sheet of water, "than which," to quote Dr. Prime again, "there is nowhere on earth one more

the missionary had labored. Having arrived there, he finds, among the converted Indians of a village on the Kennebec, some who guide him to the region of lofty mountains to the westward, where he at length attains the object of his search and finds in the Profile the fulfillment of his conception of ideal grandeur.

FURTHER DISCOVERIES

beautiful." From the base of the projection forming the chin to the top of that forming the forehead the vertical distance is from thirty-six to forty feet.[1]

A word or two as to the permanency of the material of this marvelous visual effect. Professor Hitchcock's fear, expressed more than forty years ago, that, owing to the friability of the granite of which the ledges are composed and its consequent rapid disintegration, the ledges might soon disappear, has so far not been realized. Myriads of travelers have gazed with admiration and awe upon that stern and somewhat melancholy visage looking imperturbably down the valley from its lofty situation, and myriads of persons who have not visited the spot have been made familiar with the appearance of the Old Man through pictures or other representations. Sad will be the day (may it never come!) when that marvel of Nature shall be marred or be no longer to be seen.

Regarding the discovery of the other great natural curiosity of the Franconia Notch, the Flume, there is little to tell. Indeed, beyond the bare statement that it was made at about the same time as that of the Profile, and by Mrs. Jessie Guernsey,[2] wife of

[1] According to the State Survey of 1871, when the measurement was made by young men from Dartmouth College, attached to the survey party.

[2] The name was evidently in early days pronounced in the English fashion, for it was sometimes spelled "Garnsey." Harry Hibbard's long poem "Franconia Mountain Notch," first published in 1839, contains the following stanza on the Flume: —

> "And, farther down, from Garnsey's lone abode,
> By a rude footpath climb the mountain-side,
> Leaving below the traveler's winding road,
> To where the cleft hill yawns abrupt and wide,
> As though some earthquake did its mass divide,

THE WHITE MOUNTAINS

the pioneer settler of this locality, while fishing along the brook, information appears to be lacking.

Perhaps the earliest printed description of the Franconia Notch appeared in the *New Hampshire Statesman* and *Concord Register* of September 9 and 16, 1826. It contained an account of an ascent of Mount Lafayette, which received its present name,[1] probably during the great Frenchman's stay in the United States, in 1824-25. Another early ascent of this noble peak was accomplished by Forrest Shepard, a Mr. Sparhawk, of Dartmouth College, and a guide, on the 7th of August, 1826. Mr. Shepard sent an account of his trip to Professor Silliman, which was printed in the *American Journal of Science and Arts* for June, 1827.

The summit was reached at 11 A.M. after a "rugged ascent" of several hours. The climbers were enveloped in passing clouds while on the mountain, obtaining only glimpses of the country below and around them, during occasional momentary breakings away. In the late afternoon, while there was a thunderstorm below them, they were enfolded in a slight mist, through which the sun suddenly burst, causing to their "astonishment and delight" a peculiar meteorological phenomenon. As it was described by Mr. Shepard, their shadows were seen

> In olden time; there view the rocky Flume,
> Tremendous chasm! rising side by side,
> The rocks abrupt wall in the long, high room,
> Echoing the wild stream's roar, and dark with vapory gloom."

The Guernsey farm is located about one mile south of the Flume House, and is still occupied by persons of that name.

[1] President Dwight proposed to call it Mount Wentworth. In Carrigain's map of 1816, it was called the Great Haystack.

FURTHER DISCOVERIES

reposing upon the bosom of the cloud, while around each of their shadow heads was an entire rainbow, which persisted for twelve or fifteen minutes.

A great portion of the "Crawford History" is devoted to accounts of the individuals or parties Ethan Allen Crawford entertained in his home and tavern and of the excursions made by them, under his piloting, through the Mountains, up Mount Washington, or over the Range. Among these early travelers to the region were a number of noted men, of whose visits Mr. Crawford gives interesting and entertaining reminiscences or anecdotes, drawn from his recollection or taken from entries which they made in his "album."

One of the earliest of such visitors was Chancellor James Kent, of New York, who came to the Crawford inn in the summer of 1823, accompanied by two young men. The famous jurist[1] wished to pass through the Notch, and as the stage did not then run on that route, he put up at Crawford's for the night, and arranged to secure a conveyance from the proprietor to carry his party to Conway. In the morning Crawford harnessed his two mares to a wagon and the journey was made that day. "While

[1] Chancellor Kent had just retired from his office on account of having reached the age (sixty years) which was then the age limit for the chancellorship, and was taking a pleasure tour through the "Eastern States." One of his young companions was his son, William, then twenty-one, afterwards Judge of the Supreme Court of New York and Professor of Law in Harvard University. Some books state that Chancellor Kent ascended Mount Washington, but there is nothing in the *Crawford History* to that effect. His age and the fact that at that early date the mountain could be ascended only on foot would seem to render it unlikely that he made such an arduous trip.

THE WHITE MOUNTAINS

on the way," says the pioneer, "we had an interesting time in exchanging jokes, etc."

Crawford tells, under the date of 1825, of accompanying a botanist, who was making a collection of plants of the White Mountains, in some of his tours, which occupied several weeks. This must have been Oakes, whose visits have been already mentioned.

In 1829 came another botanical explorer, Dr. J. W. Robbins, who traversed the entire Range, descending into and crossing the Great Gulf and visiting all the eastern summits for the first time for scientific purposes. The plants of the southeastern ridge had been collected by Benjamin D. Greene in 1823, and Henry Little, a medical student, also explored this part of the Mountains in that same year. About this time, also, the naturalist Nuttall botanized here and detected several species of plants, some of such rarity, it is said, that they have hardly been seen since.

Professor Benjamin Silliman, the noted scientist, made at least two excursions to the White Mountains. He visited them for the first time in May, 1828, and from memoranda taken from letters to his family and printed in the *American Journal of Science and Arts* for January, 1829, we learn that he went from Concord to Center Harbor, ascending Red Hill, and then on to Conway. On Monday, the 19th, on which day he rode through the Notch, he writes, "We ... have this day passed the grandest scenes that I have any where seen. The whole day's ride, in an open wagon, has been in the winding defile

FURTHER DISCOVERIES

of mountains, which probably have not their equal in North America, until we reach the Rocky Mountains." He describes the Notch and narrates briefly the Willey disaster, the scene of which he visited again the next day, examining the scenery, the geological phenomena, and the ruins. His letter of that day gives further details of the catastrophe and describes the slides and their effects.

Professor Silliman's second expedition to the Mountains was made in August and September, 1837, and is recorded in the *Journal* for April, 1838. On the first day of September, 1837, in company with his son and two gentlemen of Boston, he ascended Mount Washington under severe weather conditions, which rendered the trip "very arduous." They became involved in a cloud, which froze on their clothing and "tufted the rocks with splendid crystallizations of ice." The path was slippery with ice, and above the tree-line the wind blew "a frozen gale." As there were occasional outbursts of the sun, they persevered and reached the summit, where, however, the wind blew so furiously that "the strongest man could not keep his standing without holding fast by the rocks," and only a few minutes at a time could be given to the peak on account of the severity of the cold and the violent pelting of the storm. "For science," he says, "there was little to survey." He notes that the descent, although, of course, more rapid than the ascent and much less fatiguing to the lungs, was very trying to the limbs, and especially to the larger muscles and to the patella, "which seemed as if it would part with

THE WHITE MOUNTAINS

the strain." The pedestrian ascent occupied two and a half hours; the entire journey about ten hours "of strenuous and constant exertion."

Besides the elder President Dwight, accounts of whose journeys to the Mountains have been given in the preceding chapter, another member of that noted family has by his writings pleasantly associated his name with the region. This is President Dwight's nephew and pupil, Theodore Dwight, Jr., who, forced to abandon his theological studies because of ill health, became a traveler and later a metropolitan magazine editor, publisher, and philanthropist, and who was the author of numerous works, including several volumes of travel.

About 1825,[1] he made a horseback journey through New England, going up the Connecticut as far as the mouth of its tributary, the Ammonoosuc, following the latter up to the White Mountains, and thence passing through the Crawford Notch and continuing on to Boston.

The literary fruits of this tour were several. His "Sketches of Scenery and Manners in the United States" (1829), has a chapter [2] on "The White Mountains," in which he gives extensive descriptions of the scenery, an account of the Willey disaster

---

[1] I have been unable to ascertain the date of this trip. In his *Northern Traveller*, in speaking of a quarry near Concord, he notes the removal of a very large piece of rock in 1824, which he may have seen at the time. He also refers to the Notch House (Willey House) as being unoccupied in summer. Mr. Willey moved into the house in the autumn of 1825.

[2] The book contains two rude lithographic prints, one a view of the Notch and the other showing the effects of the slides. They are similar to those in his later book, *Things as They Are*.

FURTHER DISCOVERIES

with reflections upon it, a description of the house, and a long quotation having to do with the description of a storm experienced by a traveler through the Notch who took shelter from the elements in the solitary dwelling when it stood untenanted previous to the advent of the Willeys.

Again, in the later editions [1] of his guide-book, "The Northern Traveller," he includes directions for traveling through the Mountains, a brief account of the destruction of the household of Mr. Calvin [sic] Willey, and various bits of information, particularly about the first road and the turnpike through the Notch.

The detailed relation of his trip to the highland country of northern New Hampshire was, however, reserved for his entertaining volume of travels in the North and East, which was published anonymously in 1834 under the title, "Things as They Are; or, Notes of a Traveller through Some of the Middle and Northern States." [2] He writes pleasantly of the incidents of the journey and of the people he encountered, and was much impressed with the wildness and the sublimity of the scenery up the valley of the Ammonoosuc and through the Notch. Finding a

---

[1] In the first edition (1825) there are a number of pages in the appendix devoted to the White Mountains. The later editions contain an interesting cut of the Notch (Willey) House, engraved by O. H. Throop, 172 Broadway, New York.

[2] The second edition was published in 1847 with the author's name on the title-page and under the title, *Summer Tours; or, Notes of a Traveller through Some of the Middle and Northern States*. The book contains crude wood-cuts of the "Notch of the White Hills, from the North" (lower frontispiece) and of "One of the White Hills, stripped of forest and soil by the storm of 1826."

THE WHITE MOUNTAINS

party of travelers assembled at Crawford's who had arranged to make an ascent of Mount Washington, he stopped there long enough to join them in this undertaking, which he found to be "a very laborious task." It was accomplished, however, without mishap under the guidance of Mr. Crawford, who pointed out the objects of interest, such as Lake Winnepesaukee and the Androscoggin, during the occasional intervals of an unfavorable day, when the clouds for a short time broke away. The entire trip he declares was a great delight to him. He concludes with noting his thorough appreciation of the pleasure and value of the physical exertion necessary for the climb and with some reflections, suggested by the agreeableness of the experience, as to the tendency of the town dweller to indolent habits and luxury.

The summer of 1831 was marked by the coming of many visitors, chief among whom was one of the most noted of men to come to the Mountains, New Hampshire's most famous son, "a member of Congress, Daniel Webster." He arrived at Crawford's on a warm day in June and asked the landlord to go up the mountain with him. The ascent was made "without meeting anything worthy of note, more than was common for me to find," says the guide, but "things appeared interesting" to the statesman, we are told. On their arrival at the summit, Webster is reported to have made a brief address, as follows: "Mount Washington, I have come a long distance, have toiled hard to arrive at your summit, and now you seem to give me a cold reception, for which I am

FURTHER DISCOVERIES

extremely sorry, as I shall not have time enough to view this grand prospect which now lies before me, and nothing prevents but the uncomfortable atmosphere in which you reside!" As they began to descend, there was a snowstorm on the top, the snow freezing on them and causing them to suffer with the cold until they had got some distance down. They returned safely, however, to the hostelry, where Mr. Webster rejoined his women friends, whom he had left there while he made the ascent. On leaving, the next day, the statesman, after paying his bill, generously gave his host and guide a gratuity of twenty dollars. In honor of this famous son of the Granite State, his name has been given to the grand mountain [1] at the southern end of the Presidential Range, where the chain falls off sharply into the Notch, a peak which is, as Mr. Oakes has declared, "among the most unique and magnificent objects of the White Mountains."

The literary associations of the great New England romancer with the White Hills have been touched upon incidentally in sundry places in this chronicle. So important, indeed, not only in this respect but biographically and psychologically, is his connection with them — they played so important a part in his life — that the record of it demands

---

[1] Professor C. H. Hitchcock states that it is probable that the name of Mount Webster was proposed by Mr. Sidney Willard (after whom, he says, Mount Willard is named) for the peak known to earlier visitors as Notch Mountain. It is sometimes stated that Mount Willard was named by Thomas J. Crawford after Mr. Joseph Willard, once clerk of the Superior Court in Boston, who had ascended the mountain with Crawford.

THE WHITE MOUNTAINS

and deserves special and detailed treatment. Hawthorne's physical contact with the region, like that of his college classmate Longfellow, was limited, the parallel even extending probably to the number of visits and to their being made in early and in late life only. The character of the visits of the two men were, however, very different. Hawthorne's early one was a brief but comprehensive expedition through the heart of the region, while Longfellow seems to have penetrated no farther than Conway in his early days. Hawthorne's later journey thither came at the very end of his life and was cut short almost before it had begun, death overtaking the weary traveler at the gateway town of Plymouth.

Furthermore, unlike Longfellow, Hawthorne owed much to the White Mountains. They were one of the formative influences of his boyhood, much of which was passed in a wilderness home at Raymond, Maine, on the shore of Sebago Lake, where the imaginative boy could see, far away on the northwestern horizon, the peaks and slopes of the Mountains, "purple-blue with the distance and vast," or, much of the time, glitteringly white in their covering of snow.

The first decade after Hawthorne's graduation from Bowdoin in 1825 was a dismal period in his career. He returned to Salem and formed several plans of life. Authorship was, to be sure, the career that appealed to him and that Nature intended him to pursue, but it then offered little chance of a livelihood. So strong, however, was his desire to follow his bent for literature, that he determined to be, in any case, a writer of fiction, a resolve which he held

FURTHER DISCOVERIES

to in the face of the most discouraging obstacles. After the failure of "Fanshawe," he became utterly disheartened, and, despairing of success as an author, became almost a hermit. But he kept on writing, returning to his original plan of writing short stories, in which he was eventually to meet with success.

Once a year or thereabouts while he was living this solitary life in his mother's house, he used to make an excursion of a few weeks, in which, he says, "I enjoyed as much of life as other people do in the whole year's round." It is one of these expeditions, that of the autumn of 1832, that is of present interest for us. It had a profound result upon the despondent author and bore rich literary fruit. This excursion, which was to the White Mountains, Lake Champlain, Lake Ontario, and Niagara Falls, had the psychological effect of raising his spirits and of stimulating his ambition, and provided him with the materials for a number of plots for short stories. So far as the White Mountains are concerned the record of his doings there is a strikingly brief one. Writing to his mother from Burlington, Vermont, on September 16, he says: "I have arrived in safety, having passed through the White Hills, stopping at Ethan Crawford's house and climbing Mount Washington." On this same journey he doubtless visited the Franconia Notch and saw that marvelous countenance he was to immortalize in literature, but there is no record of the fact. Nor do we hear of other expeditions to the Mountains, although it is possible they were made. From such a limited acquaintance with the region as this fleeting glimpse

THE WHITE MOUNTAINS

of it afforded, what remarkable fruit was genius able to produce!

The passage of the White Mountain Notch and the defile itself were described in a sketch printed in the *New England Magazine* for November, 1835. The sight of the devastation wrought by the slides in the Notch and the story of the Willey disaster of six years before his visit suggested to his fertile imagination the theme for his allegorical tale of "The Ambitious Guest." His stay at Crawford's is vividly described in the sketch, "Our Evening Party among the Mountains." On that evening he heard the legend of "The Great Carbuncle" told, which he expanded into the beautiful tale of this title.

It was in 1840 that the idea of a story in which a human countenance gradually assumes the aspect of a semblance of the face formed of rock, and becomes at length a perfect likeness of it, presented itself to the mind of Hawthorne and was jotted down in his notebooks. Some years after this germ developed about the Franconia Profile and bore fruit in the allegorical tale of "The Great Stone Face," in which various persons, a man of wealth, a military man, a statesman (Hawthorne is supposed to have had Daniel Webster in mind when portraying this character), and a great poet, are successively acclaimed, but mistakenly, as fulfilling the prophecy that a child should be born in the valley who should become the greatest and noblest person of his time and whose countenance should in manhood be a perfect likeness of the Great Stone Face. The poet, when he comes, finds the true person in a humble

FURTHER DISCOVERIES

dweller in the valley, Ernest, a wise and simple man, beloved by all, and when approaching old age bearing a striking resemblance to the natural phenomenon.

Written in Salem in 1848, "The Great Stone Face" was submitted to Whittier, then editor of *The National Era*, and was accepted for that journal and published January 24, 1850, the author receiving twenty-five dollars for this product of his imagination. Thus ended Hawthorne's literary connection with the White Mountains.

For two or three years before his death, Hawthorne's health had been gradually failing from some mysterious malady, which sapped his physical strength and brain-power until he could work no more. Several journeys were taken in the hope that a change of climate and scene would restore his vitality and spirits, but although they had a beneficial effect upon him the improvement was only temporary. After the sudden death in April, 1864, of Hawthorne's publisher and intimate friend, William Davis Ticknor, almost at the outset of a southward journey they were taking together for their health, Hawthorne returned to his home a complete wreck.

At this juncture his college mate and lifelong friend, ex-President Franklin Pierce, came at once to Concord to offer his services in Hawthorne's behalf. He could suggest, however, nothing more hopeful than a journey to the highlands of New Hampshire, his thought being that the mountain air might reinvigorate the invalid. They had to wait several weeks for settled weather, but at length on Thursday, May 12, 1864, they started from Boston going

THE WHITE MOUNTAINS

by rail to Concord, New Hampshire, which they reached in the evening. The weather being unfavorable and Hawthorne feeble, they remained there until the following Monday, when they started on. Traveling by easy stages in a carriage, they reached Plymouth on Wednesday evening, the 18th, about six o'clock.

Seeing that Hawthorne was becoming very helpless, General Pierce decided not to pursue their journey farther and thought of sending the next day for Mrs. Hawthorne and Una to join them there. But alas! there was to be no next day for Hawthorne. Some time in the night, in Room No. 9 in the Pemigewasset House, the novelist passed quietly away, so quietly indeed that his death was not discovered by his friend until several hours afterward.

The connection of another great New England author, Emerson, with this region appears to have been limited to one visit, so far as I have been able to ascertain. This sojourn is well worthy of record, however, because made at a crisis in his career, at the time, indeed, when the young minister of the Second Church of Boston had just made known to his people his repugnance to the Communion rite and had proposed its modification. The matter having been referred to a committee for consideration, the troubled clergyman, meanwhile, betook himself, during a suspension of the church services while some repairs were being made, to the Mountains to ponder his course of action and to get spiritual refreshment.

This was in July, 1832, when he was twenty-nine

FURTHER DISCOVERIES

years old, the same year, by the way, in which his future fellow townsman, Hawthorne, made the trip through the Mountains which was so important an incident in his career, but from a very different standpoint. On the 6th, Emerson has an entry in his Journal, dated at Conway, in which he sets down the question, "What is the message that is given me to communicate next Sunday?" So it is probable that he preached by invitation in the village church.

The end of the following week found him at Ethan Allen Crawford's, where he remained over Sunday. The entry in the Journal for Saturday contains a statement which gives his idea of the benefit to be derived by withdrawing to the hills. It has an ironical touch for us when we make a mental comparison of the primitive conditions of this particular locality in that day with the busy activity and luxury which characterize it to-day.

"The good of going to the mountains," he declares, "is that life is reconsidered; it is far from the slavery of your own modes of living, and you have opportunity of viewing the town at such a distance as may afford you a just view, nor can you have any such mistaken apprehension as might be expected from the place you occupy and the round of customs you run at home."

Sunday in this environment without the outward accompaniments of religion was evidently dull and without pleasure for the sensitive soul of the philosopher, for he writes on this day, "A few low mountains, a great many clouds always covering the great peaks, a circle of woods to the horizon, a peacock on

THE WHITE MOUNTAINS

the fence or in the yard, and two travellers no better contented than myself in the plain parlour of this house make up the whole picture of this unsabbatized Sunday."

Although there are occasional references to the White Mountains, as to "Agiochook" and the "Notch Mountains," in Emerson's writings, the region seems to have made no great impression on him. He found his place of rest and refreshment amid the quieter beauties of the region in southwestern New Hampshire dominated by Monadnock, which, says Starr King, "the genius of Mr. Emerson has made . . . the noblest mountain in literature."

What more grateful honor could come to a mountain-lover than the permanent association of his name with the most striking piece of scenery of its kind in New England! Such was the good fortune of Edward Tuckerman, Professor of Botany in Amherst College from 1858 to his death in 1886, and indefatigable explorer of the White Mountains, whose name is perpetuated in the region he loved so well by having been given to the wonderful ravine on the east side of Mount Washington, north of Boott Spur. This remarkable gorge, because of the sublimity of its steep cliffs with their semicircular sweep, its close relation to the chief summit, its famous snow arch, and the comparative ease with which it may be traversed, has become by far the most widely known of the White Mountain ravines. The route of several of the early explorers [1] in ascending Mount

---

[1] Probably of Gorges and Vines in 1642. The party of Captain Evans traversed it in 1774. Mr. S. B. Beckett, author of a railroad

FURTHER DISCOVERIES

Washington, hundreds of pedestrians now pass through it every year and clamber up the side of the Mountain Coliseum, as the upper part of the gorge or the ravine proper is sometimes called.

The kindly professor, who for his contributions to our knowledge of the botany of the region well merited the local distinction conferred upon him, first visited the Mountains in 1837. He made collections in that year and the following three years, and again made botanical explorations from 1842 [1] to 1853, spending each year several months in this region. He determined the relationship and range of many species and varieties of the plants, especially the lichens, found here. Starr King, to whose book Professor Tuckerman contributed two chapters, applies to him Emerson's description of the forest seer beginning: —

> "A lover true, who knew by heart
> Each joy the mountain dales impart."

Speaking of the Mountain region when he first visited it, Professor Tuckerman says, revealing by his words his simple tastes and love of wild nature: "It was then a secluded district, the inns offering only the homely cheer of country fare, and the paths to Mount Washington rarely trodden by any who

---

guide-book to Portland, the White Mountains, and Montreal, published at the first-named city in 1853, and a gentleman from Charleston, South Carolina, made a thorough exploration of the ravine in 1852, accompanied on a part of their trip by J. S. Hall, one of the builders of the first Summit House. Mr. Beckett and his companion are responsible for the names Hermit Lake, the Fall of a Thousand Streams, and the Mountain Coliseum.

[1] His companion that year was Asa Gray.

THE WHITE MOUNTAINS

did not prize the very way, rough as it might be, too much to wish for easier ones."

It is but natural that such a lover of the mountains and the woods as Henry Thoreau should make journeys to the White Mountains, where he would expect to find so much to interest him both in the way of scenery and in the way of natural history. We are not surprised, then, to find the records of such trips in his Journal.

His first visit was made as a sort of supplement or side-trip to his famous boating excursion, the record of which forms the groundwork of his first literary venture, "A Week on the Concord and Merrimack Rivers." The bare facts of this trip to the Mountains, which was taken in September, 1839, are set down in the Journal and some details are to be found under "Thursday" in the "Week." I give the course of the journey and its incidents as recorded in the former. Having left the boat near Hooksett, as it was impracticable to proceed farther in it, the brothers, Henry and John, walked to Concord, New Hampshire, from which town they went by stage on Friday, the 6th, to Plymouth, a distance of forty miles, finishing out the day by going on foot to Tilton's Inn in Thornton. The next day they walked through Peeling (Woodstock) and Lincoln to Franconia, pausing on the way to visit the Flume, the Basin, and the Notch, and to see the Old Man of the Mountain. On the 8th the sturdy trampers went on to Thomas J. Crawford's hotel, where they stayed on the 10th. The following day was devoted to an ascent of Mount Washington, after the completion

FURTHER DISCOVERIES

of which they rode to Conway. They returned to Concord by stage on the 11th, and the next day regained their boat at Hooksett and started on the return voyage.

July, 1858, was the time of Thoreau's second visit to this region. Setting out in a private carriage with a friend on the 2d, he ascended Red Hill on the 5th, and proceeded through Tamworth, Conway, North Conway, and Jackson to the Glen House. Having previously engaged Wentworth, who "has lived here [four miles above Jackson] thirty years, and is a native," as baggage-carrier and camp-keeper, he started at 11.30 A.M. on the 7th to ascend the Mountain road. After spending the night at a shanty near the foot of the ledge, with "a merry collier and his assistant, who had been making coal for the summit, and were preparing to leave the next morning," Thoreau completed the ascent. As a result of an earlier start, he reached the Summit half an hour before the rest of his party and enjoyed a good view, which was hidden from his companions by a cloud that settled down before their arrival.

Descending the next day (with some difficulty owing to a dense fog) into Tuckerman's Ravine, over the rocks and the snow, which latter he notes was "unexpectedly hard and dangerous to traverse," the party camped about a third of a mile above Hermit Lake. While here the guide, he records, made a fire without removing the moss and it spread even above the limit of trees, "thus leaving our mark on the mountain-side." A friend for whom he had left a note at the Glen House joined them at this camp,

THE WHITE MOUNTAINS

and the party slept in the tent the night of the 8th, with some discomfort, their fire being put out by rain. The next afternoon, Thoreau, in returning from an ascent of the stream, sprained his ankle [1] so badly that he could not sleep that night, or walk the next day. So they stayed at the camp until the 12th, when, the weather clearing up, they descended and passed the night at a camp a mile and a half west of Gorham. Two days more brought them through Randolph, Kilkenny, Jefferson Hill, Whitefield, and Bethlehem to the Franconia Notch, where they camped the night of the 14th half a mile up the side of Lafayette, which peak was ascended on the 15th, a good view being had of near points. After descending, they rode to West Thornton and then began their homeward journey.

It is superfluous to add that Thoreau's record is interspersed with frequent items of information on his special interests, the birds and flowers. He concludes his account of this journey with some observations as to the best views and with a list of the plants found at different limits on Mount Washington.

Another literary visitor to the White Mountains in the pre-railroad days, of whose experiences on the excursion we have some account, was the future

[1] Emerson, when giving, in his paper on Thoreau, instances of "pieces of luck" which happened to the naturalist, mentions his fall in Tuckerman's Ravine, and states that, "As he was in the act of getting up from his fall, he saw for the first time the leaves of the *Arnica mollis*." Unfortunately, this pretty story is not in accordance with fact. Thoreau's finding of the plant took place, we learn from the Journal, the day before and not at this time. Nor was he alone and made helpless by his fall, and so in danger of perishing had not some one chanced into the ravine and been attracted by his shouts, as one account says.

FURTHER DISCOVERIES

historian of the struggle between France and England for supremacy in North America, Francis Parkman.[1] As early as 1841, his sophomore year at Harvard, the studious young man had fixed upon the writing of the history of the conflict between the two European Powers on the soil of this continent as his life-work, and even before that he had formed a passion for the woods and outdoor life. With a wisdom unusual for his years, he saw that a much wider range of knowledge and experience than could be gained in the study would be needed to equip him to handle adequately such a theme, and in this equipment a familiarity with the topography and life of the wilderness regions with which he was to deal was, he judged, a very important element. Having, as a preliminary step, begun, on entering college, a course of physical training designed to develop the utmost strength, agility, and endurance of which he was capable, he followed this up with a succession of journeys into the wilds of the United States and Canada to secure the background which he had foreseen he would need for his future work. To this preparatory training the vacations and leisure of a number of years were devoted.

In these days of railroads and summer resorts in the White Hills it is hard to think of them as a wilderness region, but such they were in 1841, when Parkman, wishing to begin his explorations by

[1] Parkman kept a diary of each of his vacation trips, the best portions of which were used in writing various books, but the part relating to his White Mountain sojourn is for the most part unpublished. His account of his adventure at the Willey Slide is quoted in C. H. Farnham's *A Life of Francis Parkman.*

THE WHITE MOUNTAINS

familiarizing himself with the wilder parts of his native New England, made, as the first of such trips, an excursion to northern New Hampshire.

Accompanied by a classmate, Daniel Denison Slade,[1] Parkman passed around Lake Winnepesaukee, and through the valley of the Saco and the Crawford Notch. Thence the pair crossed to the Franconia Range, where they spent several delightful days. They then retraced in part their course, and crossed over to the Connecticut River, whence they proceeded to Colebrook and the Dixville Notch. An ascent of the Magalloway River with Indian guides concluded the excursion. While they were sojourning at Crawford's inn (the Notch House), the ascent of Mount Washington was made. An interesting human touch appears in the record that Parkman was greatly pleased by the "strength and spirit and good-humor" shown on this occasion by a young woman, who was a member of a lively party he had fallen in with, and who had previously charmed him by the "laughing philosophy" with which she had taken a "ducking" in his company while passing through the Notch on the stage in a pouring rain. It may be added that the acquaintance so pleasantly begun ripened into a lifelong friendship.

The most noteworthy feature of this first trip of Parkman's was an exploit undertaken by him alone and characterized by him as "the most serious adventure it was ever my lot to encounter." This little excursion, which nearly cost him his life, was not a

---

[1] Mr. Slade contributed an interesting account of the trip to the *New England Magazine* for September, 1894.

FURTHER DISCOVERIES

premeditated one. While staying at Crawford's he walked one day down the Notch to the Willey House, and out of curiosity began to ascend the pathway of the avalanche. Coming to the "inaccessible precipices" which Professor Silliman had noted as preventing his further progress in ascending this place a few years before, the adventurous young man determined to scale them, and succeeded in doing so "with considerable difficulty and danger." The descent was a yet more perilous undertaking, as, in order to get out of the ravine in which he found himself, he was compelled first to climb up its steep and decaying walls to the surface of the mountain. His splendid nerve and presence of mind enabled him to achieve this well-nigh impossible and extremely hazardous climb. His badly torn clothing, his lacerated fingers, and bruised legs were material indications of the difficulty of the feat, the recital of the fact and the details of whose accomplishment astonished the company at the hotel and Landlord Crawford as well.

"The entire journey was a delight to us," says Mr. Slade, "and in Parkman especially it augmented the love for the wild and picturesque, with which he had become enamored, and upon which he expatiated most fully in his diary."

Three of America's most noted preachers and patriots of the nineteenth century, Henry Ward Beecher, Phillips Brooks, and Thomas Starr King, were lovers of the White Mountains. The pastor of Plymouth Church, Brooklyn, made a short visit to the region in the early days, and in the latter part of

THE WHITE MOUNTAINS

his life spent a portion of every summer there; the rector of Trinity Church, Boston, and Bishop of Massachusetts, tramped the hills as a young man and visited them at least once in later life; the visits of the Boston and San Francisco divine had as one result the creation of the most famous of books on these mountains.

The eloquent pastor of the Hollis Street Society of Boston appears to have first visited the Mountains in July, 1849.[1] A passionate lover of the grand and beautiful in Nature, he became interested in the region his name is to be forever associated with, through his intimacy with another enthusiast for mountain scenery. This was his elder friend and always congenial companion, Dr. Hosea Ballou, 2d, a noted Universalist clergyman, the first president and one of the founders of Tufts College. Dr. Ballou made the first of a series of visits to the White Mountains in 1844. He was, as his notebooks testify, a most careful observer, and he had made himself familiar by study with most of the great mountains of the earth. Thus he was eminently qualified to describe accurately the scenery of the New Hampshire highlands. After his first two visits he "embodied," as Mr. Frothingham puts it, "his fondness for them, in a beautiful and eloquent paper."

[1] Richard Frothingham, in *A Tribute to Thomas Starr King*, says: "He first visited the White Hills at the age of thirteen [he was born December 17, 1824], probably with his father; but I have no facts as to this visit." The author, Hosea Starr Ballou, of the *Life of Hosea Ballou, 2d, D.D.*, thinks this statement is apparently an error. King himself, in *The White Hills*, speaks of seeing Abel Crawford "in the year 1849, when we made our first visit to the White Hills."

FURTHER DISCOVERIES

This article,[1] entitled "The White Mountains," which appeared in *The Universalist Quarterly* for April, 1846, turned Starr King's attention to the White Hills, led him to visit them, and was thus a progenitor of the greater work.

King's companions on his first visit were a lifelong friend, Professor Benjamin F. Tweed, principal of the Bunker-Hill Grammar School of Charlestown and afterwards professor in Tufts College, and two others, who joined King and Tweed at Lowell. The party took the usual route of the pre-railroad days, going to Center Harbor on Lake Winnepesaukee the first day, delaying to ascend Red Hill the next morning, and in the afternoon and night traveling in an overloaded stage to Conway, part of this journey being made through a forest fire and a thunderstorm. The belated travelers did not reach their destination until half-past eleven, but they were happy in having seen a never-to-be-forgotten sight, that of the woods on fire on the entire surface of the highest summit of the Ossipee Range. The following day, which was Saturday, they proceeded through the Notch to Crawford's Notch House, where Sunday was spent. When they were standing directly in front of the Willey House, a heavy peal of thunder and the associations and scenes of the place profoundly moved them, Mr. King records. Monday morning, July 23, the ascent of Mount Washington was made on horseback, there being twelve in the

---

[1] "On this subject," says Mr. Frothingham, "I know nothing which had appeared superior to it; and well remember Mr. King's enthusiasm for the White Hills at the time of its publication."

THE WHITE MOUNTAINS

party, which included two guides. They arrived at the summit at half-past eleven, dined out on the rocks, — there was then no shelter there, — had a "most magnificent" view, as the day was "very clear," and, after having remained an hour, began the descent, which Mr. King found so much more tiresome than the ascent that he "walked more than half the way." It began to rain when they reached the summit of Clinton and most of the party were drenched when they regained the tavern. A visit to the Franconia Notch and its objects of interest completed the tour.

Mr. King repeated his visit many times, making his headquarters at Gorham, and in 1853 began to print accounts of his explorations [1] in the *Boston Transcript*. After having for ten years viewed the Mountains, in their beauty and grandeur in winter as well as in summer, he embodied the results of his observations and explorations in "The White Hills: Their Legends, Landscape, and Poetry," which was published in 1859 on the eve of his final departure for California and which was at once received with great favor.[2]

This noble volume, which one is safe in prophesying will never be equaled or superseded in its field, is thus characterized by Mr. Frothingham: "This

---

[1] A companion for several seasons in his explorations was Henry Wheelock Ripley, who prepared editions of the *Crawford History*, printed in 1883 and 1886, and who purposed to add to that work a modern history of the Mountains.

[2] Mr. King's name is preserved in the Mountains by two fine memorials, Mount Starr King in Jefferson, named in 1861, and King's Ravine, the tremendous gorge, first explored and described by him, on the north side of Mount Adams.

FURTHER DISCOVERIES

production is far more than a description of the White Hills; its rich descriptions of every variety of landscape apply to all natural scenes, and bring out their inmost meaning. There is much of himself in this volume, of his rare spiritual insight, — much of what his cultured and reverent eye saw in the beauty and the grandeur that God is creating every day."

Less notably associated with the Mountains in a literary way than Starr King, but far more memorably connected with them in a ministerial way, was the great preacher and pastor of Plymouth Church, Brooklyn's most famous citizen, Henry Ward Beecher. The year 1856 appears to be the date of Mr. Beecher's earliest acquaintance with the region. He evidently stayed at the Crawford House, then kept by J. L. Gibb. Humorously declaring himself "only a freshman, and in the first term at that," in "a university of mountains," he does not, he says, in the introductory paragraph of his paper contributed to *The Independent* at that time, "propose to set forth and write out the whole of the White Mountains." "I will give you," he continues, "just a sprig of my experience." What his readers get, however, is an altogether delightful essay,[1] the first part of which gives an account of a descent on horseback from the top of Mount Washington, an experience which gave him "one half-hour of extreme pleasure and two hours of common pleasure." It is

---

[1] "A Time at the White Mountains," one of his regular contributions, over his customary signature, a " * ", to *The Independent* (July 31, 1856). It is reprinted in *Eyes and Ears*.

THE WHITE MOUNTAINS

entirely to the "half-hour of extreme pleasure," which was a time passed in separation from his party, that this part of the essay is devoted. In eloquent and beautiful language he tells what he saw and what he thought and felt when solitary in such a place.

In the second half of the essay his descriptions of a beautiful stream, which joins the Saco near the hotel, of its pools, its "avenue of cascades" (one of which, a double one, was afterwards given his name), and its environment of forest and mountains, and of the glorious view, are charmingly done. Especially pleasing are his word-picture of the pool he selected for a refreshing plunge and his description of the witnessed actions and imagined thoughts of some trout whose "mountain homestead" he had so greatly and strangely disturbed.

Mr. Beecher's becoming an annual visitor to the White Mountains was on this wise. For nearly thirty years he had been a sufferer from that distressing malady, hay fever, which attacked him every year about the 16th of August, almost to the day. For nearly six weeks he was sorely afflicted, reading, writing, and almost all forms of mental work being impossible. Finally his attention was called to the relief that the air of the White Mountains affords many sufferers, and, trying the experiment, he happily found exemption there from the attacks of the disease. He returned year after year in the seventies to the Twin Mountain House and soon the region became one of his subsidiary pulpits, as his thirst for doing his Master's work was such as not

FURTHER DISCOVERIES

to allow him to lose any opportunity. The first year or two he rested, but after that he began holding informal services on Sundays.

The use of the large hotel parlor followed, with preaching every Sunday morning. Soon the capacity of this summer church was outgrown, and then one of the large tents used at the State fairs was secured, benches being provided for the congregation. In this, during the last two or three years that he visited the Twin Mountain House, he preached regularly every Sunday for six weeks. For a number of years also, at the request of the guests, he led the daily service of morning prayer. This, his summer parish,[1] became his most prominent field of work outside of Plymouth Church. From the neighboring hotels and near-by towns people came by hundreds to hear the famous preacher, filling the great tent. Thus he made his infirmity an instrumentality for good.

It was in the first year (1862) of his rectorship of the Church of the Holy Trinity, Philadelphia, that Phillips Brooks, tired from six months of hard labor in ministering to his large parish and in keeping the many engagements that pressed upon him, made his first visit to the White Mountains. To the vacation of this year "he had looked forward," says his biographer, "with the eagerness of a schoolboy, to whom the holiday is the most real part of his existence." Accompanied by the Reverend Charles A. L. Richards and the Reverend George Augustus Strong,

---

[1] In 1875 he published *A Summer Parish: Sabbath Discourses and Morning Service of Prayer, at the "Twin Mountain House," White Mountains, New Hampshire, during the summer of 1874.*

THE WHITE MOUNTAINS

his fellow students and close companions at the theological seminary and lifelong intimate friends, he set out, on August 4, to make the tour of the Mountains, an excursion which was not so common then as later, and which was a notable event in their lives. Phillips Brooks was not fond of exercise in those days, or indeed at any time in his life, but was endowed with rugged health. He did not like walking, or at any rate did not practice it as a regular form of exercise, but while staying in Boston in July he had taken lessons in horseback riding, which activity proved of service to him on this trip. The party made their headquarters at the Glen House, and Brooks did his share of mountain-climbing with the others. Their initial, or, as it were, practice climbs were up Mounts Surprise [1] and Hayes, two of Starr King's favorite viewpoints, near Gorham. In the course of their wanderings they were joined by Mr. Brooks's friend, the Reverend Mr. Cooper, of Philadelphia, and by his brother William, of Boston. The trip culminated in an excursion which came near to putting an end to the great preacher's career then and there. Inspired by Starr King's exuberant enthusiasm for the sublimity of the views to be gained by making such an expedition and for the physical joys of the experience, the travelers determined upon doing what was then known as "going over the Peaks," which meant crossing the Northern Peaks from Madison to Washington. When it is remembered that there were then no defined paths and

---

[1] The biography of Phillips Brooks has it "Mount Suspense," which seems to be a slip.

FURTHER DISCOVERIES

guiding marks or signs for the trampers and that guides were few, the difficulty of the excursion in those days will be at once evident. Having secured a man as guide who was said to know the way, they started from the Glen House at six o'clock on the morning of August 12, intending to make a two days' trip of it. After going two miles or so on the road to Gorham, they struck up the mountain-side. Six hours' severe labor in the hot sun and close air and over fallen timber and deep beds of moss brought them to the timber-line. They climbed Madison, crossed its two summits, dined between Madison and Adams, and, after ascending the latter, passed on to Jefferson. At the base of this peak they had meant to camp, but, as it was blowing "half a hurricane," the guide insisted that the wind was too high and the temperature too low to make camping safe for heated and tired men and that therefore they must push forward. It was at sunset that they stood on the summit of Jefferson, and there were still two or three hours of good work before them. Mr. Brooks, for the first part of the day, had stood the prolonged exertion as well as any of the party, but somewhere on the part of the way which they were now passing over, the young giant, who in those days required double rations and on this occasion had been provided for only on the scale of ordinary men, began to flag, and declared he could go no farther. He implored his companions to leave him under the shelter of a rock, with a shawl, for the night, but as, of course, they would not hear to this and as they entreated him to go on, he struggled forward for a few minutes at a

THE WHITE MOUNTAINS

time and then flung himself down exhausted for a long rest. Night came on and the way was lost in the darkness, by the guide as well as by the others. Finally they divined what was the matter with Brooks and gave him food, some one having, fortunately, an egg or two in reserve. Mr. Brooks having gained a little strength from food and rest, and the moon having risen and the wind being in their favor, they pressed on, and at last, a half-hour after midnight, the exhausted trampers reached their goal, the Tip-Top House. Tired as they were they had to sleep on the office floor, as every bed was taken. The following day they walked down the carriage road in the morning and spent the remainder of the day resting. The remaining days of the trip were passed at North Conway, where an ascent of Kearsarge was accomplished on foot, and some other expeditions were made, one of which resulted for Brooks in a sprained ankle, which accident brought his tramp abruptly to a close.

Mr. Brooks evidently enjoyed the trip, for we find him in August of the following year again tramping in the Mountains, accompanied by Mr. Richards, Professor C. J. Stillé, one of his parishioners, and his brother Frederick.[1] This tour, in the course of which he met numerous friends, was interspersed with rowing, occasional resorts to horseback riding, and mountain-climbing. One of the tramping excursions was from the Glen up Mount Washington,

---

[1] When writing to his brother to induce him to take this trip, Mr. Brooks mentions the Reverend Mr. Strong and the future Bishop of New York, Henry C. Potter, as planning to go.

FURTHER DISCOVERIES

after which the travelers returned to North Conway.[1]

The visitors who came in the early days to explore the Mountains or to see their scenic features stayed at most but a short time, far from long enough to form a strong love for the region or to enjoy its beauties satisfactorily. Probably the first city person to prolong his summer sojourns or to make frequent returns was Dr. Samuel A. Bemis, who as a boy had walked from Vermont to Boston, where he became a leading dentist and amassed a fortune. From 1827 to 1840 he spent nearly every summer in the White Hills, and in the latter year he took up his permanent residence in the glen in Hart's Location, at the base of Mount Crawford, in which Abel Crawford had lived so many years. There Dr. Bemis built the stone cottage, so well known to travelers up and down the Notch, which he made his home until his death in May, 1881.

Having lent large amounts of money to Nathaniel T. P. Davis, the proprietor of the Mount Crawford House, on mortgage, on which Crawford's son-in-law ultimately had to default his payments, Dr. Bemis was obliged to foreclose. Thus he came into possession of a vast tract of woodland, extending for miles up the Notch. This great estate the eccentric old patriarch bequeathed to his long-time superin-

---

[1] My account of these summer excursions of Mr. Brooks is drawn from Dr. Allen's *Life and Letters of Phillips Brooks*. The details of the trip over the peaks are quoted by the biographer from the Reverend Charles A. L. Richards's account of it as set down in *Remembrances of Phillips Brooks by Two of his Friends* [Richards and Strong]. (1893.)

THE WHITE MOUNTAINS

tendent, George W. Morey. Bemis Station on the railroad, Bemis Brook, Bemis Pond, and Mount Bemis, in addition to the cottage, preserve the name and memory of this lover of Nature, who is said to have named more of the mountains of this region than any other man.

VI

SOME FOREIGN VISITORS AND THEIR ACCOUNTS OF THEIR TOURS OF THE WHITE MOUNTAINS

THE next Englishman after Josselyn to visit the White Hills and to give an account [1] of his journey was Edward Augustus Kendall, Esq., a miscellaneous writer, who, during the course of his travels in this country, passed through this region by wagon in November, 1807. From Portland he proceeded to Gorham, where he first saw the Mountains, he says, after leaving the Kennebec.[2] Thence he traveled to Conway, and from there he rode over the new turnpike through the Notch and through "Briton's Woods," Bethlehem, "Lyttleton" (where he passed the night), and Bath to the Connecticut River. Owing to the lateness of the season he could not ascend any of the Mountains, the summits of which were then covered with snow. On his way thither, when he reached Hiram, Maine, on the 17th, he had experienced the first serious fall of snow, and his journey, being undertaken at this late time of year, was necessarily a hasty one. He paused long enough on the

---

[1] In his *Travels through the Northern Parts of the United States in the years 1807 and 1808*, in three volumes, published at New York in 1809. The *Dictionary of National Biography* characterizes it as "a somewhat dull account of his wanderings." His discussion of the whiteness of the Mountains and its cause has been summarized in the Introduction.

[2] He got his first view of them from some high land in Hallowell, Maine.

THE WHITE MOUNTAINS

way to eat a meal at "a small public house," twenty miles from Conway (evidently the Mount Crawford House), and speaks of passing another house, seven miles farther up (the Willey House), Captain Rosebrook's house, and the latter's son's farm in "Briton's Woods." The greatest height to which he ascended, he states, was the "Beaver Meadow" (where the Saco rises), the origin of which tract he is at pains to explain.

The derivation of place-names evidently was a subject of much interest to him, for he interrupts his narrative often to introduce extended discussions of the origin of some of those he meets with in the course of his travels. Of such names in this region, Ammonoosuc and Coös receive attention, and there is a lengthy canvassing of the signification and proper form of the name "Moose Hillock."

The tricennial period 1830 to 1860 was memorable in White Mountain travel by reason of the visits of a number of foreign tourists, who made excursions to this region a part of their American tours and who have included in the record of their travels accounts of the incidents and experiences of their trips through the Mountains. Among the earliest of these foreign visitors was a London barrister of royal name and eminently fair mind, who made a tour of North America in the years 1831 and 1832. Henry Tudor, Esq., had been an extensive traveler, and he undertook the transatlantic voyage for the purpose of visiting the only quarter of the globe that he had not seen and also for the sake of regaining his health, which was somewhat impaired. He had no intention

SOME FOREIGN VISITORS

of publishing an account of his travels (which he had given in letters to various friends), and would never have done so, he declares, had he not been displeased with the tendency of some tourists to America "to sully the fair reputation, and to depreciate whatever is excellent in the rising greatness of our transatlantic brethren." Particularly he reprobates, in his Preface, the "Domestic Manners of the Americans," pronouncing Mrs. Trollope's observations as "at once uncharitable" and as "illogical in their deductions." Moreover, he devotes a part of the body of his book, "Narrative of a Tour in North America" (1834), to some remarks upon that lady's strictures.

Our present interest in Mr. Tudor and his travels, however, lies solely in the fact that he made, in the latter part of October, 1831, an excursion through the White Mountains, going by wagon from Maine to Conway, riding through the Notch in a carriage, passing Thomas Crawfurd's [sic] hotel, and his brother's hostelry also, and crossing by way of Littleton to the Connecticut River. At the Notch House he felt, he says, an inclination to ascend the Mountains and might have done so had not a recent fall of snow rendered it impracticable. He was filled with admiration of the bold and romantic scenery, especially of the Notch, and was much impressed by the story of the destruction of the household of "Mr. Martin Willey," which he narrates with considerable fullness.

Two other foreigners who paid a visit to the region about this time were Charles Joseph Latrobe, an experienced English traveler and observer, and his

THE WHITE MOUNTAINS

friend, the Count de Pourtalès, a young Frenchman, who together made an extended tour of North America in 1832 and 1833. On their voyage to New York from Havre, they had as fellow passenger Washington Irving, who was returning to his native land after seventeen years' absence. With him they formed an intimate acquaintance on shipboard, which was resumed ashore and which led to his becoming their companion in a number of their excursions, the association being continued for the greater part of the summer and autumn of 1832. Latrobe's entertaining letters to a younger brother narrating the incidents of his travels, describing the places and persons seen, and commenting on the government, politics, manners, customs, institutions, spirit, etc., of the country in general or of particular regions, were published in two volumes in 1835, under the title "The Rambler in North America," the work being dedicated to Irving.

It was in July, 1832, that the travelers, in company with Irving, who had appointed Boston as a rendezvous previous to a visit to the White Mountains, and whom the foreigners found at the Tremont Hotel awaiting their arrival, made their journey to the northern wilderness. They approached the region via Concord, Lake Winnepesaukee, and Conway, whence they passed through the Notch and descended the valley of the Ammonoosuc. The ascent of Mount Washington was achieved by the party, but "under disadvantageous circumstances." "Upon gaining the summit," says Latrobe, "after some hours' toil and much expectation, we were

SOME FOREIGN VISITORS

enveloped in heavy mist, which set our patience at defiance, and sent us cold and wet on our downward route."

Mr. Latrobe, on the preceding day, ascended alone, "under better auspices," the summit "third in rank," and so gained a view which enabled him to give a brief description of the scenery for the benefit of the recipient of his letters. Irving being obliged to return to New York for a few days, Pourtalès and Latrobe continued on to Lancaster without him and thence crossed Vermont and proceeded to Saratoga Springs, where they kept their appointment to meet Irving again.

Of what impression the White Mountains made upon the great writer who has immortalized the Hudson and the Catskills in literature, we have no record. Writing to his brother Peter, he declares the central New Hampshire country "beautiful beyond expectation" and his course down the Connecticut River to Springfield as a passing "through a continued succession of enchanting scenes"; but he writes nothing of the White Mountains further than the brief statement, "We kept together through the mountains." Possibly the unpleasant experience encountered on the Mount Washington trip is responsible for his silence as to this region.

In the autumn of the same year (1832) as that of the visit of Latrobe and his companions, another English traveler, E. T. Coke, a lieutenant of the Forty-fifth Regiment, in the course of a comprehensive tour of the United States and the British provinces, made a trip to the Mountains, of which

THE WHITE MOUNTAINS

he has given a lively account in the second volume of his "A Subaltern's Furlough," published in 1833.

A fatiguing and rough coach journey of eighteen hours took him from Concord to Conway on the 18th of October. Such was the soldier's ambition that the next morning he started at a quarter to three to go through the Notch. The traveler (who was of an artistic bent and wished to do some sketching), on the arrival of the coach at the southern entrance to the Notch, alighted from it, and, ordering his baggage to be left at the inn beyond the pass, sat down to admire the "awful, grand and sublime spectacle, which the Notch presents." The chance rolling of a stone down the mountain-side and the starting-up of a partridge brought to his mind the thought of an avalanche and caused him to hasten his sketching work and leave the valley. He found his baggage at Ethan Crawford's, where he arrived after a toilsome journey and where he stayed several days, entertained, he notes, by his host's hunting stories. It was too windy to climb Washington on the 21st, but on the 22d, he started with a guide at 4.30 A.M. and reached the summit at 8.15, having been one and three quarters hours in covering the three miles from the base. Of the view, which he found "most extensive," he remarks, "It did not, I must confess, altogether answer my expectations, nor, to my taste, was it equal to that from Mount Holyoke, where all was richness and life."

After his descent, he proceeded to Bethlehem and thence to Littleton, where he arrived in the evening. The next day (the 23d) being cold and rainy, he

SOME FOREIGN VISITORS

remained at Littleton, but on the 24th he rode out to Franconia, and, passing through the Franconia Notch, crossed over to the Connecticut River and Vermont. On his way he visited the "Profile of the Old Man of the Mountain," about which he remarks, "No art could improve the effect, nor could any attempt be made to assist it; for, the profile being seen perfect only from one point, the slightest deviation from that spot throws all into a confused mass."

In the autumn of 1835, the noted English writer, Harriet Martineau, who was spending two years of travel in the United States, visited the White Mountains.[1] She left Boston on the 16th of September in company with three friends, going by way of Lake Winnepesaukee, which the party crossed on a steamboat and in the neighborhood of which they paused long enough to make an ascent of "Red Mountain" (Red Hill). This done, they proceeded to Conway, whence they went in a private conveyance through the Crawford Notch, stops being made at Pendexter's and the elder Crawford's, and Ethan Allen Crawford's hospitable dwelling being reached at nightfall.

Their purpose of ascending Mount Washington the next day was frustrated by a tempest of wind and snow on that peak, but the day was spent "delightfully" in climbing Mount Deception, tracing

[1] She devotes a section of volume II of her *Retrospect of Western Travel* (published in 1838), to a description of the region and a narration of the incidents of her journey. The earlier part of the trip is related in her *Society in America*. This is followed by a brief account of the Willey disaster, by a pleasant characterization of Ethan Allen Crawford and of his hospitality, and by a description of the host's ways of entertaining and amusing his guests.

THE WHITE MOUNTAINS

the course of the Ammonoosuc, and watching the storms. In the late afternoon, the tourists set out in a wagon for Littleton, passing Bethlehem ("consisting, as far as we could see, of one house and two barns"), and reaching about six o'clock their destination, where they were most comfortably entertained "at Gibb's house." The following day was devoted to an excursion to the Franconia Notch. Unfortunately, the weather was showery and cloudy, and soon after their arrival they were glad to take refuge from one pelting downpour in the Lafayette House, then just erected. Although, as she puts it, "we ... made ourselves acquainted with the principal features of the pass," she makes no mention of the Profile, whose existence was apparently unknown to her and which was doubtless on that day hidden by clouds or mist. After dinner, however, when they had duly given an account of themselves in the host's new album, they started, in defiance of the weather, to see the Flume, which she calls the Whirlpool and characterizes as "the grand object of the pass." In spite of the fact that it rained hard during their stay of half an hour there, and although they returned to Littleton in pitch darkness and arrived there wet to the skin, the experience did not discourage the writer from concluding her account with the opinion that the Franconia Defile is "the noblest mountain pass I saw in the United States."

The most famous of foreign scientists to explore the Mountains was Sir Charles Lyell, F.R.S., the eminent geologist. Early in his second visit to the United States, in 1845, he set out, accompanied by

SOME FOREIGN VISITORS

his wife, on an excursion thither from Boston, the first part of their itinerary being along the seacoast to Portland. Their course from there was to Conway, then through the Crawford Notch to Fabyan's, where they remained several days, ascending Mount Washington on horseback on October 7. Leaving Fabyan's, they journeyed to Bethlehem and the Franconia Notch, and thence traveled by stage to Plymouth, whence they returned via Concord to Boston.

Geological and botanical matters were naturally uppermost in Sir Charles's mind during the tour, but he sets down many interesting observations and remarks concerning things political, social, and religious. He records the names of many botanical specimens found, and he was particularly interested in the alpine species of plants inhabiting Mount Washington, the explanation of whose presence there he discusses briefly. At Fabyan's he found Mr. Oakes ("one of the ablest botanists in America"), who was his companion in walks about there and who was a member of the party of nine which made the ascent of the chief peak.

The geological matter that especially engaged the great scientist's attention was that of the effects of slides on the rocks over which they had passed, his object being to determine whether any of the grooves and scratches on them are caused by avalanches. As a result of his investigations at the scene of the Willey Slide, where he clambered up four hundred feet above the river under the guidance of the elder Crawford, and at other places, he became convinced

THE WHITE MOUNTAINS

that the long and straight furrows could not be due to this cause.

Although he stayed a couple of days or so at the Franconia Notch and went from there to Plymouth by stage, he does not speak of the Profile or of the Flume. Lack of time to make the side trip to the latter when on his way through the Notch may have been the reason for his silence about it. Perhaps, also, such curiosities as these did not appeal to his scientific mind.

Another foreigner of note who included a tour to the White Mountains in her course of travel in America was the Swedish novelist, Fredrika Bremer, who spent two years in this country. In August, 1851, the month preceding her departure, she paid a visit of several days to the Mountains, of which trip she has left an entertaining account,[1] with lively comments on some of the incidents of the journey and on some of the practices of fellow tourists, and especially with much description of the scenery, which impressed her greatly. That of the Franconia Notch reminded her of "the glorious river valleys of Dalecarlia or Norsland" in her native land, but was pronounced by her "more picturesque, more playful and fantastic," and declared to have "more cheerful diversity" and an "affluence of wood" and "beautiful foliage" that are "extraordinary." She declined to attempt the ascent of Mount Washington because of the difficulty of the expedition and because of the

---

[1] See volume II of her *The Homes of the New World: Impressions of America*. Translated by Mary Howitt, in two volumes (1853). The work is a transcription of her letters to her sister at home.

SOME FOREIGN VISITORS

nature of the view, visited the Flume, which interested her greatly, and saw the Profile,[1] which struck her very differently from most people. So singular is her impression of it that her characterization of it may well be given here for its interest.

The peculiarity of these so-called White Mountains is [she says] the many gigantic human profiles which, in many places, look out from the mountains with a precision and perfect regularity of outline which is quite astonishing. They have very much amused me, and I have sketched several of them in my rambles. We have our quarters here [2] very close to one of these countenances, which has long been known under the name of "the Old Man of the Mountain." It has not any nobility in its features, but resembles a very old man in a bad humor, and with a nightcap on his head, who is looking out from the mountain half inquisitive. Far below the old giant's face is an enchanting little lake, resembling a bright oval toilet-glass, inclosed in a verdant frame of leafage. The Old Man of the Mountain looks out gloomily over this quiet lake, and the clouds float far below his chin.

In this connection it may also be of interest to know that, while she was visiting in Boston, more than a year before, Charles Sumner read to her one day Hawthorne's story of "The Great Stone Face," which "poem in prose," as she characterizes it, gave her so much pleasure that she wrote a summary of it as a part of her letter sent at that time.

A mid-century visitor to America of an unusual kind and of some distinction was the Honorable

---

[1] She also mentions "Willey's House" and briefly narrates the story of the disaster and that of the fate of Nancy, as connected with a "place" called "Nancy Bridge."
[2] She stayed at the Lafayette House.

THE WHITE MOUNTAINS

Amelia Matilda Murray, a maid of honor to Queen Victoria. A brilliant woman of high social position (her mother was a lady in waiting upon two princesses and as a girl Amelia was much at court), she did not allow court life to absorb by any means her entire attention, but found time and opportunity to become an excellent botanist and artist and also to interest herself in the education of destitute and delinquent children.

In July, 1854, she started on a tour of the United States, Cuba, and Canada, not returning home until October, 1855. In the latter part of August of the first year a visit of about ten days to the White Mountains was made, of which she has left a vivacious account in her "Letters from the United States, Cuba, and Canada," published in 1856.[1]

Botany and sketching were naturally her special interests on her American tour. Immediately after her arrival she made the acquaintance of Asa Gray, who, she writes on August 4, "has proposed botanizing over part of this country with me." On the excursion with which we are concerned, he accompanied her as far as Alton Bay, whence he returned to Boston. The Mountains were approached in the usual way at that day, that is, via Center Harbor and Conway. The Honorable Miss Murray did not particularly enjoy mountain-climbing, and so re-

---

[1] An interesting sidelight on her quality is afforded by the fact that when she was reminded, on proposing to print an account of her travels, that court officials were not allowed to publish anything savoring of politics, she resigned her post rather than suppress her opinions, — she had returned a zealous advocate of the abolition of slavery. She prepared, but did not publish, a series of sketches to accompany her book. (*Dictionary of National Biography*.)

SOME FOREIGN VISITORS

fused to ascend Red Hill[1] with her party. The journey to Conway, "a drive hot and dusty but very beautiful," was made in "a kind of char-à-banc, hired for the purpose." From Conway she went to the Crauford [*sic*] House on Sunday morning, August 20, the start being made at 6 A.M. "Such a beautiful drive!" she exclaims. At her destination she found acquaintances and was induced to accompany them on a drive, after six horses, to the summit of Mount Willard. "Having once embarked in the undertaking, I was ashamed to insist upon being let off; but the ascent was really a tremendous one for any vehicle whatever; and how we ever got safely up and down again is a marvel to me," she writes. The temptation to join a party in ascending Mount Washington on horseback the next day she resisted, doubtless without much effort. She then continued her tour, going to the Profile House on the 22d, and on the morning of the following day driving to the Flume House. In connection with the Profile and Profile Lake she records: "A legend is attached to the latter, which says, that all who rise early may see the old man of the mountain take his bath in the lake." She found the scenery round the Flume House so fine that she removed there on the 24th and stayed until the morning of the 29th. On the morning of her last full day at this place, with an American acquaintance whom she found staying there, she climbed to the top of "Pemmewhasset,"

[1] This long ridge, a number of times mentioned in the text, is situated north of Lake Winnepesaukee in Moultonborough. It commands a wonderful view, whose praises have been celebrated by many writers.

THE WHITE MOUNTAINS

from which, she says, "there is a charming view up and down the valley of the Saca [*sic*]." Some one had evidently misinformed her as to the geography of the valley she was in, for, in recording her ride from the Flume House to Wells River, she writes, "The road ... runs nearly the whole way by the River Saco, the same we passed at Conway."

She has much to say in praise of the beauty of the mountain country, which appealed strongly to her artistic sensibilities. On the social side, the comfort of the hotels and the cordiality, frankness, and kindness of the people she met especially struck this English traveler, who found the hotel life "like the freedom of a very large country-house in England."

The English novelist, Anthony Trollope, he of the "nulla dies sine linea" method of doing literary work, is another famous foreigner who visited the White Mountains and gave an account of his excursion and recorded his impressions of the region in a book. Early in the course of his travels in North America, one result of which was an entertaining and fair-minded volume on the subject, he made a brief circuit tour of the Mountains. It was in September, 1861, that, on his way to Canada, he paused long enough to make the trip. His way of approach was by the Grand Trunk Railway from Portland to Gorham, and thence by wagon to the Glen House. From this starting-point he made an ascent of Mount Washington on a pony, but, as he says of this expedition, "I did not gain much myself by my labour," he evidently experienced the rather

SOME FOREIGN VISITORS

common lot of being deprived of any view by the presence of clouds. The following night was passed at Jackson, and the next day was devoted to a wagon journey to the Crawford House and a walk up Mount Willard. After spending the night at this hostelry, he completed his Mountain excursion by a ride over Cherry Mountain and thence back to Gorham.

He expresses his surprise in finding a district in New England with such fine scenery, much of which, he declares, "is superior to the famed and classic lands of Europe," and further in finding it so easily accessible and abundantly supplied with large hotels. The view from Mount Willard down the Notch he pronounces unequaled on the Rhine. The brilliancy of the autumn foliage, unapproached in any other land, he confesses to be beyond his powers of description.

VII

THE EARLY HOTELS AND THE BEGINNINGS OF THE REGION AS A SUMMER RESORT

IN an earlier chapter have been chronicled the first comings to the Mountains of inhabitants of the older and more established and populous settlements on the seacoast, who came not to stay permanently, but to pass through the region or to tarry a short time in it for the purpose of pleasure travel, or of exploration. The more noteworthy of such early visitors were, it will be recalled, men of learning, such as President Dwight and Drs. Belknap and Cutler, who made the journey, long and arduous as it was in the latter part of the eighteenth century, with a mixed motive, in which the chief element was the desire of adding to their stock of information. They had heard of the beauty and grandeur of the scenery of the Mountain district, and wished to see it for themselves, so the pleasure to be derived from viewing the landscape was an element in their reason for coming, as was also the desire for recreation; but their chief concern was ever knowledge of the natural phenomena and physical conditions of the region and of the effects of man's occupation of a wilderness and first attempts at subduing it.

These explorers or travelers, whose main interests were, as has been said, scientific, or whose minds, at any rate, were inquiring, were followed early in the

THE EARLY HOTELS

nineteenth century by a slowly increasing number of a class whose purpose in coming was entirely one of pleasure and recreation, the precursors of the multitude of summer tourists and visitors of recent days. In the preceding two chapters have been summarized the incidents of the tours of the more noted of those persons, American and foreign, who came in the early days to view the scenic beauties and wonders of the region, their experiences, and the comments they chose to make on things seen.

This growing desire on the part of travelers and pleasure seekers, to make a trip to the highlands of the north country, stimulated the residents and the local authorities to endeavor to meet the demand thus created and to turn it to pecuniary advantage, by affording facilities for making the journey and more and better accommodations for the entertainment of passers-through or sojourners. This disposition manifested itself in the building of better roads, the construction of bridle paths and trails, the establishment of stage-lines on certain main-traveled routes, and the erection of comfortable inns. Foremost among the residents of the region in this pioneer work were the members of the Crawford family. The improvements made by them and others fostered in turn the desire of making the excursion, and in consequence of this reciprocal action, and also in some measure because of the wider extension of the knowledge of the existence of such grand and beautiful scenery so comparatively near at hand, the number of travelers, as has been indicated, gradually increased. It remained for the coming of the rail-

THE WHITE MOUNTAINS

roads, the growth of the country in population and wealth, and the rise and development of the practice of spending the summer or a part of it in the country, and of the closely related custom of taking summer vacations, all circumstances occurring in or characteristic of the latter part of the nineteenth century, to make of the White Mountain district the great summer recreation ground and tourist resort it has become.

In the earlier period of this growth of the region as a resort, however, the visitors were tourists only, who devoted but a few days at most to seeing the Mountains. Many of them paused long enough, as we have seen, to make, under the guidance of the Crawfords or of others, an ascent of the chief peak, but that done and the notches visited or traversed, they passed on, in most cases never to return. It was not until late in the thirties that people came to pass the entire season or at least to make stays of any length at one place, and began to make annual returns to some village or hamlet, such, for instance, as Conway Corner or North Conway. I have spoken in another place of the pioneer in this custom, Dr. Bemis, of Hart's Location.

The first inns in the region, therefore, were opened to provide entertainment for transient guests, which included the tourists and the many persons engaged in the commercial traffic that was carried on over certain main routes of travel, especially that through the Crawford Notch, which formed the only direct connection between the seacoast and the upper Connecticut Valley. These hostelries were, as Haw-

THE EARLY HOTELS

thorne expresses it, "at once the pleasure-house of fashionable tourists and the homely inn of country travelers," and their guests were often of the motley character of a group the novelist describes, in the sketch [1] from which this quotation is taken, as spending a night at Ethan Crawford's when he was once a guest there.

The building or opening of the earliest of these houses of entertainment has been already recorded. Let the facts be again set down briefly for the sake of bringing the information into juxtaposition with other circumstances of the same kind.

The first house of entertainment in the region was built, it will be recalled, by Captain Eleazar Rosebrook in 1803 on the site of the present Fabyan House. This house was burned in 1818, shortly after Ethan Allen Crawford received it from his grandfather, and was immediately succeeded by a small house, which was moved to the site. In 1824 and 1825, Mr. Crawford added a good-sized building to this latter structure to accommodate the increasing number of summer travelers. Another addition was erected in 1832 and 1833.

Meantime, as travel through the region and especially over the new turnpike through the Notch increased, hotels and taverns of a simple type were opened along the main routes. The rude habitation known as the "Willey House" was built, as has been already mentioned, probably in the last decade

[1] "Our Evening-Party among the Mountains," one of the "Sketches from Memory," in *Mosses from an Old Manse*. Hawthorne, as has been narrated, stopped at Crawford's in the autumn of 1832.

THE WHITE MOUNTAINS

of the eighteenth century, and, not long after the opening of Rosebrook's hotel, was opened as a public house by one Henry Hill. It was kept by him and others for several years and was at length abandoned. Farther south, on Hart's Location, Rosebrook's son-in-law, Abel Crawford, began to entertain travelers at his home, which came to be known as the "Mount Crawford House," and which was kept for years by his son-in-law, Nathaniel T. P. Davis. Here Webster, Everett, Rufus Choate, and President Pierce were guests when visiting the region on fishing trips. The old house was torn down some years since,[1] its last openings to the public having been in 1872 and 1876.

The early inn at Upper Bartlett was kept for years by "Judge" Obed Hall, who had been a member of Congress. Grenville Mellen tells of stopping there in 1819 and characterizes his host as "the wonder and curiosity of his region," noting his picturesque character and rugged, honest hospitality and his abilities as a talker and story-teller.

The Honorable John Pendexter, who built the hotel, afterwards enlarged and improved and now known as the "Pendexter Mansion," in Intervale, came to the wilderness from Portsmouth [2] in the winter of 1772 or 1773, living at first in a log cabin and later in a frame house on the lowland. Another early house in this locality was Meserve's East

---

[1] In 1900. A cottage, still standing at the railroad station, was built of the sound timber.

[2] The eighty miles were made by the pioneer on foot, his wife, Martha, riding on an old horse, with a feather bed for a saddle, and he dragging the household furniture on a hand sled.

THE OLD MOUNT CRAWFORD HOUSE AT BEMIS

THE EARLY HOTELS

Branch House at Lower Bartlett, near the location of the Pitman Hall of to-day.

The great hotel locality of this region was, however, the town of Conway. Here, as the chief stopping-place at the east entrance to the Mountains, a number of taverns or inns were early established. About 1812, the Washington House, later the Cliff House, threw open its doors for the entertainment of strangers in North Conway, destined to become the principal tourist center of the town and the leading summer resort of the eastern side of the region. Daniel Eastman was its builder and proprietor. By 1825, when summer visitors began to come, the taverns in the town, besides Eastman's were, according to Mrs. Mason, Thomas Abbott's Pequawket House at Conway (formerly known as Conway Corner); Benjamin Osgood's house at Black Cat, in the lower end of the town; the McMillan House at North Conway, established by Colonel Andrew McMillan, a native of Ireland, who came there from Concord about 1764; and Samuel W. Thompson's small tavern in North Conway, situated where now stands the Kearsarge. Chatauque,[1] or Conway Corner, became, as travel increased, the starting-point for stage-lines to distant points, such as Concord, Dover, Littleton, and Portland. In these days most of the tourists came by coach from Center Harbor, but numbers, proportionately much greater than in

[1] This name was given to the village, according to Mrs. M. E. Eastman, by an old resident, who, on returning to his native town after having spent a number of years near Chautauqua, New York, remarked on the resemblance of the right-angled crossroads to the "four corners" in the New York State village.

THE WHITE MOUNTAINS

later days until the advent of the automobile, traveled by private conveyance. Mails in the pre-stage days were infrequent. In 1775, a messenger brought "the post monthly"; in 1781, the Government employed a rider to bring the mail fortnightly. From 1825 to 1829, Samuel W. Thompson carried it on horseback from Conway to Littleton once a week,[1] and after that a two-horse wagon was driven over the route until the stage-line was established.

Noted visitors to North Conway during its infancy as a summer resort were many, the town being, as has been indicated, the chief gateway to the Mountains. Some of them who wrote about their tours are named in the preceding chapters.

The artists, who early made the village a sort of American Barbizon, and who did so much to extend the locality's fame, will be dealt with in another chapter.

An important event in the hotel history of North Conway was the erection, in 1861, of the structure which constitutes the south wing of the present Kearsarge House. The enterprising Samuel W. Thompson, owner of the older hotel of the same name,[2] was the builder of the new house of enter-

---

[1] Mr. Crawford records that, in 1828, he was transporting the mail from Conway to Littleton twice a week, and that after the heavy rain of the 2d day of September, — a downpour "which was as great as the one we had two years before" and which carried away many of the newly rebuilt bridges and destroyed much of the road, — it was impossible to go with a horse. "We carried it," he says, "regularly on our backs, without losing more than one single trip."

[2] The old tavern was removed to a side street and made over into a dwelling-house. It is now used as the Episcopal rectory. I owe this information to Mr. Thompson's daughter, Mrs. L. J. Ricker, of Kearsarge Hall.

THE EARLY HOTELS

tainment and for many years its proprietor. In 1872 he completed the present hotel.

At Bethlehem the first tavern-keeper's license was granted on December 8, 1800, by Selectmen Moses Eastman and Amos Wheeler to their colleague, Captain Lot Woodbury. The need for such a house of entertainment grew out of the increasing importance of the new town as a station of commerce between Portland and northern New Hampshire. This public house of Squire Woodbury stood at the west end of the street, near where the Alpine House of to-day is situated, and was a famous tavern for many a year. Other early taverns were those kept by Thomas Jefferson Spooner, Joseph Plummer, John G. Sinclair, and the Turners, whose signboard bears the date of 1789. Gradually Bethlehem declined as a commercial place and became a summer resort only, a hotel being built before long solely for the purpose of entertaining summer visitors, now almost the only source of revenue to the town and certainly the only one for Bethlehem Street.

The building of the new Notch House on the little plateau at the northern entrance (the Gate) of the Crawford Notch has been barely mentioned in a preceding chapter. A few details may be added here. The hotel owed its origin to the thought and enterprise of Ethan Allen Crawford, then proprietor of the modest inn at the Giant's Grave. It became evident to him that an establishment for accommodating the tourists who were coming in increasing numbers was a necessity at the Notch entrance, as many wished to stop at that point and leave their

THE WHITE MOUNTAINS

horses while they pursued their way down the hill on foot to view the cascades, and on their return needed some refreshment. "Having," says Mr. Crawford, "a disposition to accommodate the public, and feeling a little self-pride to have another Crawford settled here, I consulted with my father, and we agreed to build here and place a brother of mine in the house." In the autumn of 1827, accordingly, the Crawfords prepared timber for a frame one hundred and twenty feet in length, and thirty-six feet in width; but, just as they were about to raise this, snow fell so deeply that they had to give the work up for that year. In the next winter, in the beginning of 1828, Mr. Crawford bought lumber and brick, and in the spring the building was raised and joiners put to work on it. They, with some aid from the owners, before winter set in had the outside of the building finished and the inside so far advanced toward completion that the house was a comfortable habitation. After the chief owner had bought furniture for it in Portland and had supplied it with provisions, his brother, Thomas J., moved into it in January, 1829. Owing to its newness and to its convenient location, it had a large share of the winter business and it soon became also a great place of resort for the summer tourists. Thomas J. Crawford remained its proprietor until 1852. About this time, he began to build a hotel on the site of the present Crawford House, but he got into pecuniary difficulties and was obliged to sell out to a company, of which Mr. J. L. Gibb, who had been the manager of the Lafayette House in the Franconia Notch, was the head. Mr. Gibb com-

THE EARLY HOTELS

pleted the house [1] and ran it successfully for a number of years. In 1853, when fire destroyed the other hotel of this region, the Mount Washington House, four miles distant, the Crawford House was enlarged by its enterprising proprietor and the old Notch House was repaired and refurnished to provide accommodations for the great number of travelers who came to the Mountains. Both these houses soon fell victims to the fire fiend, the time-honored old building being the first to go, in 1854. The new structure succumbed to the great enemy of summer hotels on April 30, 1859. In rebuilding it, a feat of rapid construction, which was remarkable then and would be so even to-day, was performed, but sixty days being required by the builder to replace the structure on a somewhat larger scale. And the lumber had to be drawn seventeen miles! On the night of July 4 its management was able to serve one hundred guests in the dining-room. The present Crawford House is substantially the hotel built at that time.

The history of the old hotel in the Ammonoosuc Valley, whose fate has just been incidentally mentioned, may well be recounted here. It will be recalled that Ethan Allen Crawford, because of his ill-health and his heavy involvement in debt, was finally, in 1837, obliged to give up the hotel and farm of which he had so long been the proprietor. Horace Fabyan, who had been in the provision business in Portland, took possession of the hotel in that year

---

[1] It appears to have been sometimes called after its proprietor. Henry Ward Beecher in his paper, *A Time at the White Mountains*, calls it "the Gibbs House."

THE WHITE MOUNTAINS

and kept it with increasing custom for fifteen years. Mr. Fabyan, who was destined to give his name to the hotel and railroad station of the present day, became a noted landlord of those days. In 1844, he repaired the old Willey House and its stable, and in 1845, built close to it a hotel, seventy feet by forty, which was ready to receive guests the next season. Again he extended the field of his activities by taking charge, in 1851, of the Conway House at North Conway, which was built by Samuel Thom, Nathaniel Abbott, and Hiram C. Abbott in 1850, and is said to have been then the finest hotel in the northern part of the State.

Mr. Fabyan made some repairs on the hostelry at the Giant's Grave soon after taking possession and named it the "Mount Washington House." A guest who was there that year has given an interesting account [1] of the circumstances of hotel-keeping in that day. The rate in 1837 was $1.50 a day. The price of the trip up Mount Washington was $3. This included the services of Mr. Fabyan's cousin, Oliver Fabyan, as guide and the use of horses, which were taken to a point three miles below the summit. A custom, begun by Mr. Crawford, of exhibiting for the pleasure of guests the remarkable echo to be heard at the Giant's Grave, was a feature of the entertainment at the Mount Washington House. Mr. Fabyan had a famous tin horn, six feet long, which was often sounded, with such a beautiful effect that one writer says of it, "We never heard mortal sounds to be named with the echoes of Faby-

[1] Mr. W. P. Hill in the *White Mountain Echo* for August 10, 1895.

THE EARLY HOTELS

an's tin horn." In 1845 and 1846, the whole interior of the old house was remodeled and repaired and many improvements, including new furniture and fittings for the house and a considerable amount of grading and laying-out of grounds, were made. A new building, one hundred and forty feet by forty feet and three stories high, was added to the old house, providing fifty more rooms and making a building two hundred feet long. This was completed about 1847–48.[1] The fine establishment thus created was not, however, destined to accommodate travelers for more than a few years, for, in the spring of 1853, the fire fiend again visited this site and the Mount Washington House was soon in ruins.

For nearly a score of years the White Mountain House, about three quarters of a mile west, was the only place of entertainment in this locality. The history of this house is somewhat obscure. There was evidently a hotel on this site at an early date, for Ethan Allen Crawford in the "History" mentions it a number of times and, as we have seen, has much to say of the annoyance to which he was subjected by a man who bought the place in the autumn of 1831 and took possession of it in January of the next year. Some time previous to 1843,[2] a larger

[1] Mr. Fabyan advertised in Tripp's *White Mountain Guide* of 1851 thus: "The House is large and new, having been built only three years." *The White Mountain and Winnepissiogee Lake Guide-Book* of 1846 speaks of the new building as "nearly finished."

[2] Hosea Ballou, 2d, writing in 1845, says in enumerating and locating the dwellings along the route through the Mountains, "Sixth: Half a mile farther northwest [i.e., beyond Fabyan's from the Notch House] Ethan A. Crawford's, a two-story tavern [Mr. Crawford describes it as 'the large three-story building'], built within a few years."

THE WHITE MOUNTAINS

house seems to have been built here by a Mr. Rosebrook, one of the pioneer family, members of which had established themselves at what is now Twin Mountain. It was this building, apparently, which Ethan Allen Crawford hired on his return to the Mountains in the year last mentioned and in which the remainder of his days was passed. About 1850, it was repaired and fitted up by Colonel John H. White and was opened the following June.[1] It is now the oldest hotel in the Mountains.

Passing now geographically from the rugged and impressive region of the Presidential Range and Crawford Notch to the milder but no less satisfyingly beautiful Franconia region, we find that establishments for entertaining tourists were early built and opened in this part of the Mountains.[2] What appears to have been the earliest house of entertainment in the Franconia Notch was situated about one thousand feet south of the present Flume House and on the same side of the road. It was a small affair,[3]

---

[1] According to an advertisement in Tripp's *Guide to the White Mountains* (1851). This guide-book speaks of it in the text as "a new and neat House"; Beckett's *Portland, White Mountains & Montreal Railroad Guide* (1853), describes it as "a modern built, neat and commodious establishment"; Eastman's *The White Mountain Guide-Book* (1858), says it is "on the site of the Rosebrook House."

[2] I am indebted for a number of facts to Colonel C. H. Greenleaf, of the Profile House, the senior hotel-man of the White Mountains, who has lived every summer since 1860 at this hotel, of which he became one of the proprietors in 1865.

[3] In *The White Mountain and Winnepissiogee Lake Guide-Book* (1846), the compiler, in describing the Pool, says that curiosity is situated "about ¾ of a mile from Knight's Tavern." This hostelry is also mentioned by name in Charles Lanman's descriptive piece, "The Green and White Mountains," written in 1847 and included in his *Adventures in the Wilds of the United States and British American Provinces* (1856).

THE FRANCONIA NOTCH, WITH THE LAFAYETTE HOUSE
From a Lithograph after a Drawing by I. Sprague

THE EARLY HOTELS

evidently opened for the accommodation of the passing traveler.

The first hotel of any consequence erected in this region was the Lafayette House, whose site is about five hundred feet southeast of the present Profile House and on the other side of the highway. It was built and opened in 1835,[1] as appears from Harriet Martineau's account of her excursion to the Franconia Notch in that year. Its proprietor for a number of years was J. L. Gibb, formerly of Littleton and later of the Crawford House.

About 1848,[2] the Flume House, the first hotel of that name, was built. In 1849, it was bought and opened, on June 30, by Richard Taft, a native of Barre, Vermont, then proprietor of the Washington House at Lowell, Massachusetts, to whom the Franconia Notch region in particular and New Hampshire in general owes a great debt, for what he accomplished in the development of the Mountain country as a summer resort and in the introduction of city conveniences, methods, and cuisine into hotel life in the hills. Says Dr. W. C. Prime: "Mr. Taft was a man of exceedingly quiet demeanor, but of great ability, foresight, and cautious energy ... a man of the most unswerving probity of character.

---

[1] Not 1836, as has been heretofore stated. Narrating her experiences on the day, a rainy one, devoted to this trip she says that her party took refuge from one shower in "the solitary dwelling of the pass, called the Lafayette Hotel." "This house," she continues, "had been growing in the woods thirteen weeks before, and yet we were far from being among its first guests."

[2] It must have been open under this name as early as 1848, for Oakes's *White Mountain Scenery*, published in that year, mentions it.

THE WHITE MOUNTAINS

... He commanded the respect and confidence of all men." When he began hotel-keeping at the Flume House, the price of board was $1.50 a day. The entire receipts of his first season were only eighteen hundred dollars, but, as business increased from year to year, Mr. Taft, with characteristic enterprise, acquired the Lafayette House, five miles above, and a tract of land around it, and in 1852, with his associates, George T. Brown and Ira Coffin, began the building of the Profile House. This famous hostelry was completed and opened to the public in 1853,[1] with a capacity of one hundred and ten rooms, which was increased by a large addition in 1866, the year after Colonel Greenleaf entered the firm. From 1865 to 1869, the proprietors were Taft, Tyler, and Greenleaf. In the latter year Mr. Tyler retired from the firm. In 1872, extensive additions and improvements, including the great dining-hall, were made by Messrs. Taft and Greenleaf, the new firm. The old Flume House having been burned a year or two before, the present hotel was in that same year erected on its site, the two properties being under the same ownership. The first of the group of cottages, which form such a feature of the Profile House settlement, was built in 1868.

Before leaving the early history of hotel-keeping in the Franconia Notch, mention should be made of the Mount Lafayette House, a small hotel which once stood on a spot, sometimes called the "Half-

---

[1] This is the correct date of the opening, as a letter in the *New York Herald* for July 3, 1853, makes evident, and not 1852, as is usually stated.

THE EARLY HOTELS

way Place" or "Lafayette Place," two and a quarter miles below the Profile House and near the point of divergence from the highway of the original bridle path up Mount Lafayette. Built probably in the late fifties, it was, after a short existence, burned in the spring of 1861. Still another hotel situated in this region and named after the monarch of the Franconias was the Mount Lafayette House which stood near the junction of the Gale River road with the road from the Profile House to Franconia, at the bottom of "Three-Mile Hill." It has a particular interest to literary folk and others from the association with it of Dr. W. C. Prime, author of "I Go A-Fishing" and "Along New England Roads," and his sister, the author and entomologist, Mrs. Annie Trumbull Slosson. Dr. Prime built and occupied a summer cottage in the hotel grounds, which is still standing. The hotel property was sold by Mrs. Slosson in 1908 to James Smith, of Franconia, and was burned to the ground in May, 1911.[1]

Putting on our seven-league boots and jumping in our narrative of early hotel-keeping to a beautiful valley on the eastern side of the Mountains, we will feign ourselves to have landed at Gorham in the northern part of that district. At this attractively situated mountain village, which is ninety-two miles from Portland and to which the railroad made its way in 1852, the traveler alighted from the train in the fifties and sixties of the last century at the White Mountain Station House, which, as this name

---

[1] I am indebted for this date to Eva M. Aldrich, Librarian of the Abbie Greenleaf Library, Franconia.

THE WHITE MOUNTAINS

indicates, served the dual purpose of station and hotel. This comfortable hostelry, whose name was soon changed to the more euphonious one of Alpine House, had accommodations for two hundred and fifty guests, and was long a popular place of sojourn. Gorham became at once, after the coming of the railroad, one of the chief Mountain resorts, if it did not, indeed, in the days of Starr King hold the pre-eminence. The hotel was for many years under the efficient landlordship of Colonel John R. Hitchcock, who was also a proprietor, as we shall see, of the Summit and Tip-Top Houses on Mount Washington, as well as a director in the original Mount Washington Carriage Road Company. After twenty years of existence, however, this famous hotel went the way of so many others, falling a prey to the flames in October, 1872. This disaster marked the passing of Gorham's supremacy as a resort. A second Alpine House was built in 1876. This was closed in November, 1905, and was subsequently moved across the street and made a part of the present Mount Madison House, which is a commercial hotel, open all the year round, as well as one used as a place of summer sojourn.

Traveling now in our imaginary hotel tour of the White Mountains eight miles to the southward, to the picturesque location in the valley of the Peabody River known as the "Glen," we find that the first public house on that site was begun in 1852 by John Bellows. It was not completed in time for the season of that year, but a few guests were entertained. Probably still in an unfinished state, this modest

THE OLD PROFILE HOUSE, OPENED 1853, CLOSED 1905

THE FLUME HOUSE
An Old View showing the House when Smaller than at Present

THE EARLY HOTELS

tavern, which was on the stage-road from Gorham to North Conway, was bought by Mr. J. M. Thompson, who changed its name to the Glen House, and was indefatigable in developing the property and making the region popular by building paths to the waterfalls and other points of interest, and even one up Mount Washington. Unfortunately, he was drowned in the Peabody River in October, 1869, when trying to prevent the destruction of his mill by a flood which followed an autumnal storm of exceptional severity. A few years after the lamented death of Landlord Thompson, the hotel passed into the hands of the brothers Milliken, under whose skillful management it attained great development and popularity, only to meet, after years of success, with repeated disaster, and apparently to come to an end as a large enterprise. The story of this mingled prosperity and adversity will, however, be deferred to a later chapter.

Continuing our tour, let us go farther southward on the stage-road passing the Glen House, and we shall come, after a ride of a dozen miles, to the little village which commemorates in this region the victor of New Orleans.

Jackson was late in coming to its own as a summer resort, and this quiet hamlet in a secluded glen owed its discovery as a center of landscape beauties to the artists. The pioneer painters came as early as 1847. Hotel-keeping began with the opening of the Jackson Falls House in 1858.[1] The Iron Mountain House was opened in 1861 and was burned in

[1] It was rebuilt and enlarged in 1886.

THE WHITE MOUNTAINS

1877; a new house of the same name first received guests in the season of 1885. The year 1876 was the opening year of the Glen Ellis House. In the early days Cole, Durand, Judge Story and Daniel Webster were visitors to Jackson. It is related that board was then $2 a week, the landlady doing the cooking and the landlord serving the frugal meals.

Now, Jackson is a place of many hotels and boarding-houses, as well as of summer cottages in goodly number. Right in the heart of the village, near the Wildcat River, is the Wentworth Hall, which reproduces the picturesque architecture of an English mansion of Queen Anne's time. The Thorn Mountain House, a part of the Wentworth Hall establishment, was opened on July 12, 1869, by General M. C. Wentworth, with twenty-two rooms. In 1914, the establishment consisted of these two houses and thirty-one other buildings, including a group of attractive cottages.[1] Gray's Inn has long been a leading hotel of Jackson. Its recent history is of especial interest. The first hotel of this name was burned in 1902. A new one was soon begun and was nearly completed, when it, too, went up in smoke in the winter of 1903. Nothing daunted, Landlord Gray, who was his own architect and builder, at once commenced to build another hotel. This time nothing untoward happened and a new and commodious Gray's Inn was opened the week of August 15, 1904. Open in winter as well as in summer, this hostelry was a popular place of sojourn at both sea-

---

[1] I am indebted to the courtesy of the late General Wentworth for information as to his establishment.

THE EARLY HOTELS

sons. But after about a dozen years of prosperity, Landlord Gray again met with adversity, for on February 21, 1916, the inn, together with its casino, was totally destroyed by fire. Fortunately, the one hundred and fifty guests all escaped without injury.

Let us conclude this chapter by taking a broad jump in a southwesterly direction to the extreme southern limit of the White Mountain region, — to the town of Plymouth, to be specific in our destination. In the days of its political importance and before the advent of the summer visitor, there was, of course, a transient population of considerable number in the village from time to time, but especially when the county court was in session. From soon after the settlement a tavern was in existence, conducted successively by Colonel David Webster and his son, Colonel William. In 1841, Denison R. Burnham purchased the popular and historic old Webster Tavern, built an addition, and changed the name of the inn to that of Pemigewasset House, a name which has survived a number of fires and is still retained. Under Mr. Burnham's able management the hotel became a popular one, and, after the coming of the railroad, business increased so that some time in the early fifties another addition was made and again later still another.[1]

This old hostelry was destroyed by fire in 1862, and the land was then sold to the railroad company, which immediately erected, in 1863, another hotel of the same name. This was the house in which

[1] I am indebted for information about her father's hotel to the late Abbie Burnham Greenleaf.

THE WHITE MOUNTAINS

Hawthorne died the next year. It was built on a hillside and fronted on the village street, with which its main floor was on a level, while in the rear was a lower floor in which was the railroad station. Large, commodious, and well-kept, it was long a popular place of resort. This famous old house was burned in 1908 and has been replaced by a fine modern hotel, the New Pemigewasset House, which is situated a short distance from the old location and which was opened July 1, 1913.

VIII

THE POETS AND PAINTERS IN THE WHITE HILLS

As is to be expected, the natural beauties of the White Mountains, their lofty summits, their bare or tree-clad slopes or crags, their streams, their cascades, their lakes, and their scenic curiosities, and even their few legends, have been sources of inspiration to a multitude of poets and verse-makers. Thus the pleasure afforded by some of the best nature poetry in American literature is another perennial enjoyment which we owe to the Crystal Hills. To this additional possession of White Mountain lovers, many sons and daughters of New Hampshire, whether they be children who have remained at home or children who have pitched their tent permanently elsewhere, have contributed by singing the glories of these hills in verse of greater or less merit. Among such represented in Eugene R. Musgrove's well-chosen anthology, "The White Hills in Poetry," are George Waldo Browne, James T. Fields, Charles James Fox, George Bancroft Griffith, Edward Augustus Jenks, Fanny Runnells Poole, and Celia Thaxter. The most notable singer by far in this connection is, undoubtedly, Edna Dean Proctor, who has made her native hills the theme of numerous poems of high excellence.

Preëminently, however, the poet of the White Hills is a native of the sister Commonwealth of

THE WHITE MOUNTAINS

Massachusetts, a poet whose inspiration came from summer acquaintance with them, John Greenleaf Whittier. He and his intimate friend and literary associate, Lucy Larcom, were both ardent lovers of the New Hampshire country and frequent sojourners among the Mountains or in the bordering lakeland, and both have written much verse about this beautiful region. But Whittier only, Mr. Musgrove has pointed out, has given us a series of pictures of this mountain land and has enriched American poetry with exquisite descriptions of New Hampshire scenery.

The Quaker poet's first poem having to do with the region is one published under the title, "The White Mountains," in his earliest book, "Legends of New England in Prose and Verse," which appeared at Hartford, Connecticut, in February, 1831. This short piece of verse, which seems to have been composed before the poet knew the Mountains by visual experience, is concerned with the Indian belief that Mount Washington was the abode of powerful spirits, whose voices were heard in the pauses of the tempests, and with the passing of ancient conditions.[1]

Whittier's first recorded visit to the region he was later to make one of his summer homes was for a quite different purpose. Through his interest in the anti-slavery cause and his literary activity in its behalf, the poet had attracted the attention of that

---

[1] With the title "Mount Agiochook" substituted for its original one, the poem was printed in the author's complete works, but was finally relegated to an appendix.

THE POETS AND PAINTERS

most brilliant of early anti-slavery editors, Nathaniel Peabody Rogers.[1] One of the first letters of approval and encouragement Whittier received after publishing, in 1833, the pamphlet "Justice and Expediency," in favor of immediate emancipation, was from Rogers, who then invited the young writer to visit his mountain home on the banks of the Pemigewasset in Plymouth. Their personal acquaintance was first made two years afterwards, when the invitation was accepted by Whittier. He was accompanied on this journey by the eloquent English reformer, George Thompson, who in response to Garrison's invitation had come to this country to deliver anti-slavery addresses and whom the poet had been hiding from the mobs in the seclusion of his East Haverhill home. "We drove up the beautiful valley of the White Mountain tributary of the

[1] Rogers, in 1838, gave up his law practice at Plymouth and left his native valley to reside at Concord for the purpose of editing *The Herald of Freedom*, an anti-slavery paper established a few years before. As a newspaper writer he had few, if any, equals in his day. He used to write for the *New York Tribune* under the signature "The Old Man of the Mountain." "His descriptions of natural scenery," says Whittier in his "portrait" of his friend, "glow with life. One can almost see the sunset light flooding the Franconia Notch, and glorifying the peaks of Moosehillock, and hear the murmur of the west wind in the pines, and the light, liquid voice of Pemigewasset sounding up from its rocky channel, through its green hem of maples, while reading them." His last visit to his old home was in the autumn of 1845. In a familiar letter to a friend he penned a beautiful description of his native town as seen in what was to be his farewell view of it. His health, never robust, gradually failed for some time previous to his death. Needing more repose and quiet than his duties as editor permitted him to enjoy, he bought a small and pleasant farm in his loved Pemigewasset Valley, in the hope that he might there recuperate his wasted energies. But he was not destined to enjoy this asylum, for his death occurred shortly afterward, in October, 1846. His family, however, occupied it for some years.

THE WHITE MOUNTAINS

Merrimac," writes Whittier, "and, just as a glorious sunset was steeping river, valley, and mountain in its hues of heaven, were welcomed to the pleasant home and family circle of our friend Rogers." With these friends they spent "two delightful evenings."

Early in the forties, apparently, Whittier made a journey through the heart of the Notch in a stage-coach, which leisurely mode of traveling he enjoyed greatly, and also ascended "old Agioochook." It had as its literary fruit the prologue of "The Bridal of Pennacook," the opening of which is a glorified itinerary. This poem appeared in 1844.

The poet was again in the Mountain region in the summer of 1849, sojourning there several weeks at that time. Some years afterward he again visited the Rogers family, this time for a week, before they left their home near Plymouth for the West. This was probably in 1853.

Three years later he published in *The National Era* the poem "Mary Garvin," whose prologue, beginning, "From the heart of Waumbek Methna, from the lake that never fails," deals descriptively with the Saco River, near the mouth of which the scene of the poem is laid.

In the spring of 1865, Whittier came to Campton, where his friends James T. and Annie Fields were then making their place of summer sojourn, boarding at Selden C. Willey's farm, and there the poem "Franconia from the Pemigewasset," constituting the first of his "Mountain Pictures," was expanded and modified from the first stanza composed at Lovewell's Pond in Fryeburg, Maine.

THE POETS AND PAINTERS

Soon after the close of the Civil War, the poet of freedom seems to have made his first trip to the locality in the White Mountain region which was to become his favorite mountain retreat and in which to-day his name is chiefly commemorated geographically. The success of "Snow-Bound" had rendered him not only pecuniarily independent and able to afford many added comforts and luxuries, but also had given him a firm place in the hearts of his countrymen. The days of struggle and patient endurance of adversity were over. In the summer of 1867, he made a stay at the Bearcamp River House in West Ossipee. This "quiet, old-fashioned inn, beautifully located, neat as possible, large rooms, nice beds, and good, wholesome table," was situated near the banks of the picturesque stream from which it got its name and only a few hundred yards from the railway station. In early days the public house on this site had been known as "Ames's Tavern," and afterwards as "Banks's Hotel," and the fact that among its frequenters in the primitive days were Starr King and the artists, George Inness, George L. Brown, and Benjamin Champney, is ample testimony to the satisfying qualities of the views, in which Chocorua is the dominating object, and of the environing scenes.

Amid such surroundings the inspiration came to Whittier to write an idyl of New England farm life, a companion summer piece to his winter idyl, "Snow-Bound," and so here in part was composed the charming poem "Among the Hills." His first thought was to call this poem, which combines a

THE WHITE MOUNTAINS

tender and romantic love-story with a faithful portrayal of rural scenes, "A Summer Idyl," but when it appeared in its first form, in the *Atlantic Monthly* for January, 1868, it was entitled "The Wife: an Idyl of Bearcamp Water." Before the poem appeared in the volume to which it gave the title early in 1869, the prelude had been expanded and so changed in tenor as to be a new poem and the outlines of the story filled out. This working-over and "blossoming-out" took place during that summer.

For several summers and autumns from 1875 on, Whittier spent a number of weeks at the Bearcamp River House, enjoying greatly his sojourns there because of the modest comfort, the pleasant associations, and the beautiful view. Chocorua he regarded as the most beautiful and striking of all the New Hampshire hills, and the location of the hotel he esteemed one of the most picturesque situations in the State. Besides "Among the Hills," several other poems, among them "Sunset on the Bearcamp," and "Voyage of the Jettie," were written at this, Whittier's "Wayside Inn," and celebrate the beauties of the region. The hotel was sometimes nearly filled with relatives and friends of the poet and these reunions were occasions full of enjoyment to him. He could not accompany his friends on their mountain-climbs — he did not care to ascend mountains for the prospect they afford — and on their drives, but he liked greatly to hear the reports of adventures brought to him by the younger members of his party.[1] He enjoyed also being quiet and alone.

[1] The following anecdote, related by Mr. Pickard in *Whittier-Land*,

THE POETS AND PAINTERS

Rarely was a transient guest invited to join the poet's circle, as he was usually under some constraint in the presence of a stranger.

In the summer and autumn of 1875, Lucy Larcom and he were engaged together here in the compilation of "Songs of Three Centuries," but this work "was not allowed to interfere seriously with the main object of a summer outing, rest and recreation," says his biographer.

Five years later the hotel was burned down, "much to my regret," he writes to Marshall P. Hall in May, 1881, in the same letter expressing a hope that another house will be built on its site.

In the summer of the year last named, Whittier spent several weeks at Intervale with his cousins, Joseph and Gertrude W. Cartland, who were his summer companions the remaining twelve years of his life. He much enjoyed the quiet, restful meadow

---

exhibits the poet's keen enjoyment of fun and his ability to unbend even to jollity and to the production of verse written in a rollicking vein. One day in September, 1876, a party of seven of Whittier's friends climbed Chocorua under the guidance of the Knox brothers, two young farmers and bear-hunters of West Ossipee, camping for the night on the mountain near some bear-traps. The young ladies reported to the poet the hearing of the growling of the bears in the night and other blood-curdling incidents. Shortly afterward the Knox brothers gave a husking-bee at their barn, at which Whittier and the members of his party were present. Whittier wrote a poem, entitled "How They Climbed Chocorua," for the occasion, and induced Lucy Larcom to read it as the production of an unknown author. These humorous stanzas, with their references to the incidents of the excursion and their personal mentions of the climbers, were received with great delight. The next evening Miss Larcom read to the party gathered round the fireside at the inn a humorous poem, entitled "To the Unknown and Absent Author of 'How They Climbed Chocorua,'" in which the poet was alleged to have been caught by the coat-tails in one of the bear-traps on the mountain.

THE WHITE MOUNTAINS

views and the noble distant mountain prospects of this charming spot. He loved to watch the snow-streaks on Mount Washington, which he once expressed the wish he might see all covered with snow as in winter. The beautiful pine woods near the hotel became a favorite resort of the poet, where he passed a part of nearly every day, often with a group of friends in the unconventional social intercourse he so highly prized.

Such are the outlines of the poet's connection with the White Mountains. To-day the visitor to the Ossipee region finds the northwest summit of the Ossipee Range bearing, at Sweetser's suggestion, the name of "Whittier Peak," or "Mount Whittier." The railroad station of West Ossipee has recently become Mount Whittier, while in the near vicinity is a hamlet also named in the poet's honor.

The lifelong friendship of Lucy Larcom with Whittier began in 1844,[1] during his residence in Lowell, where she was then employed in the mills and had been brought into notice as one of the leading contributors to the *Lowell Offering*, that famous magazine which attracted so much attention as a successful literary venture by factory operatives. Whittier assisted and encouraged her in her literary work and she in turn assisted him not only in compiling "Songs of Three Centuries," but in other editorial work.[2] She became, after her

[1] So Pickard, *Life and Letters of John Greenleaf Whittier;* Daniel Dulany Addison's *Lucy Larcom: Life, Letters, and Diary*, states that it was in 1843 that she first met Mr. Whittier.

[2] First in 1871 in the compilation of "Child Life: a Collection of Poems."

THE POETS AND PAINTERS

return from the West in 1853, his sister Elizabeth's dearest friend, and all his remaining life, and particularly after Elizabeth's death, the elder poet was ever thoughtful for her welfare. Kindred souls as they were, the two poets were much in each other's society, and many letters passed between them.

Early in the sixties, — to be exact, in August, 1861, — Miss Larcom began to be a regular summer sojourner among the hills of New Hampshire, a practice which had as one result the writing of many beautiful poems. Her usual place of resort at first was Campton, where, like the Fieldses, she boarded at Selden C. Willey's.[1] There "Hills in Mist," "My Mountain," "Valley Peak," and other poems were composed. Other retreats of Miss Larcom in the White Mountains, or the vicinity, were Ossipee Park, West Ossipee, Sandwich, Berlin Falls, Bethlehem, Mount Moosilauke, Center Harbor, and Bethel (in Maine). Even a mere enumeration of some others of her White Mountain poems, with mention of the places and dates of their composition, not only makes amply evident her wide and long acquaintance with the region, but suggests her ardent love of it. "Up the Androscoggin" was written at Berlin Falls in 1878; "Asleep on the Summit," on Mount Washington, in August, 1877; "Clouds on Whiteface," at North Sandwich; "From the Hills," on Mount

---

[1] In 1867, writing to Jean Ingelow, she says, "To me there is rest and strength, and aspiration and exultation, among the mountains. They are nearly a day's journey from us, — the White Mountains, — but I will go, and get a glimpse and a breath of their glory, once a year, always.... I usually stop at a village on the banks of the Pemigewasset, a small silvery river that flows from the Notch Mountains.... But I must not go on about the mountains, or I shall never stop."

THE WHITE MOUNTAINS

Moosilauke, 1891; "Garfield's Burial Day," ascending Mount Washington, September 26, 1881; and "A Mountain Resurrection," at North Sandwich, in 1863. Other poems which owe their inspiration to the monarch of the hills are, "In a Cloud-Rift," "Looking Down," and "The Summit-Flower." "Mountaineer's Prayer" was written on the summit of Moosilauke, September 7, 1892, the day after Whittier's death.

The hills gave Miss Larcom rest and the beauty of the views with their suggestions gave her inspiration for her work. Each year she tried to visit the various points she especially loved. Bethel charmed her with its majestic elms and its view of the Androscoggin and the distant mountains. At Russell's Riverside Cottage, where she was ever welcome, she frequently stayed, and on the ledge behind the house there is a little glen, in which she used to sit and read, known as "Miss Larcom's Retreat." [1] Bethlehem gave her relief from hay-fever,[2] and was always "the beautiful." From these places and from Moosilauke, her favorite summit, she frequently wrote charming letters to the *Portland Transcript*.

On the mountain just named parts of the last two summers of her life, 1891 and 1892, were spent. It was there that the news of Whittier's death came to

---

[1] "On the Ledge," written in September, 1879, celebrates the beauty of this "shelter and outlook."

[2] In October, 1885, she writes to her friend Mrs. Spalding, "I have had my 'outing' at Bethlehem; I went there hardly able to sit up during the journey, but gained strength at once, and am well now. ... I stayed there more than four weeks, and enjoyed it much. Mr. Howells and family were at the next house, and I saw them several times."

THE POETS AND PAINTERS

her. She was not long to survive her old friend and another dear friend, Phillips Brooks, for in April, 1893, she passed away, a victim of heart disease.

Longfellow's acquaintance with the region of the White Hills began early and, from a literary standpoint, promisingly. Born in a city from which they are in clear weather to be plainly seen, he became interested in them and visited them as a young man, but this acquaintance was not kept up. After he became established as professor at Cambridge, at any rate, he preferred the seashore to the Mountains, maintaining for many years a summer home at Nahant. Toward the close of his life, in 1880, he made a visit to the region, staying at the Stag and Hounds in West Campton. While there a journey was made to Mad River, which bore fruit poetically in the spirited lyric of this name, one of his last poems,[1] and his best White Mountain poem.

Slight as is, taken altogether, his association with this region, it has nevertheless a few points of interest worth a brief chronicling.

As I have mentioned when dealing with the battle of Lovewell's Pond, that fight inspired the first printed poem, so far as is known, of the youthful Longfellow. The four stanzas, with their echoes of Moore and of Scott, appeared over the signature "Henry" in the Poet's Corner of the *Portland Gazette*, November 17, 1820, when the boy was not yet fourteen years old. Five years later he recurred to the same theme, writing an ode for the

[1] It was written in January, 1882, and appeared in the *Atlantic Monthly* for May of that year.

185

THE WHITE MOUNTAINS

commemoration at Fryeburg of Lovewell's fight. Another poem belonging to this year 1825, and now relegated, like the two just referred to, to an appendix of "Juvenile Poems" is "Jeckoyva,"[1] which owes its conception to the Chocorua legend. It has a version of the story of the chief's death for its subject.

Yet another poem written in this his senior year at Bowdoin relates to the Mountains. This is the descriptive and didactic poem, "Sunrise on the Hills," which, written in his room at college, embodies reminiscently the moving sights and sounds of nature and human life observed on the occasion of a visit to the summit of Mount Kearsarge, near North Conway. This last poem, with a number of others written during his college life, the poet retained in a group of "Earlier Poems" in his complete works. Thus, "Sunrise on the Hills" and "Mad River," of more than a half-century later, represent the entire extent, so far as his own approval goes, of this poet's permanent literary association with the region.

Bryant, New England's greatest nature poet, paid a visit to the White Mountains in the summer of 1847. No poems ensued from this his first, and apparently also his last, exploration of these hills, which he had before seen only from a distance. The

---

[1] Jeckoyva is, of course, a variant of Chocorua. "Mount Jeckoyva," says the poet in an introductory note, "is near the White Hills." The poem appeared in the *United States Literary Gazette* for August 1, 1825. To this semi-monthly periodical, established in 1824 and first edited by Theophilus Parsons, afterwards a distinguished jurist, Longfellow was a regular contributor.

THE POETS AND PAINTERS

summer trip into New England, of which this excursion to the Mountains was a part, was undertaken at a time in his life when the editor of the *Evening Post* was busily engaged in the political discussions of the day and consequently found almost no time for writing verse. This circumstance doubtless accounts in large measure for the failure of his muse to be inspired by the grand and beautiful scenery amidst which he found himself during his brief sojourn in the White Hills.

He approached the Mountains by way of Augusta, whither he had come from Portland. An ascent of Mount Washington and a stay of a few days in the Franconia Notch were the chief features of his visit.

Fortunately, his impressions of the Mountains have been preserved for us by his biographer. As the passage is less familiar than other descriptive ones, we may well look for a moment with the poet's eye.

The scenery of these mountains has not been sufficiently praised [he wrote]. But for the glaciers, but for the peaks white with perpetual snow, it would be scarcely worth while to see Switzerland after seeing the White Mountains. The depth of the valleys, the steepness of the mountain-sides, the variety of aspect shown by their summits, the deep gulfs of forest below, seamed with the open courses of rivers, the vast extent of the mountain region seen north and south of us, gleaming with many lakes, filled me with surprise and astonishment. Imagine the forests to be shorn from half the broad declivities — imagine scattered habitations on the thick green turf and foot-paths leading from one to the other, and herds and flocks browsing, and you have Switzerland before you. I admit, however, that these accessories add to the va-

THE WHITE MOUNTAINS

riety and interest of the landscape, and perhaps heighten the idea of its vastness.

I have been told, however, that the White Mountains in autumn present an aspect more glorious than even the splendors of the perpetual ice of the Alps. All this mighty multitude of mountains, rising from valleys filled with dense forests, have then put on their hues of gold and scarlet, and, seen more distinctly on account of their brightness of color, seem to tower higher in the clear blue of the sky. At that season of the year they are little visited, and only awaken the wonder of the occasional traveller.

It is not necessary to ascend Mount Washington to enjoy the finest views. Some of the lower peaks offer grander though not so extensive ones; the height of the main summit seems to diminish the size of the objects beheld from it. The sense of solitude and immensity is, however, most strongly felt on that great cone, overlooking all the rest, and formed of loose rocks, which seem as if broken into fragments by the power which upheaved these ridges from the depths of the earth below.

So many have been the landscape artists who have made occasional or frequent sojourns for longer or shorter periods in the White Mountains, and who have plied the instruments of their profession to good purpose there, that, if the records of their stays in the region had been kept and a catalogue of the pictures that were the outward and visible signs of their communion with the natural beauty and grandeur of their surroundings could be compiled, a sizable volume would be required to contain such material. But such a record, which might be styled the "art history" of the White Mountains, cannot be prepared or, at any rate, can be only very in-

THE POETS AND PAINTERS

adequately set forth, for in most cases the artists' visits to this region were but episodes in busy careers. In many cases, indeed, the fact of such personal association with the Mountains is borne witness to solely by some picture which reproduces a scene or prospect to which it owed its inspiration, or, at most, by a few of such pictures. Often, again, the only accessible record of such association that apparently exists is the mere statement that such and such an artist frequented a particular locality, set down incidentally in a guide-book or in a magazine article on the place.

As to the paintings themselves, they are so thoroughly and so widely distributed among the collections of individuals and of the smaller public galleries, few being in the great galleries of the country, that the preparation of a respectable, not to say adequate, list of White Mountain paintings would be well-nigh an impossibility.

A chronicle of the region would, however, be sadly deficient without some brief record, or at least mention, of the painters who have done so much to spread abroad a knowledge of its scenic attractions. Furthermore, so intimate, indeed, was the association with the White Mountains of the earlier American landscape artists, who constitute our first really native school, that they are sometimes called collectively the "White Mountain School." More usually, however, from the circumstance that so much of their work depicts the river and mountain scenery of eastern New York, they are known as the "Hudson River School."

THE WHITE MOUNTAINS

Such, then, being the importance of the White Mountains in American art, and such, as I have outlined, being the difficulties, especially for a layman, in acquiring knowledge of the artists' personal contact with the region and of the pictures that resulted therefrom, I approach the treatment of the subject with considerable hesitation. I shall have, therefore, to content myself with setting down such information, meager as it is, as I have been able to gather from various sources, not with the thought that what I shall present has any pretense to completeness or adequacy, but with quite the contrary mental attitude toward it, namely, one of apology for being unable to do more than merely touch upon some of the more readily accessible bits of information relating to the subject.

Mr. Crawford, in his "History," notes the visit of a painter to the Mountains as early as July, 1824, "who took some beautiful sketches of the hills and likewise of the Notch," but we are not informed as to his name.

Not long after this pioneer visit of an unnamed artist, two of the earliest and most noted of American landscapists, Thomas Doughty and Thomas Cole, found their way thither, and they have had many successors in discovering and depicting with the brush the beauties of the region.

Of the connection with the Mountains of the latter, who made his summer home chiefly in the Catskills, and who is regarded as one of the fathers of the Hudson River School, we are fortunate in having some record, for his own account of his first

THE POETS AND PAINTERS

visit to the White Mountains has been preserved. It was in the autumn of 1828, that with a friend, Henry Cheeves Pratt, Cole explored the region, making a tour which was to result in a number of striking pictures. Early in October, they climbed Chocorua, which early became and has remained the favorite mountain of the painters, as it has been also of the poets. This ascent was "both perilous and difficult" on account of the windfalls, consisting of prostrate tall pines and gnarled birches heaped together in wild confusion. But the artists felt themselves amply rewarded by the "mighty and sublime" prospects which opened on their vision. "With all its beauty the scene was," says Cole, "too extended and map-like for the canvas." "It was not for sketches," he continues, "that I ascended Chocorua, but for thoughts; and for these this was truly the region."

After remaining several hours on the peak, they descended to the village, arriving after dark. On October 6, the two footed it, with their baggage on their backs, through the Crawford Notch. Cole notes that the distance is twelve miles and that there is not a house except the deserted Willey House, of whose location he says, "It is impossible to give a true picture of this desolate and savage spot." They paused, however, long enough to make some sketches before proceeding up the gorge.

Two days later, Cole went alone, Pratt having left him, to Franconia "through the Breton woods on the bank of the Ammonoosuck." From Franconia he walked through the Franconia Notch, hav-

THE WHITE MOUNTAINS

ing set off with the expectation of the coach's overtaking him, but he reached the southern end of the Notch some time before it arrived there. His description of the Notch and of his walk is well worth giving, particularly noteworthy being his account of the impression the Great Stone Face made upon him: —

There is nothing of the desolate grandeur of the other Notch. The elements do not seem to have chosen this for a battle-ground, and the hoar mountains do not appear wrinkled by recent convulsions. One of the two lakes, you here meet with, is presided over by the Old Man of the Mountains [sic], as the people about here call it. . . . The perfect repose of these waters, and the unbroken silence reigning through the whole region, made the scene peculiarly impressive and sublime: indeed, there was an awfulness in the deep solitude, pent up within the great precipices, that was painful. While there was a pleasure in the discovery, a childish fear came over me that drove me away: the bold and horrid features, that bent their severe expression upon me, were too dreadful to look upon in my loneliness: I could not feel happy in their communion, nor take them to my heart as my companions. . . . In spite of a timid excitement, and the prospect of a shower, I sketched several trees by the road-side. In the course of my walk, I came to a bark-covered hut, in the midst of burnt trees, with a swarm of unwashed, uncombed, but healthy-looking children, who ran out to stare with amazement at the passing stranger. I reached, at length, a better-looking abode, where the horses of the coach were to be exchanged, and awaited its arrival. From the door I made a sketch of the mountains, to the surprise and admiration of the people of the house, who put me down for a surveyor making a map. The long-looked-for coach at last came down, and gave me a pleasant ride into Plymouth.

A VIEW NEAR CONWAY
After a Painting by Thomas Cole

THE POETS AND PAINTERS

The following winter, Cole produced at least two spirited pictures of Chocorua, his "Autumn Scene—Corway Peak" and his "The Death of Chocorua," the former of which is now in the gallery of the New York Historical Society, and the latter of which became widely known through the "very much admired" steel engraving of it by George W. Hatch. During this winter or the following one, he painted his "White Mountains," purchased for the Wadsworth Athenæum, Hartford, a "View near Conway," exhibited in 1830 at the Royal Academy in London, and a "View from Mount Washington."

Cole was again in this region, we learn from a letter, for several weeks in the summer of 1839. Not only did he paint actual reproductions of White Mountain scenes, but he used ideas and material acquired here in pictures that were not localized views. One of his most attractive paintings, "The Hunter's Return," for instance, is a composition, but one noble mountain in the background is copied from a spur of the White Hills.

Besides being a painter of note, Cole not seldom meditated the thankless Muse, and the White Mountains were a source of inspiration in this phase of his creative activity. During the year 1835, he found leisure to compose a dramatic poem, in twelve parts, called "The Spirits of the Wilderness," the scene of which is laid among the Mountains. This work, declared by his biographer to be "of singular originality, and much poetic power and beauty," was, in the spring of 1837, rewritten and "prepared in a measure for publication."

THE WHITE MOUNTAINS

Mr. Pratt also recorded his impressions of his trip through the Notch, in his "View of the White Mountains after the Late Slide," which was engraved by V. Balch for *The Token*, in 1828.

I have found almost no record of Doughty's sketching among the Mountains. He must, however, have visited the Crawford Notch in or about the early thirties, for an engraving by George B. Ellis of a drawing by him of "The Silver Cascade" was published in *The Token* for 1835, and an engraving, by F. J. Havell, of his painting of the same waterfall appears in N. P. Willis's "American Scenery."

One of the fathers of American landscape and leaders of the Hudson River School, A. B. Durand, who was also one of the original members of the National Academy of Design, painted a number of pleasing White Mountain pictures. In 1857, he produced for Mr. R. L. Stuart the large work "White Mountain Scenery, Franconia Notch," now in the Stuart Room of the Galleries of the New York Public Library. It is recorded that the purchaser was so pleased with the picture that he made the amount of the check given in payment for it larger than he had agreed to pay. In the following year, Durand sojourned for weeks in the summer in North Conway and West Campton. "New Hampshire Scenery" was painted for Mr. A. A. Low in that year, and the same year Mr. Stuart purchased from the artist the smaller canvas "Franconia, White Mountains," also now in the New York Public Library. His "On the Pemigewassett" was purchased

THE POETS AND PAINTERS

by a citizen of Brooklyn. In 1876, he painted "Sunset on Chocorua," which was purchased by a Hoboken patron of art.

Another eminent landscapist who has connected himself with the White Mountains is George Loring Brown, known, from his skill as a copyist of Claude Lorraine, as the "American Claude." After a long residence abroad, he returned in 1860 to his native land and devoted himself in part to executing views of American scenery. One of his places of sojourn while sketching in the Mountains was, on the authority of Mr. Sweetser, Wilson's farm, two miles from Jackson, where noble and extended views are to be had. His most noted White Mountain picture, "The Crown of New England," was painted in 1861, and gives the view of Mount Washington as seen from the slope below the road, west of the old Mount Adams House at Jefferson Highlands. It was purchased by the Prince of Wales (Edward VII) during his visit to the United States, and hangs in the gallery of Windsor Castle.

One of our principal sources of information concerning artists who frequented the White Mountains in the early days is the "Sixty Years' Memories of Art and Artists"[1] of Benjamin Champney, who, at his death at the age of ninety in December, 1907, was the oldest and most beloved of North Conway's summer residents and who was the pioneer among the artists who have made the grandeur and beauty of that region's scenery known.

Mr. Champney first visited his future summer

[1] Published in 1900 at Woburn, Massachusetts, his winter home.

THE WHITE MOUNTAINS

home in 1838, in company with "a young artist friend," the imaginations of the two students having been so "inflamed" by the study of a series of illustrations drawn by an English artist, W. H. Bartlett, and engraved in London for N. P. Willis's "American Scenery," published there in 1838-39, that they devoted their first sketching trip to a study of the same scenery.

After some years of study in Europe, beginning in 1841, where he became intimate with other art students who were to associate themselves in later years with White Mountain scenes, and among whom were A. B. Durand, J. W. Casilear, and J. F. Kensett, Mr. Champney returned to America to practice his profession of landscape artist. As the result of an agreement with Kensett to go on a sketching trip to the White Mountains, Champney and Kensett went in the summer of 1850 to Fryeburg. Casilear, having been sent for to join them, did so, and the three friends for six weeks "reveled in the beauty" of the Saco Valley. Having made a reconnaissance of North Conway, they decided to go there at once. They had interviewed Landlord Thompson, of Kearsarge Tavern, who had agreed to take them in "for the magnificent sum of $3.50 per week with the choice of the best rooms in the house," it being then the middle of August and there being not a guest in town. "You won't like me," said Mr. Thompson, as reported by Champney. "I'm a kind of crooked fellow, and you won't like me, but you can come and try it." They did like it, being made to feel at home and being supplied with

THE POETS AND PAINTERS

a generous table of good old-fashioned cooking, and the landlord they liked also as they got acquainted with him, ever ready as he was to enter into any project for exploring the country and hunting out new beauties. Delighted with the surrounding scenery, they lingered in North Conway two months. Late in the season they painted Mount Washington, white with snow, from Sunset Hill. After his return to New York, Kensett made a large painting of this view, "The White Mountains and Valley of the Saco, from Sunset Hill, North Conway," which became very widely known, especially through an engraving made of it by James Smillie.

About the middle of October, Champney and the others left North Conway, making a trip on foot through the Crawford Notch and on to Franconia, sketching as they went and being heartily welcomed and urged to come again another year by the landlords of the two or three then deserted Mountain houses.

Champney returned the next summer with a reinforcement of two Boston artists, Alfred Ordway and B. G. Stone, and found a New York contingent, headed by Casilear, already established at the Kearsarge House. The other New Yorkers were David Johnson,[1] John Williamson,[2] and a nephew of A. B. Durand, and they "made a jolly crowd," says Champney.

Again, in 1852, Champney returned to North

[1] Johnson painted a picture of "Echo Lake" (1867), and exhibited at the Centennial a view of the "Old Man of the Mountain."
[2] One of the most notable pictures of Williamson, who was of Scottish birth, is "The Summit of Chocorua by Twilight."

THE WHITE MOUNTAINS

Conway, this time bringing with him Hamilton Wilde. Other artists had preceded them thither, and the little coterie nearly filled the dining-table in Thompson's old house. Every year brought fresh visitors to the hamlet, as news of its attractions spread, until in 1853 and 1854 the meadows were dotted with great numbers of white umbrellas. Samuel Colman,[1] a pupil of Durand, R. W. Hubbard,[2] Sandford R. Gifford,[3] and A. D. Shattuck,[4] of New York, settled themselves at an old farmhouse situated near the Moat Mountain House and later remodeled and occupied by Mr. George Wolcott.

After his wedding tour in 1853, Champney brought his bride to the Kearsarge House. Wilde, W. A. Gay,[5] and other artists were there, and the little hostelry was crowded and more popular than ever. In the autumn of that year Champney bought Lewis Eastman's old-fashioned house in the lower part of the valley, and in the summer of 1854 the artist was domiciled in it, verandas and dormer windows being added and new rooms being finished the next year. The carpenter-shop on the place was transformed into a spacious studio with a top light.

---

[1] Colman's "Conway Valley" was bought by a citizen of Brooklyn.

[2] Hubbard was a pupil of Professor Morse and of Daniel Huntington. He painted "High Peak — North Conway," in 1871.

[3] "His painting of Echo Lake is a very successful attempt to combine cloud, water, forest, and mountain scenery in a harmonious whole." S. G. W. Benjamin in *Our American Artists*, series I. 1879.

[4] Shattuck, a native of New Hampshire and a brother-in-law of Colman, painted an "Autumnal View of the Androscoggin, with the White Mountains in the Distance," and a view of Mount Chocorua.

[5] Gay, a pupil of Robert W. Weir and of Tryon, painted various pictures having to do with this region, including a "Mount Washington" in the Boston Athenæum.

THE POETS AND PAINTERS

This building, which was to be so long occupied by its owner for artistic uses, was formally dedicated to such purposes in 1855 by a reunion of Champney's friends and a speech by Deacon Greeley, of Boston. Kensett,[1] who was Champney's most intimate friend, visited him just as the studio was completed, and painted, Champney thinks, the first pictures made there.

J. W. Casilear [2] has been already mentioned as an associate of Champney and Kensett at North Conway in the early days. Together these friends explored and sketched along Artists' Brook, whose laughing, bubbling waters, picturesque nooks, and transparent pools make it one of North Conway's

---

[1] John Frederick Kensett was born in 1818 at Cheshire, Connecticut, and died in 1872. He was one of the shining lights of the so-called "Hudson River School" and painted many White Mountain pictures, among them "Mount Washington, from North Conway" (1850); "Sketch of Mount Washington" (1851), now in the Corcoran Gallery of Art, Washington; "Franconia Mountains" (1853); "White Mountain Scenery" (1859), now in the New York Public Library; "Glimpse of the White Mountains" (1867); and "New Hampshire Scenery," an elaborate view of the White Mountains, which belongs to the Century Club, New York. Champney writes of him: "Kensett was more to me than any other [of his school], for I had known him so intimately, and had struggled with him through want and difficulties abroad. . . . His brilliant studies brought back from the Catskills and White Mountains were marvels of clever handling and color. No one seemed able to give the sparkle of sunlight through the depths of the forest, touching on mossy rocks and shaggy tree-trunks, so well as he. . . . I know that to-day his pictures are considered old-fashioned, that they are wanting in solidity and broad massing of forms, but that does not take away from them the lovely feeling of color and crispy touch they possess."

[2] His "Scene in New Hampshire" was painted in 1877. Champney thus characterizes his work: "His pictures are more delicate and refined than either Cole's or Durand's, but not so vigorous. . . . There is a poetic pastoral charm in all his work, pleasing to the eye, and possessing beautiful qualities." He also painted Chocorua.

THE WHITE MOUNTAINS

chief charms. The most noted of American landscapists, George Inness, was also for a time a frequenter of North Conway, using as a studio "the ugly little building," once the academy, which was situated near the Kearsarge House and which was torn down in 1887. Inness also sketched in the West Ossipee region, having been, as has been noted, a guest at one of the predecessors of Whittier's favorite haunt, the Bearcamp River House.

Thomas Hill, famous as a painter of the Sierras and the Yosemite, during his second residence in New England, in the last of the sixties, was one of the artist-colony at North Conway and painted at this period the thrilling picture [1] called "White Mountain Notch — Morning after the Willey Slide," an engraving of which forms the frontispiece of Thompson's revised edition of "Willey's Incidents."

An artist connected in a melancholy way with North Conway is James A. Suydam, who died there September 15, 1865. In company with Sandford R. Gifford he was about to make a sketching tour of the White Hills, whence they were to go to Lake George. Suydam, not feeling very well, decided to

---

[1] Benjamin thus describes it: "Mr. Hill has laid the scene of this large and powerful painting there [in the Notch at the Willey House location]. The top of the mountain is enveloped in a dense canopy of dun, lowering clouds, and a shadow like the threat of doom broods over the fated valley. It is long years since I saw that painting, but the impression it left upon me I am sure could only have been made by a work of real power, inspired by genuine imagination." Of his facility, Champney thus writes: "In one afternoon of three hours in the White Mountain forests, I have seen him produce a study, 12 x 20 in size, full of details and brilliant light. There is his greatest strength, and his White Mountain wood studies have not been excelled."

THE POETS AND PAINTERS

rest at North Conway while his companion went into the Mountains to study. Gifford rejoined his friend in time to be with him in his last hours. In Suydam's death "American art met," says Daniel Huntington, "with more than a common loss." His only White Mountain picture, "Conway Meadows," was purchased by a citizen of Washington.

Mention of Huntington reminds one that this eminent portrait painter also painted Mountain landscapes. His "Chocorua Peak, New Hampshire," dating from 1860, was purchased in 1861 by Mrs. R. L. Stuart, of New York, and now hangs in the Stuart Room of the New York Public Library.

The late Homer Martin also visited and painted in the Mountains in his early days. His "Madison and Adams from Randolph Hill," depicting "two snow-capped mountains rising into a cold cloudy sky," was apparently produced in 1862. It was given in 1891 to the Metropolitan Museum of Art.

Mr. Champney, who passed so many summers with keen delight in North Conway, and who has described its beauties so enthusiastically, says that at one time the village and the neighborhood of Artists' Brook were almost as famous as Barbizon and Fontainebleau after Millet, Rousseau, and Diaz had set the fashion. Artists of repute from all sections of the country came, but, he remarks, "Fashions change, and fads and whims come along to turn the current to the seashore, where the greatest simplicity of form prevails." His own studio was the resort of many from this country and even from

THE WHITE MOUNTAINS

foreign lands. Many of his Mountain canvases are owned in and around Boston.

Albert Bierstadt, of Rocky Mountain fame, was a visitor here both in his earlier and his later years.[1] His "On the Saco, New Hampshire," was painted in 1886. S. L. Gerry was another frequenter of the region. His best-known Mountain picture is his "The Old Man of the Mountain."

Jackson, as has been said, was early discovered by artists as a center of rare landscape beauties. Boardman, Geary, Clark, Hoit, and Brackett are named as the pioneers there, the first of whom came, as has been previously noted, as early as 1847. Chester Harding, the portrait painter, to whom we owe the likeness of Abel Crawford, was also a visitor there. G. S. Merrill long occupied as a studio a deserted Free-Will Baptist church at the angle formed by the junction of the Dundee Road with the Black Mountain Road. In more recent times artists in great numbers have summered in Jackson. One who helped to a great degree to make known the beauties and wonders of the White Hills, the late Frank H. Shapleigh, of Boston, may be mentioned. For fifteen years, beginning in 1877, he had a studio at the Crawford House. Later, he built the quaint and otherwise attractive cottage, "Maple Knoll," behind the Jackson Falls House. Among his pictures are views of "The Northern Peaks" and "Mount Washington."

---

[1] In 1869, according to Benjamin Osgood, the guide, Bierstadt was a guest at the Glen House, and it was he who found Landlord Thompson's body.

THE POETS AND PAINTERS

Campton and West Campton have attracted many artists. Among those who frequented this district in the early days are included Durand, Gay, Gerry, T. Addison Richards, Griggs, Pone, and Williams.

Church's Falls, on Sabba-Day Brook in Albany, perpetuate the association of F. E. Church, who painted them, with the Mountain region. The Scottish-American artist William Hart was another who has depicted Chocorua, while H. B. Brown, of Portland, noted especially for his spirited reproductions of coast scenery, painted a striking view of the Crawford Notch, looking up, which is familiar from its reproduction in photogravure.

Another artist who deserves a mention in this fragmentary chronicle of White Mountain art is Godfrey N. Frankenstein, who was of German birth and who died in Springfield, Ohio, in 1873. He painted many sketches of the scenery of this region, two of which, "Mount Washington, over Tuckerman's Ravine" and "The Notch of the White Mountains from Mount Crawford," are lithographed in Oakes's "White Mountain Scenery." In his honor his friend, Dr. Bemis, gave his name to the imposing cliff just above Bemis Station on the Maine Central Railroad.

IX

THE LATER SCIENTIFIC EXPLORATIONS OF THE MOUNTAINS

ACCOUNTS have been given in preceding chapters of the visits to the Mountains of some of the eminent scientific men of the early days and mention has been made of the results of their explorations. During later years, this region, so accessible to the earlier settled part of the country and possessing so many features of interest from the standpoint of science, has, naturally, been the theater for field work of a host of scientists and naturalists. Space can be taken to record the names and explorations of only the more noted of such observers and to summarize the activities and results of some of the more systematic examinations of the natural phenomena of the region.

A scientific event of the first years of the fifth decade of the nineteenth century, which concerned the Mountains to a considerable extent, was the first geological survey of New Hampshire. An inventory of the natural resources of the State, an account of which sort was what passed at that period for a geological survey, had been recommended for New Hampshire by several governors, but without success until Governor John Page in 1839 advocated such an undertaking and the legislature of that year passed an act providing for it.

LATER SCIENTIFIC EXPLORATIONS

Acting under the authorization of the legislature, Governor Page appointed, as State Geologist to conduct the work, Dr. Charles T. Jackson, of Boston, a chemist and mineralogist of repute, who became world-famous later in connection with the discovery of anæsthesia.

An annual appropriation of two thousand dollars for three years was authorized in the act for carrying out its provisions; but, the laboratory work proving more difficult and extensive than was anticipated, additional appropriations were necessary from time to time, bringing the total cost of the Survey up to nine thousand dollars, exclusive of the expense of publishing the reports.

Dr. Jackson, although he had already conducted similar surveys of Nova Scotia and Rhode Island, was one of the most primitive of State surveyors in his methods. Trained abroad under Élie de Beaumont, he had adopted that scientist's erroneous theories of mountain-building, which rendered his geological work on the Mountain region largely futile. Moreover, when we learn that Dr. Jackson devoted but very little of his own time to the field work and that it was carried on for the most part by untrained and unpaid assistants, we are not surprised to find that the Survey accomplished so little of real scientific value.

The summers of three years, beginning with 1840, were occupied in collecting minerals and soils, which were analyzed in Dr. Jackson's laboratory in Boston during the winters following. Much of this field work was done in the White Mountains.

THE WHITE MOUNTAINS

This Survey, however, possesses for us another than its scientific interest, and that lies in the personnel of the assistants. In the summer of the first year, M. B. Williams and Josiah Dwight Whitney, later the famous geologist and head of the California State Survey, were employed in the field work, which closed for that year with a tour in August to the White Mountains.

Williams was again in the field the following summer. Whitney, who found the work most congenial, and who, then undecided as to his future career, was counseled by his chief to adopt the latter's profession, gained in the winter of 1840-41 his first professional success, an appointment to the Survey as a paid assistant. His duties were to assist Dr. Jackson in the latter's laboratory in Boston in the analyses of the minerals collected the preceding summer. This work lasted only through the winter, and in the spring the future geologist ended his connection with the Survey. In the published report of the State Geologist, portions of which were Whitney's and Williams's own composition, it is told that their party were the first persons to reach the top of Mount Washington on horseback.[1] The report also contains seven full-paged lithographed plates of New Hampshire scenery from drawings by Whitney,[2] a number of which were of White Mountain views.

[1] Abel Crawford, as affirmed by his son Ethan, was actually "the first man that ever rode a horse on the top of Mount Washington," he being the guide on this historic occasion. Dr. Jackson was also of the party.

[2] I am indebted for information as to Whitney's connection with the Survey to Edwin Tenney Brewster's *Life and Letters of Josiah Dwight Whitney* (1909).

LATER SCIENTIFIC EXPLORATIONS

In 1841, Edward Everett Hale was, at the instance of his friend, William F. Channing, who had become an assistant on the Survey, appointed a junior member of it, and the two were in the field that summer, as was Channing also the following year. In September, Hale and Channing made a trip up the South Branch of Israel's River, in search of large sheets of mica alleged to have been found there. They continued up over one or more of the Northern Peaks and Washington and returned the next day to the old Fabyan tavern. Dr. Hale thus recalls his first ascent of Mount Washington, in "Tarry at Home Travels": "The first time I stood at the Tip-Top House [1] was at ten o'clock at night in the first week of September, 1841, with a crowbar in my hand as I pressed upon the door. It was after a tramp which had lasted seventeen hours and had taken us over Jefferson and through one or two thunderstorms."

The advance in geological and mineralogical knowledge after the middle of the nineteenth century and the improvement in field and laboratory methods in these sciences having rendered the results of the earlier geological survey largely obsolete, the State authorities in the sixties determined upon undertaking a more thoroughgoing investigation of the physical conditions and resources of the State. They were further urged to this action by a number of considerations which arose from the character of the early Survey. The first inventory of the natural resources of New Hampshire, made under the direc-

[1] See pp. 229, 230.

THE WHITE MOUNTAINS

tion of Dr. Charles T. Jackson, was conducted, as has been intimated, in a very primitive manner, and the barometrical and other observations were incomplete. More attention was paid to minerals and their localities and to soils as affecting agriculture than to structural geology, and so the reports deal largely with mineralogical, metallurgical, and economic descriptions and statements. Moreover, the State authorities did not think it important to color the geological map attached to the final report, which last fact makes it hard to understand many things that otherwise might have been evident.

From the reports and map, therefore, it is difficult to deduce any very satisfactory notions of geological structure. Again, Dr. Jackson, as has been said, held erroneous theories as to mountain-formation, which invalidated his conclusions as to the geological structure of the State. Furthermore, the illustrative collection of rocks and minerals deposited by Dr. Jackson at Concord had been destroyed by fire.

A new survey was, on all these accounts, a pressing need. Accordingly, at the June session of the legislature of New Hampshire in 1868, a bill was passed to provide for the geological and mineralogical survey of the State, which bill received the approval of Governor Harriman on July 3.

The appointment as State Geologist of C. H. Hitchcock, son and pupil of the eminent Professor and President Edward Hitchcock,[1] of Amherst Col-

---

[1] In 1841, President Hitchcock ascended Mount Washington from the old Notch House, and wrote about the rocks in a paper upon glacio-aqueous action in North America.

LATER SCIENTIFIC EXPLORATIONS

lege, and himself professor of geology at Dartmouth College, was a natural and fitting one. Professor Hitchcock's character, equipment, and experience — he had been Assistant State Geologist of Vermont and State Geologist of Maine — insured an accurate, comprehensive, and otherwise adequate prosecution of the work.

While it is not the province of this narrative to give a history of the Survey, still so much of its activity related to and centered about the White Mountains that a summary of the explorations in that region must necessarily embody an outline of a large part of the entire field work.

The day, September 9, 1868, after he received notice of his appointment, Professor Hitchcock, although the season was almost too late to commence work, started for Lisbon to begin the examination of the Ammonoosuc gold field. There was time, naturally, for little more than a reconnaissance of that district for the purpose of laying out future work.

J. H. Huntington, of Hanover, and George L. Vose, of Paris, Maine, having been appointed assistant geologists, the former was made principal assistant, while to Mr. Vose was assigned the White Mountain region as his special subject or definite area to investigate. He was expected to pay especial attention to the topography, and, in addition to the delineation of the geological structure, to furnish the most accurate map of the region ever drawn.

Field work for 1869 was begun in May on the

THE WHITE MOUNTAINS

Ammonoosuc gold field, which received more attention than any other portion of the territory and concerning which a comprehensive report, with a colored geological map of the most interesting part of the area, was printed in pamphlet form. This map, with its accompanying descriptions, is of historical importance as containing the germ of the geologists' notions and opinions as to the structure of all New England.

Mr. Vose spent a few weeks of this year among the White Mountains, taking a large number of observations for the purpose of fixing the exact position of many of the high peaks and also making observations upon the geology of the region. By this means the latitude and longitude of Passaconaway, the northern Kearsarge, Whiteface, and Chocorua were ascertained. From Kearsarge and Chocorua, he drew accurate sketches of all the mountains as seen along the New Hampshire horizon, using a six-inch theodolite for the purpose. In August he resigned his position on the Survey.

During the winter of 1869–70, as narrated in full in another place, Mr. Huntington carried out, with Mr. A. F. Clough, the winter occupation of Moosilauke. In May, 1870, Mr. Huntington made a trip on foot to determine the relative altitude of the passes along the principal White Mountain Range between the Crawford House and Waterville, an expedition which was attended with considerable labor owing to the fact that much snow was still remaining.

By this time in the progress of the Survey, the

LATER SCIENTIFIC EXPLORATIONS

geologists had begun to understand the structure of the White Mountains, "which knowledge proved to be the key to that of the rest of the State." This field of research having been left vacant by the resignation aforesaid, the State Geologist himself assumed the duty of exploring the territory.

The area for investigation for 1870 included especially the region, about thirty miles long and twelve or fifteen wide, bounded by Israel's, Moose, Peabody, Ellis, and Saco Rivers. The laboriousness of the work of exploration is plainly indicated when it is stated that the area was nearly an unbroken forest, traversed only by bridle paths and roads used for the ascent of Mount Washington in summer. The plan of campaign pursued was to visit systematically with the hammer and barometer every one of the numerous peaks and valleys which make up this tract. So numerous were the localities requiring visitation that six members of the class of 1871 of Dartmouth College were invited to assist. J. H. Huntington, Dr. Nathan Barrows, and E. Hitchcock, Jr., also furnished aid in this work. The Survey party lived among the mountains, in extempore camps, until the explorations and observations had been made. Animated by the desire to discover the real geological structure of the region, the members of the party did not rest until all the nearly inaccessible peaks and ravines had been explored. Often the exertion necessary to procure a single specimen was greater than that required to pass over Mount Washington on foot by the paths, involving, as it did, traveling through primeval forest, full of under-

THE WHITE MOUNTAINS

brush, fallen trees, and other obstacles. Many of the results of the exploring work were thus, Professor Hitchcock remarks, "acquired only through infinite toil."

The first result of this laborious and painstaking survey of the Mountain region was the construction by the State Geologist of a physical model [1] of the area. This is about five feet in length, and is on the scale of one hundred and forty rods to the inch horizontally, and of one thousand feet to three fourths of an inch vertically.

The White Mountain explorations of 1871 [2] included a thorough examination of the area lying between the Saco and Pemigewasset Rivers and north of Sandwich. This work, which continued uninterruptedly for a month beginning just after the middle of June, was carried on with the assistance of eleven members of the graduating class of Dartmouth College, who proffered their services and who labored cheerfully and effectively, all contributing something of value. Two of them discovered a new lake (Haystack Lake) on the northwest side of Mount Garfield (then called "The Haystack"); two others found a still larger one upon the

---

[1] After this had been exhibited in public, it was learned that a plaster model of the White Mountains had been fashioned several years before by Rev. Dr. Thomas Hill, formerly president of Harvard College. Dr. Hill's model was upon a much smaller scale, about eighteen inches square, and it showed all the ridges and valleys from Gorham to Conway and Littleton. It was built upon the basis of Bond's map of 1853, and showed great familiarity with the structure of the Mountains.

[2] In the winter of 1870–71 occurred the first winter occupation of Mount Washington, by Huntington and others, as related elsewhere.

LATER SCIENTIFIC EXPLORATIONS

east side of Mount Kinsman; others measured the length of the Profile and explored the Devil's Den on Mount Willard. Soon after the disbanding of the first party, a new one was formed, some of the members of which remained two months longer exploring the country as far south as Sandwich.

A still larger party than the first of the preceding year was organized for work in 1872. It included thirteen members of the class of 1872 of Dartmouth College, and two members of the class of 1873. One section of it was engaged in making a plane-table survey of the southwest portion of the Mountain area, for the purpose of perfecting the map. The remainder of the party examined, under the guidance of Mr. Huntington, the rocks along the Saco Valley and in Albany, being occupied in this work for a period of three weeks.

Although the exploration had been essentially completed in 1872, Messrs. Hitchcock and Huntington visited a few points about the Mountains in 1873 and later years for the sake of completing their knowledge of them. In 1875, Professor Hitchcock made a special reëxamination of the Saco Valley, and in July of that year he made observations in the Crawford Notch along the line of the new railroad, Professor J. D. Dana examining with him the rocks in the neighborhood of the second cut from the Crawford House. In the course of this field work two flumes, Hitchcock and Butterwort, were discovered on Mount Willard by Professor Hitchcock.

Such are in outline the main features of the work of this Survey so far as it concerned the White

THE WHITE MOUNTAINS

Mountains. The results of this great State enterprise are embodied in the three monumental volumes on the geology of New Hampshire,[1] published by the State of New Hampshire (1874–78), the first two of which contain a vast amount of information concerning the scientific aspects of the White Mountains, with many illustrations, maps, and diagrams relating to them.

It remains, before I am done with this topic of the scientific exploration of the Mountains, to set down briefly the facts and circumstances relating to the activities of one or two other investigators in this field than those whose work under State auspices has just been described.[2]

---

[1] Volume I contains: "History of Explorations among the White Mountains," by Warren Upham; "The Distribution of Insects in New Hampshire," by William F. Flint; and "Scenery of Coös County," by J. H. Huntington. The geology of the White Mountain district is given in volume II (1877). Volume III contains little about the Mountains. The maps include a large contour map issued in sections and a colored geological map in sections.

[2] Among early geological explorers of this region who published articles embodying the results of their observations are Oliver P. Hubbard, M.D., Henry D. and William B. Rogers, and Professor J. P. Lesley. Dr. Hubbard studied the geology and mineralogy of the Mountains and published an outline of the results of his investigations in the *American Journal of Science and Arts* for April, 1838. In the same journal for March, 1850, he printed the results of his study of the condition of trap dikes as evidence of erosion. The Rogerses explored the Notch in July, 1845, and published a joint article on the geological age of the White Mountains in the *American Journal of Science and Arts* for May, 1846. Professor Lesley visited the region in 1849 and subsequent years, and in 1857 made a section along the Grand Trunk Railway. In the *Proceedings* of the Academy of Natural Sciences of Philadelphia for 1860, he stated briefly the results of some observations made in the White Mountains during that summer. Among those who have dealt with the glacial phenomena are, besides Agassiz, Professors C. H. Hitchcock, Alpheus S. Packard, and Warren Upham.

LATER SCIENTIFIC EXPLORATIONS

The beloved teacher, Louis Agassiz, made a journey here the first summer (1847) after his arrival in America. At that time he "noticed unmistakable evidences of the former existence of local glaciers," which, he says, "were the more clear and impressive to me because I was then fresh from my investigation of the glaciers in Switzerland." Beyond the mere statement, in a letter to Élie de Beaumont, of the fact of his having seen some very distinct moraines in some valleys of the White Mountains, he at that time made no report upon the glacial phenomena of the region, publishing nothing in the way of a detailed account of the observations, because he did not then have time to study the difficult problem closely enough. Opportunity to revisit the region for a more careful examination did not present itself until twenty-three years later. As a result of a prolonged stay among the Hills in the summer of 1870, however, he was able to trace the contact of the more limited phenomena of the local glaciers, which succeeded the all-embracing winter of the Glacial period, with the more widespread and general features of the drift. In a paper, published in the *Proceedings* of the Nineteenth Meeting of the American Association for the Advancement of Science, held in that year, were set forth the general facts then ascertained, which were all that the space admitted. He described especially the fine moraines in Bethlehem and vicinity, which particularly interested him, noting the various kinds, defining their locations, and indicating the course and extent of the glaciers which occupied the re-

THE WHITE MOUNTAINS

gion.[1] Very fittingly, in honor of the great scientist, his name has been bestowed upon the prominent hill in that town, formerly known as "Peaked" or "Picket Hill," and now visited annually by so many persons for its magnificent panoramic view.[2] He is commemorated also elsewhere in the Mountains, the striking rock formation on the Moosilauke Brook in Woodstock, where the water of the stream rolls through deep black basins hollowed out of the solid granite, having been named the "Agassiz Basins" shortly after his visit to the locality.

Agassiz's personal friend and scientific associate of long standing, — they had been intimates from boyhood and colleagues in Switzerland, — Arnold Guyot, compelled to abandon his work in Europe because of the political disturbances of 1848, followed his friend to this country, which he was destined, like his friend also, to make his place of abode thereafter. Although Guyot finally settled at Princeton, while Agassiz was attached to Harvard, the two friends kept up their intercourse and shared all their scientific interests.

The Princeton professor, who made geography his specialty, began as early as 1849 a series of investigations of the physical structure of the Appalachian Mountain system and of measurements of its altitudes from New Hampshire to Georgia. In that

[1] What one mountain jehu remarked of Agassiz and his assistants, after witnessing the apparently strange antics of the scientific observers, has happily been preserved. "They said they was 'naturals,' and I should think they was!"

[2] A noble tribute to the great man is the poem of Charlotte Fiske Bates (Madame Roget), entitled "Mount Agassiz." It is printed in Musgrove's *The White Hills in Poetry.*

LATER SCIENTIFIC EXPLORATIONS

year he made the first of a series of four summer excursions devoted to the barometric exploration of the White Mountains, and he continued his work until he had spent five years over New Hampshire, the Green Mountains of Vermont, and the Adirondacks and other elevated regions in the State of New York. Among his companions, who constantly made corresponding observations to his, were Mr. Ernest Sandoz, who was with him in nearly all his excursions, Mr. Émile Grand Pierre, who accompanied him during three summers, and Alexander Agassiz, Edward Rutledge, and Herbert Torrey, then young men, who gave him active assistance in the White Mountains.

In 1851, Professor Guyot measured Mount Washington by barometric observations, and obtained the height of 6291 feet,[1] only two feet under the now accepted altitude, ascertained by Captain T. J. Cram by spirit leveling in 1853. He continued his explorations in the White Hills from time to time. In 1857, he made ascents of Mounts Washington, Willard, and Carrigain.[2] The association of his name with the region has been made perpetual by the conferring of it upon one of the peaks of the Twin Mountain Range.

Notable scientific work has been done in the Mountains in the domain of entomology by Samuel

---

[1] In his memoir "On the Appalachian Mountain System," published in the *American Journal of Science and Arts* for March, 1861, he changed his figures to 6288.

[2] The itinerary of his expedition of this year, with letters written while *en route*, is given by S. Hastings Grant, one of his companions, in *Appalachia* for June, 1907.

THE WHITE MOUNTAINS

H. Scudder, a pupil of Agassiz and the first of the vice-presidents of the Appalachian Mountain Club and the first editor of *Appalachia;* by Mrs. Annie Trumbull Slosson, noted also as a story-writer; and by J. H. Emerton, the authority on spiders.

The explorations of the earlier botanists in these happy hunting-grounds of the plant-lover have been narrated. Additional information as to the scientific aspects of the plants of the Mountains and as to the plants of different localities has been furnished by a number of later investigators. The volumes of *Appalachia* contain many valuable articles and notes on botanical matters, as well as on other scientific phenomena of the region, by members of the Appalachian Mountain Club who are scientists by profession or who find their recreation in the making of observations or explorations as amateurs. The literary naturalists, Bradford Torrey, Frank Bolles, and Winthrop Packard, whose main interest is ornithological, have also written about the flowers and their haunts found in wandering afoot among the Hills. The writers just mentioned have descanted pleasingly, even if sometimes too exclusively for the general reader, upon the birds which make their spring and summer sojourn here.

The story of an exploring feat, of the nature of a satisfaction of curiosity rather than of scientific inquiry, may well find space here. This is the descent to the Devil's Den, a dark-mouthed cave high up on the sheer cliffs of the south side of Mount Willard, where it is plainly seen from the Notch. This perilous undertaking was twice accomplished during the

LATER SCIENTIFIC EXPLORATIONS

last century by daring explorers. There is a tradition that Abel Crawford visited it many years ago and found the bottom bestrewn with bones and other ghastly remains. Be that as it may, curiosity was early aroused as to what this lofty hollow, inaccessible by any way affording foothold, might contain. According to Spaulding, the credit of first visiting the place belongs to F. Leavitt, Esq., who, by means of a rope let down from the overhanging rock, succeeded in reaching the level of the cavern. Finding, it is said, a collection of skulls and bones of animals scattered about the entrance, the explorer lost all desire to enter the dismal den, and, after dangling but a short while at this perilous height, gave the signal to be drawn up. "As the old *Evil One* has such daily business with mortal affairs," remarks Mr. Spaulding, with quiet humor, "rather than believe that to be his abode, it appears more just to conclude that alone there the mountain eagle finds a solitary home."

In 1870, as has been mentioned, the cavern was explored by members of the Geological Survey party, let down, by means of one hundred and twenty-five feet of rope from the summit of the mountain. "Our explorers," says Professor Hitchcock, ". . . discovered nothing mysterious about this locality, but would not advise visitors to explore it again without better facilities for going and coming than they enjoyed."

X

THE COMING OF THE RAILROADS — THEIR LATER EXTENSIONS

As a glance at the map of the White Mountain region will suggest, there is in this country probably no other summer-resort area, and certainly no other mountain district of anything like its extent, that is to-day provided with such an abundance of railroad facilities, rendering it at once easy of access and convenient for local travel. Indeed, this is so much the case that it may be affirmed that, like some other parts of New England, it is possibly oversupplied with such means of transportation. In these automobile days the railroad has ceased to play so great a part as it once did as a carrier of people to and through the Mountains, but in former days it was an essential and very great element in the growth, and, indeed, in the very existence, of the region as a summer resort.

As a necessary preliminary, therefore, to an account of that development, as well as for its own intrinsic interest, a brief outline of the chief steps by which the railroads approached the Mountains from different points and of the building of the local extensions would seem to be pertinent at this point.

The first railroad to reach the region was the Atlantic and St. Lawrence Railroad, which was projected to run from Portland, Maine, to Island Pond,

THE RAILROADS

Vermont, and which was chartered successively in 1845, 1847, and 1848, by the three States it was to cross. Construction was begun July 4, 1846, and was completed as far as Gorham, New Hampshire, early in 1852. The entire line from Portland to the western terminus in Vermont was opened in January of the following year. At the latter place this railroad was to connect with the St. Lawrence and Atlantic Railroad, a line from Montreal to that point in Vermont, the two roads, with the interchanged names, thereby forming a continuous route between the two cities. The Canadian line was completed and opened for business in July, 1853. On the evening of the 18th of that month, the first train from Montreal arrived in Portland, where it was received with the ringing of bells, a salute of thirty-one guns, and various other formal and informal manifestations of joy at the consummation of this great work. About this time the amalgamation of a number of Canadian lines into one Grand Trunk Railway was effected, and to this system the Atlantic and St. Lawrence Railroad was leased for 999 years on August 8, 1853.

The route of the Atlantic and St. Lawrence Railroad, which is now known only by the general name of the Grand Trunk, and which is the one that has present interest for us, is, when approaching the Mountains, up the beautiful valley of the Androscoggin River, through Shelburne and Gorham. It thus passes to the north of the White Mountains, and so has been superseded for the most part, as a means of access to the region, by the railroads from

THE WHITE MOUNTAINS

the south and another railroad from Portland reaching directly the resorts among the Mountains. At the time of the completion of this first railroad to Gorham, there were only five public houses from which the summit of Mount Washington could be reached in a day, which statement will give the reader, familiar with the accommodations of to-day, some notion of the development of the region since the coming of the railroads.

The advance of the railroads from the south was a slow one, forty years elapsing from the time the early railroads out of Boston were opened before a traveler could reach the heart of the Mountains from that city entirely by rail.

The Boston and Lowell Railroad was opened for travel June 26, 1835. Three days before this opening of the road to Lowell, the Nashua and Lowell Railroad Company obtained a charter to build a road from the State line northwardly in the Merrimac Valley. The line was opened to Nashua, December 23, 1838. The surveys for the next link, the Concord Railroad, were made by Loammi Baldwin, Jr., William Gibbs McNeill, and George Washington Whistler,[1] the father of the artist, and the pioneer passenger train ran into Concord [2] Tuesday evening, September 6, 1842, a great gathering of rejoicing

[1] Major Whistler went to Russia in 1842 to superintend the construction of the railroad from St. Petersburg to Moscow, and died in that country seven years later. William Gibbs McNeill was his brother-in-law.

[2] A favorite route to New Hampshire from New York about 1850 was by steamer to Norwich, Connecticut, and thence to Concord via the Norwich and Worcester Railroad, opened in 1840, the Nashua and Worcester Railroad, and the Concord Railroad.

THE RAILROADS

people being on hand to welcome it. This was only twelve years after the first steam railway, the Liverpool and Manchester, was built.

North of Concord two lines were soon under construction, and in a little more than ten years Littleton was reached. Here, however, the advance was halted for two decades.[1]

The Northern Railroad of New Hampshire started from Concord, proceeded up the Merrimac to Franklin, and then struck over to a point on the Connecticut River near the mouth of its tributary, the White River. It was opened to Lebanon in November, 1847, and to White River Junction in the town of Hartford, Vermont, in June, 1848. There it connected with the Vermont Central Railroad (later the Central Vermont) and with the Connecticut and Passumpsic Rivers Railroad, lines then under construction. With the latter, which was in operation to Wells River as early as 1849, it formed a route much used, though somewhat less direct, by travelers to the Mountains in the early days as an alternative to the one about to be mentioned. The Northern Railroad became a part of the Boston and Maine system in 1890.

The Boston, Concord, and Montreal Railroad, the other line and the one which has more of interest for us as that which eventually became a link in the principal through route from Boston to the White Mountain region, was chartered on December 27,

[1] A correspondent, "Pennacook," of the *New York Herald*, writing from the Flume House, June 15, 1853, speaks of the approaching opening of the railroad to Littleton, and adds, "No railroad should ever be constructed farther into these mountains than Littleton."

THE WHITE MOUNTAINS

1844. It was to start from Concord or Bow, and was to extend to some point on the west bank of the Connecticut River opposite Haverhill or to Littleton. Construction was immediately undertaken by the enterprising and courageous people who lived along its way, and on May 22, 1848, there was an opening of the road to Sanbornton (now Tilton). On this occasion the new engine, "Old Man of the Mountain," and cars painted sky-blue, were deemed peculiarly appropriate for a line whose future travel would largely consist of traffic to and from the White Mountains. Plymouth was reached in January, 1850, and Wells River, May 10, 1853. Late the same year, in December, the White Mountains Railroad was opened to Littleton. Twenty years later, this latter line became by purchase a part of the Boston, Concord, and Montreal Railroad.

In 1856, when the Boston, Concord, and Montreal Railroad, which was peculiarly a New Hampshire enterprise, was on the verge of bankruptcy, John E. Lyon took charge of it. To his courage, initiative, and persistency were due the extensions built into the north country beyond Littleton between 1869 and 1878.

This railroad-builder was, it may be mentioned in passing, concerned in many other enterprises connected with the development of the White Mountains as a resort. Besides being associated with Mr. Marsh in the Mount Washington Railway, he was instrumental in the rebuilding of the Pemigewasset House at Plymouth and in the building of the Fabyan House and of the Summit House on Mount Wash-

THE RAILROADS

ington, and was one of the incorporators of the Moosilauke Mountain Road Company.

The further extensions of the White Mountains Railroad referred to were to Lancaster, to which point the road was opened October 31, 1870; to Groveton, reached on the national holiday two years later; and to Fabyan by way of Wing Road, to which terminus the road was opened July 4, 1874. Two years afterwards, the railroad was extended from Fabyan to the Base in time to be opened early in July, and thus the stage service over the turnpike from Fabyan to the Mount Washington Railway was superseded. The Profile House and Bethlehem were for some years longer accessible only by stage, but in 1879 a narrow-gauge road was opened to the former and in 1881 to the latter. These branch lines, which are operated only in the summer, remained narrow-gauge until 1897, when the change to standard-gauge was completed.[1]

What these extensions meant to the development of the region as a summer recreation ground and tourist center will be at once evident to any present-day frequenter of the White Mountains, when he recalls that for more than a score of years Littleton was the northern terminus of the White Mountains Railroad, and that Bethlehem, the Profile House and the Franconia Notch, the Crawford House and Notch, and other places were accessible only by long and tedious, and often otherwise unpleasant, stage rides.

[1] I am indebted to the Boston and Maine Railroad, and particularly to Mr. G. E. Cummings, superintendent of the White Mountains Division, for information as to the time of this change of gauge on the Profile and Franconia Notch Railroad.

THE WHITE MOUNTAINS

The openings of two more branch lines remain to be chronicled. North Woodstock, now become a considerable summer resort, was connected by rail with Plymouth in 1883. Ten years later, a road twenty miles long was opened to Berlin. This started at the old terminus on Jefferson Meadow of the Whitefield and Jefferson Railroad, opened in 1879, at a point near to which starts the spur, opened in 1892, to the Waumbek Hotel, and passed through Randolph and Gorham.

All of these railroads in the Mountain region now form a part of the Boston and Maine Railroad system, which controls nearly all the railroads in the Granite State.

The lines up the Connecticut River from Springfield, Massachusetts, which city was connected by rail with Hartford, Connecticut, in 1844, were opened at various times. The principal links in the northern part of this the most direct route from New York City to the White Mountains were the Connecticut River Railroad, opened to South Vernon, January 1, 1849; the Vermont Valley Railroad, Brattleboro to Bellows Falls, opened in 1851; the Sullivan County Railroad, Bellows Falls to Windsor, opened in February, 1849, and sold October 1, 1880, to the Vermont Valley Railroad; and the Connecticut and Passumpsic Rivers Railroad, from White River Junction on. All these lines were eventually leased to the Boston and Maine.

Another important means of rendering the Mountains accessible by rail was undertaken in the early seventies in the construction of the Portland and

THE DOUBLE GATE OF CRAWFORD NOTCH

THE RAILROADS

Ogdensburg Railroad, so called, some one has facetiously remarked, because it started from Portland and never reached Ogdensburg. To two brothers, citizens of the State of Maine, belongs the credit for the building of this railroad, which vies with the Mount Washington Railway as a conception and achievement and in scenic interest. General Samuel J. Anderson, of Portland, was the foremost promoter of the road and its first president. "Being," says Mrs. Mason in her article on Conway, "a gifted and persuasive speaker, it was easy for him to induce the town of Conway to raise five per cent of its valuation for the building of the road." John Farwell Anderson, of South Windham, Maine, was the engineer. Maintaining that the gorges of the Crawford Notch could be bridged, he accomplished the feat after it had been repeatedly declared impossible by other engineers. The company was chartered in February, 1867, and in four and a half years the line reached North Conway. It was opened to Fabyan in August, 1875. Some idea of the difficulties and expense of construction and operation may be gained from the facts that of the total ascent of 1890 feet from Portland to Crawford's, 1369 feet are included in the thirty miles between North Conway and the latter place, and that between Bemis and Crawford's the rise is 116 feet to the mile for nine consecutive miles. Such structures on the right of way as the Frankenstein Trestle [1] and the Willey Brook Bridge are striking evidences of the skill and genius of the engineer.

[1] The old trestle was replaced by a new steel one in 1895.

THE WHITE MOUNTAINS

Less than a year after the Portland and Ogdensburg was opened to North Conway, the Eastern Railroad, now a part of the Boston and Maine, reached Conway. To-day the rail connection between the two, which form together another through route from Boston to the Mountains, is at Intervale. In 1888, the former road fell into the hands of the Maine Central and was renamed the Mountain Division of that railroad. The following year the line was extended from Fabyan to Scott's Mills via the Twin Mountain House and Whitefield, thus completing a route passing entirely through the heart of the Mountains. A later extension to the northward, from Quebec Junction to North Stratford, opened in 1891, made the Maine Central a means of access to the region from Canada.

XI

THE HOTELS ON MOUNT WASHINGTON — THE CARRIAGE ROAD, AND THE MOUNT WASHINGTON RAILWAY — HOTELS AND SHELTERS ON OTHER SUMMITS

The steps in two connected enterprises — one the supplying of shelter for visitors to Mount Washington and the other the providing of means of making the ascent for others than persons coming on foot or on horseback — form perhaps the most interesting series of events in White Mountain history. The joint story covers a long period of time and is a record worthy of the strong men who by their courage and energy have made New Hampshire famous. I have already told of the building of the earlier footpaths and the bridle path and of the first shelter erected on the Mountain. This latter, it will be recalled, consisted of Ethan Allen Crawford's three stone cabins, which, soon after their erection in 1823, were abandoned. Mr. Crawford followed these with a large tent, which he spread near a spring of water not far from the Summit and which was provided with a sheet-iron stove. Because, however, of the violent storms and wind, this new shelter could not be kept in place and soon wore out.

Soon after the bridle path was opened, a rude wooden shelter of about a dozen feet square was built,

THE WHITE MOUNTAINS

but its existence was short,[1] and it is not known what became of it. This is the "Tip-Top House," that Dr. Edward Everett Hale tells of entering, in September, 1841.

The first hotel on Mount Washington was built in 1852, and owed its construction to the enterprise of Nathan R. Perkins, of Jefferson, and Lucius M. Rosebrook and Joseph S. Hall, both citizens of Lancaster. This difficult work was begun in May, and on July 28 the hotel, the "Summit House," was opened to the public.

All the lumber for the sheathing and roof had to be carried upon horses from a sawmill near Jefferson Highlands. A chain was hung over the horse's back and one end of each board was run through a loop at the end of the chain, two boards being carried on each side of the horse. The drivers, D. S. Davis and A. Judson Bedell, walked behind carrying the farther end of the boards. Mr. Rosebrook, it is said, carried the front door up the Mountain on his back from the Glen House. Such were the obstacles that were overcome by these energetic men.

This structure, which stood on the north side of the peak, was built largely of rough stones blasted from the Mountain and was firmly secured to its rocky foundation by cement and large iron bolts. Over the low, sloping gable roof passed four stout cables. It was enlarged the following year, when Mr. Perkins was in charge and a half-interest had

[1] Colonel Charles Parsons, of St. Louis, who visited Mount Washington in 1900 for the second time, remembered that this shelter was in existence in 1844, when he walked up the Mountain. (From his "Reminiscences" in *Among the Clouds*.)

MOUNT WASHINGTON

been sold to Nathaniel Noyes and an associate, and an upper story with a pitched roof was added. It withstood the storms of winter for more than thirty years, being used, after the building of the second Summit House, as a dormitory for its employees until 1884, when it was demolished.

The success of this undertaking led to the erection of a rival house, the famous Tip-Top House, which was opened in August, 1853. Samuel Fitch Spaulding, of Lancaster, was the builder, and his associates in the project and in the management of the hotel were his sons and a nephew, John Hubbard Spaulding, the author of "Historical Relics of the White Mountains." It was built of rough stones, similarly to the Summit House, measured eighty-four by twenty-eight feet, and had originally a deck roof, upon which the visitor might stand and thus have an unobstructed view. A telescope was kept there in pleasant weather. Competition between the two hotels was keen the first common season, but in 1854 Mr. Perkins disposed of his interest in the Summit House to the Spauldings, who managed the two houses for nine seasons. Mary B. Spaulding (Mrs. Lucius Hartshorn), daughter of Samuel F. Spaulding, managed the Tip-Top House for three seasons. In a letter written a few years ago she gives a vivid description of the difficulty of managing a hotel on the Mountain at that day. Everything had to be brought on horses' backs from the Glen House, and fresh meat, potatoes, milk, and cream were absent from the menu. Among the supplies kept on hand were bacon, ham, tripe, tongue, eggs, and rice, and

THE WHITE MOUNTAINS

pancakes, johnnycake, fried cakes, and varieties of hot bread and biscuit were served. The number of guests for dinner was very uncertain and could be roughly estimated only from the number of visitors at the foot of the Mountain and from the weather conditions. Among her guests she names Jefferson Davis, Charles Sumner, Horace Greeley, and William H. Seward.

C. H. V. Cavis, engineer for the carriage road, was for one year manager of the Tip-Top House. In his day, according to Mrs. Cavis, in order to estimate the number of guests for dinner, some one went to what is known as Point Lookoff, overlooking the Lakes of the Clouds, and counted the ponies in the cavalcade coming along the bridle path from Crawford's. Others came from the Glen and from Fabyan's. Landlord Cavis kept some cows on the plateau, since known as the "Cow Pasture," near the seven-mile post of the carriage road.

The first woman to sleep in the house after its opening in August, 1853, was a Mrs. Duhring, of Philadelphia, who came up on horseback from the Crawford House and walked down. Twenty-four years later she revisited the Mountain.

From 1862 to 1872, the lessee of the Tip-Top House and Summit House was Colonel John R. Hitchcock, who was also the proprietor of the Alpine House in Gorham. He paid a rent of two thousand dollars a year after the first year. Colonel Hitchcock connected the two houses, and, after the completion of the carriage road, an upper story containing seventeen little bedrooms was added to the

MOUNT WASHINGTON

Tip-Top House. Mrs. Atwood, the housekeeper of the Alpine House, had charge of the Summit hotels, visiting them twice a week in a specially constructed light two-horse carriage. During the Hitchcock régime, in which baked beans, brown bread, and other simple dishes were chief features of the bill-of-fare, the business, especially after the building of the railway, far outgrew the accommodations. After the building of the new Summit House, the Tip-Top House was used by hotel and railway employees for a few years. From 1877 to 1884, the printing office of *Among the Clouds* was in the old hotel, its front room being equipped for that purpose in the former year. After that use of it ceased, the building, owing to dampness, fell somewhat into decay and came to be visited only as a curiosity. In 1898, an observatory was constructed at the western end to afford a good place from which to watch the sunsets.

But this ancient landmark was not destined to remain a curiosity only. As the sole survivor of the fire which devastated the Summit just before the opening of the season of 1908, the venerable structure had necessarily to be restored to its original purpose of a place of entertainment and shelter. As such it continued to be used until the opening of a new Summit House in 1915.

The next structure to be built on the Summit after the erection of the Tip-Top House was an observatory. Built in 1854, by Timothy Estus,[1] of

---

[1] So Spaulding. Professor Hitchcock, in *Mount Washington in Winter*, gives the builder's name as Timothy Eaton.

THE WHITE MOUNTAINS

Jefferson, it was a framework forty feet high supported by iron braces at the corners. It was provided with a sort of elevator operated by a crank and gearing and capable of accommodating eight persons at a time. This observatory, which cost about six hundred dollars, was abandoned as a complete failure after being used a part of the first season. It stood until the summer of 1856, when it was torn down.

No further buildings were erected on Mount Washington until after the building of the carriage road and of the railway, when the necessary structures for carrying on the operation of these means of visiting the Summit were erected. Soon the increase of business due to these agencies for making the peak more accessible necessitated the provision of greater accommodations for the shelter of visitors. From time to time, also, buildings for various other uses were added to the Summit settlement. The recording of the history of the later hotel and of the other structures referred to, however, properly follows the stories of the carriage road and the railway, and will be set down in due course after the latter have been related.

The construction of the first-named means of access to the summit of Mount Washington is a work which bears eloquent witness to the enterprise, courage, and persistence of its projector and builders. The road, which extends from the Pinkham Notch Road, near the site of the Glen House, to the Summit, is eight miles long and makes an ascent of forty-six hundred feet, the average grade being one foot in

HALFWAY HOUSE ON THE CARRIAGE ROAD

MOUNT WASHINGTON

eight and the steepest, one foot in six. To General David O. Macomber, of Middletown, Connecticut, belongs the credit for originating this undertaking. The Mount Washington Road Company was chartered July 1, 1853, with a capital of fifty thousand dollars. The company was organized at the Alpine House, in Gorham, on August 31 of that year, General Macomber being chosen president. The road was surveyed by Engineers C. H. V. Cavis and Ricker. Two incidents of the surveying period have been preserved by John H. Spaulding. One is the measurement of the height of the Mountain by actual survey made by the engineers in 1854, who arrived at 6284 feet as a result. The other incident was the dining, on July 16 of that year, of President Macomber, Engineer Cavis, and Mr. Spaulding in the snow arch. It was then two hundred and sixty-six feet long, eighty-four feet wide, and forty feet high to the roof. Mr. Spaulding records that, during the time spent in this somewhat rash action, icy cold water constantly dripped down around them and a heavy thundershower passed over them.

Construction was begun by Contractors Rich and Myers in or about the year 1855,[1] and within a year two miles were completed and further construction was under way. The section ending at the Ledge just above the Halfway House, a total distance of four miles from the beginning, was finished in 1856. Then the pioneer company failed, because of the great cost of construction. A new

[1] Mr. Spaulding notes that in June, 1855, the road is "in rapid progress towards completion."

THE WHITE MOUNTAINS

company, the Mount Washington Summit Road Company, was, however, incorporated two or three years later, and this company finished the road in 1861. Joseph S. Hall, one of the builders of the Tip-Top House, was the contractor for this work, and John P. Rich, the first contractor, was the superintendent. The road, which is splendidly built and which winds up the Mountain in long gradual lines of ascent, places where there are steep grades being rendered safe by stone walls on the lower side, was opened for travel on August 8, 1861.

The first passenger vehicle which arrived at the Summit — an old-fashioned Concord stage-coach with eight horses — was driven by George W. Lane, for many years in charge of the Fabyan House stables.[1]

The memory of Mr. Rich, who had so much to do with the construction of the road and who died in California in 1863, has been preserved by a tablet set in a rock by the roadside near the Glen and bearing a suitable inscription. Witness to the excellence of the engineering and construction work on the road, as well as of the care with which it has been maintained, is borne by its use for now more than fifty years and its well-preserved condition.

Striking as was this achievement in rendering the top of New England's highest mountain more ac-

---

[1] Landlord Thompson, of the Glen House, drove to the Summit in a light wagon with one horse, just before the road was completed, thus beating his rival for the honor, Colonel Hitchcock. Two men assisted in keeping the wagon right side up as he drove over the uncompleted last section of the road. Landlord Thompson was also in the first coach driven up.

MOUNT WASHINGTON

cessible, it was soon to be surpassed in boldness of conception and skill and successfulness of execution by another undertaking directed to the same end. I refer to the building of the Mount Washington Railway, the first railway of its kind in the world. The projector of this enterprise was Sylvester Marsh, a native son of New Hampshire and a Yankee genius. The idea that it was wholly practicable to apply the principle of the cog rail to a mountain railroad and the carrying out of the conception was only one of this ingenious New Englander's services to the world. Having gone West in the winter of 1833–34, when thirty years old, Mr. Marsh became one of the founders of Chicago, prominent in the promotion of every public enterprise there. He was the originator of meat-packing in that city and the inventor of many of the appliances used in that process, especially those connected with the employment of steam. The dried-meal process was another of his inventions.

When on a visit to his native State in 1852, he one day made an ascent of Mount Washington with a friend, the Reverend A. C. Thompson, of Roxbury. It was while struggling up the Mountain, or perhaps a little later, that the idea came to him that a railway to the Summit was feasible and could be made profitable. Very soon he set to work and invented the mountain-climbing mechanism, and then with characteristic energy and perseverance he fought his project through to completion against much opposition and ridicule. In 1858, he exhibited a model of the line to the State Legislature and asked

THE WHITE MOUNTAINS

for a charter to build steam railways up Mount Washington and Mount Lafayette. The charter was granted on June 25 of that year, one legislator, it is said, suggesting the satirical amendment that the gentleman should also receive permission to build a railway to the moon. Pecuniary support for so apparently ridiculous a proposal was difficult to obtain, and before anything could be done the breaking-out of the Civil War postponed action for several years more. Finally a company was formed, the necessary capital being furnished by the railroads connecting the White Mountain region with Boston and New York. At the outset, however, Mr. Marsh had to rely chiefly on his own resources, but little encouragement being received until an engine was actually running over a part of the route. Construction of the railway was at length begun in May, 1866, nearly eight years after the granting of the charter. In order to render its starting-point accessible, a turnpike from Fabyan's to the Base was begun in April of that same year.

As the railway is so important in the history of mountain railways a brief description of its mechanical features may not be out of order. The road is of the type known as the "cog road," or the rack and pinion railroad. The indispensable peculiarity of the invention is the heavy central rail, which consists of two parallel pieces of steel connected by numerous strong cross-pins or bolts, into the spaces between which the teeth of the cog wheels on the locomotive play. As the driving-wheel revolves, the engine ascends or descends, resting on the outer

MOUNT WASHINGTON

rails, which are of the ordinary pattern and which are four feet seven inches apart.

The first locomotive, which was designed by Mr. Marsh and was built by Campbell and Whittier, of Boston, was used until entirely worn out. Exhibited at the World's Fair in Chicago in 1893, it is now in the Field Museum of Natural History. It had a vertical boiler and no cab, and thus resembled a hoisting engine in appearance. The present type of locomotive was designed by Walter Aiken,[1] of Franklin, New Hampshire, who was the man to work out the practical details of Mr. Marsh's idea and who supervised the construction of the road. The engine is furnished with two pairs of cylinders and driving gears, thus guaranteeing ample security in case of accident. The car is provided with similar cog wheels to those on the engine and with brakes of its own, insuring safety independent of the engine. There are separate brakes on each axle of the car and an additional safety device on both it and the engine in the form of a toothed wheel and ratchet. This latter mechanism affords the greatest protection against accident, as it prevents the wheels of the car or of the engine from turning backward. It is, of course, raised during the descent, but it can be

---

[1] From an article by Mr. Aiken in *Among the Clouds* for September 1, 1877, it appears that Herrick Aiken, of Franklin, about 1850 conceived the idea of ascending Mount Washington by means of a cog railroad. He went so far as to build a model of a roadbed and track with the cog rail and to make two ascents of the Mountain on horseback for the purpose of determining the feasibility of the route, etc.; but he was dissuaded from undertaking the project by prominent railroad men whom he consulted and who thought it impracticable and unlikely to be profitable.

THE WHITE MOUNTAINS

dropped instantly into place in an emergency. The car is pushed up the Mountain and descends behind the locomotive, and is not fastened to it. The train moves very slowly, so slowly, indeed, that a person can easily, if necessary, step on or off while it is under full headway. Seventy minutes are required to make the trip up. The safety appliances, the powerfully constructed locomotive, the moderate speed, the constant inspection, and the experienced men concerned in the operation of the road have eliminated the element of danger from the trip. No passenger has yet been injured in all the years since the road's opening.

The route was surveyed and located by Colonel Orville E. Freeman, of Lancaster, New Hampshire, a son-in-law of the pioneer, Ethan Allen Crawford. Very appropriately, the course of the railway is substantially that of the latter's early path to the Summit. The length of the road is about three and one third miles, and the elevation overcome is about three thousand seven hundred feet. The average grade is one foot in four and the maximum thirteen and one half inches in three feet, or one thousand nine hundred and eighty feet to the mile. With the exception of the railway up Mount Pilatus in Switzerland, the Mount Washington Railway is the steepest in the world of the type of which it is the pioneer. The road is built on a wooden trestle all the way except a short distance near the Base, where the track lies on the surface of the ground.

But to return to its history. The first quarter of a mile was finished in 1866, and a test was made

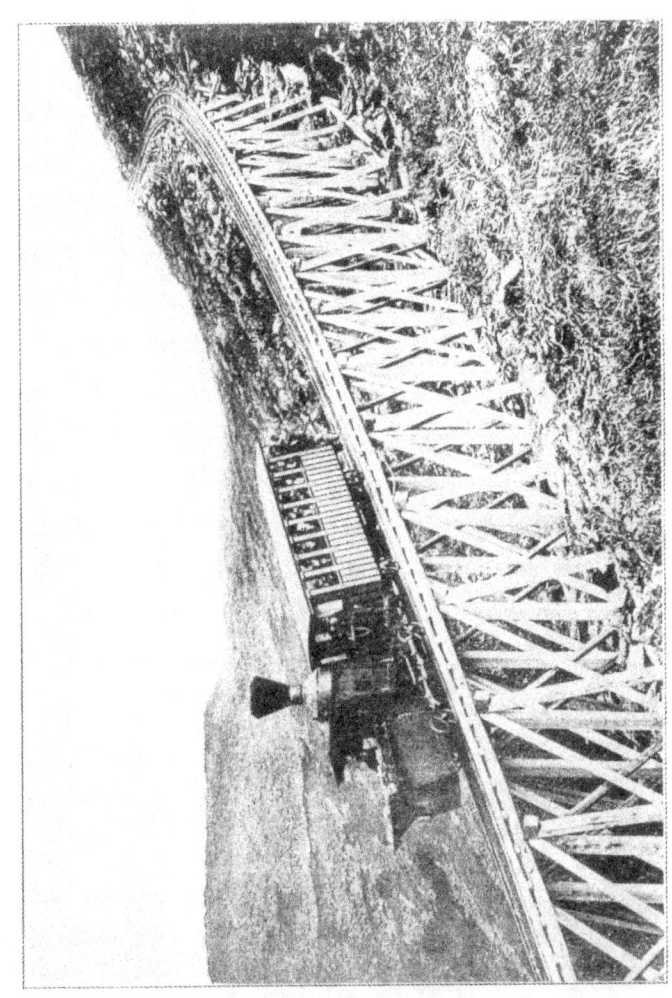

JACOB'S LADDER, MOUNT WASHINGTON RAILWAY
Showing the Early Type of Locomotive with Vertical Boiler

MOUNT WASHINGTON

which demonstrated the practicability of the invention. A half-mile more was completed in 1867, and on August 14, 1868, the railway was opened to Jacob's Ladder.[1] Before work on it stopped that year, construction was carried to the Lizzie Bourne monument. The road was finished the following year, being opened to the Summit for business in July. The cost of construction and equipment was $139,500.

At the time of its completion, the nearest railroad station was at Littleton, twenty-five miles distant. Every piece of material for the construction of the railway and the locomotive and cars, had to be hauled through the woods, it should be remembered, by ox teams.

I have spoken of the beginning of the construction of the turnpike to the Base. This was completed in 1869, and for many years afforded the only means of access to the railway, passengers being brought by stage over it from Fabyan's. It was owned for some years by the Boston and Maine Railroad, but has recently been turned over to the State.

A word more as to the railway's projector and inventor. Leaving Chicago, he returned to live in New Hampshire, settling at Littleton in 1864. He passed the closing years of his life in Concord, where he removed in 1879 and where he died in December, 1884, at the age of eighty-one, a public-spirited and highly respected citizen. He was asked to build the

[1] This name was transferred to the railroad from the path, having been given to the steep crag at this place, many years before the building of the railway.

THE WHITE MOUNTAINS

railway up the Rigi in Switzerland, which is patterned to some extent after the Mount Washington Railway, but he declined.

During the latter's construction, a Swiss engineer [1] visited the American railroad, and he was allowed to take back with him drawings of the machinery and track.

After the Swiss railroad was completed (1871), Mr. Marsh said of it, "They have made a much better road than mine. Mine was an experiment. When proved to be a success, they went ahead with confidence and built a permanent road."

A noteworthy incident of the first season of the Mount Washington Railway was the visit of President Grant, whose first term had begun the preceding March. His trip up Mount Washington was made in the course of a tour through the Mountains that summer with Mrs. Grant and some of their children. Another episode of this excursion has been

---

[1] This was Mr. Nicholas Riggenbach, then superintendent of the Central Swiss Railway, who took the first steam locomotive into Switzerland in 1847, and who appears to have independently conceived the idea of a new system of track and locomotives for the ascent of mountains. On August 12, 1863, he took out a patent for a rack railway and a locomotive for operating the same, but nothing further seems to have been done with the idea by him until after the visit to America mentioned in the text. On his return he associated himself with two others, got a concession, and built the road up the Rigi. The rack rail designed by Riggenbach is a distinct improvement upon that used by Marsh. Instead of a round tooth, it employs a taper tooth, which experience has shown to be preferable, inasmuch as it not only insures safe locking of the gear at different depths, but resists more efficiently the tendency of the gear-wheel to climb the rack — a further security against derailment. Riggenbach's type of tooth, with modifications, is that now used on rack railways. (From F. A. Talbot's *Railway Wonders of the World*. 1913.)

MOUNT WASHINGTON

preserved.[1] The general, as is well known, was a great lover of horses. One can imagine, therefore, his keen enjoyment, as he sat on the box with the driver, Edmund Cox, of a stage-coach which traveled, drawn by six horses, from the Sinclair House in Bethlehem to the Profile House, more than eleven miles, in fifty-eight minutes.

Accidents on the carriage road, so strong are the vehicles and horses used and so careful and reliable the drivers employed, have been few. The first by which any passengers were injured, and the only serious one I have found recorded, occurred on July 3, 1880, about a mile below the Halfway House. A company of excursionists from Michigan had been visiting the Summit that day, and the last party of them to descend, consisting of nine persons, were thrown violently into the woods and on the rocks by the overturning of the six-horse mountain wagon in which they were riding. One woman was instantly killed and several other occupants were more or less injured. The husband of the dead woman was riding at her side and escaped with a few bruises.

It seems that the driver, one of the oldest and most experienced on the road and one who had himself uttered the warning, "There should be no fooling, no chaffing, and no drinking on that road," had failed to practice what he preached, and, while waiting for his party at the Summit, had indulged in liquor. This lapse, most serious under the cir-

[1] Recorded by Alice Bartlett Stevens in the *Granite Monthly* for February, 1903.

THE WHITE MOUNTAINS

cumstances, was discovered shortly after starting, and the passengers thereupon left the wagon and walked to the Halfway House, four miles down. There, on being assured by one of the employees of the Carriage Road Company that there was no dangerous place below that point, and on his telling them further that he thought it would be safe for them to ride the remainder of the way with the same driver, they resumed their seats, only to meet, a few minutes later, in rounding a curve at too great a speed, with the sad mishap that has been described.

As has been already stated, no passenger has ever been even injured on the Railway. The only mishap of any consequence, and a most peculiar one, occurred about the middle of July, 1897, when a train consisting of a locomotive, passenger car, and baggage car was wrecked. A heavy gust of wind struck the train, which was standing near the Summit, with such force as to start it off down the line. It was found that about a quarter of a mile down the engine and baggage car had jumped the track, had turned over and over while falling a hundred feet or more into the gulf, and had become total wrecks. The man sent out to investigate on a slide-board reported that he saw nothing of the passenger car, but it was later discovered that this had left the track at a curve near Jacob's Ladder, had turned over, and had been completely demolished. Fortunately no one was on board.

Mention has just been made of the slide-board. This interesting contrivance was invented to meet the need of rapid transit for the workmen employed

MOUNT WASHINGTON

in track repairing and the like. By this means an experienced rider can go from the Summit to the Base in three minutes. The slide-board is about three feet long, rests lengthwise on the center rail, and is grooved so as to slide on it. The braking mechanism, by which the board is kept under such perfect control that it can be stopped almost instantly whenever necessary, is very simple. On either side of the board is pivoted to it a handle, to which is attached, near the pivot, a piece of iron bent in a peculiar form so as to project underneath the rail. By pulling up the handle this piece of iron is made to grip the flange of the rail very tightly.

It was formerly the practice for the roadmaster or his assistant to descend on a slide-board before the noon train every day, going slowly enough to make a careful inspection of the track. The death of an employee in performing this hazardous act a few years ago, which accident cost the Railway Company several thousand dollars in damages and made evident the liability to mishaps of this kind, has caused the discontinuance of the use of this dangerous means of conveyance.

A picturesque employment of the slide-boards in former days was as a "newspaper train." This novel enterprise was carried on in the early nineties, when the coaching parades at Bethlehem and North Conway were at their height, and there was thereby created a great demand for the issues of *Among the Clouds*, which contained accounts of the festivities. So that readers in those towns might have copies of

THE WHITE MOUNTAINS

the paper at their breakfast tables, some of the skillful coasters used to transport the morning edition down the Mountain before daylight.

After the completion of the railway, steps had immediately to be taken to remedy the woefully inadequate provisions for feeding and sheltering visitors, and, accordingly, in 1872, was begun the building of the second "Summit House," the famous structure which for thirty-five summers entertained so many people of various walks in life, — guides, trampers, railroad officials, scientific and literary men and women, clergymen, and just ordinary persons, — and which had a wealth of associations connected with it, and especially clustered about its office stove. The undertaking was financed by Walter Aiken, manager of the Mount Washington Railway, whose tall, stalwart form and sterling manhood is one of the memories of the early days, and President John E. Lyon, of the Boston, Concord, and Montreal Railroad, whose contributions to the development of the Mountains have been already mentioned. The hotel, which was completed early in 1873 and opened in July of that year, was of plain outward apppearance, but of the most rigid and solid construction possible for a wooden building. The difficulties of erecting so large a structure — it could accommodate one hundred and fifty guests — on a site where severe weather often prevails, are obvious as well as are the necessities for strong construction and for anchorage by bolts and cables. Two hundred and fifty freight trains were required to carry up the lumber, and the cost of the hotel, exclusive of the expense for freight (estimated at $10,000), was $56,599.57.

The excellence of the construction is evidenced by the fact that the solid frame withstood gales of one hundred and eighty-six miles an hour by actual record by the anemometer and very likely of higher unrecorded rates when no instrument or observer was there to tell the tale. Its cheerful office, with its great stove, was a welcome place to many a traveler arriving by railway, by carriage road, or by trail. Many a day weather conditions were such that visitors were marooned in the office during their entire stay on the Summit and were devoutly grateful for the hotel's hospitable shelter. Almost every evening of the season found a group of travelers whiling away the time enjoying the genial warmth of the stove and exchanging experiences of their mountain trips.

Notables who made longer or shorter stays there at various times, as recalled by Editor F. H. Burt of *Among the Clouds*, were Lucy Larcom, the poet; William C. Prime, editor, traveler, author, and angler; his sister-in-law, Annie Trumbull Slosson, entomologist and author, who came year after year for longer and longer sojourns and who latterly regarded the hotel as her home; the botanist, Edward Faxon; the entomologist, J. H. Emerton; E. C. and W. H. Pickering, the astronomers; the naturalist and author, Bradford Torrey; and among the cloth, Rev. Dr. W. R. Richards and Rev. Dr. Harry P. Nichols.

Day visitors of prominence were legion. Some names of such, culled from the pages of *Among the*

THE WHITE MOUNTAINS

Clouds in 1877, are those of President Hayes [1] and Mrs. Hayes, who, accompanied by William M. Evarts, Charles Devens, and D. M. Key, of the Cabinet, made their visit to the Summit on August 20; the Reverend and Mrs. Henry Ward Beecher on the same day; Vice-President Wheeler, on August 29, and in September, Sir Lyon Playfair, the eminent British statesman and scientist. Other noted visitors whose names are found in the records of later years were P. T. Barnum, General Joseph Hooker, General McClellan, Lord Chief Justice Coleridge, of England, who came on August 30, 1883, Phillips Brooks, Speaker Cannon, Lieutenant Peary, and Señor Romero, the Mexican Minister. In 1880, the eminent Scottish professor, William Garden Blaikie, spent "a night on Mount Washington," an account of which experience he gave in a typically British article with this title, published in *Good Words* in June, 1881. He went up by train and walked down the carriage road. As there was a cloud on top when he arrived, he walked down below to see the view and the sunset. "Nothing could be finer," he declared, than the dawn he witnessed.

The versatile English writer and scientist of Canadian birth, Grant Allen, was another foreign visitor to Mount Washington who deserves a passing mention. From his graphic and often facetious account of his brief visit to the Mountains in 1886, written for *Longman's Magazine*, we learn that he made the ascent by train and that he was much

[1] This was President Hayes's fifth visit to the Summit.

MOUNT WASHINGTON

interested in the botany — his specialty — and the gastronomy of the region.

The first proprietor of this new Summit House was Captain John W. Dodge, of Hampton Falls, New Hampshire, who also became postmaster by Government appointment when the Mount Washington post-office was established July 1, 1874, and who died in June of the following year. For nine seasons, a period ending with 1883, his widow, Harriet D. Dodge, successfully managed the house. Charles G. Emmons had charge for the two following seasons, and from 1886 to the end, the hotel was leased to the Barron, Merrill, and Barron Company by the railway company into whose hands, after the deaths of Mr. Aiken and Mr. Lyon, their interest passed. The Summit House was enlarged by the addition of an ell in 1874 and extensive improvements were made in 1895, 1901, and 1905.

From time to time, as need arose or circumstances required, buildings for various uses were erected on the Summit until a considerable summer settlement had been created. Besides such essential structures as the train shed, built in 1870 and subsequently blown down in a winter gale and rebuilt,[1] and the stage office, erected in 1878 by the owners of the carriage road for the accommodation of the agents and drivers of the stage line and sometimes used as sleeping quarters by trampers, several buildings came into existence for special purposes, which

[1] A third train shed — the one burned — was built about 1890. The second one, having become disused and dilapidated, was taken down in 1904.

THE WHITE MOUNTAINS

structures demand more attention than mere mention, either because of their uses or because of their associations.

When in May, 1871, the Government took up the work of maintaining weather-bureau service on the Summit, the observers, who were at that period detailed for this duty the year round by the Signal Service of the Army, were quartered in the old railway station, but in 1874 a wooden building, one and a half stories high, the so-called "Signal Station," was erected for their use.

At the beginning of 1880, the buildings on the Summit were the old Summit House, which, as has been stated, was then used as a dormitory for the hotel employees, the old Tip-Top House, the front room of which then served as the printing-office of *Among the Clouds*, the stage office, the train shed, the Signal Station, and the Summit House. Two more buildings were added to the group during the years soon following, to stand with the others until that fateful evening in June, 1908, when the results of so many years' development were reduced in a few hours to ashes and blackened ruins.

In the year first named the railway company erected a strong wooden tower, twenty-seven feet high and of pyramidal shape, on high ground near the southwest corner of the Summit House. It overlooked all the buildings and became a favorite observatory. For several summers it was used by the United States Coast and Geodetic Survey in the triangulation of the region. In 1892, the tower was carried up another story and, during that season

SUMMIT HOUSE AND OBSERVATORY, MOUNT WASHINGTON
ABOUT 1895

THE NEW SUMMIT HOUSE ON MOUNT WASHINGTON
ERECTED AND OPENED IN 1915

MOUNT WASHINGTON

only, a powerful searchlight was operated on it. Having fallen into decay and having become unsafe, this, the second observatory built on the Mountain, was pulled down in 1902.

Four years after the erection of the tower came the last addition to the group of buildings. This was a home for the Mountain newspaper, *Among the Clouds*, which had outgrown its quarters in the old Tip-Top House. In the autumn of 1884 was built the compact and cozy little office so well known to visitors for nearly twenty-five years. It contained a fully equipped printing-plant, with a Hoe cylinder press and a steam engine (superseded a short time before the great fire by a seven horse-power gasoline engine). Many a tourist here saw for the first time a newspaper plant in operation.

The same year saw another change in the Mountain buildings, for, as has been recorded before, the old Summit House was that year taken down, a wooden cottage being erected in its stead. Mention having just been made of the printing-office of *Among the Clouds*, and the establishment of that newspaper belonging chronologically to the period now under review, accounts of this unique journalistic enterprise and also of another similar undertaking may perhaps be interjected at this point.

The distinction of being the first and for many years the only newspaper printed regularly on the top of a mountain, and the further distinction of being the oldest summer-resort newspaper in America, belong to Mount Washington's daily journal.

THE WHITE MOUNTAINS

It was founded in 1877 by Mr. Henry M. Burt, of Springfield, Massachusetts, who had been connected with the *Springfield Republican* and various other papers, among them the *New England Homestead*, which he founded. In 1866, Mr. Burt published "Burt's Guide to the Connecticut Valley and the White Mountains," the preparation of which brought him first to Mount Washington. While spending a stormy day at the Summit House, in 1874, the thought of printing a newspaper on top of the Mountain came to him, resulting in the starting of *Among the Clouds* three years later, the first issue appearing on July 18, 1877. This unique and daring undertaking gained the admiration of all visitors, and the paper with so peculiarly appropriate a name soon filled a recognized position in White Mountain life. For eight summers it was printed in the old Tip-Top House. Thereafter until 1908, it was published in its own building, the erection of which in 1884 has been recorded. The genial editor, during the twenty-two years in which he conducted the paper, gained a host of personal friends among those frequenting the White Mountains and those carrying on business in the region. Since his death in March, 1899, his son, Frank H. Burt, has been its editor and publisher.

Before the great fire of 1908 deprived *Among the Clouds* of its well-equipped and appropriately located home, two editions were printed daily, the principal one being issued in the early morning. At 1 P.M. the noon edition, containing a list of the names of visitors arriving by the morning train, was ready

MOUNT WASHINGTON

for purchase as a souvenir by the traveler before the train departed on the downward trip.

Besides recording all events of interest relating to Mount Washington, together with news of the leading Mountain resorts, many articles of historical and scientific value have appeared in its columns, all of which contents have combined to make a complete file of *Among the Clouds* at any time, and now especially since the fire, a treasure indeed.

In view of the staggering blow that the paper received in the loss of its home and equipment before the opening of the season of 1908, it was thought best to omit for that summer the daily edition, which was done. Thus, for the first time in a generation the history of the summer's events had to go untold. The enterprising editors, however, far from being discouraged and from giving up all for lost even that season, showed their quality by preparing a "magazine number," containing a very complete and interesting record of the fire by pen and camera, and many facts and reminiscences concerning Mount Washington.

The failure to rebuild the settlement upon the Summit is responsible for *Among the Clouds* not being able to regain its ancient and proper seat, but publication was resumed on July 5, 1910, and the paper is now temporarily established at the Base.

The other journalistic enterprise referred to is that of a newspaper long widely known among Mountain visitors, *The White Mountain Echo and Tourists' Register*, the founding of which is almost contemporary with that of *Among the Clouds*. It

THE WHITE MOUNTAINS

was in 1878, at Bethlehem, that *The Echo* was started, the date of the first issue being July 13, and it has continued to be published there since. It is not, however, a local paper, but is devoted to the interests of the entire White Mountain region. Its founder and editor for twenty years, Mr. Markinfield Addey, had an interesting career. He was an Englishman, who, after serving in the publishing house of Chapman and Hall, had become a publisher on his own account. In 1857, when he was thirty-nine years old, his eyesight failed and he retired from business. The following year he came to America, where his eyesight improved. Twenty years later he founded *The White Mountain Echo*. Having entirely lost his sight in 1898, he gave up the editorship of *The Echo*, and returned to England, settling at Louth, in Lincolnshire. There he lived twelve years longer, dying November 18, 1910, at the age of ninety-two. He was "a bright, cheerful little man, of a very sanguine nature," always active in promoting by his pen and his influence the good of the Mountain region he had come to love so well. He lived to know of the carrying-out of many of the improvements he so earnestly and so long before had advocated.

The only White Mountain summit other than Mount Washington, upon which anything more than a temporary shelter exists to-day, is Mount Moosilauke. The beautiful Mount Kearsarge [1] of the Bartlett-Conway region formerly bore upon its

---

[1] Now to be called, in accordance with a decision (1915) of the United States Board of Geographic Names, "Mount Pequawket."

MOUNT WASHINGTON

top a small hotel, built, in 1848 or 1849,[1] by Caleb Frye, Nathaniel Frye, John C. Davis, and Moses Chandler, which was kept open for several years and then fell into disuse. Andrew Dinsmore bought it in 1868 or 1869, put it in thorough repair, and reopened it. The weather-beaten old structure was blown down in a tempest in November, 1883. Mr. Dinsmore collected the fragments and rebuilt the structure on a smaller scale. This has been abandoned of late years and is rapidly falling into decay. It is now the property of the Appalachian Mountain Club, the building and ten acres on the summit having been given to the Club in 1902 by Mrs. C. E. Clay, of Chatham, New Hampshire. A small one-room house of logs and poles was built on Mount Moriah by Colonel Hitchcock, of the Alpine House, probably in 1854. A road up having been constructed under his auspices, that mountain for a time rivaled Mount Washington in popularity. In the sixties a rude house for the protection of climbers stood on the crest of Mount Lafayette, but, except for the low stone walls, it had disappeared by 1875.[2]

Moosilauke was first climbed by Chase Whitcher, who, in 1773, when a boy of twenty, came from Salisbury, Massachusetts, and settled in Warren, devoting himself to hunting. On this occasion he was following a moose. He is said to have thought

---

[1] So Mrs. Mason. Sweetser says, "built in 1845."
[2] The substantial Peak House on Mount Chocorua, which was built in the early nineties, was not located on the summit, but at the base of the cone. This house was blown down on September 26, 1915.

THE WHITE MOUNTAINS

the summit "a cold place."[1] Mrs. Daniel Patch, the first white woman who ever stood upon this summit, evidently had a different reception as to weather from that given to Whitcher, for she thought it a pleasant place, and, having brought her teapot with her, made herself a cup of tea over a fire kindled from bleached hackmatack boughs.

The Tip-Top House of Mount Moosilauke — it was first called the "Prospect House" and is also sometimes spoken of as the "Summit House" — was originally a low and massive stone building, erected in 1860 by Darius Swain and James Clement. It stands on the south side of the crest or north peak.

The house was opened on July 4, 1860, with a grand celebration, in which more than a thousand people took part. Music was furnished by the New-

---

[1] The first printed account of an ascent appeared in the *American Monthly Magazine* for November, 1817, in an article on "The Altitude of Moose-Hillock in New Hampshire, ascertained barometrically," by Alden Partridge, Captain of Engineers. Captain Partridge, who was a graduate of West Point, founded in 1820 a military school at Norwich, Vermont, which was incorporated in 1834 as Norwich University. He was president of it until 1843. He appears twice in the pages of the *Crawford History*. In the autumn of 1821, he came to Mr. Crawford's with a number of cadets, and Mr. Crawford, being unable on account of lameness to act as guide, Mr. Rosebrook, his nearest neighbor, was sent for to pilot the party up Mount Washington. Again, on October 2, 1824, Captain Partridge came to Crawford's with fifty-two cadets. Taking a part of them with him, he went to "the camp" for the night, so that he might have the next day for making some barometrical observations. The remainder of the cadets, who overran the somewhat meager accommodations of Crawford's house, — some sleeping in beds, some on the floor, some in the barn, and some, for a time, even out-of-doors beside the fence, — made the ascent the next day, meeting the captain and his companions coming down. Captain Partridge computed the height of Mount Washington to be 6234 feet.

SUMMIT OF MOUNT WASHINGTON IN 1854
TIP-TOP HOUSE, OLD SUMMIT HOUSE, AND FIRST OBSERVATORY

TIP-TOP HOUSE ON MOUNT MOOSILAUKE

MOUNT WASHINGTON

bury brass band, and the citizens, a whole regiment of them, marshaled by Colonel Stevens M. Dow, marched and countermarched upon the mountain-top. The Honorable Thomas J. Smith delivered a patriotic oration, and the celebration concluded with a performance by a company of real Indians, who sang, danced, and sounded the war-whoop. Another incident of the day was the driving of a large two-horse pleasure wagon up the mountain by Daniel Q. Clement.

William Little was the first landlord of the Prospect House. Following him, Ezekiel A. Clement kept it for one season, and afterwards James Clement was "mine host" for years and years. The opening of the Prospect House stimulated several citizens of Warren to begin the keeping of summer boarders.

An occurrence of the first season of the hotel was the visit, on August 29, of Philip Hadley, ninety years old, who walked all the way from his home in Bradford, Vermont, to the top of the mountain.

The Moosilauke Mountain Road Company was incorporated in June, 1870, by John E. Lyon, Joseph A. Dodge, Daniel Q. Clement, Samuel B. Page, David G. Marsh, G. F. Putnam, and James Clement. The length of the road, which was immediately put under construction, is four and a third miles. The ascent is not difficult, and the road is kept in good condition. It starts from Merrill's Mountain House, at the base of the mountain, and meets the long ridge a short distance north of the south peak, and thence follows the ridge in a northerly direction.

THE WHITE MOUNTAINS

After the completion of the carriage road, the number of visitors to the summit was, naturally, much increased. In consequence the house was enlarged in 1872 by the addition of a wooden ell a story and a half high, and in 1881 a wooden superstructure was added to the original stone house, the capacity being thus raised to from thirty-five to fifty guests. The remoteness of Mount Moosilauke from the centers of White Mountain summer life and its position off the main routes of travel have made its summit a place far less visited by frequenters of the Mountains and tourists than it would otherwise be and less than it merits for its own beautiful configuration [1] and for the wonderful views in all directions.

[1] "With one bold curve it [the ridge] sweeps away in air.... There can be nothing finer than this curving crest," wrote the late Colonel Higginson in 1880.

XII

SOME NOTEWORTHY WHITE MOUNTAIN "CHARACTERS"

A NAME sometimes given to the Summit of Mount Washington in the early days was "Trinity Height," which must have been current before 1845, as it occurs in the "Crawford History," published in that year. It has also been handed down in connection with a peculiar episode recorded by Mr. Spaulding. In 1850, a man afflicted with religious mania regarded himself as having obtained by lawful title ownership of the top of Mount Washington, and, erecting gateways upon all the bridle paths, he exacted one dollar as toll from every person who ascended. He also issued in the papers of the day a flaming proclamation, of which the following is said to be a true copy: —

PROCLAMATION.

FOURTH OF JULY ON THE WHITE MOUNTAINS.

There will be a solemn congregation upon Trinity Height, or Summit of Mount Washington, on the Fourth Day of July, A.D. 1851, and 1st year of the Theocracy, or Jewish Christianity, to dedicate to the coming of the Ancient of Days, in the glory of his Kingdom, and to the marriage of the Lamb; and the literal organization in this generation of the Christian or purple and royal De-

THE WHITE MOUNTAINS

mocracy (let no man profane that name!), or the thousand thousands, and ten thousand times ten thousand of the people of the Saints of the most high God of every nation and Denomination into the greatness of God's kingdom and dominion under the whole heavens; and there will be a contribution for this purpose from all who are willing, in the beauty of holiness, from the dawn of that day.

        JOHN COFFIN NAZRO,
                Israel of Jerusalem.

"The appointed fourth of July was," says Mr. Spaulding in his book, "as dark and rainy as any, perhaps, that ever shrouded Mount Washington in wildly-flying clouds; and Nazro, meeting with strong opposition in toll-gathering, relinquished his temple-building designs, and, throwing away his gate-keys to the entrance of this mighty altar, retired to United States service, where, perchance, he may be now plotting the way to fortune among the clouds."

Years after the erection of the old Tip-Top House, a wrinkled, tanned, thin-faced man, who signed, "John C. Nazro, U.S.N.," was one day among the crowd registered at the hotel. Chaplain Nazro stated that the object of his visit was to collect the rents from those who were trespassing upon his rights. His friends, anticipating personal injury to him if he pressed his claims, dissuaded him from doing so. Being told by the occupiers of the houses that they paid annual rent to David Pingree, of Salem, Massachusetts, he took that name and address, but nothing was ever heard further from him.

It appears that Nazro's claim to the top of the Mountain originated in a joke practiced upon him

WHITE MOUNTAIN CHARACTERS

by Thomas Crawford, with whom he sojourned at the Notch House for some time. Mr. Crawford proposed to give him, in exchange for the manuscript of a history of the White Mountains, a good title deed to the Summit of Mount Washington, and, upon the manuscript being forthcoming, a written agreement was entered into, Crawford little thinking that any action would be taken in connection with it. The deed was, however, duly registered in the Coös County Registry of Deeds at Lancaster, and possession was then taken of the property in the manner already related.

A peculiar character whom many people still remember was the "Man at the Pool," John Merrill. In his time, indeed, he was as much an object of interest as that Franconia-Notch attraction itself. According to his own account he was born in Bristol, New Hampshire, in 1816 or thereabouts. In the course of his wanderings, he came to the Pool in 1853, and on this first visit he happened to meet a party of forty sight-seers who wished to get near to the fall. To accommodate them he set to work and constructed a rude boat, which he lowered down to the river by means of a rope. Thus, by chance he found what was to be his summer vocation for many years, as he was induced to return annually, and thus became an institution at the Pool. He spent his summers there until about 1887. His winters he was accustomed to pass in Wisconsin, from which place *The White Mountain Echo* last heard from him in 1888, when he made a request that the paper might be sent to him.

THE WHITE MOUNTAINS

From the Pool he carried away annually enough money to provide a comfortable living for the rest of the year. Indeed, it is said that the gratuities given him by tourists for paddling them over the Pool and for expounding to them his cosmogony were in the aggregate far from inconsiderable. While he was undoubtedly an oddity, it is hinted that there was method in his peculiarity, some of his notions and characteristics being assumed for their value in extracting money from visitors to this beauty spot.

Visitors to Bethlehem in the seventies and earlier used to see or hear about the aged eccentric, Sir Isaac Newton Gay, who celebrated his eighty-second birthday there, July 16, 1878. Although born in Old Ipswich, Massachusetts, he had at that time lived eighty-one years in Bethlehem, his family having been the seventh to arrive in the town. In 1855, he built a one-story loosely constructed building in the beeches opposite the Maplewood Inn. Not only was the man himself an oddity, but his "château" as well. Its interior, his front garden, and every nook and cranny in the vicinity of his domicile formed together a curiosity-shop of accumulated fragments. He followed the occupation of farming all his life, and entirely lost one eye by an accident which happened to him while working in the field. "If I had n't been a born philosopher," he is said to have remarked on one occasion, "I should have been a subject for the lunatic asylum." Questioned as to his peculiar name, he averred that it was given to him by his mother, and declared that it "suits me and I have always borne it."

WHITE MOUNTAIN CHARACTERS

There died near the end of April, 1912, the most picturesque of latter-day White Mountain characters, "English Jack," known to thousands of visitors to the region as the "Hermit of the White Mountains" or the "Crawford Notch Hermit." Jack spent his summers in an old shanty, which became known as the "House that Jack Built," and which was situated, at no great distance from the highway, in the woods above the Gate of the Notch. His house — "ship" he preferred to call it — was reached by paths from several directions, signboards indicating the way thither. Here in a low-ceilinged room Jack received his visitors. From the sale of picture postcards of himself, of a booklet containing what purports to be his life-story, told in rhyme by James E. Mitchell, and of other souvenirs, he acquired a considerable revenue.

He usually had some trout in a small aquarium just outside his door. Besides fish, it was commonly reported that snakes were sometimes articles of diet with him.[1] Asked about this rather queer taste attributed to him, he replied, "Well, they never ketched me at it, anyhow." For a beverage other than the cool sparkling water of the near-by brook or spring, Jack brewed a kind of beer out of hops and roots which grew near his hut, with which stimulant he sometimes regaled his visitors.

This singular individual, whose real name was John Alfred Vials (or Viles), was ninety years old when he died.

[1] *Among the Clouds* for July 25, 1877, tells of his eating half of an uncooked striped snake, "with apparent relish." This was done in the presence of a party of people from the Crawford House.

THE WHITE MOUNTAINS

According to the "Story of Jack," he was born in London and left an orphan at twelve, with one pound in gold as his whole fortune and with the sole ambition of going to sea. For days and days he frequented the docks seeking an opportunity to ship as cabin-boy, but in vain. Nobody would take him, and at last, tired and homesick, he sat down to cry. A five-year-old girl came toddling up and told him not to cry, saying that she was looking for her father's ship and that she was lost as well as he. Hand in hand, Jack and little Mary walked along the hot street, a sad pair. Mary suddenly saw her father on top of a passing omnibus, but he did not hear her call to him, so occupied was he in talking with his sailor mate. With quickness of mind and action, Jack pushed Mary through a door and ran after the omnibus, which he caught and mounted, blurting out, "Your little girl is gone!"

At that the father at once started off with Jack to find Mary, which they did to the father's and little daughter's great joy. When Jack told his tale, the grateful Bill Simmonds took the friendless lad home with him, and he and his wife cared for him. When Bill went to sea again, he got Jack a berth as cabin-boy on his ship. After sailing together for eight years in different ships, Bill and Jack, who had by this time become an able seaman, shipped in the good ship *Nelson* for the Indian Ocean. Jack, Mary, and her mother had forebodings that all would not be well on this voyage, but the men laughed them off and joined the crew.

Nothing untoward happened until the ship was

THE HOUSE THAT JACK BUILT

WHITE MOUNTAIN CHARACTERS

in the Indian Ocean, when one Sunday afternoon a terrible gale struck it. After running for hours before the hurricane, the ship was wrecked upon a small desert island. Jack, Bill, and eleven others were all that were saved out of the crew of forty-two. Water, fortunately, was found, but the only food to be had, after a water-soaked cask of bread was consumed, consisted of mussels, crabs, limpets, snakes, and the like. Before the rainy season came on, disease and death had reduced the company to four. For nineteen months the four lived on what they could pick up on the barren shore, and then Bill succumbed, his dying wish being that Jack would look after his wife and Mary and tell them about his end.

A week or so after Bill's death, there came a violent hurricane and when the storm had cleared off a sail was seen. The shipwrecked men's signal had been seen also, and the ship, an American one, rescued them. Jack's two companions died before they could reach home, and he alone of all the *Nelson's* company returned alive to London. When he had reported to the owners the fate of the ship, Jack started in search of Mary and her mother. After many days he learned that Bill's wife was dead and that Mary had been taken to the workhouse. Jack at once took her out and placed her in a school, paying her board for a year, and then took ship on a vessel bound for Hongkong. All went well with the sailor both on the outgoing and on the return voyage. Immediately after the ship's arrival at Liverpool, the anxious Jack took the train for

THE WHITE MOUNTAINS

London. When, however, he reached the school, he received the heart-crushing news that Mary had died just a month before.

Eventually, and against his wish, Jack recovered from the severe sickness caused by this blow to his hope and love. He then joined the navy, with the thought that death might overtake him in that service, but although he fought in many skirmishes and battles his life was spared through all. He tells in the "Story" of fighting in Africa to free the slaves, of going with Inglefield to search for Sir John Franklin's crew in the frozen North, and of serving through the Crimean War and in the Indian Mutiny. After traveling land and sea for many years, Jack left old England and came to America. Drifting to the Crawford Notch to work on the railroad, he came to like the region so much that he took up the life of a hermit there in the summer months. He used to spend his winters hunting, trapping, and making souvenirs to sell to his summer visitors. Latterly, in the winter, Jack lived with a family at Twin Mountain.

He was well read, it is said, in history and literature. He had spent much time and money in searching through advertisements and otherwise for his relatives, but, as he met with no success in this, he came to the conclusion that they were all dead. He had a kind heart. One way in which he manifested this was by assisting orphans and other unfortunates among the Mountains.

XIII

CASUALTIES ON THE PRESIDENTIAL RANGE —
THE TERRIBLE EXPERIENCE OF DR. BALL
— SOME DESTRUCTIVE LANDSLIDES

In the summer months the ascent of Mount Washington or the traversing of the Presidential Range is, if ordinary prudence be exercised, attended with only a trifling element of danger; just enough, it may be thought, to give a little added zest to the pleasures attending the excursion. The trails, moreover, are now so well worn and marked that guides are not needed. Indeed, if climbers would refrain from tramping alone, there would be almost no danger at all. A piece of recklessness on the part of a climber, an accident, and the remote chance of being overtaken by a storm are the causes of any peril which may be attached to the trip. The contingency of a cold and blinding storm above the tree-line is, of course, much greater in the autumn months than in the summer; the winter ascent is obviously hazardous as well as often extremely arduous. However, no fatalities have as yet occurred in the latter season, when the climb is not often attempted by any but experienced mountaineers in parties.

It was ascents made in October and September that led to the earliest losses of life on the Mountains. Furthermore, it was not until after the middle of the nineteenth century that Mount Washing-

THE WHITE MOUNTAINS

ton and the other peaks of the Presidential Range began to take their toll of human life. In view of the great number of ascents made before that time and of the circumstances that often the climbers were inexperienced persons and that in many cases untrodden and unmarked courses were passed over, the early record of no lives lost is remarkable. Much of the credit for the safety of such expeditions must rightfully be given to Ethan Allen Crawford and other guides of the pioneer days, to whom not a few climbers owed their freedom from injury or from a worse fate.

The first person to perish on the Mountains was the victim of his own rashness and obstinacy. Frederick Strickland, the eldest son of Sir George Strickland, an eminent member of Parliament, came to Thomas J. Crawford's Notch House one day in the latter part of October, 1851. An heir to large estates, a graduate of Cambridge University, and a cultivated scholar, he was then about thirty-five years of age. The next day after his arrival at the hotel, he set out, in company with another Englishman[1] and a guide, to ascend the mountains via the Crawford Bridle Path. On the summit of Clinton they encountered deep snow and a wintry wind,[2]

---

[1] So Mr. Willey, whose account is very circumstantial. The later accounts say nothing of the other Englishman. Mr. Willey gives the date of the ascent as October 19, and states that the body was found on the second following day.

[2] Mr. Willey says, "When they reached Mount Pleasant, the guide and the other Englishman, on account of the cold, and snow on the mountain, proposed to return." The later accounts say the party encountered a snowstorm. Mr. Spaulding, like Mr. Willey, says nothing of a snowstorm.

CASUALTIES ON PRESIDENTIAL RANGE

under which conditions the experience of the guide had taught him that it was imprudent to go on and so he advised a return. Strickland, however, was determined to proceed, and, delivering his horse over to the guide, he persisted, in defiance of the weather and the advice of the guide, in continuing the ascent on foot and alone. The guide and the other gentleman returned to Crawford's.

It had been the plan of Strickland to descend to Fabyan's, so Mr. Crawford sent his baggage there, with a message to the effect that its owner might be expected to stay there that night. As the young man did not put in an appearance, Landlord Fabyan thought he had returned to the Notch House. The next morning, Mr. Crawford, when passing, inquired for the Englishman, and when it was found that he had been seen at neither inn, the proprietors became alarmed and started in search of him. They tracked him to the summit of Washington and thence down the Ammonoosuc River, but found that day only some of his clothes. On the following day, they, with others, continued the search, and, after some time, the party discovered his dead body lying face downward in the stream. The unfortunate man had evidently fallen exhausted over a precipice.

It was nearly four years after the perishing of the young Englishman, Strickland, before another death was added to the record of fatalities on the Mountains. This time the life lost was that of a young woman, Miss Lizzie C. Bourne, of Kennebunk, Maine, daughter of Edward E. Bourne, Judge of

THE WHITE MOUNTAINS

Probate of York County. But she can hardly be called a victim of the Mountain's rigor, as her death was mostly due to a physical weakness, to the aggravation of which the difficulty of climbing the final mile or two against a gale of wind contributed. The chief element in the pathos of the occurrence is the knowledge that she was so near shelter and restoratives. The place of her succumbing being near the railroad track and the Summit House, and its proximate location being marked by a board monument, the fact of her fate has thereby become more widely known than that of any other person who has perished on the Presidential Range.

The story has been often told. In company with her uncle, George W. Bourne, and his daughter, Lucy, she started from the Glen House about 2 P.M. on September 14, 1855, the party's intention being to pass the night on the Summit. They walked up the carriage road as far as it was then built and left the Halfway House at four o'clock to complete the ascent by the path, which lay plain before them. Mr. Myers, the occupant of the House, tried, on account of the lateness of the day, to prevail upon them to stay there overnight, but "they were determined," he is reported to have said, "to go." About five o'clock, two sons of Samuel F. Spaulding, one of the proprietors of the Tip-Top House, met them about two miles below the Summit. They were then progressing well and evidently anticipating no trouble in finishing the climb. The weather was clear, but a high wind was soon encountered, against which they struggled until after dark. Then,

CASUALTIES ON PRESIDENTIAL RANGE

as Miss Lizzie showed signs of increasing exhaustion, as they were entirely ignorant of the proximity of the Summit, and as the darkness obscured the way and a cloud hid the Summit House, it was deemed impossible to proceed farther that night. So the young women lay down in the path, and Mr. Bourne, with great difficulty, succeeded in building a rude stone wall to shelter them from the gale. So far as his niece was concerned, however, his efforts proved vain to save her, for about ten o'clock he found her dead, the principal cause of her death being some organic disease of the heart. Her companions passed the night in safety, discovering at daybreak the melancholy fact of their nearness to the Summit. Miss Bourne, who was but twenty-three years old,[1] was buried in Hope Cemetery at Kennebunk, where was set up a large monument, which was intended, as its inscriptions testify, for the top of Mount Washington, but whose erection there was prevented by the temporary failure of the projected road.

The year following the death of Miss Bourne was marked by the Mountain's claiming of another victim, and, as in the case of the young Englishman, the fatality was due to the traveler's attempting the ascent without companions. On August 7, 1856, Benjamin Chandler, an elderly man of Wilmington, Delaware, started up the path from the Glen late in the afternoon, but was caught in a storm and

[1] The former board monument on the mountain-side gave her age as twenty; her age is given correctly on the present three-sided wooden monument.

THE WHITE MOUNTAINS

wandered from the trail. Two men who arrived at the Tip-Top House that day, at dark or a little after, reported passing an old gentleman halfway up and remarked that he would hardly get up alone that night. After making some inquiries, a guide started out with a lantern, but when he had gone nearly a mile, his light was put out by the wind. He then returned, having got no answer to his shouts, and the proprietor of the hotel concluded that the old gentleman must have stopped for the night with the road workmen camping at the Ledge. Search was resumed the next morning, but, as it was in vain, it was thought that the traveler might have turned back and have left the Mountain. Late in September, however, his son, David Chandler, came in search of his father and offered a reward for his recovery, and thus informed the people of the Mountain region that he was still missing.

For nearly a year Mr. Chandler's fate was unknown, although much time was spent in searching for his remains. Finally, in July of the next year after his disappearance, Ambrose Tower, of New York, came across a skeleton about half a mile east of the Summit. A gold watch, considerable money, a railroad ticket, and other articles were found with the skeleton, and there is no doubt of its being that of the unfortunate Benjamin Chandler, who was about seventy-five years old when he met his sad fate. In his memory the neighboring ridge has since been called Chandler Ridge.

Eighteen years after the death of Mr. Chandler, Harry W. Hunter, twenty-two years old, a printer

CASUALTIES ON PRESIDENTIAL RANGE

of Pittsburg, Pennsylvania, perished near the Crawford Bridle Path about half a mile from the summit of Mount Washington. Again the victim was a lone climber. On September 3, 1874, he left the Willey House in the early morning, after writing home that he was about to start to make the ascent. He did not appear at the Summit, and nothing was known of his fate until July 14, 1880, when three Amherst students who were climbing the Mountain saw what looked to be the body of a man partly hidden under an overhanging rock on the side of the cone. The object proved to be the remains of the unfortunate printer. Just how the young man met his death, of course, can never be known. The weather records for the day show that the weather was fair in its early part, but that a high wind was blowing at the time when he might have been on the portion of the trail northward from Mount Clinton, and that it rained from 3 to 9 P.M., at which latter time the temperature fell to 30°. Such conditions are sufficient to account for his fate. Very likely, exhausted by his exertions and chilled by the cold rain, he crawled into the crevice for such poor shelter as it afforded and there succumbed to heart failure. The place where his body was found is marked by a board monument, grim reminder of the peril of an unaccompanied trip over the Crawford Trail.

A peculiar accident, and one which furnishes a warning against similar temptings of fate, was responsible for another untimely and unnecessary death on the side of Mount Washington. On July 24, 1886, Sewall E. Faunce, a Boston boy, fifteen

THE WHITE MOUNTAINS

years old, when climbing through Tuckerman's Ravine, rashly stepped under the snow arch, which fell and killed him.

Eight years later, on July 2, there was a narrow escape from a similar fatality, which might have involved the loss of several or many lives. A party of fifty members of the Appalachian Mountain Club, which was holding a field meeting at the Summit, were making an excursion through Tuckerman's Ravine on that day. They had passed through the snow arch and had barely emerged, when one hundred feet of it fell, fortunately injuring none of them, although fragments of the snow struck several.

In the cases of the five persons who had lost their lives on the Range up to the time of the casualty now to be related, the bodies had been immediately, or, in one instance, eventually, recovered. That of the sixth victim, however, has never been found, and the circumstances and manner of his perishing and the resting-place of his remains are solely matters of conjecture. On Sunday, August 24, 1890, Ewald Weiss, a violinist of the Summit House orchestra, set out alone to visit the summit of Mount Adams. In fair weather the trail, as far as the base of the cone of that mountain, is not difficult to traverse or to follow; nor is the distance great. However, a severe storm came up and some time during it Weiss evidently met his death, as he was never seen afterward. That, bewildered by the storm, he wandered from the path and went or fell down into one of the ravines and there perished, or that one of the large jagged rocks with which the cone of

CASUALTIES ON PRESIDENTIAL RANGE

Adams is largely covered rolled from its place and crushed him, concealing his body from view, are two plausible guesses which have been made as to the mystery of his fate. In July, 1891, after two young men had reported finding, on the precipitous eastern face of the so-called Mount John Quincy Adams, a watch which was at first identified at the Summit House as that of Weiss, Professor J. Rayner Edmands and Charles E. Lowe, the well-known guide, started from the Ravine House to make a search for the remains or for traces of Weiss. At this time they found footprints which made them conclude that the violinist intended to reach Mount Madison, which discovery opened the whole of that peak as a hunting-ground for the unfortunate man's remains. Professor Edmands conjectured that Weiss may have fallen over an amphitheater of cliffs forming a branch of the Great Gulf.[1]

It was ten years after the mysterious death of the violinist Weiss before the death-toll of the Presidential Range received any further accessions. Then came the most unexpected and striking, so far, of the tragedies of climbing in the White Mountains, the double fatality which is constituted by the deaths of Curtis and Ormsbee on the Crawford Trail. Occurring at the time of year it did, it made a profound impression upon visitors to the Mountains in that season and in the following years, because of the demonstration the casualty afforded of the possibility, even in summer, of peril from weather

---

[1] From a letter of Professor Edmands to *The White Mountain Echo*, published in the issue of that paper for August 1, 1891.

THE WHITE MOUNTAINS

so violent as to be too much for even the most athletic and hardy to cope with successfully.

William B. Curtis,[1] of New York, a noted American amateur athlete, known to many friends as "Father Bill" Curtis, started, in company with Allan Ormsbee, of Brooklyn, also famous for his athletic prowess, to go up the Crawford Path on Saturday afternoon, June 30, 1900. It was their intention to join the members of the Appalachian Mountain Club, who had gone up by train that day, at the Summit House, where the Club was about to hold a field meeting. A storm was threatening, but as Curtis knew the trail well, the thought of harm was not seriously entertained. During the ascent, however, one of the most furious storms [2] ever known in the summer season broke upon them. Rain and hail, which changed to sleet and snow, were accompanied by a gale of nearly one hundred miles an hour.

---

[1] Mr. Curtis, who was at the time of his death sixty-three years old, was the founder of the Fresh Air Club of New York and one of the founders of the New York Athletic Club. He took up mountain-climbing late in life and was accustomed to climb alone and in all sorts of weather, thinly clad.

Mr. Ormsbee, who was in his twenty-ninth year, was a member of the Crescent Athletic Club of Brooklyn and of the Fresh Air Club.

[2] During this, "the storm of a century," which raged for sixty hours, more than forty panes of glass were broken in the Summit House. The temperature fell from 48° on Friday to 25° on Saturday morning, before the storm. Rev. Dr. Harry P. Nichols and his son, Donaldson, came up by the Montalban Ridge in this same storm and had a hard struggle to reach the Summit. They arrived at the open Boott Spur at 11 A.M. on Saturday, and by alternate rushings and crouchings they succeeded in crossing Bigelow's Lawn in two hours. On the cone the sleet was bitter and the rocks crusted with ice. Every one hundred steps required a pause behind some sheltering rock to recover breath and normal heart action.

CASUALTIES ON PRESIDENTIAL RANGE

All day Sunday the Club members were confined absolutely in the hotel, their minds filled with anxious forebodings as to the fate of the two trampers, whom they were powerless to aid in any way. When the terrible storm at length ended on Monday, and fair weather permitted a search to be made for the two men, the body of Curtis was found about noon, by Louis F. Cutter, lying on the path about two miles down, in the vicinity of the Lakes of the Clouds. Ormsbee's body was found late in the afternoon, by Professor Herschel C. Parker, within five minutes' walk of the Signal Station, at a point off the path, which he had reached after climbing, by efforts almost superhuman, over the icy rocks.

The two men were seen at 1.30 P.M. on the fatal Saturday, when they were on the south side of Mount Pleasant, by James C. Harvey, a workman from the Crawford House, who, with a companion, was engaged in cutting out growth on the path. He started after them and shouted, but did not succeed in overtaking or in stopping them. They signed the Appalachian Mountain Club roll in the cylinder on Mount Pleasant, giving the date and this note as to the weather: "Rain clouds and wind sixty miles — Cold." They were last seen alive by two Bartlett men, Charles Allen and Walter Parker, who had been employed by a camping party in the woods south of Mount Washington, and who, when on their way down, met Curtis and Ormsbee north of Mount Pleasant. Neither of the climbers made any reply to a warning to turn back.

The probable course of events may be inferred to

THE WHITE MOUNTAINS

be this: Mr. Curtis doubtless fell on the ice-coated rocks, for he had received a blow on the head sufficient to render him senseless. Ormsbee, failing to restore him, hastened, after providing such temporary shelter as he could for his companion, toward the Summit, which he knew was the nearest point where aid could be secured. There, two miles away, were many sturdy mountaineers.

If this hypothesis is correct, Curtis must have regained consciousness after Ormsbee had left him, and have endeavored to struggle on, for his body was found some distance beyond the place, under the lee of the larger of the Monroe summits, where evidence was found of an attempt to make a rude shelter.

Or, to give another supposition, when resting at this temporary refuge and taking counsel as to what course to pursue, they may have decided that there was no hope of survival unless they kept in motion, and so may have continued on from there, Curtis's fall occurring not long afterward on the spot where his body lay, and Ormsbee having then pushed on to get assistance. Or, again, Curtis may have been a few steps behind his companion and have fallen without the latter's knowledge in the thick fog and perhaps darkness.

However that may be, the pitiless storm and mountain were too much also for Ormsbee. Along the remaining portion of the trail he must often have fallen and so have severely injured himself, for his body was covered with cuts and bruises. Even after encountering such mishaps, although he must

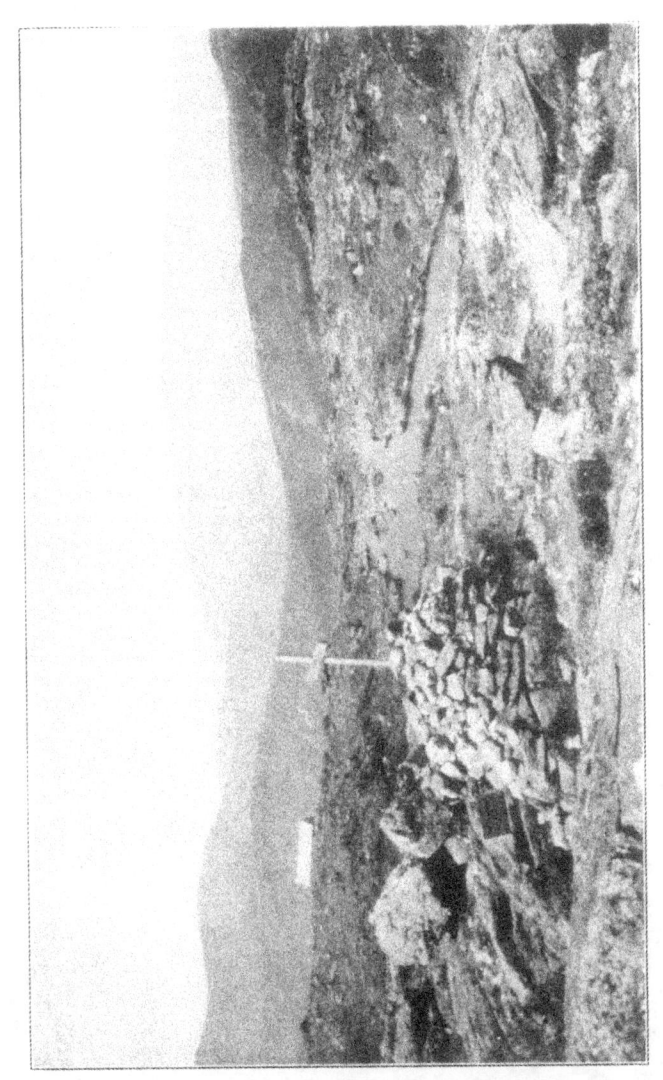

CURTIS MONUMENT, LAKE OF THE CLOUDS, AND A. M. C. HUT

CASUALTIES ON PRESIDENTIAL RANGE

have realized that the struggle to save his own life and that of his friend was probably hopeless, the heroic man did not immediately give up. His lacerated hands showed that he must have dragged himself for some distance over the jagged rocks before death overtook him.

The spot where Curtis's body was found is conspicuously marked by a pile of stones surmounted with a wooden cross and by a bronze memorial tablet fastened to the adjacent rock, and bearing this inscription: "On this spot William B. Curtis perished in the great storm of June 30, 1900. Placed by Fresh Air Club of New York." Fifteen hundred and eighty feet farther up the trail the Appalachian Mountain Club built the next summer a wooden shelter [1] where trampers may take refuge from the storms which sometimes sweep over the exposed southern trail, with the idea of minimizing the danger of such fatalities as have just been narrated.

The place where the stout-hearted Ormsbee's body was found is also marked by a wooden cross and a bronze tablet provided by the Fresh Air Club.

The latest fatality in the White Mountain region, which occurred in 1912, is in some respects the most singular of all. It is unlike all the other casualties in that the unfortunate man was not a pleasure-seeking tramper, in that he got off the dangerous upper mountain tract alive, and in that he was seen after he had reached the valley district by several persons, and yet was finally lost.

John M. Keenan, eighteen years of age, of Charles-

[1] Moved in 1915 about half a mile farther north.

THE WHITE MOUNTAINS

town, Massachusetts, was a new member of a party of engineers, who for two summers had been surveying the right of way for a proposed scenic railway up Mount Washington. Keenan arrived at the surveyors' camp at the Base of the Mountain on Friday, September 13, and the next day began his work as rear flagman. His duties for the next few days kept him near the Base, but on Wednesday, the 18th, he went to the Summit with a party of experienced engineers. After reaching the Summit the surveyors descended the cone to a point below the Ormsbee monument and in the direction of the Lakes of the Clouds. The chief gave instructions and placed his men in various positions, Keenan being told, as a man unfamiliar with the ground, to remain at his station until he was signaled to come up to the Summit, or, if it clouded up, to stay there until they came for him.

Although the sky was overcast and the wind on the top was blowing more than fifty miles an hour, the Mountain was free from clouds the early part of the forenoon. The surveyors had not been long separated, when a heavy cloud, in which objects could scarcely be seen ten feet away, enveloped the Mountain. Coming to the conclusion, after a little while, that conditions were not likely to improve, but rather appeared to be getting worse, the chief decided to go back to get Keenan and to go then up to the Tip-Top House. On reaching the position where Keenan had been stationed, they found that, contrary to orders, he had left. This was at 10 A.M. The party searched in that vicinity until noon with-

CASUALTIES ON PRESIDENTIAL RANGE

out success, and then went to the Summit, whither it was thought the lost man might have gone. Finding that he was not there, and learning on telephoning to the Base that he had not arrived at that point by the afternoon train, as was thought possible, the alarmed men took up the search again and continued it, but in vain, until nearly dark, when they had to desist on peril of losing their own lives.

When the surveyors arrived at the Base that night and told the story of Keenan's disappearance, word was at once sent to the various Mountain centers to be on the lookout for the missing man. The bell on the Summit was kept ringing all night, while at the Base the steam whistle was blown at intervals.

Thursday a large party, composed of the surveyors and others, made a fruitless search of the entire cone of Mount Washington in dense clouds. The search was continued Friday under dangerous weather conditions, as the clouds had not lifted and the fall in temperature had caused the rocks to become coated with ice. That night word was received from the Honorable George H. Turner, of Bethlehem, who with Dr. Gile, of Hanover, had been out making a tour of inspection of State roads on that day, that between 11.30 A.M. and 12 M. they had passed a man who answered the description of Keenan, at a point on the Pinkham Notch Road about two miles below the Glen House. The man was standing beside the road and appeared almost demented. As the automobile passed, he

THE WHITE MOUNTAINS

waved his arms and pointed toward Mount Washington, but did not speak. Unfortunately, Mr. Turner did not know until he reached Fabyan that a man had been lost.

This information made it evident that Keenan had succeeded in getting off the Mountain. How he accomplished this will never be known. He naturally at the outset traveled with the wind, which course would take him into Tuckerman's Ravine. Down the precipice he must have managed to slip, slide, crawl, and fall, evidently arriving at the Pinkham Notch Road in sound physical condition, a remarkable outcome under the circumstances.

The searching party, which was spending the night on the Summit, was communicated with, and told to go at daybreak to the Glen House and start a search from there. Several experienced guides had in the mean time been hired by the railway company and they also were ordered to the Glen. When the party arrived at its new field of search, Fire Warden Briggs was found at his camp and inquiry was made of him as to whether he had seen anything of the lost young man. It was then learned that the fire warden had met a man answering Keenan's description on Friday morning, when coming down a lonely log road near the point where Mr. Turner passed him. From what the stranger said there is no doubt that he was Keenan. His mental condition was evident from his rambling and somewhat unintelligible talk, in the course of which he said he was looking for the Keenan farm. Briggs at the time had not learned of any one having been lost. Knowing that

CASUALTIES ON PRESIDENTIAL RANGE

there was no such farm in that region, he did not credit this and some others of the man's statements.

After being brought down to the State road and being shown the way to the Glen House, Keenan bade Briggs good-bye and started about 11 A.M. in that direction. Briggs then went to his camp, and, being accustomed to meet strange-looking persons in that locality during the summer, he gave no further thought to the man he had seen until the searching party visited his camp.

During the disagreeable weather which continued through Saturday, the searchers covered carefully the ground between the Darby Field and the Glen House, but without avail. Sunday the 22d, the first clear day after Keenan was lost, they were joined by fully one hundred voluntary searchers from Gorham and other places in the Mountains, and, although every foot of ground on both sides of the road for more than a mile was gone over and other ground was covered and Milliken's Pond drained, no trace of Keenan was found. His father, Lawrence J. Keenan, came on from Boston and was with the searchers all day Sunday, returning to his home that night satisfied that a thorough search had been made and that there was no chance of finding his boy alive. Search was discontinued on Monday, except by the experienced guides and a few of the surveyors, who went again over the territory.

In the mean time it was rumored that a man by the name of Lightfoot, who was following Mr. Turner in an automobile, had picked up a man thought to be Keenan. This story, which was at

THE WHITE MOUNTAINS

first contradicted and thought to be false, turned out to be true, and, when its details became known, it threw a new light on the mystery. Lightfoot, a chauffeur of Bethlehem, was carrying the highway officials' baggage in his own car behind them. About noon, and about half a mile beyond the Glen House toward Jackson, he was stopped by a young man who asked him for a ride and got into the vehicle. Although Lightfoot knew that a surveyor had been lost on the Mountain, he did not until later, after seeing Keenan's picture in a Boston paper, connect the coatless and evidently demented passenger with the missing man.

The chauffeur carried Keenan about two miles, and at his request let him out at the deserted lumber camps near the Darby Field, not looking, in the hard rain, to see just where he went after getting out. When this story was told a few days later, another searching party was organized and the territory where the poor fellow was last seen was covered, but without success. The most likely supposition as to what became of him is that he wandered in his dazed, helpless way up some of the old log roads and through the thick woods toward Mount Washington, until, exhausted from hunger and exertion, he sank down.[1]

The record of having endured probably the most terrible of experiences, and certainly the most prolonged of all encounters, with the fury of the Moun-

---

[1] I am indebted for my account of this casualty to Reginald H. Buckler's very full and comprehensive account published in the issues of *Among the Clouds* for July 15, 16, and 17, 1913.

CASUALTIES ON PRESIDENTIAL RANGE

tain weather in the history of White Mountain climbing, and of having, in spite of unexampled hardship and great agony, survived to tell the tale, belongs to Dr. B. L. Ball, a Boston physician. His almost miraculous escape from death under the conditions he met with was due in part to his medical training, which made him know the fatal consequences of permitting himself to go to sleep, and in part to the fortunate chance, as it turned out, that it was raining when he began his ascent and also when he continued it on the second day from the Camp House, which circumstance caused him to take his umbrella.

Dr. Ball had been an extensive traveler, having visited only a short time before this adventure the Philippine Islands and Java, where he had successfully achieved on the third trial the difficult ascent of the cone of the Marapee. He had crossed the Bernese Alps, wading much of the way in deep snow, and had, against the protestations of guides, persisted in climbing a snowy peak near the Bains de Leuk, also in Switzerland. So he was an experienced mountaineer, thus well prepared for coping with any conditions he was likely to meet with in climbing Mount Washington.

Dr. Ball had intended to make his excursion to the White Mountains as early as midsummer of 1854, when he had just returned from Europe, as he "was desirous of comparing some of the finest American scenery" with that he had just seen abroad. But his engagements prevented, and the summer of 1855 was also occupied, much of the

THE WHITE MOUNTAINS

time with the preparation and publication of his "Rambles in Eastern Asia," so that it was the middle of October before he was free to carry out his design.

He had regarded October as too late, thinking that the autumnal scenery must have lost much of its attractiveness and that the weather would be too cool on the Mountains, but friends had told him that he would probably be repaid for the journey even as late as the first of November. Added to this encouragement was the inducement that two former traveling companions in the Philippine Islands had started about the middle of October to visit the White Mountains and Niagara Falls to take sketches and would be at the Mountains at the end of a week, where he had partly arranged to meet them. While he was awaiting a prospect of pleasant weather, the 23d of October arrived, promising to be the beginning of a period of such weather. The previous evening in making a call at a friend's house, he met and conversed with the Reverend T. Starr King, whose description of the grandeur and beauty of the scenery, and expression of a wish to view the Mountains in autumn and in winter, gave him an additional motive for visiting them at this season.

Dr. Ball then resolved to go, his intention being to make an expeditious trip and to return on the third day. The engagements of his friend, Dr. A. B. Hall, who had expressed a desire to accompany him, preventing that gentleman's leaving for two or three days, Dr. Ball determined to go alone. When at

CASUALTIES ON PRESIDENTIAL RANGE

length his mind was made up to attempt the excursion, he, by making haste, reached the railroad station just in time for the train for Portland. Arriving at that city a little after dark, he was disappointed to find that there was no train for Gorham that night. When he arose the next morning, a greater disappointment was his, for it was raining hard and bid fair to continue stormy. Had he obeyed his first impulse, he would have returned to Boston, but the second thought that it might possibly clear in a few hours, and that if he should get but a glimpse of the Mountains he would return better satisfied with his trip, made him resolve to proceed to Gorham, where he arrived about 11 A.M. Inquiring of the train conductor as to the location of the Mountains, and being told that he would not be able to see them in such weather short of the Glen House, he decided to go thither. So engaging a horse, he set off on horseback, with his valise in front of him and his umbrella up to protect him from the rain. On arriving at the hotel he found a dense fog prevailing. It had been his intention to stop there but a half-hour and then to return, but, after inquiring for his two friends who, he was informed, had not been there, he engaged in conversation with the landlord, Mr. Thompson. The latter in the course of their conversation told him of the carriage road then under construction, of the Camp House and Ledge, four miles up, and of the bridle path to the Summit. This information caused Dr. Ball to change his mind about his length of stay and to form the purpose of walking up the road a distance, perhaps as

THE WHITE MOUNTAINS

far as the Camp House, which design, in spite of Mr. Thompson's discouraging declaration that there would be nothing to see and his warning against attempting to go to the Summit, he immediately put into execution. Although it was raining hard, he felt stimulated by the cool, invigorating air and so continued his walk, to find himself in less than two hours at the end of the road and at the foot of the Ledge. Here a less determined man would have been satisfied to stop, particularly under the weather conditions then prevailing, but the doctor concluded he would go to the top of the Ledge, and accordingly, he clambered up there, "without much difficulty." Perceiving higher land beyond, he started for it, but progress became very slow and fatiguing, with a chilling wind blowing, the rain freezing upon him, and his feet breaking through the crust of snow at every step. So after about an hour's traveling, he turned to retrace his steps. In the gathering darkness, he ran down and managed after much difficulty eventually to reach the Camp House, where, arriving encased in ice and thoroughly chilled, he was hospitably received by its occupants, J. D. Myers and two others, everything in the way of restorative measures that kindness and experience could suggest being done for the unexpected guest. Accepting an invitation to remain until the next day, he passed a comfortable, but sleepless, night.

Little did he think, when he awakened in the morning, of what was before him, of the terrible experiences his persistency was to bring upon him that day and the two following, and of the suffering

CASUALTIES ON PRESIDENTIAL RANGE

and even agony he was to be subjected to for weeks and months afterward. When he walked out to view the prospect, the weather had softened, and although clouds hung over the Mountain, there was little rain, and they seemed likely to break away. The bridle path was pointed out to him, and, as it was then free from snow, he formed the project of making a short trip over the Ledge and perhaps of going on to the Summit, persuading himself to this course chiefly by reflecting that he was already halfway up and that a convenient opportunity might not present itself another season.

Despite the warnings conveyed in the not altogether encouraging remark of Mr. Myers as to the inadvisability of attempting such a trip at such a time and in his recital of the circumstances of the then recent death of Miss Bourne, Dr. Ball determined to go, and so, after an almost untasted breakfast, started out, shod with his host's "much too large," but stout, thick boots, provided with a cane presented to him by the same kind-hearted man, and protected from the sprinkle by the providential umbrella.

At first he made good progress, and with little fatigue he reached the top of the Ledge, where, however, the view was, owing to the fog, of but very limited extent, only the Camp House and its immediate surroundings being visible. Soon, as he went on, the path became no longer discernible, losing itself so gradually that its termination could not be detected. Pressing on, following the rise of land and passing what he calls the "first mountain,"

THE WHITE MOUNTAINS

the way became more difficult and fatiguing, his feet breaking through the crust and being often difficult to extricate. His natural determination and the lure of an occasional breaking-away of the clouds made him continue on, when the greater consumption of time than anticipated and the increasing difficulty counseled abandoning the project. "Between the second and third mountains," the air grew disagreeably cold, the rain changed to sleet and soon to fast-falling snow, and the wind increased. Pressing forward, he at length, after many wanderings from his course, reached "the summit of the third mountain." There he was at a loss what direction to take, but, believing that he was three-fourths of the way up, and having been told that he would find provisions, materials for fire, and clothes and bedding for the night at one of the two houses on the Summit, on he resolved to go.

In spite of the piercing cold and the violent wind, which made the storm difficult to face, and the clouds of snow, which rendered it impossible to see more than a very short distance, this man of indomitable will and amazing hopefulness, lured by the thought that he was within half or three-quarters of a mile of comfortable shelter and the possibility that the storm might in a short time be over, went on with renewed energy. He walked as fast as his partly benumbed legs would permit, buffeting the cold storm. Many times the wind threw him to the ground, but, although his face became covered with ice, a row of icicles two inches long depended from his cap, and his eyelashes were filled with icy globules,

CASUALTIES ON PRESIDENTIAL RANGE

and although he began to think the condition of affairs had become somewhat desperate, he resolved, believing that he was on the "fourth mountain," to try for the Summit House.

After an hour's painful exertion against a storm which, instead of abating, appeared to increase, and in which he could advance only by plunging forward by aid of his cane in the intervals of the gusts, he arrived upon a piece of comparatively level ground, which he took to be the summit of Mount Washington. His self-congratulation upon his supposed success was damped by the condition that now confronted him, for, if the storm had seemed violent elsewhere, in this exposed place it had a fury that was indescribable. "If ten hurricanes had been in deadly strife with each other, it could have been no worse," he says. His freezing hands and benumbed limbs and the increasing laboriousness of respiration admonished him that he must find the Summit House if he would live. So he groped on with the greatest difficulty in the whirling snow, seeking the desired shelter, blown along or prostrated by turns by the powerful wind, and aware that he was becoming frozen.

Twice he went in the direction of darker shades which he thought might be the hotel, only to find on reaching the objects that they were piles of rocks, in one case evidently a landmark or a monument. Unwilling to give up, although coming to think that the mountain he was on might not be the Summit, he persevered for a while longer in his search, but in vain. Seating himself in the slight

THE WHITE MOUNTAINS

shelter of a rock, to consider the best course to pursue, he remained there until he became aware that he was as if riveted to the ground and that a delightful drowsiness was stealing over him. Knowing that he must rouse himself, he raised himself with considerable effort, and, reluctant even then to abandon his project, made one more trial, which ended as had his other exertions. This time he found that the land descended in every direction and, knowing that he could not hold out much longer, he finally decided to make his way back. It was then, as he judged, about the middle of the afternoon, so delay was dangerous and some degree of haste was demanded.

At first, in retracing his course he tried to find his footprints in order to follow them back, but they were irregular and at times partly obliterated or lost altogether, so that much time was consumed in searching for them. Finding his strength rapidly failing from the cold, he believed it more prudent to abandon search entirely, and, guided only by the fall of the land, to undertake the descent. The furious wind enveloped him in snow, he was compelled to gasp and hold on to the rocks for minutes at a time, and frequently a sudden gust threw him down, causing him to receive many bruises from the hidden stones.

Before he had proceeded far, he came upon a stake standing a few inches above the snow. Advancing he saw others and noticed that they were at regular distances. They were surveyors' marks for the contemplated road to the Summit; and when

CASUALTIES ON PRESIDENTIAL RANGE

the doctor realized what they were, he at first had the thought of trying to follow them up to the goal of his desire, but various considerations, such as the possibility of their not extending all the way, his condition, and the lateness of the day, decided him to go downward only. So on he went as best he could, and at length a patch of thick, stunted brushwood appeared before him, indicating that he had reached the line of vegetation. Here he soon could discover no more stakes, and to his consternation observed that night was fast coming on. Being in doubt what course to pursue and knowing nothing as to where he was, he continued downward for some little time against many obstacles, until the gathering darkness made it evident that he should have to pass the night out on the Mountain. Perceiving that he was fast freezing and knowing that his own exertions were all he had to depend upon, he looked around for shelter, but in vain. Finally, stopping on a flat rock, and casting his eyes about, he saw a small recess between it and a low patch of firs. Then he found a use for the umbrella, for opening it over him, and below the firs, he utilized it as a shelter, fortunately finding a strong root at hand in the snow, to which he managed, with great difficulty on account of the numbness of his hands, to fasten the handle by means of a small cord. After a short rest, he set to work, with all his remaining strength, pulling up the tough bushes by the roots and piling them upon the umbrella to protect it from the wind. The sides of his camp he made tight with crusts of snow and tops of fir trees. At-

THE WHITE MOUNTAINS

tempts to build a fire were unsuccessful because of the dampness of the wood and the force of the storm. In this frail shelter the doctor passed the night — the longest of his life, he pronounces it. Knowing too well the fatal consequence of indulging in even a few minutes' sleep, and feeling that, with his stiff and frozen feet and the freezing chill of his body, he might be soon overpowered, Dr. Ball exerted himself to his utmost to keep awake. By taking constrained positions, now leaning on one elbow, then on the other, now changing from side to side, now taking a forward position, then a backward one, now extending at full length and now drawn up, he succeeded in preventing sleep. During the whole night the storm swept down the mountain-side, with such violence that he feared many times it would carry away the umbrella and leave him exposed to certain death.

But no such disaster happened, and at length morning — it was Friday, October 26 — dawned. The snow had ceased falling, but the keen wind still blew hard and clouds obscured the sun and shut out all the view below him, while above the air was clear. It seemed to him, so numb was he, that he had become a part of the Mountain itself, but arousing himself and exercising to restore warmth and animation to his feet, he contrived with the aid of his cane to ascend to the line where vegetation ceases, to reconnoiter. But nothing to guide him could be seen, clouds being above him and below. Searching diligently for the stakes, he was unable to find them beyond this place, and so was disap-

CASUALTIES ON PRESIDENTIAL RANGE

pointed of any guidance they might furnish him. It was difficult to determine on what course of action to pursue. He had no wish to go toward the supposed Mount Washington, — the mountain, he learned afterward, was Mount Jefferson, — which was on the right. Reasoning that if he made a circuit of the Mountain he should somewhere cross his track of ascent, which he might follow down, he started off toward the left. The ground was covered with snow to the depth of eight or ten inches, and he could travel but slowly on account of his weakness and various difficulties in the way. At nearly every step his feet broke through the crust, and he several times had to make considerable détours to avoid obstacles. Vainly he tried to quench his burning thirst with ice, which he broke from the rocks.

He traveled for about two hours toward a place which showed some appearance of a path, and about noon, as he judged, he arrived near it, but to his disappointment, he could discover nothing that looked like an outlet.

Discouraging as it was, there was no other course but to retrace his steps. It had taken him four hours to reach where he now was, and, knowing that it would take at least as much time to return, he walked along as fast as the nature of the way and the clumsiness of his frozen feet would permit. As he approached the place of the previous night's shelter, the clouds cleared away so that he could see below, but nothing was visible but forests and another range of mountains beyond them. Hearing a clinking noise he looked around and saw upon the

THE WHITE MOUNTAINS

top of the bluff two men, apparently standing together. Thinking now that help was at hand, he hallooed repeatedly. But his voice died away on the wind, and, discerning no movement in them, he at last concluded that they might be rocks with shapes like men, and, although he did not give up trying to attract their attention, he continued on. It was impossible for him to reach them. The men — for men they were and not rocks — were two guides who had been sent out to look for Dr. Ball by Landlord Thompson, of the Glen House. They found the doctor's tracks and followed them to within half a mile of his place of shelter, but night coming on, they despaired of finding him and returned home. Probably on account of the high wind no sound of his voice reached them.

Arriving near the place where he had spent the painful previous night, Dr. Ball observed that the sun was sinking, and, as the clouds gathered around closer and thicker and the cold was intense and piercing, and as, moreover, in his weakened condition he could do nothing in the way of searching for an outlet farther on to the right, he was soon forced to the melancholy conclusion that he must pass another night on the Mountain. Failing, after about half an hour's search, to find a more comfortable place in which to stay, he, with some difficulty in the storm and darkness, made his way to the sheltering rock and fastened his umbrella in the same place as before, endeavoring, but with not much success, to close it in more securely than it had been the night before.

CASUALTIES ON PRESIDENTIAL RANGE

The second night passed much like the first. It stormed and snowed all night, the snow drifted in a good deal, and the wind came in violent gusts, threatening to destroy at times his only shelter. His sufferings from thirst were almost intolerable, his throat and stomach feeling as if they were scorched. The crusts of frozen snow alleviated his distress only while he was swallowing them. His respiration became short, his lungs apparently becoming incapable of inflating to more than about half their natural capacity, he continually experienced a severe pain in his left side, his pulse was accelerated, but much reduced in force, labored, and very intermittent, and his entire muscular system was affected with uncontrollable shaking. Sleep was warded off by keeping the mind active by a multiplicity of thoughts and by taking constrained positions as on the night before. He would have given way, he feared, had he made the effort only to keep awake, with no other exercise of the mind than thinking of the cold.

The long night was over at last and the breaking of dawn gladdened the heart of the sufferer. On looking off, after a while, he saw through the dry brush a building several miles away in the valley below on the other side of a large forest. He was somewhat perplexed as to the identity of the house, although he knew of no other house very near the Mountain, his confusion being due to his mistaking Mount Jefferson for Mount Washington, which latter is not visible from the place where he was.

When he realized that the building was not a

THE WHITE MOUNTAINS

product of his imagination, he crawled forth to the front of the rock to reconnoiter, supporting himself on it and stamping his feet to restore animation to them. After about two hours he was able to walk, and then with painful steps he ascended to the tract above the brush to get a clear view to aid him in determining the course to be pursued. Deeming it unwise to take a straight line down the Mountain and through the forests to the Glen House, because of the obstacles and the chances of losing his way, he decided that he ought to encircle the Mountain in the opposite direction from that of the previous day, and, accordingly, he started off in that direction, hobbling along in his enfeebled condition, his mind supported by the hope that each step was bringing him nearer the outlet.

Toward the middle of the day he halted upon an elevated flat rock to look about and lay out a course as free as possible from impediments. Before, however, he could adopt his plan of taking a range, if possible, a hundred feet higher up the Mountain, as he was about to move on, to his "joy and astonishment," he saw a party of men just coming into view around the angle of the bluff. They appeared to be looking for some object in the snow. Without any thought that they were searching for him, Dr. Ball shouted to them, whereupon they all stopped short and looked at him with manifest amazement. Soon Mr. Hall, one of the proprietors of the Summit House and the leader, recovering somewhat from his surprise, came forward and then stopped and put several questions to the doctor. From his

CASUALTIES ON PRESIDENTIAL RANGE

manner of asking them and receiving the answers was made evident his wonder, for it seemed as if he could not bring himself to believe that the answerer was actually the man who had left the Glen House Wednesday afternoon. Mr. Hall's companions, all experienced guides, gathered around and looked at Dr. Ball, too astonished to speak. The party had followed his tracks, but, losing them in the brush, they were endeavoring to rediscover them by extending their line, when they heard his shout.

So parched and dry was Dr. Ball's mouth and throat that he could not swallow food. Unfortunately, his rescuers had provided nothing to drink, so he was unable to obtain any relief from his thirst until they had gone some distance on their return, when two swallows of water were obtained from a rock which had a small hollow at the top. Now that the doctor had not to rely upon himself, his strength was less and he could not walk so firmly as before. Throwing his arms around the necks of two of the party, he walked on, with this assistance, between them. After a while they came to the regular path and then they descended the Ledge to the Camp House, where Mr. Myers welcomed the doctor as one from the dead. The distance to the place where he was found was about a mile and a half and from his encampment about two miles. On Dr. Ball's remarking that he believed he would have reached the Camp House alone, as he was at last on the right course, Mr. Hall expressed a different opinion and called his attention to the clouds which had gathered and had shut in the view.

THE WHITE MOUNTAINS

Here the doctor's feet were examined and, being found still frozen, were plunged into cold water from melted snow and ice to remove the frost. After being somewhat rested, he was placed upon a horse, which, for many years accustomed to the Mountains, carried him very steadily, guardedly stepping around or over stones, stumps, and other obstacles, for a mile and a half over the new road. When they came to the finished part of the road, Mr. Thompson, who had arranged with the party to be informed, by means of signal flags, when Dr. Ball's body should be found, and who had watched the men with a telescope as they advanced over the Mountain and returned, met them with his horses and carriage. Welcoming the doctor "back alive," Mr. Thompson observed, "You have been through what no other person has, or probably will again, in a thousand years."

The sufferer, having been transferred to the carriage and covered with blankets, which protected him from the cold and the rain, arrived at the Glen House about five o'clock in the afternoon, progress being necessarily slow because of his sensitive body. Welcome, indeed, to him was the substantial hotel, and even more grateful, if possible, to him were the sympathetic faces and solicitous words of the inmates.

Here, under the kind ministrations of the women of the household, he was made as comfortable as he could be. A physician from Gorham was in attendance on the patient, and the latter's brother, Dr. S. Ball, of Boston, came to look after him. For a few

CASUALTIES ON PRESIDENTIAL RANGE

days his sufferings were comparatively light. There was general prostration of his system, with some fever, an insatiable thirst, and frequent violent tremblings of the body, due to chills. His feet and hands were as if dead and were discolored to blackness, distorted by swelling, and covered with water-blisters. Above the injuries the pain was severe, and at times, when cramp set in, excruciating.

After having remained about a week at the Glen House, the doctor was sufficiently recovered to be driven to Gorham, riding very comfortably on a sofa placed in a carriage, whence the train was taken to Boston. There, under the care and treatment of his brother, Dr. S. Ball, and Dr. H. Barnes, after remaining for twelve weeks in a very helpless condition, his general health was quite restored, and his injured members were by the 1st of March, 1856, again usable to a moderate degree.

Such is the record of this remarkable case of sixty hours' exposure on the Mountains.[1] Mr. Hall truly remarked in a letter to the doctor's brother, "There is nothing in the history of the White Mountains to compare with this case of your brother; and I am very sure its parallel will not be known in time to come."

By a curious irony of fate, this man, who survived the cold snowstorm and freezing wind of the White Mountains and endured such bitter sufferings from frost, died, four years later, at the age of thirty-nine, in Chiriqui, Panama.

To a chapter dealing with casualties may perhaps

[1] My account of Dr. Ball's experience is drawn from his own book, *Three Days on the White Mountains*, published in 1856.

THE WHITE MOUNTAINS

appropriately be added a brief record of some noteworthy convulsions of Nature, which altered, for a time at least, the appearance of the Mountain landscape, and which in one case since the famous disaster of 1826 resulted in the loss of human life. Landslides of greater or less magnitude have always been frequent occurrences in the White Mountains. Torrential rains acting upon the loose thin soil of the upper portions of the slopes, or upon the surfaces of high areas denuded of trees by fire, are usually responsible for these natural phenomena. In the prehistoric days they were, as has been noted, one of the causes of the Indians' dread of the loftier summits, the aborigines attributing the noise which attended the slides to the supposed superior beings with which their superstition peopled the higher regions. In historical times several slides have occurred which are memorable for their extent or for the damage they have done. The most noted of all is, of course, the Willey Slide of 1826, which has been recorded in an earlier chapter.

In the autumn of 1869, exceptionally heavy rains were experienced in the White Mountain region and in consequence a number of disastrous avalanches occurred. On October 4, there was a landslide on Carter Dome, by which the mountain was stripped to its bed ledges for a distance of nearly a mile on its north and west sides. An indirect result of the storm which caused this slide was the death of Mr. Thompson, proprietor of the Glen House, who, as has been told elsewhere, when attempting to avert the destruction of his mill was swept away by

CASUALTIES ON PRESIDENTIAL RANGE

the torrent of water and débris which rushed down the narrow glen of the Peabody River.

At this time a slide of immense magnitude devastated a vast area on Tripyramid, that mysterious triple-crowned mountain in the Waterville region. The denuded area has a length of two and a half miles and varies in width from thirty feet at the upper extremity, which is but two hundred feet below the top of the peak, to more than a thousand feet at the lower end, where the accumulated débris spreads over the meadows.

Again, in 1885, Tripyramid was the scene of slides greater than that of 1869. They occurred about the middle of August after several hard rains. In both cases, owing to the wilderness nature of the region, the slides were attended with no loss of life or property.

A striking freak of Nature, which formerly added to the interest of that great scenic feature at the southern entrance of the Franconia Notch, the famous Flume, was the suspension of a huge boulder between the walls of the narrowing upper part of the canyon. There it was held, doubtless for centuries, tightly gripped by the opposing cliffs, midway between the rim and the floor of the chasm, and under it thousands of visitors passed with no thought of the possibility of its ever being dislodged. The enormous rock was, however, swept away on June 20, 1883, when an avalanche, caused by heavy rains on the peaks above, crashed down through the Flume. As compensation for the carrying away of the boulder, the landslide lengthened and deepened

THE WHITE MOUNTAINS

the gorge and added to its attractions two new waterfalls, one of them the very beautiful cascade at its head.

On July 10, 1885, the great slide took place on Cherry Mountain, descending the Owl's Head peak on the north side. Its débris — broken trees, mud, rocks, and earth — was carried to the foot of the mountain, making a two-mile track of devastation, and was mostly deposited on the farm of Oscar Stanley, where it wrecked the house, killed several cattle, and mortally injured Donald Walker, one of the farmhands. For years the vast scar of this slide, known as the "Stanley Slide," was plainly visible from Jefferson, but of late years it has become overgrown again and so is now much less conspicuous.

XIV

WINTER ASCENTS OF MOUNT WASHINGTON — THE WINTER OCCUPATION OF MOUNT MOOSILAUKE AND OF MOUNT WASHINGTON — THE U.S. SIGNAL SERVICE ON MOUNT WASHINGTON

THE winter ascent of Mount Washington, a feat now, in these mountaineering days, rather frequently accomplished by hardy members of the Appalachian Mountain Club, by sturdy collegians of the Dartmouth Outing Club, and by a few others, is an excursion of considerable difficulty and not a little danger. It often gives opportunity for some real Alpine mountaineering,[1] and thus offers the nearest approach in the Eastern United States to such mountain-climbing as is undertaken in the summer in the playground of Europe and in the Canadian Rockies.

The first ascent in winter was not made for pleasure, as are all of the ascents of the present time and as were many of those achieved in the past, but in the performance of a duty. Lucius Hartshorn, of Lancaster, son-in-law of Samuel F. Spaulding, one of the proprietors of the Tip-Top House, was a

[1] That the climbing of "the crown of New England" in winter is regarded as in the same category with and as comparable with the most strenuous mountaineering exploits, is borne witness to by the fact of the inclusion of an article on "Mount Washington in Winter," by Edward L. Wilson, in the volume on *Mountain Climbing* in "The Out-of-Door Library," in which volume the companion articles have to do with the Alps, and Mounts Ætna, Ararat, and St. Elias.

THE WHITE MOUNTAINS

deputy sheriff of Coös County, and as such was employed by his father-in-law, in the winter of 1858, to go up the Mountain and make an attachment of property at the Summit, in connection with litigation as to the title. The noted guide, Benjamin F. Osgood, of the Glen House, who died in December, 1907, at the age of seventy-eight, was Mr. Hartshorn's companion in this first scaling of Mount Washington in winter, which was done on the 7th of December in the first-named year. Their course was up the carriage road to the Halfway House and thence over the crust to the top. Mr. Osgood, who had piloted many distinguished men through the Mountains in the old Concord coaches or on horseback over the Mountain trails, and who had a large fund of reminiscences of the early days, used often to tell of his thrilling experience on this historic occasion.

Some of the details of their stay on the Summit and of the descent are given in a contemporary issue of the *Coös Republican*. On arriving, they immediately took measures to enter one of the houses, which, as these were covered with snow, was a work requiring time. Unable to force an entrance at the doors, they finally got in through a window, on which the frost was a foot and a half in thickness. The interior of the hotel was like a tomb, the walls and all the furniture being draped with some four inches of frost, while the air was extremely biting, and the darkness was such that a lamp was necessary to enable them to distinguish objects. As delay was dangerous in the extreme, the two men, the

CLIMBING MOUNT WASHINGTON IN WINTER

THE SUMMITS IN WINTER

legal duty having been performed, prepared to return. Upon emerging, they saw to the southwest a cloud, which was coming on toward them with alarming swiftness and which rapidly increased in volume. Knowing that to be caught in this frost cloud would probably be fatal, they hurried on and just managed to reach the woods, at the base of the Ledge, when it enfolded them. So icy and penetrating was it that to have encountered it on the unprotected part of the Mountain would have been to have perished in its enveloping pall. The intrepid pair reached the Glen in safety, where they received a hearty welcome from their anxious friends.

Another noteworthy winter ascent was accomplished on February 10–11, 1862, by John H. Spaulding, Chapin C. Brooks, and Franklin White, a photographer, all of Lancaster, who spent two days and nights in the old Summit House.

From a graphic account of the visit, written by Mr. Spaulding, we learn that they started from the Glen House at eight o'clock in the evening on the 10th in bright moonlight with ample packs and provisions. Walking slowly up the carriage road on snowshoes in the still night, they arrived at the Ledge after midnight. In this first portion of the ascent, the glittering crust, the tree-shadows across their path, and the white, winding road and contrasting evergreen thickets all combined to form a most beautiful scene, while at the place of rest a weird picture was presented to them, formed by the ruins of the great barn built the previous season, and by the fire-scathed trees, standing in bold relief in

THE WHITE MOUNTAINS

the moonlight, with the glittering Ledge itself and the dark old shanty in the background. Kindling a fire at the shelter, they drowsed until daybreak on an old straw bed laid on a snowdrift. At sunrise they began the onward march, without snowshoes, advancing by cutting steps in the ice. At five miles up, a wide ice-field was encountered, necessitating the cutting of deep steps, and at about six miles, a deep drift impeded their progress and prevented them from following the road. Here lunch was taken, and they found the thermometer to register in a rising wind 27° above zero. Storm-clouds over toward Mount Carter warned them to hasten on, which they did as rapidly as circumstances would permit. As they approached the top, they were enwrapped in a heavy black cloud, which froze upon them. On arriving at the Summit, the hardy climbers found the two houses covered with glittering ice and with curious frost feathers standing out on the northerly side. Walking up a drift, they broke away the ice from the south gable-end window of the Summit House, and, taking out the window, entered the attic. As soon as possible a stove was brought up from a lower room, some wood secured from the Tip-Top House, and a fire kindled. This done, the doughty trio, after further fortifying themselves by piling up a barricade of mattresses around the stove, passed a fairly comfortable night. But their stay had to be prolonged beyond its intended duration of a single night, for in the morning they found themselves in the midst of a fierce snowstorm, and on that account they were compelled to endure, as

THE SUMMITS IN WINTER

it turned out, a siege, the storm driving by their enforced habitation for thirty-six hours. Some idea of the Arctic conditions within the hotel may be gained from the facts that snow and ice lay piled all about from three inches to five feet deep, that the furniture was set in feathery white casings, and that snow-wreaths and icicles were everywhere on the walls and roof. Most magnificent scenes that beggar all description were witnessed; the sun was seen to set in a vast "snow-bank," and a hundred glittering peaks were beheld in the moonlight. A return to the Glen in another thick snowstorm completed a trip with which they afterwards felt "perfectly satisfied."

These two winter ascents are all that are on record previous to the winter of 1870–71, during which, as will be related farther on, ascents were numerous.

Before recording any more of these alpine experiences, however, the steps which brought about the establishment of a meteorological station on New England's highest summit, including especially the winter occupations of Moosilauke and Washington, demand notice. The two expeditions just mentioned, the stories of which are now to be narrated, not only demonstrated the possibility of human beings successfully braving the frost and storms of the Arctic winter of the summit of Mount Washington and enduring the inconveniences and privations incident to winter life in such a place, but also showed the feasibility of making and recording weather observations under such circumstances.

The project of a winter stay on Mount Washing-

THE WHITE MOUNTAINS

ton was a long-cherished one in the minds of J. H. Huntington and C. H. Hitchcock, graduates of Amherst and associates on the geological surveys of Vermont and New Hampshire.

The former, whose acquaintance with the White Mountains dated back to 1856 and 1857, first raised the question of the possibility of such an undertaking while accompanying an expedition, along Lake Champlain, of a survey party led by the latter in 1858.[1] At the same time he expressed a willingness to make the experiment. After Mr. Huntington had tried in vain to secure the pecuniary support of the Smithsonian Institution by appealing to Professor Joseph Henry, who declined to undertake the enterprise at that time on account of the many obstacles in the way, and after Professor Hitchcock, who visited the White Mountains for the first time later in that year, had also made an unsuccessful appeal to the same source, the project had to be abandoned. It was revived ten years later, when Professor Hitchcock was appointed State Geologist, and Mr. Huntington, recalling the old conversations about spending a winter on Mount Washington, applied for and received the appointment of an assistant on the geological survey.

Application for the use of the Tip-Top House for scientific purposes during the winter of 1869–70

[1] In 1859, Jonathan Merrill, a then recent graduate of Dartmouth College, conceived the idea of spending a winter on Mount Washington. He received the encouragement of Professor Henry, of the Smithsonian Institution, and was given permission to occupy one of the houses; but an unexpected snowstorm delayed some of his preparations, and this and other considerations compelled him to abandon the adventure.

THE SUMMITS IN WINTER

failed to secure the consent of the lessee, Colonel Hitchcock, of the Alpine House, a fortunate refusal for the applicants, as it proved, for Professor Hitchcock having, in a conversation with William Little, of Manchester, made known to that gentleman his disappointment at not being able to secure quarters on Mount Washington, unexpectedly and to his great delight received from him the offer of the use without charge of the house on Mount Moosilauke. This proffer being communicated to Mr. Huntington, he accepted it without a moment's hesitation, so eager was he to spend a winter at such a height.

Supplies were carried to the summit of the Benton mountain and preparations were made to begin Arctic housekeeping the latter part of December. Huntington's expected companion having been compelled, in consequence of being offered an advantageous situation in Georgia, to give up his plan of spending the winter in a far different climate, the vacant position of fellow observer was filled by A. F. Clough, of Warren, a photographer by profession and a great lover of Nature. The experiences of this sojourn on Moosilauke proved not only valuable in and for themselves, but also as preliminary to the stay on the higher mountain the following winter. From a scientific standpoint, moreover, the stay here proved of great interest. Indeed, it is affirmed that so unusual were a number of the meteorological phenomena observed here that in some respects those of Mount Washington did not equal them.

The first attempt to ascend the mountain for the purpose of carrying up wood and other supplies and

THE WHITE MOUNTAINS

of fitting up a room in the house failed because of a high wind with driving snow, which forced the men back by its fierceness and made the bridle path impassable with huge drifts. A lame, frost-bitten, and discouraged group of men ate their evening meal at the foot of the mountain, the only cheerful and hopeful person being James Clement, the pioneer of this mountain. The next day, November 24, 1869, being clear and bright and everything seeming propitious, another attempt to reach the summit was made, and this one was crowned with success. Two fine days and one cloudy one were experienced, in which period of time the preparatory work was completed. Provisions were not taken up until late in December, when they were transported on two large hand-sleds drawn by a horse. A furious storm arose the night of that expedition, making venturing out extremely hazardous; but, having no fodder for the horse, the descent had to be made the following day in intense cold and in a wind so fierce that the men could not keep their footing and were several times nearly blown over the crest of the ridge. On the last day of December, Messrs. Huntington and Clough ascended the mountain for their winter stay.

In a chapter of the book "Mount Washington in Winter," Mr. Huntington tells in a most interesting way the story of the sojourn on this perhaps finest of New England viewpoints. Many were the grand and beautiful scenes beheld by the two observers from this outlook, over the snow-covered country in the various atmospheric conditions experienced, the summits of Mounts Washington, Lafayette, and

THE SUMMITS IN WINTER

the others, sublime in their canopy of snow, often glittering in the bright sunlight above the clouds, or presenting ashy pale or dark, forbidding aspects under the shadows of the clouds, or being suffused with rosy light at sunset. Hardly had the two men got settled in their new quarters, when, on the 2d of January, they were visited by a terrific storm, which changed from snow at daylight to sleet and then to rain, and which continued with unabated violence until 9 P.M., after which hour there were lulls, midnight finding it considerably diminished in fury. At eight in the morning the velocity of the wind was seventy miles, and at twelve noon, when the storm had become "a perfect tempest," Mr. Clough, determined to know the exact rate, succeeded, by clinging to the rocks, in placing himself where he could expose the anemometer and not be blown away himself, and found the velocity to be ninety-seven and a half miles an hour, the greatest ever recorded up to that time.

Amid Arctic conditions and surroundings such as might be expected on so high and exposed a place, about two months were passed. When the last of February arrived, the weather being extremely cold and the winds violent and their supply of wood being nearly exhausted, it was deemed advisable to descend. This action was attended with much peril in a wind blowing seventy miles an hour and in a temperature of zero or lower, but was accomplished safely, in spite of the facts that on the highest part of the ridge, Huntington, as he tells us, was frequently blown from the ridge, and that the sled was blown out of Clough's hold and its standards broken on a projecting rock. Compelled by this mishap to go back some distance to secure another sled, Clough, after a severe struggle in which he was almost overwhelmed several times, eventually managed to achieve his purpose, and, when the reloading, no easy task under such conditions, had been effected, the travelers soon succeeded in reaching the protection of the woods.

This stay on Moosilauke having demonstrated the possibility of living on a mountain-top in the winter and having fed the desire for the winter occupation of the loftier summit, early in 1870, Messrs. Hitchcock and Huntington began to contrive ways and means to this end. Renewed application for the Tip-Top House being refused in April, negotiations for the use of the engine-house or station that the Mount Washington Railway Company was intending to erect on the Summit were opened with the president, Mr. Marsh, by letter and interviews, and eventually the desired permission was obtained, although the building was not completed.

Efforts to obtain the necessary funds from State and National authorities,[1] scientific bodies, and individuals were unavailing. The Government would

[1] Probably the first attempt to establish a scientific observatory on Mount Washington was made in 1853 by D. O. Macomber, president of the Carriage Road Company. A circular was issued, setting forth the importance of such an enterprise and arguments in favor of erecting a permanent building on the top of Mount Washington for scientific purposes. A petition to Congress, dated December 1, 1853, asking for an appropriation of $50,000 and offering on the part of the road company to build an observatory for the use of the Government was presented, but nothing came of the project.

THE SUMMITS IN WINTER

not sanction any special arrangement to furnish any newspaper exclusively with weather reports (in return for pecuniary support, which one New York journal offered on this condition), and it seemed probable that the undertaking would have to be abandoned when assistance came from an unexpected quarter. In July, Mr. Durgin, of the Sinclair House in Bethlehem, informed Professor Hitchcock that a relative by marriage, S. A. Nelson, of Georgetown, Massachusetts, was very much interested in the meteorology of Mount Washington and would like to join the expedition. Mr. Nelson proposed, in case he should be permitted to be one of the party, to devote himself to raising funds, which, after the formal invitation extended had been accepted by him, he set about doing. Beginning in September, he succeeded in obtaining, by late December, when he joined the party on the Mountain, more than eight hundred dollars.

The Chief Signal Officer, General A. B. Myer, offered in September to furnish insulated telegraph wire sufficient to connect the Summit with the Base, which, together with the necessary instruments, was duly received the following month. In November, he informed Professor Hitchcock that he would detail for duty with the expedition an expert operator and observer, with a complete set of meteorological instruments, and requested that one weather report might be forwarded to him daily by telegraph, to be bulletined along with those from other stations and to be furnished to the principal daily journals.

Many other obstacles, more especially such as

THE WHITE MOUNTAINS

were connected with the purchase and transportation of supplies, the preparation of the building for occupancy, and the procuring of additional funds, were eventually overcome, with the generous help of the railway company and with the assistance of additional subscribers secured as the result of a new appeal.

The members of the expedition as finally organized were: C. H. Hitchcock, State Geologist, with office at Hanover, connected by telegraph with the Summit; J. H. Huntington, in charge of the observatory; S. A. Nelson, observer; A. F. Clough, of Warren, and H. A. Kimball, of Concord, New Hampshire, photographers, the former the original artist of the expedition and the latter one who applied for and received permission to join the party; and Sergeant Theodore Smith, observer and telegrapher for the Signal Service.

The evening of October 8, Mr. Huntington and a carpenter from Berlin Falls ascended, finding that Professor Hitchcock and several other men on pleasure bent had preceded them to the Summit for a brief visit. From the 10th to the 22d, the two former worked at fitting up the room, laying the telegraph wire, and making other necessary preparations. At length, everything being ready, Mr. Huntington promptly climbed the Mountain at the time appointed, November 12, and on the 13th began to take and record daily meteorological observations.

The dauntless Huntington[1] remained there alone

[1] The deep and narrow chasm, "less a ravine than a gulf," to the

OBSERVER, SUMMIT OF MOUNT WASHINGTON
ABOUT 1875

THE SUMMIT HOUSE IN WINTER, ABOUT 1875

THE SUMMITS IN WINTER

until November 30, when the two photographers, accompanied by Charles B. Cheney, of Orford, and C. F. Bracy, of Warren, arrived after a most thrilling experience in a wind of seventy miles an hour and a temperature down to zero or below. In this ascent Mr. Kimball became so extremely exhausted that his reason tottered and he became indifferent to his fate, and he would have perished had it not been for heroic measures to save him used by Messrs. Clough and Cheney. At the foot of Jacob's Ladder the men became separated, three of the party leaving the railroad track, while the other, Mr. Bracy, remained on it. The latter, after a narrow escape from death by falling through the trestle to the gorge beneath, reached the Summit about seven o'clock. The others, failing to get any answer from him in the roar of the tempest, made their way slowly by repeated short advances after brief rests in a prostrate position. Three hours or more of this ascent were made in the darkness of a moonless night, and it took half an hour's time to make the thirty rods from the Lizzie Bourne monument to the observatory. The incidents of this perilous adventure in such tempestuous weather, and under such other conditions as have been noted, rendered the experience unforgettable by its participants and make the account of it,

north of Tuckerman's Ravine, was named "Huntington's Ravine" in his honor, by his companions in this expedition. Professor Huntington was an indefatigable explorer of the White Hills. Sweetser, whose guide-book explorations were made in 1875, says of him: "To the last-named [Professor J. H. Huntington] the public owes all the best features of this *White Mountain Guide-Book*, since he accompanied and practically directed the most arduous surveys and pioneering expedition of the Guide parties."

THE WHITE MOUNTAINS

as narrated in detail in "Mount Washington in Winter," impressive to the imagination of the reader.

Sergeant Smith arrived on December 4, and on the 21st of that month Professor Hitchcock and Messrs. Nelson, L. B. Newell, Eben Thompson, and F. Woodbridge came up, making the party complete, with some visitors.

Mr. Nelson and Sergeant Smith spent the entire winter on the Mountain, Professor Huntington most of it, and Messrs. Clough and Kimball a part of it. Professor Hitchcock joined his associates at the Summit from time to time, his last stay being from April 26 to May 1.

Visitors were fairly numerous and ever welcome. Some of them have been already named. L. L. Holden,[1] "Ranger" of the *Boston Journal,* visited the Summit twice, once in February with another newspaper man, P. B. Cogswell, of the *Concord Daily Monitor,* and Mr. Clough as companions, and again from April 29 to May 9, his companions this time in the ascent being Professor Huntington, who had been down for a day or two to fulfill a lecture engagement, and Eben Thompson, of Dartmouth College, a previous visitor. Other visitors were Messrs. Walter and Charles L. Aiken, George C. Procter, and Michael ("Mike") Mularvey (of Marshfield) in February; the late Benjamin W. Kilburn, of Littleton, one of the pioneers in the art of stereo-

---

[1] Mr. Holden's description of his ascent in February and his account of his ascent, experiences during his stay, and descent in the spring are printed in *Mount Washington in Winter.*

THE SUMMITS IN WINTER

graphic photography, Edward L. Wilson, editor of the *Philadelphia Photographer*, whose article on "Mount Washington in Winter" has been mentioned, and "Mike" on March 1 and 2; Dr. Rogers and Mr. Nutter, of Lancaster, in March; Messrs. Clough and Cheney again, in April.[1] Seventy ascents in all were made that winter by the indefatigable Professor Huntington and others.

The winter passed very pleasantly. There was much to do in keeping the telegraph line open and repairing breaks, in making the meteorological observations, in housekeeping, in maintaining a comfortable or at least livable degree of warmth within the house, in taking photographs, in writing reports, etc., and in various other duties.

The lowest temperature experienced was 59° below zero at three A.M. on Sunday, February 5. The mean temperature for January 22 was $-28.5°$, and for February 4 was $-35°$. All day and all night of the former date the wind raged, at times blowing in gusts of every direction and of high velocity. With two fires maintained at red heat all night, two of the party sitting up for that purpose (there was little sleep for anybody), the room was cold.

Saturday, February 4, was a strenuous day, as besides the intense cold the wind was very high, some of the gusts before morning undoubtedly attaining a velocity of one hundred miles an hour.

[1] This ascent, the most difficult one of the winter, was made on the 5th, in a furious snowstorm, the temperature being nearly zero and the wind at one time blowing more than eighty miles an hour. The men succeeded in it only because of their superior powers of endurance.

THE WHITE MOUNTAINS

The house rocked and trembled and groaned, movable articles were continually on the move, — books, for example, repeatedly dropping from the shelves. In "*sawing* off" a piece of salt pork, which operation was like "cutting into a block of gypsum," Mr. Nelson was out only five minutes, but froze his fingers. The butter for the Sunday morning breakfast had to be cut, with a chisel and hammer, from the tubs, which stood in the outer room.

The highest wind velocity recorded was ninety-two miles an hour at seven o'clock in the evening of December 15, 1870, when the most severe storm of all that they experienced raged. After that hour it was not safe to venture out with the anemometer, for the wind kept increasing, reaching, it was estimated, at its highest a velocity from one hundred and ten to one hundred and twenty miles. During this storm so great was the force of the wind that three-inch planks bolted across the opening in the shed where the train enters were pressed in four or more inches and the whole building had an unpleasant vibratory motion.

On many days the high winds and stormy conditions confined the observers to the house; observations were often taken under great difficulties and at considerable peril on this account; and many a night sleep was well-nigh impossible on account of the roaring of the wind, the creaking and groaning and oscillation of the building, and the noise due to the driving of particles of ice by the wind against it. Repairing the telegraph line, a frequent necessity, gave occasion for some arduous and often dangerous

THE SUMMITS IN WINTER

trips down the railway, and many times other trips were taken which entailed severe exposure.

Altogether, the "expedition" was a most notable one, not only for its scientific importance, but also for its human interest as demonstrating what severe conditions of winter cold and wind and storm human beings can successfully endure for a prolonged period. I have devoted so much space to it not only because of this intrinsic interest, but because of the attention it attracted at the time and of its historical importance.[1] From time to time there appeared in the newspapers references to the occupation of the summit of Mount Washington, expressing the opinions of various writers, either upon the facts reported or upon the general prospects of the adventure. Many regarded the project as idiotic, lunatic, or perfectly chimerical, and the participants in it as a party of maniacs.

True to the American tendency to burlesque, many of the articles about the expedition were of a facetious character, one writer even preparing what purported to be an official report of the expedition, with a burlesque journal of "each day's proceedings."

Convinced that Mount Washington was a desirable place for a weather station, the feasibility and value of winter observations on it and from it having been by this expedition amply demonstrated,

[1] All of the information here summarized, and much more, is contained in that most entertaining, instructive, and otherwise interesting volume, *Mount Washington in Winter*, prepared by all the members of this remarkable expedition as their "official report" to those friends who furnished the means for establishing and maintaining this Arctic observatory.

THE WHITE MOUNTAINS

the United States Signal Service, immediately upon the departure of the voluntary observers, took up, on May 13, 1871, the work of carrying on meteorological observations, and thereafter maintained the station continuously until the autumn of 1887 and in summer for five years more. During this period an immense amount of valuable data as to the weather conditions of this point was obtained and recorded.

Great were the hardships endured by these servants of the Government and thrilling were some of the incidents of this service on a mountain-top. At four in the morning one day in January, 1877,[1] the wind reached the velocity, never equaled elsewhere, of one hundred and eighty-six miles an hour. In this gale was blown down the engine-shed, used by the winter party of 1870–71, and by the Government observers until the erection of the Signal Station in 1874, and the board walk leading from the hotel to the Signal Station was demolished, the boards being carried as if they were straws and scattered far and wide in wild confusion over the top and sides of the Mountain.

This almost inconceivable velocity was equaled at least once subsequently and a rate of one hundred and eighty miles an hour was attained several times. In February, 1886, in one of the greatest storms ever

[1] I get this date from Drake, *The Heart of the White Mountains*. The author tells, in chapters VII and VIII of his "Second Journey," of his ascent and descent by the carriage road and stay on the Summit in May, 1877, when he saw the boards scattered about and was informed that the engine-house had been blown down in the January gale. Private Doyle's story, as narrated farther on, is given in this source.

THE SUMMITS IN WINTER

known, the mercury dropped to 51° below zero and the wind lashed the Summit with a fury which threatened to sweep it clear of the works of man. One building was torn down, some of its constituent parts being flung violently against the stanch little Signal Station, which, fortunately, was so protected by a tough thick coating of frost feathers that its doors, windows, and roof escaped. During this gale, when a rate of one hundred and eighty-four miles was recorded, the anemometer itself was carried away from its bearings.

Private Doyle, who was on duty in the station at the time of the great storm of January, 1877, has related his recollections of it. Anticipating, from the aspect of the heavens in the afternoon preceding the gale, when the clouds spread for miles around — an ocean of frozen vapor — and became, late in the day, so dense as to reflect the colors of the spectrum, that some great atmospheric disturbance was impending, the observers made everything snug for a storm. By nine in the evening, the wind had increased to one hundred miles an hour, with heavy sleet, making outside observations unsafe. At midnight, the velocity of the storm was one hundred and twenty miles and the thermometer registered $-24°$. Within the house, with the stove red, it was hard to get the temperature above freezing, and water froze within three feet of the fire. The uproar was deafening. At one o'clock, the wind rose to one hundred and fifty miles, raising the carpet a foot from the floor, and dashing all the loose ice on top of the Mountain against the building in one continuous volley. Not

THE WHITE MOUNTAINS

long after came a crash of glass. With the greatest difficulty the two men, working in the dark, succeeded in closing the storm-shutters from the inside. Hardly had they done this, when a heavy gust burst them open again, apparently as easily as if they had not been fastened at all. After a hard tussle, they again secured the windows by nailing a cleat to the floor and using a board as a lever. "Even then," said Private Doyle, "it was all we could do to force the shutters back into place. But we did it. We *had* to do it." The remainder of the night was spent in an anxious and alarmed state of mind, as was but natural when they did not know but that at any moment the building would be carried over into Tuckerman's Ravine and they swept into eternity with it. Doyle and his companion took the precaution to wrap themselves up in blankets and quilts, tied tightly around them with ropes, to which were fastened bars of iron. But these desperate measures to afford a possible chance of safety in case the station succumbed to the gale proved unnecessary, for the stout little building, anchored to the rocks by cables, successfully weathered this gale and all others.

Many similar experiences were encountered by these observers and others. Sometimes the frost feathers so obscured the windows that lights were required in the daytime; at other times the wind tore so through the building that the lamps could not burn.

On account of the dreadful solitude of this remote and lonesome place and for fear of accidents, the Government always maintained at least two men in

THE SUMMITS IN WINTER

the station and sometimes there were three or four, including a cook, and a cat and a dog.[1] Their duties were multifarious and their time was fully occupied. Seven observations had to be made daily, the recording-sheet of the anemometer had to be changed at noon, and three of the seven observations had to be forwarded in cipher to the Boston Station. There was much routine office work, including the receiving and sending of letters, and the filling of blank forms with statistics. The battery and wire of the telegraph outfit demanded much attention, and the making of repairs, often involving the risk of the observers' lives in storm and cold in searching for and mending a break, was no inconsiderable part of their work. The stock of food supplies was replenished in September, the "refrigerator" (the top story of the station) being stocked with meat and poultry already frozen. The water supply came from the frost feathers, a stock of which was always kept on hand, and an icy cold drink of which could always be found on the stove, unless the cook failed of his duty.

The personnel of the station was changed frequently. Sergeant Smith, who was detailed to accompany the voluntary expedition, was relieved, toward the end of May, 1871, by Sergeant M. L.

[1] Many visitors to the Summit in former days were acquainted with the beautiful St. Bernard dog, "Medford," whose graceful form and pleasing traits made him a favorite with all. Brought to the Mountain when he was a few months old, "Medford" spent his summers at the Summit House and his winters at the Signal Station with the weather observers, whom he often accompanied on their trips down the Mountain for the mail. One of the best-known dogs in the country in his lifetime, he was often inquired for after his death.

THE WHITE MOUNTAINS

Hearne. The saddest and most harrowing experience of any observer befell this gentleman. On February 26, 1872, his assistant, William Stevens, died of paralysis. For a day and two nights, Sergeant Hearne was alone with the dead body, as no one could come up on account of the hurricane and cold. "I look years older," he wrote, "than when it occurred." When aid came, a rude coffin and sled were made and a solemn procession of men moved slowly down the mountain-side over the snow with the mortal remains of the unfortunate observer.

Sergeant O. S. M. Cone, who spent one summer and winter only (1877–78) at the station, when relieved because of sickness, improvised a sled with a kind of safety brake and attempted with his companion, D. C. Murphy, and with his trunk, to coast down the track. When about halfway down, the brake gave way and the sled and its passengers were hurled from a high trestle. Almost miraculously they escaped death, Cone, however, being seriously injured.

A melancholy interest attaches to the connection of one observer with the station, in view of his sad fate a few years after his service here. Sergeant W. S. Jewell, who was in charge from 1878 to 1880, was given this detail at his own request, that he might fit himself for service in the Arctic regions. A member of the ill-fated Greely expedition, he was the first of that unhappy company to succumb, perishing from starvation in April, 1884.

Naturally, during the winters that the Summit was occupied, ascents were numerous, as the hardy

THE SUMMITS IN WINTER

climbers knew that there was a warm welcome and a comfortable shelter at the end of their climb. The numerous ones made during the first winter of occupation have been already mentioned. Several difficult or perilous ones are recorded by Edward L. Wilson as participated in by him. Mention has already been made of his ascent with B. W. Kilburn in March, 1871.[1] Photography was the principal object of these gentlemen, who together made five visits to the Summit in winter.

In the 1871 ascent, the travelers followed in the main the course of the railroad track, and all went well until long after the tree-line was passed, although they had found walking on snowshoes, with seventy-five pounds of photographic paraphernalia (the "wet" process was all that was then known) and other baggage to carry, warm work. Soon after they had passed the halfway point on the railway, they entered a cloud and were assailed by a cold northeast sleet-storm, in which they could not see a yard ahead. Suddenly the wind became more violent and erratic so that they could not stand alone. Joined arm in arm, they advanced sidewise with the greatest difficulty up the steepest part of the climb in the darkness, passing Jacob's Ladder, for which they looked as a landmark to guide them, without seeing it. They floundered on, confused and bewil-

[1] Mr. Kilburn kept a camera and photographic apparatus at the Summit for seven years from 1871 and came up every winter, witnessing some terrible storms and having some severe experiences in taking his famous winter views. He once saved Sergeant Hearne's life, when the latter was overcome at Jacob's Ladder, by carrying the observer bodily up the remaining one and a half miles of icy track.

THE WHITE MOUNTAINS

dered by the storm, for some time as best they could, and at length suddenly came upon the engine-shed, where they were made welcome by Messrs. Nelson and Smith.[1]

The fifth and last ascent of the two photographers was made March 2, 1886. This time there was no heavy baggage to carry, as the "dry" processes of photography had been invented. They were met before they reached the tree-line by "Medford" and two members of the Signal Service, to whom they had telegraphed their start from the Base. Leaving their snowshoes at the tree-line, they made their way first on the rock and crust, which were so discouragingly wet and slippery that they left them for the cog rail. This proving too dangerously icy, as a last resort they betook themselves to the cross-ties, on which there were a few inches of new snow. Over this hard road they succeeded in reaching the Summit. At times it required desperate effort to hold their own against the wind, and on Jacob's Ladder they were forced to resort to "all-fours," and more than once to lie flat and hold firmly to the sleepers until a gust had spent its strength. "Taken altogether," Mr. Wilson declares, "this was the most difficult ascent we made."

A most perilous ascent, which nearly cost the climber his life, is narrated by the writer just quoted. It was performed by Sergeant William Line, who served on Mount Washington three years (1874–77), and occurred on November 23, 1875. The day was

[1] This ascent and others are pleasantly described by Mr. Wilson in the volume *Mountain Climbing* (1897).

THE SUMMITS IN WINTER

unpromising, and against his better judgment he left Fabyan at about 9 A.M., with the mail for the Summit. All went well as far as the foot of Jacob's Ladder, which point was reached at one o'clock, after two hours of hard work from the Base. There the snow was several feet deep, and the gusts began to increase in force and frequency, so that he could advance only by a few steps in the lulls, being compelled to lie flat in the intervals of high wind. Once his body was blown up against the cross-ties of the railroad and held there for some time. At length he succeeded in approaching the Gulf Station-House, which it seemed for a time impossible to reach, as he could not stand in such a wind, or even breathe facing it. Finally, by lying down and, feet first, backing up the drift near the building, and by falling down the other side of the drift, he gained the house. After several futile attempts to continue his ascent, he returned to the building to pass the night. Here he found to his consternation that he had lost his match-box, and that his life depended upon his being able to light a single damp match which he had in his vest-pocket. Luckily he was successful in igniting it. In the morning he resumed his way and was making good progress, when, near the Summit, he met his exceedingly anxious companion, Mr. King, coming down the Mountain in search of him. Hardly had they arrived when they heard voices, and soon Mr. Kilburn and two other men appeared coming up out of the fog. The photographer had been informed by telegraph about midnight that the observer was lost and had immediately started from

THE WHITE MOUNTAINS

Littleton to go in search of him, requesting the others to join him.

Professor Huntington, who made many ascents, some of them dangerous, during his winter stay on the Mountain in 1870–71, made what is recorded as the most perilous one, late in November, 1873, when the thermometer stood at 17° below zero and the velocity of the wind was seventy-two miles an hour.

Place aux dames! The first women to climb Mount Washington in winter were — worthy offspring of a noble sire! — two daughters of the pioneer, Ethan Allen Crawford. Mrs. Orville E. Freeman, of Lancaster, New Hampshire, and Mrs. Charles Durgin, of Andover, New Hampshire, in company with their brother William H. Crawford, of Jefferson, and their nephew Ethan Allen Crawford, of Jefferson Highlands, accomplished the feat on a mild afternoon in January, 1874, walking up the railroad track and spending the night in the Signal Station. At the outset they did not anticipate going to the top, but, finding progress not so very difficult, they kept on. They made the entire distance in three hours. Mrs. Freeman described the trip as "glorious fun" and expressed the hope that all her women friends might enjoy the pleasure of making it in winter. The winter ascent was not again, however, made by a woman until Dr. Mary R. Lakeman, of Salem, Massachusetts, achieved it with a party of Appalachians, who walked up from the Glen House by the carriage road in February, 1902.

XV

LATER HOTELS

I HAVE already set down, in a previous chapter devoted to the subject, such facts as I have been able to gather regarding the early hotels of the White Mountain region, bringing the chronicles of hotel-keeping there down to 1870, or thereabouts. In the seventies the building of the extensions of the already existing railroads and of an entirely new main line to the Mountains, the Portland and Ogdensburg, greatly stimulated travel thither, thousands of summer visitors coming where hundreds came before. As a necessary consequence of this increase of travel, an era of hotel construction and enlargement began, to continue for a period of thirty years, or until the advent of the motor age, with its changed conditions of summer recreation, put an end to the old order of things in summer resorts and especially to hotel development along the old lines. During this period of thirty years or so from 1870 on, there came into existence, then, many hotels and boarding-houses. These, by reason of the attractiveness of their location, the excellence of their cuisines, and the general high degree of comfort and convenience provided, have done much to draw visitors to the region and to increase and to spread far and wide that high repute of White Mountain hospitality which the older hotels had created by the excellence of their accommodations.

THE WHITE MOUNTAINS

Of these places of entertainment some are still taking care of patrons as satisfactorily as ever without increased room, but many more have been either largely rebuilt or succeeded by more capacious and elegant houses on the same sites, while yet others have succumbed to the fire fiend and have never been rebuilt. Space can be taken to narrate the history of only a few of the more important of these establishments.

Systematic attempts at the development of Bethlehem as a summer resort began toward the close of the Civil War. In 1859, the Sinclair, now the leading hotel of Bethlehem village, was a small two-story and a half gable-roof house — a "well-kept stage tavern with a few rooms for boarders." As business increased, additions had to be made from time to time and the older portions of the structure had to be modernized. Thus, the huge and commodious hostelry of to-day has developed by successive increments and alterations.

In 1863, the Honorable Henry Howard, of Providence, Rhode Island, who was afterward governor of that State, was visiting the region with a party, and, the coach in which he was coming down Mount Agassiz being overturned and most of its occupants severely injured, several weeks were necessarily spent in Bethlehem until the injured ones recovered sufficiently to go to their homes. During this stay Governor Howard spied out the land and was greatly impressed with the healthfulness and attractiveness of the village's location. Becoming convinced that Bethlehem had great possibilities as a summer re-

LATER HOTELS

sort, he made extensive purchases of land there, and showed his faith in the opinions he had formed as to the future of the place by selling building-lots on credit and by lending money to those who were disposed to go into the summer-hotel business.

When it was discovered that, in addition to its unusual general healthfulness, Bethlehem afforded speedy relief to visitors who were afflicted with hay-fever, a new element was added, for many people, to the charms of the place. The adoption of Bethlehem as the headquarters of the American Hay-Fever Association has made the fame of the village nation-wide.

Since the time of Governor Howard's activity in promoting the development of Bethlehem, houses for the care of summer boarders, who have become the town's chief, and indeed almost its only, source of revenue, have multiplied until they are counted by the score. The people of the town were, it is said, somewhat slow to appreciate their opportunity, but when, at length, the destiny of the place became evident to them, they were very willing to hasten its development, and provision was made for a water supply, sewer system, and other adjuncts necessary to make the village an attractive place of residence. The spirit of enterprise has ever since characterized the town and no steps have been left untaken to attract summer visitors. Bethlehem's frequenters number annually many thousands. In August and September, in the height of the hay-fever season, the village is the place of sojourn of many victims of this distressing malady, who return year after year, thus constituting a permanent clientèle for the hotels

THE WHITE MOUNTAINS

and boarding-houses, and there are also staying in the village many other people, who enjoy the wonderful air, the coolness, the fine views, and the pleasant life of this highest of New Hampshire villages.

Another man whose name has become indissolubly connected with Bethlehem was Isaac S. Cruft, a Boston merchant, who came to the village in 1871. His business sagacity made him realize the soundness of Governor Howard's belief as to the possibilities there and led him to acquire a large tract of land for summer-resort purposes. This property, known as the "Maplewood Farm," is situated about a mile east of the center of Bethlehem at the point on the highway to Fabyan where the Whitefield road joins it. The comfortable farmhouse then standing on this sightly location was remodeled and opened as a hotel. The new resort immediately sprang into favor. In 1876, Mr. Cruft erected on the site an elegant and spacious hotel, the celebrated Maplewood. Its magnificent distant view of the Presidential Range and the excellence of its appointments soon caused the hotel to grow into high favor, necessitating the building, in 1878, of a large addition. Maplewood, which has its own railroad station and post-office, a group of cottages, a large and attractive casino and spacious grounds, and which provides every comfort and luxury that can be thought of and facilities for all kinds of indoor and outdoor diversion, has long been a fashionable resort and has ever ranked among the foremost of the great Mountain hotels.

The Twin Mountain House, located in the Am-

LATER HOTELS

monoosuc Valley five miles west of Fabyan, with stations on the Boston and Maine and Maine Central Railroads, was built in 1869-70. It was at first a small house, — only a cottage, — but by additions and changes it soon became a capacious hostelry, now one of the landmarks of the Mountains. Its first proprietor was Asa Barron, whose son, the late Colonel Oscar G. Barron, was brought here, a boy of nineteen, in 1869. For two years, Oscar Barron was associated with C. H. Merrill, who was the manager of the hotel; but in 1872, Mr. Merrill went to the Crawford House, where he remained until the close of the season of 1907, and young Barron became the manager. During the next six years the Twin Mountain House developed, under the landlordship of Colonel Barron and his father, until it became famous, its cuisine and its social life being "justly celebrated." It was also highly reputed as a hay-fever refuge. These were the days of its glory. Henry Ward Beecher returned year after year. President Grant was a visitor, and many distinguished persons of the literary and social world enjoyed the hospitality of the Barrons. The prestige then acquired still lingers about the old house. In 1878, Asa Barron leased the Fabyan House, and four years later the noted hotel firm of Barron, Merrill, and Barron was formed, which association has been continued ever since. The Twin Mountain House has remained under the proprietorship of the company of this name, which also conducts the Fabyan House, the Crawford House, and the hotel on the summit of Mount Washington.

THE WHITE MOUNTAINS

Mention has just been made of the Fabyan House. As the building of that famous hotel in the Ammonoosuc Valley follows in time that of the Twin Mountain House, the narration of its origin and subsequent history may well come here. After the burning of Horace Fabyan's Mount Washington House, in the spring of 1853, there arose a legal controversy over the ownership of the land constituting the original hotel site of the Mountains, which prevented the immediate rebuilding of the hotel. During the autumn of 1858, the stables, which the previous fire had spared, were struck by lightning and destroyed. The legal difficulties must have dragged along, for the traveler through the Ammonoosuc Valley, between Crawford's and Bethlehem or Franconia in the fifties and sixties, saw only ruins at the Giant's Grave and found the White Mountain House, about a mile farther on, the only house of entertainment in this vicinity.

At length, a stock company, called the Mount Washington Hotel Company, and composed of Messrs. Hartshorn, Walcott, and Sylvester Marsh, was chartered, and, in 1872, work was begun on a new hotel at the Giant's Grave, which mound was at that time removed to obtain a level site.[1] This, the present hotel, called the "Fabyan House" in honor of the proprietor of the previous hotel here, was opened to guests in 1873. After the opening of the White Mountains Railroad to this point in 1874 and after the completion of the Portland and Ogdensburg from the east as far as here in the following

[1] Sweetser characterized this as "a needless act of vandalism."

LATER HOTELS

year, this location, as the place of changing cars in the journey through the Mountains and as the starting-point for the trip up Mount Washington, soon became the busiest of White Mountain railway centers, which it has remained to this day.

The first landlord of the Fabyan House was John Lindsey, one of the old-time stage-drivers of this region. He, with his partner, Mr. French, remained in charge until 1878, when, as has been already noted, the hotel was leased by Asa Barron, of the Twin Mountain House, who with his son, Oscar, left the latter that year and came here. Then began Colonel Oscar G. Barron's famous connection with the Fabyan House, which lasted for thirty-five years. To his genial hospitality and thorough knowledge of hotel-keeping the Fabyan House chiefly owes the popularity which has characterized it through all these years.

Colonel Barron's warm-hearted personality endeared him to all who in any way came in contact with him. His services to the town of Carroll and to the White Mountains in general, as by his efforts to further and upbuild the summer-resort business and by his advocacy of the bill for making the Crawford Notch a State reservation, made his death in January, 1913, a heavy blow to the White Mountain community.

Another well-known and popular hostelry in this locality is the Mount Pleasant House, a half-mile east of the Fabyan House, which, as erected in 1876 by John T. G. Leavitt, was a very different-looking structure from the one the traveler sees to-day. In

THE WHITE MOUNTAINS

1881, Joseph Stickney became interested in it and rebuilt it. Abbott L. Fabyan, son of Horace, managed it for ten years for Barron, Merrill, and Barron, to whom it was leased. In 1895, it was transformed into virtually a new establishment, the present large and comfortable hotel, which achieved a high reputation under the skillful management of the firm of Anderson and Price.

The story of the Glen House, the celebrated hotel on the east side of the Presidential Range in the valley of the Peabody River, has been brought down elsewhere to the death by drowning, in 1869, of its first landlord, Mr. Thompson. Two years later, the hotel passed to the control of Charles R. Milliken and his brother, Weston F. Milliken. These enterprising business men believed that increased patronage would follow efforts to provide accommodations superior to those travelers had been putting up with, and in their hands the house took a new start and developed into a first-class hotel. This type of management, combined with the advantageous location of the Glen House, far from the noise and bustle of railways and villages, and commanding one of the grandest views in the Mountains, soon put it in the front rank of popular favor. An era of prosperity set in, during which addition after addition was made to the old structure until it became an aggregation of buildings. This increase of business and favor continued unbroken until the autumn of 1884 arrived. The last guests had gone and the house was being closed on October 1 for the season, when it was suddenly discovered to be on fire. The fire,

THE FIRST GLEN HOUSE

THE SECOND GLEN HOUSE, 1885-1893

LATER HOTELS

fanned by a strong northeaster, spread with great rapidity. Soon all was a mass of flames, and in two hours what had constituted a good-sized village in itself was but a heap of ashes.

The destruction of this hotel, in which so many thousands had been entertained, was a heavy blow, not only to the proprietors, but to the traveling public. Without a hotel the region was at once thrown back into its primitive solitude, and, moreover, an important link in the chain of Mountain tours was broken. It was a public misfortune.

Although the pecuniary loss the complete destruction of the Glen House involved was a serious one, its proprietors were not disheartened, but immediately took steps toward the building of a new hotel on the same site. The old building was, as has been indicated, a growth, and was in no sense a modern structure. It was decided to erect in its place a homogeneous building, attractive in its architecture and characterized by simple elegance and solid comfort in its appointments. The architect chosen, F. H. Fassett, planned a house in the English cottage style. It was nearly three hundred feet long, was three stories in height above the basement, and was provided with a veranda of about four hundred and fifty feet in length. Within, both the public rooms and the private rooms were pleasing in their appearance and commodious, while their furniture and fittings were in good taste and often luxurious.

The design was so far carried into effect that a new hotel was opened to the public for the season of 1885. It was, however, not fully consummated until

THE WHITE MOUNTAINS

the season of 1887, when the huge and attractive structure, with its accommodations for five hundred guests, stood complete, as if risen, phœnixlike, from the ashes of the old. The new Glen House immediately sprang into high favor with the Mountain sojourners of the well-to-do variety and was soon enjoying a large patronage. But, alas! the years of its existence were to be few. It would almost seem as if there were a curse upon this site similar to that which tradition had attached to the Giant's Grave location on the other side of the Range, for on Sunday evening, July 16, 1893, this magnificent structure caught fire from some unknown cause and in a few hours the site was again desolate. This disaster, by which a property of about a quarter of a million dollars was either destroyed or, by the destruction of the means of accommodating visitors, rendered largely valueless, was an overwhelming one to the proprietors and to the locality itself. The Glen House has not so far been rebuilt. The stables remain, and in them are kept the horses and wagons for the ascent of Mount Washington by the carriage road. The business of carrying passengers up and down the Mountain, conducted here, has kept the Glen from being abandoned. Of recent years the building which was used as the servants' quarters of the hotel, and which escaped the fire, accommodates a few guests, usually those of the pedestrian class or persons of similar simple tastes, under the name of the Glen House.

The new house of 1885–93 had too brief an existence to acquire much in the way of a tradition, but

LATER HOTELS

about its famous predecessor of 1852–84 gathered many happy memories. Many noted persons visited it either as regular guests or as transients who had come to make the stage trip to the summit of Mount Washington. One famous habitué of the old house has his memory perpetuated in a roadside spring not far away. He, "Josh Billings," was a great trout fisherman, and in the seventies he used to practice his favorite diversion upon the streams in this vicinity, even penetrating, in his quest for the speckled beauties, into the lower sections of the Great Gulf. Those who visited the Glen House in those days often saw him, "deep-eyed and hirsutely aureoled, and talking much of trout in language which, even in its spoken form, reveals how preciously distinct, subtle, and blessed its orthography must be."

The history of the hotels in the Franconia Notch has been already brought down to the year 1872, when the present Flume House was built. The next event in this locality, the building of the Profile and Franconia Notch Railroad, has also been recorded. The scenic beauties and natural curiosities of the district have always attracted many visitors, and hotels of the highest rank have been maintained there to minister to the wants of permanent and transient guests. The great hotel, the Profile House, at the northern entrance of the Notch, particularly, is one of the famous summer-resort hotels of America. The hotel and the group of cottages, with the railroad station, the stables, etc., constitute a little world in themselves. The fine appointments, the cuisine, the opportunities for amusements of various

THE WHITE MOUNTAINS

kinds, the social life, and other features of the Profile House have always secured for it a liberal patronage of refined and cultured people, many of whom have made the settlement their summer home for many years. In 1898, a stock company was formed to hold the Franconia Notch property. Business having increased and the famous old hotel having come to be regarded as inadequate, the erection of a new hotel was decided upon by the owners. Accordingly, in the autumn of 1905, the old house was torn down, and on July 1, 1906, the New Profile House, a caravanserai of luxurious appointments, was opened to the public.

So numerous were the houses of entertainment that date from the period of which I am writing that it would take considerable space merely to name them. I shall tarry but to give the principal facts concerning a few others at important places before closing this record of the Mountain hotels with an account of the building of the great Mount Washington Hotel at Bretton Woods.

The Sunset Hill House at Sugar Hill was built in 1879 and the Deer Park at North Woodstock was opened in 1887. The now celebrated Waumbek Hotel at Jefferson was the result of a remodeling completed in 1889, the plain but substantial house built thirty years before being thereby transformed into the commodious and elegant structure of to-day. A popular hotel of to-day which represents an interesting development is the Mountain View House at Whitefield, which, beginning from a farmhouse, where a passing traveler obtained shelter in 1866,

MOUNT WASHINGTON HOTEL, BRETTON WOODS

LATER HOTELS

has become by successive additions, the last opened in 1912, a large and attractive house. In September, 1899, the Willey Hotel, which Horace Fabyan had built in the Notch many years before, was, with its companion building, the historic old Willey House, burned to the ground.

It remains now only to relate the circumstances of the most considerable hotel-building enterprise ever undertaken in the White Mountains, that of the erection of the Mount Washington. This particular undertaking differed in conception from most similar projects of recent years in that the hotel was erected on a site that had never before been occupied. It is said that the original builders of the Mount Pleasant saw the advantages of the location and entertained a vague idea of sometime building there. Nothing at any rate came of the plan, however, until the late Joseph Stickney, of New York, a capitalist of New Hampshire birth, who, as we have seen, had become owner of the Mount Pleasant House early in the eighties, entered upon the development of the project and carried it through to a successful conclusion. As the result of this gentleman's enterprise and command of large means, one of the most magnificent summer hotels in the world stands about a mile from Fabyan upon a little plateau seventy or eighty feet above the Ammonoosuc River, with its eastern outlook toward Mount Washington and the Presidential Range. The architect was Charles Alling Gifford, of New York, and the style of the architecture is of the Spanish Renaissance. The general shape is that of a capital letter

THE WHITE MOUNTAINS

Y, and prominent features are two octagonal towers, five stories in height, between which is the main portion of the structure. The foundation is of granite, the blocks where exposed being left in a rough finish, and the superstructure is of wood, covered with light-colored cement, laid upon a steel network, the whole building being as nearly fireproof as possible. The kitchen is in a detached building. The interior of the hotel is fitted with every convenience, comfort, and luxury that experience can suggest and the liberal expenditure of money provide.

Active work was begun on the hotel in June, 1901, and construction was carried rapidly forward, so that the hotel was opened to the public July 28, 1902. The company owning this hotel and the Mount Pleasant also owns an extensive tract of land, much of it virgin forest, around the hotels. Roads, bridle paths, and trails have been built in this area, the immediate grounds of the Mount Washington have been elaborately laid out, and every facility for outdoor games and amusements has been provided. In the summer the Mount Washington and its appurtenances constitute a city in themselves, so far as completeness of equipment and of provision for every possible demand of guests is concerned.

XVI

EARLY TRAILS AND PATH-BUILDERS — THE APPALACHIAN MOUNTAIN CLUB AND ITS WORK IN THE WHITE MOUNTAINS

THE building of the first paths to the summit of Mount Washington by the Crawfords, as well as that of the bridle path thither from the Glen House, has been already mentioned. Probably the first path made on the Northern Peaks was the Stillings Path, which, starting from the Randolph-Jefferson Highway in Jefferson Highlands, extended for nine miles to a point about a mile from the Castellated Ridge, whence Mount Washington could be reached over the slopes of Jefferson and Clay. It was this path that was used in carrying up the lumber for the Summit House of Rosebrook and Perkins, and so it is known to have been in existence as early as 1852. In 1860 or 1861, a partial trail over the peaks to Mount Washington, some sections of which are still in existence, was made by Gordon the guide. It was in 1875 that the first path up Mount Adams, which is the oldest of those now maintained on the Northern Peaks, was constructed by William G. Nowell, a very active trail-builder in later years, and Charles E. Lowe, a guide long favorably known to visitors to that region, and from 1895 to his death in 1907 proprietor of the Mount Crescent House at Randolph. Until 1880, Lowe's Path, as it was

THE WHITE MOUNTAINS

named, was maintained as a toll-path. It is now an Appalachian Mountain Club path. In 1876, Professor J. Rayner Edmands had Mr. Lowe cut a branch path through King's Ravine, and in the same year Mr. Nowell built the first camp on the Northern Peaks.

An early path up Mount Washington from the south was completed in 1845 by Nathaniel T. P. Davis, proprietor of the Mount Crawford House. About sixteen miles long, it leaves the Saco meadows near the present Bemis Station, passes up between Mounts Crawford and Resolution, ascends the Giant's Stairs on the southwest side, runs along the Montalban Ridge to Boott Spur, and finally crosses Bigelow's Lawn to the Crawford Path. Much of the course of the Davis Path being not particularly interesting and its length being so great, it did not become popular, and so it was abandoned in 1853 and was for many years actually obliterated for all but a very small portion of the way. Professor Huntington, however, ascended by it in 1871, and W. H. Pickering and W. S. Fenollosa followed its route in the main or where possible, in an excursion to Mount Washington via Mounts Crawford, Resolution, Davis, and Isolation in 1880. In August and September, 1910, under the direction of Warren W. Hart, Councillor of Improvements of the Appalachian Mountain Club in that year, this ancient path was reopened.

A path-builder whose name became early connected with the Glen side of the Mountain, and is permanently associated with Tuckerman's Ravine,

TRAILS AND PATH-BUILDERS

is the late Major Curtis B. Raymond, of Boston, for many years an explorer and ardent lover of the Mountains. Major Raymond first visited the Ravine in 1854. In 1879, he opened the well-known Raymond Path, which leaves the carriage road two miles up the Mountain and ascends by easy grades to the snow arch. This was in the main an old route, that of the bridle path which was cut by Landlord Thompson, of the Glen House, but which had in course of time become more or less obstructed by falling trees. From the Raymond Path a side path diverges to the celebrated Raymond Cataract, while the Appalachian Mountain Club Crystal Cascade Path, also opened in 1879, joins it a quarter of a mile or so below Hermit Lake. In 1891, Major Raymond improved his path, and, after his death in February, 1893, his widow maintained the path for some years. It was reopened in 1904 and is now an A.M.C. path. These two paths with the trail from the snow arch to the Summit, laid out by F. H. Burt and others in 1881 and now maintained by the Club, constitute a continuous route through Tuckerman's Ravine to the summit of Mount Washington.

Benjamin F. Osgood, for many years head porter of the Glen House and noted as a guide, has been already mentioned in the latter and other connections. He was also something of a path-builder, for in 1878 he opened a path to Mount Madison from a point near the Glen House, and in 1881 built a path from Osgood's Falls on the Mount Madison path to Spaulding's Lake, or just beyond it, at the head of the Great Gulf. The Osgood Path fell into

THE WHITE MOUNTAINS

disuse after the burning of the Glen House, but was reopened in 1904. In 1907, the Appalachian Mountain Club relocated its lower end and adopted it as an official path.

The founding of the Appalachian Mountain Club in 1876 marks the beginning of a new epoch in the exploration, study, and pleasure use of the White Mountains, for, although the Club has "taken all outdoors for its field," it is to this region that the major part of its attention has been directed. Indeed, the White Mountains may be regarded as peculiarly an A.M.C. preserve.

Three years before this important event, what is believed to be the first organization of the sort ever attempted in America was formed in the White Mountain Club of Portland, Maine. Its object was, however, amusement rather than exploration and scientific study. It had been by members of this then future club that Carrigain was early visited (only Professor Guyot and party had previously been there), Professor George L. Vose and Mr. G. F. Morse, with J. O. Cobb for a guide, accomplishing this difficult climb on September 20–21, 1869.

On August 29–31, 1873, a second ascent of this mountain was made, this time by a party of six men from Portland or its vicinity, with two local men hired as guides. This is known in the White Mountain Club annals as "the famous Carrigain party," and, indeed, the expedition was a memorable one because of an action taken during it. The first day was spent — because the guides knew nothing

TRAILS AND PATH-BUILDERS

of the country — in futile wandering over the worst kind of obstructions. The men were without water, and so, when, in the late afternoon, they came again upon Carrigain Brook, which they had crossed early in the day, they camped for the night. There and then the White Mountain Club was founded. The next day the ascent of the mountain was achieved by the new club.

The beginnings of the Appalachian Mountain Club were on this wise. The project of forming an organization "for the advancement of the interests of those who visit the mountains of New England and adjacent regions, whether for the purpose of scientific research or summer recreation," had been for some time a subject of discussion among scientists and others residing in or near Boston who were mountain-lovers. The suggestion of such a club must date back many years. At length definite action looking toward its realization was taken. The initiative came from Professor E. C. Pickering, who, on January 1, 1876, issued fifty cards of invitation to a meeting, at the Massachusetts Institute of Technology in Boston, "of those interested in mountain exploration." Professor Charles E. Fay was chairman of this first meeting, held on January 8. After three preliminary meetings, the first regular meeting was held on February 9, when a permanent organization was formed, the original number of members being thirty-nine. Professor Pickering, to whom unquestionably belongs the honor of founding the Club, was naturally chosen as its first president.

THE WHITE MOUNTAINS

As the interest in the Club grew and the scope of its activities became enlarged and more defined, it was soon evident that it would be advisable for it to have a legal standing, and so early in 1878 a corporation was formed to enable the Club to hold and defend a legal title to any property of which it might become possessed. The number of incorporators was one hundred and fifty, the same name was retained, and the objects of the Club were set forth as "to explore the mountains of New England and the adjacent regions, both for scientific and artistic purposes; and, in general, to cultivate an interest in geographical studies." The first meeting of the corporation was held on March 13, 1878; at the eighth corporate meeting, on January 8, 1879, a resolution was passed dissolving the "voluntary, unincorporated association heretofore known by the name of the Appalachian Mountain Club."

When one comes to pass in review the activities of the Club in the White Mountains during the years since its founding and to record its services in the exploration of the region and in the promotion of the pleasure of visitors, and especially of those who are fond of mountaineering, one must declare at the outset that time would fail him to tell of a tithe of the Club's doings and benefactions. In the way of commendation of the organization's work, it may be said that all who love to follow a trail up and over the Mountains, and to live in the open, owe to the Appalachian Mountain Club an ever-increasing debt for its contributions to the opportunities and facilities for their enjoyment of the White

THE MOUNT PLEASANT TRAIL

A. M. C. HUTS ON MOUNT MADISON

TRAILS AND PATH-BUILDERS

Mountains, and will, one and all, wish to utter a fervent "Amen" to Dr. Hale's simple benediction, "Blessings on the Appalachian Club."

One will have to be content also with little more than a mere enumeration of some of the more important of the Club's explorations, path-building and other constructive undertakings, and other activities.

It is the custom of the Club to hold one general field meeting in the summer of each year. Most of these gatherings have been held in the White Mountains, a goodly number of them, the first in 1886, at the Summit House on Mount Washington. Other places of meeting have been the Crawford House, the Profile House, North Conway,[1] Jefferson, Jackson, Bethlehem, and North Woodstock.

A winter excursion is now a feature of the Club year. The earliest of these was made in 1882, in the first days of February. Jackson was the headquarters on this occasion, when a ride through the Notch to Fabyan was taken.

The first important building work ever undertaken by the Club is the provision for shelter on the Northern Peaks, in the form of a stone cabin or hut at the Madison Spring, which is located on the south flank of Mount Madison in the depression between that peak and Mount Adams. The advisability and feasibility of having a place of refuge at this point having been demonstrated, construction was begun in August, 1888, the masons going into

[1] The first field meeting, that of 1876, was held there, ascents being made of Kearsarge and Willard

THE WHITE MOUNTAINS

camp on the 21st and finishing the walls in about three weeks. Then ensued a prolonged spell of extraordinarily stormy weather, and it was with the greatest difficulty that the roof was got on and the hut made tight for the winter. As originally constructed, the building's inside dimensions were sixteen and one half by twelve and one quarter feet, and it was seven feet high at the eaves and eleven at the ridge of the roof. The walls are about two feet thick and are constructed of flat stones carefully fitted and pointed inside and outside with Portland cement. The plans were furnished by J. F. Eaton and the original cost was about eight hundred dollars. The work of construction was completed in 1889. In 1906, the hut was enlarged by the building of a compartment for women. Still further provision for the comfort and convenience of pedestrians was made by the erection of a second building in 1911, which was opened for use in 1912. This "hut" contains two rooms, one a living-room for the caretaker and the other a kitchen and dining-room in which to prepare and serve meals to the guests.

Continuing its policy of promoting the interests of those vacationists who prefer to tramp, and especially of improving existing facilities for their convenience and protection while on an extended trip, the Club, in 1914, replaced with a stone hut its log cabin in the Carter Notch, which building had served as a shelter in that region for ten years, but which had proved unsatisfactory in location and in several other ways. For this new camp in this deep wild cleft in the Carter-Moriah Range, which

TRAILS AND PATH-BUILDERS

lies east of the Presidential Range, a better situation than that of the old cabin was chosen. The latter was close under the western slope of Carter Dome, but the new structure is in an open place beside the southern one of the two beautiful tarns in the middle of the Notch and commands a pleasant outlook down the Wildcat Valley toward Jackson. This, the third of the Club's stone huts, has accommodations for thirty-six persons, with separate heated rooms for men and women.

The most recent building enterprise of the Club is the Lakes of the Clouds Hut, which was constructed in the early summer of 1915 and opened to the use of the mountain-climbing fraternity in August. It is located on a little terrace on the Mount Monroe side of the larger of the two lakelets from which it gets its name, faces the south, from which direction the bridle path approaches it, and, although not situated directly on the path, is only a few rods from it. In planning the kind of structure to be erected at this situation, which, unlike those of the other A.M.C. huts, is in a place from which it is a long, and in violent weather a dangerous, way to the protecting timber of lower levels, it was thought advisable to depart somewhat from the type of hut previously built and to construct one in which the tramper — who, if caught at this point in a storm, must perforce wait it out there — would be able to pass a more comfortable time than is possible in the older kind of hut, with its low walls and few and narrow windows. So the new hut was provided with somewhat higher stone walls, — it is

THE WHITE MOUNTAINS

not, like the first Madison Hut, built into the side of the mountain, — and, as a special constructive feature, with several large plate-glass windows, consisting not, however, of single panes, but of large lights set in steel frames. In the lighter and otherwise more attractive interior thus made possible, a person imprisoned during a driving tempest would have a rather pleasant experience, being able not only to stay there in comparative comfort, but also to watch the antics of the storm; while in clear weather, if it happened to be too cool or too windy to remain outside with pleasure, a sojourner at this camp would find it far from disagreeable to sit within and view the prospect down the Ammonoosuc ravine and away to the distance. Accommodations, not luxurious but comfortable, are provided for twelve women and twenty-four men.

A new convenience for mountain-climbers, introduced in 1915, was the establishment of wireless telegraph service at the Madison, Lakes of the Clouds, and Carter Notch Huts, radio outfits being installed at each, so that thereby intending visitors might be enabled to reserve accommodations from hut to hut or from the world below by telephoning to the Madison Hut.

Other shelters of a less permanent character have been built by the Club in various parts of the Mountains, as, near Hermit Lake in Tuckerman's Ravine, on the Crawford Path,[1] and on Mount Liberty in

---

[1] The shelter on this trail was built in 1901, as has been stated in connection with the recital of the story of the perishing of Curtis and Ormsbee. In 1915, on the erection of the Lakes of the Clouds Hut,

A. M. C. HUT ON MOUNT MONROE

MOUNT MONROE HUT INTERIOR

TRAILS AND PATH-BUILDERS

the Franconia Range; and it is one of the ambitions of this benevolent organization to establish a chain of huts and camps throughout the Mountains as one of its agencies for achieving its purpose of cultivating the tramping habit and the love of woods and mountains.

On the Northern Peaks are a number of privately built camps, such as the Log Cabin, constructed by William G. Nowell in 1890, and the Cascade and Perch Camps, built in 1892-93 by the late Professor Edmands, of Harvard Observatory, a member of the Appalachian Club, who at his own expense constructed also many miles of paths on the Presidential Range, including the Gulfside Trail, the Randolph Path, the Israel Ridge Path, the Edmands Path from between Mounts Franklin and Pleasant down the side of the latter, and the Westside Trail.

These paths and many others are now maintained by the Club. Not a few have been newly constructed and a number of older ones have been reopened. The work of path-making was almost immediately taken up by the Club after its organization and has since been a very important feature of its work. In 1876 and afterward, Lowe's Path up Mount Adams was improved, and in that and the following year, the Jackson-Carter Notch Path, another Club path, was built by Jonathan G. Davis. A Club path to Tuckerman's Ravine from the Crystal Cascade was, as we have seen, opened in 1879. In 1878 and 1894, paths were opened along Snyder Brook on the side

it was removed to a point, about half a mile farther north, where the Boott Spur Trail meets the Crawford Path.

THE WHITE MOUNTAINS

of Mount Madison, sections of which paths were incorporated in the graded Valley Way from Appalachia Station to the Madison Hut, a path built by Professor Edmands in 1895–97. In 1882, a trail was built by the Club over the Twin Mountain Range. The Air Line Path up Durand Ridge to Mount Adams was built as to its lower part by Messrs. W. H. Peek, E. B. Cook, and L. M. Watson, in 1883–84, and in the latter year a trail to the Castellated Ridge on Mount Jefferson was made under the direction of William G. Nowell. The old Fabyan (originally Crawford) Path to Mount Pleasant was reopened by the Club in 1886, but, being little used, it soon became overgrown again.[1] A path up Mount Garfield[2] in the Franconia Range was opened in 1897. The Boott Spur Trail, which utilizes a mile of the old Davis Trail before it joins the Crawford Trail, dates from 1900. Six years later, the Glen Boulder Trail was opened to the summit of Mount Washington.

Club paths are now to be found over the entire Mountain region. There are, for instance, trails up Mount Moosilauke and a path ascending the Franconia Range from the south through the Flume. The Club is now devoting its attention to the perfecting of an organic system of main through-route paths, by which it will be possible to traverse nearly all the principal ranges and valleys from end to end and to cross from one valley to another.

[1] In 1900, this path was again reopened, this time by Mr. Anderson, of the Mount Pleasant House, and Professor Edmands, who had it cleared and improved. A new road was made then to the foot of the mountain.

[2] So named in 1881, at the suggestion of Frances E. Willard.

TRAILS AND PATH-BUILDERS

Reservations are owned by the Club in various parts of the Mountains, notably at North Woodstock, Appalachia, Shelburne, the Glen Ellis Falls, and the Crystal Cascade.

Another undertaking of the Club is the maintenance on most of the less-frequented summits of copper cylinders containing paper and pencil, for recording ascents and the names of the climbers. This was a systemization of a matter hitherto left to individual initiative and only sporadically attended to. As it may be of some interest to the reader to have set before him the circumstances connected with the previous attempts of this nature alluded to, a brief narration of them may therefore be pardonably interjected here.

Mention was made in the early pages of this chronicle of one or two cases in which visitors to the top of Mount Washington left on the Summit a record of their achievement in mountaineering.[1] In 1824, Ethan Allen Crawford attempted to make provision for those who wished to leave their names, carrying up a thin piece of sheet lead, eight or ten feet in length and seven inches wide, which was put round a roller he made for the purpose. He also made an iron pencil for use on the lead, by which means he thought visitors could much more quickly and easily register their names "than they could carve them with a chisel and hammer on a rock." The party of vandals from Jackson, already spoken of as carrying off the brass plate placed on the

---

[1] See the accounts of the expeditions of Belknap's party (p. 31); of Brazer and Dawson (p. 84); and of Dr. Bigelow (p. 37).

THE WHITE MOUNTAINS

Mountain in 1818, also took away at the same time (1825) Mr. Crawford's sheet of lead, which is said to have been run into musket balls.

The next placing of a register on a White Mountain summit is credited to the famous guide, Benjamin F. Osgood, who on August 12, 1854, placed a roll, probably in a bottle, on Mount Adams. By 1866, it contained twelve names, it is said, and ten years later twenty. Lastly, L. L. Holden, of the *Boston Journal*, in his account, in "Mount Washington in Winter," of the excursion of Mr. Nelson and himself to Mount Adams on the 6th of May, 1871, tells of their inscribing their names "upon an old sardine box which had evidently served as a sort of visitors' register for nearly a dozen years."

The Appalachian Mountain Club took up this matter of providing means for registration of ascents in the first summer of its existence, William G. Nowell placing a Club bottle on the summit of Mount Adams on July 22, 1876, as the roll placed in this receptacle records. On August 23 of the next year, the bottle was replaced by an A.M.C. cylinder. The successive rolls on Mount Adams are in good order and form a continuous, or nearly continuous, record. Their history is marked, however, by one noteworthy occurrence, for in June, 1894, the cylinder was struck by lightning and destroyed. It was promptly replaced. On the new roll of that year, it is recorded that a small party suffered to some extent from the shock of that stroke. The year 1876 appears to be the date that Mount Madison first received a register.

TRAILS AND PATH-BUILDERS

The last of the Club's activities I shall mention in this fragmentary and, considering the merit of its achievements, far from commensurate, account of them, is one of the most important. This is its means of disseminating among its members and to the world in general the information, scientific and other, acquired by explorations, the reports of the various departments of the Club work, and the like. The Club's journal, *Appalachia*, was established immediately after the Club's founding in 1876, and the first number appeared in June of that year. The idea of publishing papers by members of the Club in an official periodical was conceived by the entomologist, Samuel H. Scudder, the Club's first vice-president and second president. He determined the form and character of the magazine, gave it its euphonious and now widely known name, and was its first editor. As a large part of the contents of the journal relates to the White Mountains, the volumes constitute a scientific and topographical record of them of inestimable value.

XVII

THE GREAT FIRE ON MOUNT WASHINGTON — OTHER RECENT EVENTS OF INTEREST

ASIDE from the establishment of the White Mountain National Forest, to be dealt with in the next chapter, the most notable event in recent White Mountain history is an occurrence which has already been several times mentioned incidentally, the great fire of the night of Thursday, June 18, 1908, by which the active portion of the settlement on New England's highest point was in a few hours wiped out and the Summit thrown back to the primitive conditions of half a century before. This most disastrous conflagration not only was a serious setback to the business interests concerned, — a reparable injury, — but, by its removal of a number of ancient landmarks about which were clustered memories and associations of many a sort, it occasioned a sentimental loss which cannot be recovered. For it was with genuine sorrow that the news of the fire came to thousands throughout this country and in distant lands, and particularly was the destruction of the hotel lamented by those who as permanent summer guests had enjoyed the hospitality and shelter of the Summit House, and by those whose occupations were in connection with the enterprises conducted on the Summit.

Many had been the pleasant gatherings around the office stove enjoyed by the little Summit colony

FIRE ON MOUNT WASHINGTON

or "family," as they called themselves. To them, such was their attachment to their summer home, the passing of the old structure was like the loss of a dear human friend. Wrote Annie Trumbull Slosson, a regular sojourner at the Summit: "I know . . . that no new hostelry . . . will ever be to us, the little band of habitués, of annual dwellers therein, of devoted pilgrims seeking each summer a loved shrine, just the same as the dear old Summit House. Of late years it had been my home, my *homiest* home. . . . Dear old house! I loved every timber, every clapboard of it."

As a spectacle the fire, involving so many buildings situated at such an elevation, and occurring, as it did, in the early evening of a clear day, was naturally a brilliant and far viewable one. As in addition to these circumstances the fire was early discovered and the news of it soon communicated to the Mountain towns and villages, many inhabitants of the localities from which Mount Washington is visible were enabled to witness this unforgettable sight and even to watch the conflagration's progress.

There is a dramatic element, too, in the time of year of the fire's occurrence, for it was while preparations were going actively forward for the summer. For several days previous to that calamitous Thursday, the railway men had been employed during the day in putting things in readiness. The section of track along the platform had just been reconstructed, the following Sunday the manager and other employees of the hotel were due to arrive, and the opening was set for the 29th.

THE WHITE MOUNTAINS

On the fateful day, work had been done under the direction of Superintendent John Horne in making the Summit House habitable for the summer. Between 4.30 and 5 P.M. the employees' train left for the Base, but before its departure a party of young people from Berlin arrived, who had come over the Range from the Madison Hut and were intending to pass the night in the stage office. Everything was apparently right when the railway employees departed.

It had been a beautiful day, and there was a brilliant sunset. After the sun had gone down, the light still lingered on the peaks, as it was nearly the longest day of the year. No one thought of any disaster being about to happen. The railway men had settled themselves for a quiet evening's rest; others were enjoying the beauty of the evening sky.

It was at the Fabyan House, probably, that the first discovery of the fire from below was made. A number of persons connected with the hotel, or staying there, as they came out from supper caught sight of a glow on the Summit House. The bookkeeper of the hotel, who first saw it, called to his friends to come to see the "pretty sight." One of the latter, the clerk, soon detected a suspicious flickering of the light and so hurriedly summoned Colonel Barron, who was at the cottage, by telephone. At first the latter thought it was the reflection of the sunlight, but soon an outburst of flame revealed the light's true nature, and an alarm was at once telephoned to the Base, where, such is the station's position in relation to the Summit, no sign

FIRE ON MOUNT WASHINGTON

of the fire had been discovered. Immediately a train was made ready and a force of employees under Superintendent Horne started for the Summit. Not until the Gulf Tank was reached were the flames visible from the train. As the top was approached, it could be seen that the hotel was already a mass of flames and that it would be impossible to run the train to the platform. So a stop was made a short distance below the water tank, and the remainder of the way was made on foot. When the men arrived, the roof of the Summit House had already gone, the fire was working its way to the cottage, the stage office had fallen in, the home of *Among the Clouds* was ablaze, and the train-shed had been completely destroyed. The walk leading to the Tip-Top House was at once cut away, as the fire had begun to creep along it, but this precaution proved unnecessary, as the high wind kept the flames from traveling farther in that direction. Soon the Signal Station caught from the fire in the ruins of the train-shed, and the crest of the peak was an unbroken line of flame. Nothing could be done to stay the work of destruction, and the powerless men could only watch the progress of the flames and think of what it meant.

When the fire was seen at the Glen House, the housekeeper immediately telephoned to the office at Gorham of the E. Libby & Sons Company, the firm which controls the carriage road, and to the Halfway House. The superintendent of the road, George C. Baird, at once prepared to start for the Summit in a wagon. Before he left, four boys of the Berlin party arrived, having hurried down to give the alarm.

THE WHITE MOUNTAINS

Near the five-mile post the remainder of the party were met, one of whom, a teacher, said the flames had first been seen breaking from a window in the corner of the hotel nearest the printing-office. Some of them had entered to try to put out the fire, but it had gained such headway that they were unsuccessful. They also tried to telephone, not knowing that the telephone had been disconnected. Superintendent Baird reached the Summit in time to see the fire at its height.

Before midnight the fire had burned itself out and the Crown of New England was covered with a desolate heap of embers and ashes, charred timbers, and ruined metal work, the Tip-Top House alone of all the Summit buildings being left to watch over this sad scene of devastation.

The buildings destroyed have been already named. Besides the Tip-Top House, the flames also spared the two stables, a few hundred feet below the Summit. The high wind was the means of saving the upper stable, as the gusts blew off the blazing pieces of wood which fell on the roof of that building before they had time to do more than scorch the shingles.

The destruction of all but one of the buildings made a great alteration in the sky-line of the top of Mount Washington as seen from below, restoring it nearly to the appearance it had about 1855. The tall chimney of the hotel, however, which remained standing for some time, stood out like a monument and was a striking object from all the country round.

Plans for rebuilding the hotel were at once talked of, and it was at first thought that by extraordinary

THE FIRE ON MOUNT WASHINGTON AS SEEN FROM GORHAM

FIRE ON MOUNT WASHINGTON

efforts a new hotel might be ready for use by the first of August. When, however, it was remembered that it took two years to build the destroyed hotel and two hundred and fifty trains to carry up the material, and that on account of the exposed position and the uncertain weather conditions work on the mountain-top was both difficult and dangerous, it was seen that reconstruction would have to proceed slowly.

Meanwhile, the only thing to do was to restore the Tip-Top House to its original use as a hotel, and, accordingly, steps were at once taken to that end. The railway ties and supporting timbers, which had been burned, and the rails, which had been twisted out of shape, were replaced by almost superhuman efforts as soon as the 29th day of June, so that the first regular passenger train made its trip on that day, according to schedule. The repairs on the Tip-Top House were also hastened along. The old partitions, floors, and sheathing were taken out and replaced by new material, the windows were again exposed to daylight, and the observatory room at the back was fitted up as a kitchen. Soon the old house, unused as a hotel for an interval of thirty-five years, was, under the conduct of the staff of the Summit House, entertaining visitors in the plain but cheerful and comfortable manner of a half-century before.

And such were the conditions of hospitality that obtained on Mount Washington for seven years after the fire; for, although plans were made for the early erection of a new wooden hotel on the Summit,

THE WHITE MOUNTAINS

and, on the 27th of July, 1910, the cornerstone was laid and work begun on the foundation of a building on the Summit House site, no new building crowned Mount Washington until the summer of 1915.

The foundation just mentioned was completed, but further work was not carried on, as the adoption of more elaborate plans, which provided for the erection of a massive Summit House of stone, concrete, steel, and glass, whose center should be on the very apex of the peak, and for the building of a scenic electric railway, twenty miles long, up Mount Washington, were about that time decided upon by the railroads interested. But the depression in business in New England and the failure of the project for combining the two principal railroads of this section into one system prevented the consummation of the plans, and the undertaking, which, on any such scale as here outlined, would seem to have been, even under the most favorable conditions, a chimerical one, was abandoned. The surveys, however, were made and the lines of the proposed building staked out. The survey, also, of the railroad, which was laid out to circle the Mountain several times in ascending it, was begun on July 4, 1911, and was completed in October, 1912.[1]

---

[1] The roadbed was to be constructed of rock and the grade was to be uniformly six per cent. The cost was estimated to be upwards of a million dollars, and the time required for construction about two years. The route starts at the Base Station, goes up Mount Jefferson to the very edge of the Castellated Ridge, crosses the west slopes of Jefferson and Clay, and winds around the cone of Mount Washington two and a half times, passing close to the head wall of Tuckerman's Ravine, Boott Spur, and the Lakes of the Clouds. The necessary permission for building the road and appurtenances was granted to the

OTHER EVENTS OF INTEREST

The year 1915 was rendered a memorable year in the annals of Mount Washington by two events, the construction and opening of a new Summit hotel and the occurrence of another fire, by which an ancient landmark was for the most part destroyed.

After the abandonment of the project, just outlined, of building a scenic railway up the Mountain and a very costly hotel on the Summit, nothing was done for a year or so about constructing a new house there. But the idea of having some kind of shelter for visitors more commodious and comfortable than was furnished by the old Tip-Top House was not given up by the persons most concerned in the matter, the officials of the Concord and Montreal Railroad Company, which controls the Mount Washington Railway. At length it was decided to build a modest structure, using the accumulated profits of the little road to pay for it, and plans for a new building on this basis were completed in the autumn of 1914.

As most of the people who come to the Summit remain but a few hours, it was thought advisable in designing the interior to adapt it to serve principally as a station and restaurant, but the provision of comfortable accommodations for those visitors who desire to spend a night in order to witness the impressive sunset and sunrise, or who wish to remain for a longer time, was by no means disregarded.

Last summer saw the materialization of these

Concord and Montreal Railroad by the New Hampshire Board of Public Service Commissioners in July, 1912. One result of the survey is the most accurate map ever made of Washington, Clay, and Jefferson.

THE WHITE MOUNTAINS

plans, and Mount Washington is now again crowned with a Summit House, and one equal in appointments and in comfort to any mountain-top hotel in the world. The new house, which is one hundred and sixty-eight feet long, thirty-eight feet wide, and one and one-half stories in height, is constructed of wood, has its outside walls shingled, and rests upon the foundation already mentioned as having been completed some years ago upon the site of its predecessor. The building was framed at Lisbon during the winter and the frame was hauled to the Base in the early spring. Work was commenced on the Summit on May 10, about twenty men, who boarded in the Tip-Top House, being employed. Although the workmen had to contend in May with snow, frost, terrific winds, clouds, and rain, which rendered it impossible to work at all on some days, and with more or less bad weather later, good progress was made and the hotel was completed in time to be opened about a month before the close of the season.

To avoid having to resort to the usual practice of anchoring the building to the Mountain with stout chains in order to hold it on its foundation, the sills of this substantial structure are sunk in the solid concrete and then secured with heavy iron bolts, each post is fastened to the sills with wrought-iron straps, and the second half-story is similarly bound to the first-floor plates.

The main floor is given up mostly to the office, restaurant, and other public rooms, while the guest-rooms and employees' rooms are on the floor above.

OTHER EVENTS OF INTEREST

The hotel is heated with steam, lighted with electricity, and supplied with water from the Lakes of the Clouds, which is pumped from the Base into a large tank located on the highest point of the Summit.

The opening of the new house took place on August 21, in the presence of prominent railroad officials, various members of the Appalachian Mountain Club, many residents of the Mountain towns, and others. Among the special features of this celebration, which was such an event as Mount Washington had never seen before, was a flag-raising, a dinner, an address on "The Old Times and the New," by Rev. Dr. Harry P. Nichols, to whom was given the honor of being the first to register, and an illumination by means of rockets of many colors and red lights, for which latter railroad fusees were used. This display, which began at 9 P.M. and lasted for half an hour, was given a spectacular finish by the descent of the railroad in three minutes by the veteran roadmaster Patrick Camden on a slideboard, carrying gleaming red lights. He was followed by the train similarly illuminated, and the final note was struck by the firing of a dynamite salute at the Glen House. Unfortunately, clouds prevented the illumination of the Summit being seen at distant points, and the success of the idea of lighting up various Mountain peaks with bonfires in honor of the event.

The New Summit House had been opened but a week, when Mount Washington was the scene of another spectacular event, the burning of the famous

THE WHITE MOUNTAINS

old Tip-Top House, which very nearly involved its sister building in its own fate. Providentially, the wind during the fire was from the northeast and so carried the flames directly away from the new building, which otherwise would not have been spared.

The blaze was discovered at seven o'clock on Sunday morning, August 29, and in an hour's time the roof and other woodwork were entirely consumed, and only the stone walls, which did not crumble at all, were left standing. The fire, which is supposed to have been caused by a defective chimney, was fed by quantities of paint and oil stored in the building, and spread so rapidly that the occupants, a cook and four carpenters employed on the Summit House, were not able to save many of their belongings. The only object connected with the building that was saved was the old weather-beaten sign over the door, which was rescued from the burning structure by a grandson of John H. Spaulding, one of the builders and early landlords of the ancient hotel.

The fire was visible for miles around, and appeared so large that when first seen at the various resorts among the Mountains, many feared that the new house was burning. The news soon spread that it was the old Tip-Top House that was on fire, and so thousands of people witnessed from afar the spectacular passing of one of the most famous landmarks in New England. The destruction of the old house so soon after its mission was fulfilled, of affording a shelter to visitors during a period when it was so much needed, added the last touch of pathos to

OTHER EVENTS OF INTEREST

the history of this venerable monument of early enterprise. But the Tip-Top House is not to remain a ruin or to disappear from the landscape, for it is the announced intention of the railway company to restore it so far as possible to its former appearance by rebuilding the wooden roof on the old walls.

The chronicle of events relating to Mount Washington would be incomplete without some mention of the famous "Climbs to the Clouds" of a few years since. The rapid progress in the development of the automobile about the beginning of the twentieth century and the successful construction of powerful steam and gasoline vehicles stimulated manufacturers and owners to test the hill-climbing capabilities of the new mechanical means of transportation. Naturally the attention of enthusiastic motorists was drawn to the Mount Washington Carriage Road as furnishing the most difficult piece of hill-climbing in the East and thus the finest possible test of the quality of a machine in this respect, and also the opportunity for making records in a new and exciting form of sport.

Permission having been obtained to make use of the road in this way, Mr. and Mrs. F. O. Stanley, of Newton, Massachusetts, made on August 31, 1899, the first ascent by automobile, the machine being a steam one. The first officially timed ascent of the Mountain by automobile was made on August 25, 1903, when the trip took one hour and forty-six minutes. The following year, on July 11 and 12, the first automobile climbing contest was held. Harry S. Harkness made a record of 24 minutes, $37\frac{3}{8}$

THE WHITE MOUNTAINS

seconds, and F. E. Stanley one of 28 minutes, $19\tfrac{2}{5}$ seconds.

These records were surpassed in the second "Climb to the Clouds," which took place on July 17 and 18, 1905. In this contest the best time was made by W. M. Hilliard, 20 minutes, $58\tfrac{2}{5}$ seconds. Bert Holland in a steam car made the ascent in 22 minutes, $17\tfrac{3}{5}$ seconds.[1] The climb has been made on a motor cycle in 20 minutes, $59\tfrac{1}{5}$ seconds, Stanley T. Kellogg achieving the feat.

A distinguished visitor to the summit of Mount Washington in 1907 was Ambassador James Bryce, who, accompanied by Mrs. Bryce, Rev. Dr. Harry P. Nichols, and a few others, walked up the Crawford Bridle Path late in the season. Mr. Bryce (as he was then), who is an enthusiastic mountaineer and a former president of the English Alpine Club, enjoyed greatly the walks and climbs in the neighborhood of Intervale, where the summer home of the British Embassy was established that year. The unfavorable weather he was so unfortunate as to experience on the Summit did not spoil the enjoyment of the visit for the genial British gentleman, whose delightful personality is most pleasantly remembered by all who were privileged to meet him at that time.

Much interest has been taken in late years in Lost River, a small stream in the Kinsman Notch. About seven miles west of North Woodstock, this

[1] A related automobile feat may be noted here. This is the record climb of Tug-of-War Hill (so-called), the steep ascent from the south to the Gate of the Notch, which was achieved in July, 1906, in the time of 2 minutes and 48 seconds.

LOST RIVER

OTHER EVENTS OF INTEREST

mountain brook passes for a distance of about half a mile through a remarkable series of glacial caverns, which is the third great curiosity in the Franconia Mountain region, the Profile and the Flume being the other two. In these dark and gloomy caves, which are from forty to seventy-five feet deep, the water of this mountain brook disappears from sight and at times from sound. This unique natural wonder, which far surpasses the Flume in its surprises and its massive rock structure, was discovered about 1855 by R. C. Jackman, of North Woodstock. About 1875, when he returned to live in North Woodstock after an absence of some fifteen years, he cut a footpath to the caves, and for a number of years he acted as a guide to this and other scenic attractions of the region. Fortunately, in 1912, the Society for the Protection of New Hampshire Forests acquired a forest reservation of one hundred and forty-eight acres surrounding and including the caves, the owners generously offering to give the land if the Society would buy the standing timber on the tract. A legacy and gifts enabled the Society to accept the offer, the sum required being about seven thousand dollars. Further gifts have made it possible to provide bridges, ladders, and trails to render the caverns accessible, and to build a comfortable shelter for the use of visitors.

Two important highways built in the early years of the present century should receive at least a brief mention because of interesting circumstances connected with them. One is the John Anderson Memorial Road, named in honor of the senior mem-

THE WHITE MOUNTAINS

ber of the noted former hotel firm of Anderson and Price, of Bretton Woods. Mr. Anderson, who was the son of General Samuel J. Anderson, of Portland and Ogdensburg Railway fame, did much for the White Mountains.

The road came into existence in this way. Desiring to find a way from Bretton Woods to the Franconia Notch which would be shorter than the existing road via Bethlehem and Franconia Village, and which would avoid the long climbs on that route, Mr. Anderson, with a party from Bretton Woods, in the autumn of 1902, explored the region lying between that locality and the Franconia Notch. The route for a road was surveyed by R. T. Gile in November of that year, and a final location was made by him in the summer of the next year. In the autumn of 1903, a bridle path was constructed under the supervision of the State Engineer and opened. In July, 1905, the State began the work of developing the bridle path into a highway, which was constructed that summer and autumn. After Mr. Anderson's death, which occurred at Ormond, Florida, in February, 1911, his name was fittingly attached to this new State Road, which runs from near Twin Mountain to the Profile Golf Links.

The other highway, the Jefferson Notch Road, besides being one of convenience, is because of its location one of the grandest drives in the State. Rising, as it does, to an elevation of three thousand and eleven feet, it commands magnificent views. When the construction of this road was agitated, the New Hampshire Legislature appropriated six

OTHER EVENTS OF INTEREST

thousand dollars for the purpose, on condition that the additional expense should be defrayed by private subscription. Toward the needed amount several hotel companies, the Boston and Maine Railroad Company, and the citizens of Jefferson Highlands contributed forty-five hundred dollars.

The southern division, to which the State Highway Commissioners have given the name Mount Clinton Road, as much of its course lies along the slope of that mountain, was built by Contractor Thomas Trudeau, of Pierce Bridge, and was opened November 8, 1901. The Commissioners, Messrs. John Anderson, C. H. Merrill, and E. A. Crawford (the third of the name), were, however, unable to find contractors willing to undertake the task of constructing the northern or Jefferson division. Mr. Crawford then came to the rescue and personally constructed the road. In carrying the project through to a successful conclusion, he had to meet many difficulties, which included bad weather, construction through forest and rock and over the crest of a ridge, the holding together of a force of sturdy mountain men, and the pledging of his own credit for the funds required in the prosecution of the work.

The first trip over the road was made on August 9, 1902, when Mr. Crawford drove a three-seated buckboard, drawn by two horses and containing six other persons, from the Base Station of the Mount Washington Railway to his house in Jefferson Highlands. The formal opening was held on Tuesday, September 9, 1902, when Mr. Crawford drove over the road in an eight-horse wagon, in which were

THE WHITE MOUNTAINS

Governor Chester B. Jordan and his councillors. At the summit of the road the party was met by a cavalcade from Bretton Woods. After an exchange of bugle salutes, a dismounting, a handshaking, and general congratulation, the horsemen escorted the governor's party to the Mount Washington Hotel, then recently opened, where luncheon was had. Among the party at the opening was the venerable Stephen M. Crawford, son of Ethan Allen Crawford, the pioneer.

This road, so auspiciously opened, was nearly destroyed by the tremendous downpour of June 11 and 12, 1903, but it was repaired and in July, 1904, reopened.

Of late years the Jefferson division has been usable only for horses by fording, as the bridges over two streams had not been replaced. After the Legislature of 1914 had failed to make an appropriation for reopening the road so as to make it passable by automobiles, the Bretton Woods Company and a prominent summer resident of Jefferson Highlands jointly undertook to rebuild the road at their own expense. In 1915, it was advertised to be open, but the frequent rains of that summer rendered it rather unsafe or at any rate difficult to travel over.

XVIII

THE LUMBER INDUSTRY IN THE WHITE MOUNTAINS — THE PERIL OF THE FORESTS — THE WHITE MOUNTAIN NATIONAL FOREST — OTHER RESERVATIONS

BUT one other important event, and that one which is still in process, remains to be recorded before this chronicle shall be completed by having been brought down to this present. The event referred to is the creation and increment of the White Mountain National Forest.

In order to arrive at a proper understanding of the circumstances which gradually made evident the necessity for action of this sort, it is essential to review briefly the history of lumbering in this region and to give also some facts relating to the local effects of the reckless cutting of the trees practiced by settlers and lumbermen, and, further, some information regarding the destructive effects here and there in the Mountains of that other menace to the life of the forest, the forest fire. When this shall have been done, I shall rehearse as briefly as I may the steps in the rather prolonged process which proved necessary to bring about the desired action in respect to the White Mountain forest on the part of the Federal Government, and shall conclude with some brief statements as to the other reservations in the region.

THE WHITE MOUNTAINS

From the first settlement of the region of northern New Hampshire, lumbering has been a leading industry there. In the earlier settled towns along the coast there was from the beginning a demand for building material and ship timber, and so the settlers in the river valleys among the Mountains soon recognized the commercial value of the veteran white pines. Moreover, the forests were regarded as more or less of an obstruction to agriculture and as therefore to be removed as soon and as rapidly as possible. The histories of the early days of various towns bear witness to the beginning and development of the lumber industry. An account of Shelburne in 1800 speaks of the prodigal use of the best trees for the frames of houses and for the making of shingles, baskets, chair bottoms, ox bows, etc., all the rest of the timber cleared, it is stated, being piled and burned on the spot; and the record goes on to say: "Logging was always a standard industry, and the timber holds out like the widow's meal and oil. All the pines went first; nothing else was fit for building purposes in those days." The "Crawford History," in recording the chief facts regarding the settlement and growth of Conway touches upon the activity of the early inhabitants of that town in this direction: "They soon began the lumber business by floating logs and masts down the Saco to its mouth, where they received bread stuff and other necessaries of life in exchange."

By the middle of the last century the industry had become well established as one of the region's principal ones. It is stated that the white pine was

LUMBER INDUSTRY AND FORESTS

then still abundant, although vast quantities of it had already been sent to the market, the largest and best of such trees being used for the masts of vessels.[1] Berlin, now become, because of its neighboring forests and its water power, such an important industrial center, even then had three large sawmills employing each about fifty men, besides several small ones. The value of the lumber product in New Hampshire multiplied nine times in the last half of the nineteenth century and nearly doubled in the decade 1890–1900.

So vast, however, were formerly the forests in the valleys and on the lower slopes of the Mountains themselves that the supply of timber seemed inexhaustible, and as, therefore, no thought of a possible future scarcity ever entered the minds of the early lumbermen, no care, naturally, was taken by them in cutting off the trees.

But an important discovery in connection with one of the leading manufacturing industries of New England was destined to affect very greatly the forests of the northern region, not only as to quantity but also as to kind. Until about 1870 nearly all paper was made from rags. Since that time, in the making of many cheaper grades of paper, and especially that used for newspapers, wood fibers have been almost entirely substituted for rags, the fibers

---

[1] In colonial days it was specially stipulated in the royal grants that white and other pine trees, "fit for masting our royal navy," were to be carefully preserved for that use, the cutting for any other purpose of any tree marked with the broad arrow being, under British law, a felony punishable by a heavy fine and involving also forfeiture of the rights of the grantee, his heirs and assigns.

THE WHITE MOUNTAINS

being transformed into paper pulp by mechanical and chemical processes. What this change has meant for the White Mountain forests, with their abundance of spruce, the chief tree used for the purpose of making paper pulp, may be gathered from the statement that during the decade between 1890 and 1900 the growth of the paper and wood-pulp industry in New Hampshire exceeded that made in any other State, the value of the product increasing from $1,282,022 in 1889 to $7,244,733 in 1899. This increase was well maintained in the next census period, the value of the product rising in 1909 to $13,994,251, an increase of ninety-three per cent over that of 1899.

Other wood industries also materially affect the forests of northern New Hampshire. These are the production of rough bobbins, in which various species of birch, the sugar maple, and the beech are used; the manufacture of shoe-pegs, utilizing the paper and the yellow birch; the crutch industry, in which the wood of the yellow and the paper birch and of the sugar maple is employed; and the manufacture of excelsior, spools, rakes, chairs, veneering, ladder rounds, etc.

The statistical and other information just given will furnish some indication of what has been the effect of human industry in wood on forest conditions in this region. Before considering, however, the results of this great industrial development, as shown in the forests themselves, let us turn our attention to the other agency imperiling the tree-life of the region.

LUMBER INDUSTRY AND FORESTS

Forest fires of greater or less extent and severity have been an accompaniment of lumbering and land-clearing from settlement days. But the introduction of the steam railroad as a common carrier and as an adjunct of the logging industry, and the increase in the number of persons who resort to the woods for pleasure, have in more recent times greatly increased the number and the danger of such fires, and have operated to render the fire question one of the first importance to forest maintenance. Many of the fires that occur run over logged land, but often considerable areas of virgin forest are destroyed by this agency.

The White Mountain region has, fortunately, not been visited by such catastrophic fires as have occurred in some other regions, but, nevertheless, a number of destructive ones have devastated large areas. One in the Zealand Valley, in 1888, starting, as is supposed, from a burning match dropped by a smoker, ran over twelve thousand acres which had been lumbered for spruce saw timber, destroying the remaining small spruce and the hardwood on the tract, together with about two million board feet of saw logs.

Much more extensive and destructive fires occurred in the spring of 1903, burning over more than a tenth of the total White Mountain area and entailing a loss at the time, to say nothing of the future, estimated conservatively at more than two hundred thousand dollars. About ten thousand acres of this was in a part of the Zealand Valley which escaped the fire of 1888. About eighteen thousand acres

THE WHITE MOUNTAINS

were burned over in the townships of Kilkenny and Berlin in the region to the north of the Pliny and Crescent Ranges and in the vicinity of the Pilot Range. Another large tract devastated in that year was in the upper part of the Wild River Valley in the Carter Range region. The Twin Mountain Range and the lower slopes of Mounts Garfield and Lafayette suffered greatly from a fire, in August, 1907, which lasted several days and burned over about thirty-five thousand acres, mostly of land that had been cut over. Much timber was thereby consumed and the forest growth retarded for thirty years.

As to the causes of forest fires, it may be confidently affirmed that the most prolific one is the railroad locomotive, and it is probable that the great fires of 1903 in the Mountains may be ascribed to this cause. As bearing on this point may be recorded the fact that a division superintendent in the White Mountain region had in his office, on September 12 of that year, five hundred and fifty-four separate reports of fires causing greater or less damage to neighboring property during that year.

In view of the danger from fire, by far the most serious one affecting the White Mountains as a summer resort, as the very existence of the region as such depends directly upon the protection of the forests from this destroyer of landscape beauty, the Forest Service of the National Government recommended, some ten years ago, the adoption of legislation for the organization of an adequate fire service by the State of New Hampshire. Happily, it

LUMBER INDUSTRY AND FORESTS

can be recorded that the State adopted the recommendation and now has one of the best fire systems in the United States, under the direction of a State Forester and with fire wardens and deputy wardens in every town. In bringing about this fortunate condition the Society for the Protection of New Hampshire Forests has played a most important part, as it has also in initiating and promoting many other movements affecting the forests of the White Mountain region.

Let us return now to a consideration of the lumbering industry and its effects on the White Mountain forests. By their careless methods of cutting, the early settlers and lumbermen removed large portions of the virgin forest in the valleys and on the lower slopes, which were easy of access, and by their selection for lumber purposes of the valuable conifers, — the spruce, the white pine, the hemlock, and the balsam, of which the primeval forests were mostly composed, — they brought about a great change in the character of the forests, the hardwoods, through being present in mixture with the original conifers, and thus causing the growth that came up after lumbering to be of their kind, coming to be in great preponderance. So comparatively small, however, was the ratio, of the amount of timber cut to the vast amount of forest in the region, and so considerable, even though slow, was the reproduction, especially of hardwoods, on the cut-over land and on land originally cleared for pasture and agricultural purposes but subsequently abandoned as unprofitable, that no apprehension of the

THE WHITE MOUNTAINS

Mountains being some time in the future denuded of their forest covering came into the minds of lovers of the region in the earlier period of its use and growth as a summer vacation land.

Let me briefly set down also some economic facts and conditions which have operated adversely to the welfare of the forests. Down to 1867 the State of New Hampshire owned the greater part of the White Mountain region. The policy of the State being, however, to dispose of its public lands as fast as possible, large tracts were in consequence sold for almost nothing. In the year just named, Governor Harriman, acting in pursuance of this policy, was induced to part with this domain for the paltry sum of twenty-six thousand dollars. A most unfortunate sale for the State this proved to be in the light of future circumstances. Had the region remained in the possession of the Commonwealth there would have been saved much expense and time, and much anxiety and effort also, in connection with the important matter of the preservation of the district's forests and of its beauty, which is in such large measure dependent upon them.

The new owners of this rich domain, so lightly parted with, were speculators, who cut off as rapidly as they could the mature timber in order to pay the taxes and to obtain as much profit as possible. At length the increasing scarcity of spruce lumber and the tariff on building materials impelled the owners, who for the most part had remained the same persons as had originally bought the land, to cut the trees below the line of their maturity. These

LUMBER INDUSTRY AND FORESTS

considerations urging to destructive cutting were strongly reinforced by the further inducement arising from the demands of the wood-pulp industry, which operated to cause some owners to cut down the spruce, poplar, and birch trees to mere saplings, and others to clear off the trees entirely, especially in places, such as the higher slopes, where logging is difficult. In the former case a quarter of a century or more is required to restore the forest; in the latter, often fires ran over the denuded area, consuming not only all vegetation, but also destroying the humus and other organic matter in the soil and thus causing the land to be lost to forest production. In the vicinity of Whitefield, Berlin, and Gorham the forests were so cut off by about 1890 as to lay waste the country, while in the Zealand Valley reckless lumbering and destructive fires had produced at that period a condition of extreme desolation over a large tract. The aim of the lumbermen in these well-known instances of destructive cutting was evidently to wrest the last dollar from the land, the pecuniary side of the forests being naturally that on which they chiefly regarded them. In process of time every valuable timber area was either bought by the large lumber and paper companies, or, when still held by the original owners, was subject to contracts which called for the cutting of the trees under certain conditions of stumpage.

Such being the state of affairs toward the beginning of the last decade of the nineteenth century, persons interested in the White Mountains as a summer resort and in the preservation of the region's

THE WHITE MOUNTAINS

natural beauties for the use and enjoyment of the people, watching the progress of the injudicious and often ruinous lumbering operations, began to be alarmed for the future of the region and to agitate for a change of policy. In the first number (February 29, 1888) of *Garden and Forest*, a quondam weekly periodical conducted by Professor Charles Sprague Sargent, the historian Parkman had a brief article in which he made a plea for the preservation of the forests of the White Mountains on the ground of their importance as elements of the scenery that attracts so many summer visitors. He averred that the Mountains owe three fourths of their charm to their primeval forests and prophesied that if they are robbed of their forests they will become, like some parts of the Pyrenees, without interest because stripped bare. If proper cutting is practiced, he declared, this unfortunate result will be avoided and also some droughts and freshets saved. Later in the same year the editor advocated the purchase of all the forest region by the State or by the railroads, and stated that, unless one of these plans or some other looking to the permanent safety of the forests is adopted, the region and its usefulness would be ruined. In the *Atlantic Monthly* for February, 1893, Julius H. Ward, author of "The White Mountains" (1890), published a more extended article with the title, "White Mountain Forests in Peril." In this he sounded the note of warning very strongly, telling of the wasteful and destructive lumbering, — "unwise and barbarous," he characterized it, — giving a number of typical instances of the results of

LUMBER INDUSTRY AND FORESTS

such cutting, and asserting that a few lumbermen have it in their power "to spoil the whole White Mountain region for a period of fifty years, to dry up the east branch of the Pemigewasset, to reduce the Merrimac to the size of a brook in summer, and to bring about a desolation like that which surrounds Jerusalem in the Holy Land." The protection and preservation of these forests should be regarded as a national problem, he declared, the White Mountains with their forests being "worth infinitely more for the purpose of a great national park than for the temporary supply of lumber which they furnish to the market." He suggested that if the one or two large owners should adopt the regulation, already followed by one company, of cutting no tree below twelve inches at the butt, they would practically settle the whole matter. His idea was that the State through a forest commission should purchase from the owners of woodland in certain regions an agreement that they would not cut trees below a certain size.

Other writers took up the advocacy of measures to preserve the White Mountain forests, and, aided by the establishment of a scientific forestry programme by the National Government and the popular interest taken in the subject of conservation, an agitation in favor of a forest reservation in the region was started, which eventually became nation-wide and which was destined after many vexatious delays to reach fruition.

In the first year (1901) of its organization the Society for the Protection of New Hampshire For-

THE WHITE MOUNTAINS

ests advocated and engaged actively in work for this object, and during the whole course of the movement it has taken a prominent part in furthering it. In 1902, a meeting, called by the Reverend Edward Everett Hale, was held at Intervale, for the purpose of opening a campaign for a national White Mountain Forest Reserve. Dr. Hale worked early and late for this end and it is a matter of regret that his death came before his faith became a reality.

Early in the following year the Legislature of New Hampshire passed a bill, approved January 10, favoring the proposal to establish a White Mountain reserve and giving the State's consent to the acquisition by purchase, gift, or condemnation according to law, of such lands as in the opinion of the Federal Government may be needed for the purpose. At the same session also was passed a resolution authorizing and directing the State Forestry Commission to procure a general examination of the forest lands of the White Mountains by employees of the Bureau of Forestry in the Department of Agriculture at Washington, the expense not to exceed five thousand dollars and the report of the investigators to be laid before the next session of the General Court. The examination thus provided for was begun in May of that year and was carried on during the summer months. The printed report,[1] with its maps and plates, is a comprehensive and

---

[1] To this report, entitled "Forest Conditions of Northern New Hampshire," which was prepared by Alfred K. Chittenden, an assistant forest inspector, and which was published by the Bureau of Forestry of the United States Department of Agriculture in 1905, I am much indebted.

LUMBER INDUSTRY AND FORESTS

illuminating survey of the forest conditions of northern New Hampshire at that time, and their causes. It embodied a number of recommendations, most of which have since been adopted and put into effect.

It was suggested, by some of the opponents of the proposal to have the National Government purchase forest lands in the White Mountains, that the State of New Hampshire should herself acquire for a State Reservation these lands that she had once practically given away. But it was soon realized that it was impossible for that small and comparatively poor State to follow the lead of large and wealthy States such as New York, Pennsylvania, and Michigan, and, moreover, New Hampshire would have to take over a proportionately much larger area than these States had done. An alternative suggestion was then made, which was that the New England States should combine to make the desired purchase, it being argued that the rivers that rise within the White Mountain region contribute largely to the prosperity of all the New England States save one, and that New Hampshire ought not to be expected to burden herself with debt for the benefit of her neighbors. This solution of the problem was not, however, seriously regarded as a feasible one, inasmuch as the neighboring States could not be expected to buy lands outside their own borders for the creation of a forest reserve over which they could have no control, and inasmuch as, furthermore, concerted action for such an object on the part of so many legislatures would be well-nigh an impossibility.

THE WHITE MOUNTAINS

It was soon patent, therefore, to friends of the project of creating a White Mountain reserve that it could be brought about only through acquisition of the region by the National Government, and, accordingly, a vigorous movement was begun looking toward the consummation of such a result. After years of agitation, carried on in Congress and out of it by favorably disposed legislators, societies, newspapers, and individuals, in all parts of the East, against tremendous opposition on the part of politicians and others, success was at length achieved, a striking instance of the effect of public opinion when widespread and persistent.

Space cannot be taken to do more than outline the successive steps in Congress from the initiation of the project there until the legislation was consummated.[1] On November 11, 1903, Senator Hoar, of Massachusetts, presented to the Senate resolutions of the General Court of his State in favor of enacting national legislation to protect the forests of the White Mountains. On the 10th of the following month, Senator Gallinger, of New Hampshire, introduced a bill calling for the appropriation of not more than five million dollars, one million to be immediately available, to enable the Secretary of Agriculture to purchase land suited to the purpose of a national forest reserve in the White Mountains, in total extent not to exceed one million acres. This bill was referred to the Committee on Forest Reser-

[1] I am indebted, for information as to the course of congressional action down to the end of the Sixtieth Congress (March 3, 1909), to an article, "The Fight for the Appalachian Forests," by Edwin A. Start, in *Conservation* for May, 1909.

LUMBER INDUSTRY AND FORESTS

vations and the Protection of Game, to which Senator Gallinger had, as a member of the Republican Committee on Committees, procured the assignment of his colleague, Senator Burnham. A bill was introduced in the House, also, by Representative Currier, of New Hampshire. The Senate Committee to which the Gallinger bill had been referred reported favorably upon it, Senator Burnham's report, which was the first official notice of the Northern project, discussing clearly all phases of the matter and demonstrating strongly the importance, commercial and other, of protecting the forests. The Fifty-eighth Congress passed into history without taking any action on the bills, and new ones were promptly introduced in the Fifty-ninth Congress.

So strong, however, was the opposition in Congress to this largely New England matter, which was regarded by many legislators as a sentimental project without economic basis, that it was soon evident to friends of the measure that it could be carried only through combination with the earlier and related Southern one for creating a national forest reservation in the Southern Appalachians, which would thus enlist a much wider support.

Accordingly, a bill uniting the two projects, which had been prepared by a committee appointed by the American Forestry Association at its annual meeting in January, 1906, to be offered as a substitute for the separate measures, and which had been accepted by all interested, was immediately laid before the Senate Committee on Forest Reservations and the Protection of Game. This union bill, which called for an

THE WHITE MOUNTAINS

initial appropriation of three million dollars, was promptly reported to the Senate by that committee in lieu of the two bills already introduced.

The only accomplishment in this direction, however, of the Fifty-ninth Congress, which ended March 2, 1907, was the passage of a bill appropriating twenty-five thousand dollars for the survey of the two regions by the Department of Agriculture. This investigation was conducted during that summer by the Forest Service, and a valuable report, recommending the purchase of five million acres in the Southern Appalachians and six hundred thousand acres in the White Mountains, was made by the Secretary of Agriculture to the Sixtieth Congress.

When new bills were introduced in the first session of the Sixtieth Congress in both Senate and House, it was evident that there was a great and growing support behind the project, and this fact caused the opposition in the House to stiffen and to take another than the economical tack. A very strong case for the measure was presented at a hearing before the House Committee on Agriculture in January, 1908, but the adverse majority in the committee was not to be overcome without further struggle. The constitutionality of a bill looking to the purchase by the National Government of lands within a State for forest reserves had early been questioned in the House, and it was now decided to refer this aspect of the matter to the House Judiciary Committee, which action was taken in February. Finally, late in April, that tribunal gravely reported that it was its

LUMBER INDUSTRY AND FORESTS

decision that the Federal Government had no power to acquire lands within a State solely for forest reserves, but could purchase such lands only to protect the navigability of rivers, thus resting the validity of all such measures upon the Interstate Commerce Clause of the Constitution. The pending bills, not being thus limited in purpose, were declared to be unconstitutional. The Senate bill was then modified to meet this opinion, and in its new form was passed by the Senate in the closing days of the session. When received in the House, it was referred to the Committee on Agriculture, to the majority of which it still proved unacceptable.

Thus a bill for national forest reserves in the Southern Appalachians and in the White Mountains had already passed the Senate a number of times before the opening of the second session of the Sixtieth Congress, in December, 1908, but had not been as yet permitted to come before the House. At length, to meet the objections to the Senate bill of the House Committee on Agriculture, on the score of its unconstitutionality, a substitute for the Senate bill which would be acceptable to a majority of the committee, and which, it was hoped, would pass the House, was prepared by Representatives Weeks, of Massachusetts, and Lever, of South Carolina, with the assistance of Representative Currier, of New Hampshire. This new bill, which was accepted by the committee and reported to the House in January, 1909, was fittingly given the name of Representative (now Senator) John W. Weeks, a native of Lancaster, New Hampshire, who worked

THE WHITE MOUNTAINS

indefatigably in and out of the House to promote the project of a White Mountain reserve, and who, fortunately, had been appointed to the Committee on Agriculture by Speaker Cannon, in deference to the clamor which arose when the Speaker appointed Representative Scott, of Kansas, an opponent of the project, as chairman, instead of Henry, of Connecticut, the ranking member. To overcome the objection to the appropriation of money mainly for the benefit of certain sections and to draw the teeth of Representatives who were bitterly opposed to the project, the bill was made absolutely general in its terms. It provided for the appropriation for the current year of one million dollars and for each fiscal year thereafter of a sum not to exceed two million dollars "for use in the examination, survey, and acquirement of lands located on the headwaters of navigable streams or those which are being or may be developed for navigable purposes," until this provision should expire by limitation. No locality was mentioned, and the bill therefore applied to the whole United States; but, as the headwaters of the rivers of the West were already largely protected, it was understood that the first purchases were to be made in the White Mountains and Southern Appalachians and the bill was regarded as a bill relating to these regions.

Into the Weeks Bill were incorporated provisions from the Scott Bill[1] (one fathered by the chairman

[1] The Scott Bill passed the House and was referred in the Senate to the Committee on Commerce, by which it was pigeonholed. It was in no way acceptable to the friends of practical Appalachian forest legislation.

LUMBER INDUSTRY AND FORESTS

of the House Committee on Agriculture and designed to sidetrack the measure) permitting States to combine for the purpose of conserving the forests and the water supply and appropriating one hundred thousand dollars to enable the Secretary of Agriculture to coöperate with any State or group of States in this object.

In this form the bill looking to the protection of the White Mountain forests eventually passed the House on March 1, 1909, by a close vote, but it failed of consideration in the Senate in the closing days of the session. This killed the bill so far as that Congress was concerned.

In the Sixty-first Congress, the Weeks Bill again passed the House, June 24, 1910, the day before the close of the second session. Finally, in February, 1911, during the third session of this Congress, the bill passed the Senate and became a law when President Taft signed it on March 1.[1]

By the Weeks Act, a new doctrine in government was asserted, in that Congress decreed that the nation had an interest in the headwaters of navigable streams and might properly spend public money in the acquisition and protection of watersheds. Evidently suspicious, however, that there was opportunity for fraud, Congress had insured efficiency and honesty in the administration of the

[1] The act, as it went on the statute book, appropriated one million dollars for the fiscal year ending June 30, 1910, and a sum not exceeding two million dollars for each fiscal year thereafter, the provisions appropriating these sums expiring by limitation on June 30, 1915. The first one million dollars was never appropriated because the limit of time specified for its use expired before the bill became a law.

THE WHITE MOUNTAINS

law by a number of checks, which, while doubtless necessary, were not conducive to speedy action. The work of considering and passing upon lands recommended for purchase and of fixing the prices was entrusted by the act to a commission, to be known as the National Forest Reservation Commission, and to consist of three Cabinet officers, two members of the Senate, and two members of the House.

At its first meeting the Commission decided to spend the entire appropriation in the White Mountains and the Southern Appalachians. During the four months between the passage of the bill and the end of the fiscal year, the United States Forest Service got quickly to work, secured offers of land amounting to about seventy-five thousand acres, and completed the examination of thirty-seven thousand acres. The Geological Survey, whose report that the control of the lands offered will promote or protect the navigation of streams upon whose watersheds they are was by the act a necessary preliminary, made no report on the White Mountain lands until the following year. About thirty thousand acres were purchased in the South, but the greater part of the two million dollars appropriated for the fiscal year ending June 30, 1911, reverted, because unused, to the United States Treasury. To remedy this loss and to prevent a recurrence, an amendment to the Weeks Act was introduced in the House by Representative Weeks and in the Senate by Senator Gallinger, reappropriating the three million dollars not used, but intended for

LUMBER INDUSTRY AND FORESTS

use in the original bill and making the whole sum available until used. This amendment was accepted in part by Congress, the remainder of the allotments being rendered available until used.

At length, the Geological Survey having early in 1912 rendered a favorable report upon the desirability of acquiring certain White Mountain forest lands that had been offered, for the regulation and protection of the streams having their source in that region, the first purchase under the law was authorized June 16 of that year, when 30,365 acres, mostly on the northern slopes of the Presidential Range, were accepted.

Since this beginning of a national forest was made, the process of acquiring lands in the White Mountains has gone on, although more slowly than some of its advocates approve, to be sure, because of the difficulty of establishing titles and because of the extortionate prices demanded by some owners. By the middle of 1914, the area purchased amounted to 138,572 acres and included some seven thousand acres in the Moosilauke region, more than sixteen thousand acres on the north slopes of Mounts Garfield and Hale, thirty-one thousand acres on the northern Presidential Range and the Dartmouth Range, some four thousand acres in the Wild River Valley, and more than four thousand acres on Wildcat, Spruce, and Iron Mountains. To the great delight of lovers of the White Mountains it was announced, early in September, 1914, that the Government and the owners of Mount Washington had come to an agreement on the purchase price for it,

THE WHITE MOUNTAINS

that the foresters were satisfied with the terms, and that the National Forest Reservation Commission had approved the purchase and had at the same time sanctioned the acquisition of four other tracts. The purchase of these areas, aggregating 85,592 acres, was consummated later in the year and the Government holdings were thereby increased to 224,164 acres, acquired at a cost of $1,600,147.50. This is about one third of the acreage, 698,086, originally laid out for purchase.

The tract on the Presidential Range includes all of the great central peak itself, with its flanks and spurs, and six other peaks as well, Clay, Jefferson, and Adams of the northern group, and Monroe, Franklin, and Pleasant of the southern. Nor is this all, for included in this purchase is also that long southerly ridge, the Montalban, which extends for eight miles from Boott Spur down to the lower end of the Crawford Notch at Bartlett. This purchase of 33,970 acres is by far the most important one yet made by the Government for the White Mountain National Forest, both from a sentimental and from an economic standpoint, as it comprises the grandest part of the Mountain scenery and contains very considerable areas of virgin forest and the fountain-heads of the Connecticut, Androscoggin, and Saco Rivers.

Of the four other tracts alluded to, one is even larger than the area on the Presidential Range just spoken of, for it comprises 45,170 acres. This holding covers the sides of two distinct mountain ranges in the towns of Bartlett and Albany. The other

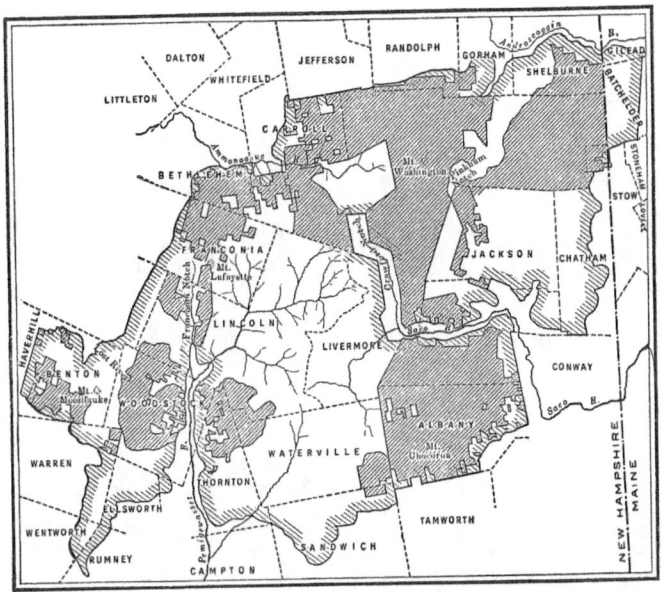

THE WHITE MOUNTAIN NATIONAL FOREST

The complete reservation as planned by the National Forest Reservation Commission, consisting of about 698,000 acres, is shown by the shaded boundary-line. The territory acquired to date (1916), amounting to about 272,000 acres, is indicated by the full shading. The upper part of Crawford Notch is a State Forest Reservation.

LUMBER INDUSTRY AND FORESTS

three include 5615 acres on the side of Mount Whiteface in the Sandwich Range, and two small areas, one of 710 acres on the lower slopes of Mount Parker in the Montalban Ridge and the other of 127 acres along the Oliverian Brook in the town of Benton, near the western boundary of the purchase area.

During 1915, further and substantial progress was made in the acquisition under the Weeks Act of tracts of land for addition to the White Mountain National Forest domain, the total area and cost being brought up at the end of the year, in round numbers, to 272,000 acres and $1,800,000, respectively. One tract purchased includes some twenty-three thousand acres in the Franconia Notch, extending south from the land previously acquired at Eagle Cliff to a point beyond the lumber village of Johnson and containing portions of Mounts Lafayette, Liberty, and Flume on the east and Mounts Pemigewasset, Kinsman, Jackson, and Cannon on the west. Another region acquired is the entire watershed of the Zealand River, between the Twin Mountain and Rosebrook Ranges. The most important acquisition, however, was the last one of the year, which comprises all of the Bean Grant, a large area adjoining the Crawford House property and lying east and northeast of it. Included in its confines are portions of Mounts Webster, Clinton, Jackson, and Pleasant, of the Presidential Range, whose many streams feed two of New England's principal rivers, the Saco and the Connecticut, while on the lower slopes of the latter three moun-

THE WHITE MOUNTAINS

tains stands some of the finest primeval spruce and fir forest yet remaining in the whole section. On the south this tract borders the New Hampshire State Forest in the Crawford Notch, on the west its boundary follows the State Road from Crawford's along toward the Jefferson Notch and the valley of Israel's River, while on the north the area joins the earlier purchases on Mount Washington and the Northern Peaks. At the close of the year some other tracts had been examined for purchase, but had not been acquired.[1]

Thus, as the matter now stands, somewhat more than one third of the official purchase area has been acquired, and an excellent beginning has been made in a great conservation project. As, however, the appropriations under the Weeks Law (of which, as we have seen, about three million dollars, of the original eleven million dollars provided for, did not become available) ceased with the fiscal year ending June 30, 1915, it will be necessary, for the carrying to completion of the undertaking, that Congress should make further appropriations. It is strongly held, by those organizations and individuals that have been all these years deeply interested in the inception and progress of this Government enter-

[1] It is a pleasure to make acknowledgment of my indebtedness for information about National Forest acquisitions, etc., to Mr. Allen Chamberlain, whose interesting articles on White Mountain National Forest and on Appalachian Mountain Club subjects have been especially helpful to me in both connections; to Mr. J. St. J. Benedict, Supervisor, United States Forest Service, and to Mr. Philip W. Ayres, Forester of the Society for the Protection of New Hampshire Forests, who, both in his official capacity and by his own personal interest and activity, has done so much for the cause of which he is the official representative.

LUMBER INDUSTRY AND FORESTS

prise, that it is of the highest importance that the programme of purchases so well begun should be continued without interruption, as otherwise a great economic loss to the Government will result, not only from the failure to acquire valuable timber lands and to protect further the mountain watersheds, but from the failure to utilize the existing machinery created for the work of acquisition and the intimate knowledge of conditions now possessed by the force of experts that has been trained.

The Secretary of Agriculture was, accordingly, memorialized by a group of interested organizations, North and South, and he has recommended the continuation of the appropriations. With his approval and that of the Forest Reservation Commission, Congress has been asked to appropriate for the purpose of carrying out the purposes mentioned in the Weeks Act the sum of two million dollars for each of the fiscal years ending on the 30th day of June, 1917, 1918, 1919, 1920, and 1921.

The State of New Hampshire has done its part. Besides the enabling legislation with reference to the Federal Government's acquisition of lands within the State and the establishment of the splendid forest-fire protection system already mentioned, the State Legislature, acting under the stimulus of agitation started by that voluntary organization which has done so much for the forestry interests of the State, the Society for the Protection of New Hampshire Forests, passed in 1911 a bill for the purchase of the Crawford Notch, which was in danger of disfigurement from logging operations. The Society proposed the purchase and invited the coöperation of commercial bodies, clubs, and individuals in furthering the project. The Appalachian Mountain Club, many women's clubs, the Boston Chamber of Commerce, and a number of newspapers were among those actively interested in it.

Finding that definite information was a necessary preliminary to legislative action, the Society carried through, at an expense of seven hundred dollars, a careful examination and survey of the Notch, and prepared a report embodying an account of the kind, amount, location, quality, and value of the timber, with maps and estimates.

The bill, as originally introduced, called for an appropriation of one hundred thousand dollars, but it was amended by the House so as to make the appropriation indefinite by empowering the governor and council to issue bonds for a sum sufficient to acquire the Notch. Through a failure to engross the amendment, the bill was signed by the governor without it. Discovering after the legislature had adjourned that the bill was defective, the governor requested a review of it by the supreme court of the State and by the attorney-general, which resulted in a decision that, although the State was without power to issue bonds in the premises, it might, under the right of eminent domain, take any lands in the Crawford Notch that it could pay for from current funds not otherwise appropriated. Under this unfortunate circumstance the State was unable to buy the whole of the Notch, but it did purchase in 1912 the upper and more picturesque part, extending six

LUMBER INDUSTRY AND FORESTS

miles south from the Crawford House, at a cost of sixty-two thousand dollars. Much credit is due to Governor Bass and his council for carrying through the matter of purchase, despite the defective bill.

By way of conclusion to this account of the history of the National and State Reservation projects in the White Mountains, it may be well to bring together and summarize the information relating to such areas which have been set aside for the use and enjoyment of the people in this region, as they existed at the end of the year 1915. The National Forest then covered 272,000 acres. The State Forestry Commission held some six thousand aeres in the Crawford Notch, three hundred acres on Bartlett Mountain, one hundred and thirty acres above Livermore Falls in Campton, and forty acres in the town of Conway, including the Cathedral and White Horse Ledges, presented by citizens to the State. The Society for the Protection of New Hampshire Forests owned one hundred and forty-eight acres in the Lost River region and some twenty acres in Tamworth, consisting of forested roadside strips known as the "Chocorua Pines." The Appalachian Mountain Club had many holdings, including the following: one acre at the Madison Spring on Mount Madison, thirty-six acres along Snyder Brook in Randolph, thirty-seven acres at the Lead Mine Bridge in Shelburne, the Joseph Story Fay Reservation of one hundred and fifty acres in Woodstock and Lincoln, ten acres on the summit of South Baldface Mountain and ten acres on the summit of Mount Kearsarge (Pequawket), both in the town of

THE WHITE MOUNTAINS

Chatham, twenty-eight acres at the Glen Ellis Falls, and twenty-eight acres at the Crystal Cascade, both in the Pinkham Notch region. All honor to those organizations and individuals to whose advocacy and persistent activity this happy condition of things is due!

XIX

THE CHANGES IN THE CHARACTER OF WHITE MOUNTAIN TRAVEL AND BUSINESS IN RECENT YEARS

THE advent of the automobile, with its almost immediate leap into general use for touring, greatly to the regret of many, including some landlords, has largely transformed in character the summer hotel and tourist business in the White Mountains, as well as elsewhere. While the volume of travel has increased, the majority of the visitors to the region are now of the transient variety, making in most cases but a fleeting stay at any one place and consisting largely of those who are "doing" the Mountains in their "motor-car." Many of these make only a rapid passage through the region on some of the main lines of travel, such as that from Plymouth through the Franconia Notch to Bretton Woods, and thence on through the Crawford Notch, pausing not much longer at various favored stopping-places than the time required to consume one of the hostelry's famous meals, or at most to spend a night. As a result, some of the capacious and luxurious houses of entertainment at strategic points on the approved and well-advertised automobile routes are now doing a highly profitable business in catering to the wants of patrons of this sort. Some tourists make their headquarters at a central point and from

THE WHITE MOUNTAINS

there tour in their machines to the various points of interest about the Mountains, but, even in these cases, the length of sojourn is usually comparatively short. On the other hand, resorts not on these favored routes have suffered in the amount of their patronage on account of this change in the purpose of the summer visitors, not only because they fail to receive their share of these migratory sojourners, but because some of their old-time permanent clientèle are now numbered among that class. The railroads serving the region also have suffered a considerable loss in the volume of passenger traffic, owing to this change from the use of public to that of private conveyances, which is somewhat of a reversion in type of travel to the conditions of pre-railroad days.

While, as has been intimated, there are many real lovers of the Mountains who regret the passing of the old order, with its simplicity and restfulness, and its more leisurely ways of seeing the country, by walks or delightful drives after two, four, or more horses in the old-fashioned mountain-wagons of a bygone day, there are others who feel differently about it. Writes Ralph D. Paine in *Scribner's Magazine*, in describing the pleasures of automobiling in the White Hills: —

In other days many of the finest views of this beautiful region were denied the visitor unless he tramped it with a pack on his back. Now the hillsides have been blasted and the gullies filled to make it no more than a flight of a few hours from the Franconia gateway, across the mountains and out through Crawford Notch to the highway that leads southward through North Conway and Intervale.

CHANGES IN TRAVEL AND BUSINESS

Gone is the old simplicity and quiet summer life of Fabyan's and Bethlehem and Crawford's, when the same guests returned year after year for the same placid existence, the young people at tennis and walking tours, their elders gossiping in rocking-chairs along the hospitable piazzas. Nor is it to regret the passing of the old order of things. Where one pilgrim discovered the White Mountains then, a hundred enjoy them now. The region has ceased to be a New England monopoly and is a national possession. At Bretton Woods and its vast hotel seventy per cent of last summer's [1912's] guests were motorists.

Whatever may be thought of this opinion in general, and while it is a cause of gratification that many more people are enabled to enjoy the Mountains, even though they may gain only fleeting glimpses of their beauties, it must be said that the statement in the first sentence of the quotation is almost as true to-day as "in other days." For, owing to the physical character of the country, "many of the finest views" are still and must be ever reserved for him who knows the real "joys of the road," the pedestrian with or without the pack on his back. Nature has forever established as impassable to vehicles many routes of the region and has placed many of its chief attractions in spots inaccessible to any but the foot traveler. So the saunterer who keeps off the beaten track may still enjoy to the utmost the delights of the woods, the ravines, and the trails. He will always hold in fee simple the right to enjoy not only very many of the most charming and of the grandest prospects, as has been said, but numbers also of the special wonders and beauties of various localities.

THE WHITE MOUNTAINS

It may well be that when this often mad rush to get somewhere and this desire to "do" the White Mountains as a part of a motor tour shall have spent their novel force, a reaction will set in, and the old-time placid sojourn in a particular resort — there are still many people who cling to the milder form of summer pleasure — will be again in fashion. In any case, there is room enough for both classes of visitors and each type may, if it will but seek it, find a place to its liking.

Another change in White Mountain business which has arisen in late years and which deserves notice in this concluding chapter is the development of the region as a winter resort. In earlier days few urban residents other than hardy members of the Appalachian Mountain Club ever thought of venturing, let alone actually going, into the White Hills for a winter pleasure trip. In those bygone days at that season the Mountains were almost as deserted and solitary as the Himalayas themselves, and even the aforesaid pioneers in what was destined to be an epoch-making movement in vacationing were regarded as overenthusiastic for outdoor life, if not more or less foolhardy, in betaking themselves in winter to this land of ice and snow, where they might be at the mercy of blizzards, avalanches, and other terrors, real or supposed, of winter life in high altitudes. So the Appalachians not only had a monopoly of winter pastiming there, but were often hard put to it to find accommodations other than those furnished by the Club shelters. Gradually, however, the number of the "snowshoe section" of the

CHANGES IN TRAVEL AND BUSINESS

Club increased, the newspapers and magazines began to take knowledge of these romantic excursions to the snow-covered solitudes of the Granite State, and at length the railroad companies, needing only the pioneer work of a widely known outdoor organization to build upon, took up the matter of providing facilities for such expeditions in a systematic way, and the winter vacation in the north country became an accomplished fact. Meanwhile, a few of the more enterprising proprietors of White Mountain summer hotels discerned the drift of things and tried the experiment of keeping open in winter also. The new idea that a winter vacation could be enjoyed, with the comforts of a modern hotel, in cold New England as well as in warm Florida or California, immediately found favor with the public; and now, where a decade or so ago, there were but three or four hostelries prepared to entertain winter guests and few sojourners at that season in the White Hills, there are a dozen or more hotels catering to the demands of this class of patrons, who are numbered by the hundreds.

THE END

INDEX

Abbott, Thomas, 159.
Abnaki, group of Indians, 2.
Abnakis, at St. Francis, 9.
Academy of Arts and Sciences, American, 32.
Adams, Mount, named, 78; Phillips Brooks on, 135; first path, 345; Air Line Path, 356; provisions for records on, 358.
Adams, Mount John Quincy, 275.
Adams, town. *See* Jackson, 59.
Addey, Markinfield, 254.
Addison, Daniel Dulany, 182.
Agamenticus, Mount, 5.
Agassiz, Alexander, 217.
Agassiz, Louis, his explorations, 215; Mount Agassiz, 216; Agassiz Basins, 216; poem on, 216.
Agassiz, Mount, named, 216; coach overturned, 332.
Agassiz Basins, 216.
Agiocochook or *Agiochook*, xxix; legend of origin, 13.
Aiken, Charles L., 318.
Aiken, Herrick, 239.
Aiken, James, 64.
Aiken, Walter, and the Mount Washington Railway, 239; second Summit House, 246; on Mount Washington in winter, 318.
Air Line Path, 356.
Albany, town, dying of cattle in, 13; forest purchase in, 398.
"Album" of landlord, 107, 146.
Alden, Reverend Timothy, xxx.
Aldrich, Eva M., 169.
Algonquian family of Indians, 2.
Allen, Dr. A. V. G., 137.
Allen, Charles, 277.
Allen, David, 96.
Allen, Grant, 248.
Alpine House (Gorham), 170.
"Ambitious Guest, The," 86, 116.

American Foresters, Society of, its *Bibliography*, xiv.
American Forestry Association, 391.
American Hay-Fever Association, 333.
American Philosophical Society, 29.
Ames, Moses, 40.
Ames's Tavern, 179.
Amherst, General Jeffrey, 54.
Amherst College, 120, 208, 310; students find Harry Hunter's body, 273.
Ammonoosuc gold field, 209, 210.
Among the Clouds. xiii, xv; housed in old Tip-Top House, 233; "newspaper train," 245; office built, 251; history, 251–53.
"Among the Hills," 179.
Anasagunticooks, the, 2.
Anchors, made at Tamworth Iron Works, 69.
Anderson, John, 338, 356, 373, 374, 375.
Anderson, John Farwell, 227.
Anderson, General Samuel J., 227.
Anderson and Price, 338.
Androscoggin, the, xxxi.
Aneda, 19.
Appalachia, founded, 359; first editor, 218, 359.
Appalachian Mountain Club, the, *Guide*, xiii; summit of Mount Kearsarge given to, 255; and snow arch, 274; shelter on Crawford Path, 279, 354; winter ascents, 305; and various paths, 346, 347, 348; founded, 348, 349; incorporated and voluntary association dissolved, 350; its work and activities, 350–57, 358, 359; advocates Crawford Notch purchase, 402;

411

INDEX

its reservations, 403, 404; winter expeditions, 408.
Applebee, Zebedee, 58.
Apthorp. *See* Littleton.
Arosagunticooks, the, 2.
Art history of White Mountains, 188.
Artists' Brook, 199.
Ascents, registration of, 31, 37, 84, 357, 358.
Aspinquid, St., 5.
Asquamchemauke, 48.
Atkinson, Theodore, 52.
Atlantic and St. Lawrence Railroad, 220, 221.
Atwood, Mrs., 233.
Auger, screw-, first, 69.
Austin, the Misses, 79.
Automobiles, on Mount Washington, 371, 372; on Tug-of-War Hill, 372; 405–08.
Avery, James, 57.
Ayres, Philip W., 400.

Baedeker, Karl, xiii.
Baird, George C., 363, 364.
Baker, Captain, of Newbury, his expedition against Pemigewasset Indians, 48.
Bakers River, 48.
Balaam, the Indian, 8.
Baldwin, Loammi, Jr., 222.
Ball, Dr. B. L., 285–301.
Ball, Dr. S., 300, 301.
Ballard, Rev. Edward, as to meaning of Agiocochook, xxx.
Ballou, 2d, Dr. Hosea, 128; quoted as to hotels existing in 1845, 165.
Banks's Hotel, 179.
Barker, John, at Notch (Willey) House, 92, 93.
Barnes, Dr. H., 301.
Barnum, P. T., 248.
Barron, Asa, 335, 337.
Barron, Colonel Oscar G., 335, 337; and Mount Washington fire, 362.
Barron, Merrill, and Barron (Company), and Summit House, 249; firm formed, 335; Mount Pleasant House, 338.

Barrows, Dr. Nathan, 211.
Barstow, George, 6.
Bartlett, early citizens, 52; settled, 60; forest purchase in, 398.
Bartlett, ——, collegian, 28.
Bartlett, W. H., 196.
Base of Mount Washington, the, railroad extended to, 225; turnpike to, 238, 241; *Among the Clouds* at, 253.
Bass, Governor Robert P., 403.
Bates, Charlotte Fiske, 216.
Bean, David, 67.
Bean Grant, 399.
Bearcamp River House, Whittier first comes to, 179; frequents, 180; burned, 181.
Beaumont, Élie de, 205, 215.
Beaver Meadow, 140.
Beckett, S. B., 120, 121.
Bedell, A. Judson, 230.
Beecher, Henry Ward, his connection with White Mountains, 127, 131–33, 335; at Crawford House, 131, 163; on Mount Washington, 248.
Beede, Daniel, 67.
Belknap, Jeremy, his *History of New Hampshire*, xxv; quoted, xxv, xxvii; Agiocochook, xxix; quoted, 2, 3; map, 10, 31; Great Carbuncle, 15; records explorations, 24, 25; quoted, 25; on Crawford Notch, 25; tour of White Mountains, 27 *ff.*; unable to climb Mount Washington, 30; battle of Lovewell's Pond, 44, 45; motive for visiting Mountains, 154.
Bellows, John, 170.
Bemis, Dr. Samuel A., his connection with White Mountains, 137, 138; and G. N. Frankenstein, 203.
Bemis station, 55, 73, 346.
Benedict, J. St. J., 400.
Benjamin, S. G. W., on S. R. Gifford's painting, 198; on Thomas Hill's painting, 200.
Bent, Allen H., quoted, ix; his bibliography, ix, xiv.

INDEX

Berlin, N.H., granted, 59; Lucy Larcom at, 183; railroad reaches, 226; sawmills at, 379; forest fire, 382; destructive lumbering, 385.
Berlin Falls. *See* Berlin.
Bernard, Sir Francis, 58.
Bethel, Maine, Indian raid, 65; Lucy Larcom at, 183, 184.
Bethlehem, President Dwight visits, 35; granted and settled, 60; President Dwight on, 61; early history, 61; Harriet Martineau quoted on, 146; first taverns, 161; Lucy Larcom at, 184; William Dean Howells at, 184; Agassiz describes moraines at, 215; railroad to, 225; General Grant at, 243; coaching parades, 245; *White Mountain Echo*, 254; Sir Isaac Newton Gay, 262; development of as a resort, 332–34.
Bierstadt, Albert, 202.
Bigelow, Dr. Jacob, 31; explores White Mountains, 35, 36; his account of the Mountains, 37.
Bigelow's Lawn, 37.
"Billings, Josh," 341.
Black flies, Josselyn on, 24.
Blaikie, William Garden, 248.
Blanchard, Joseph, 48.
Boardman, artist, 202.
Bolles, Frank, natural history, 218; summer home, 69.
Bond, Professor G. P., map, 19, 212.
Boott, Dr. Francis, with Dr. Bigelow, 36; explores the Mountains again, 37.
Boott Spur, 22, 31, 36, 37.
Boott Spur Trail, 356.
Boston, England, 20.
Boston and Lowell Railroad, 222.
Boston and Maine Railroad, 223, 225, 226, 228, 241, 375.
Boston Athenæum, 198.
Boston, Concord and Montreal Railroad reaches Plymouth, 50; leased to the Boston and Lowell, 50; early history, 223, 224.

Botany and botanical explorations, 32, 33, 35, 37, 38, 108, 121, 124, 147, 218.
Boulder in Flume, 303.
Bourne, George W., 270, 271.
Bourne, Lizzie C., 269–71.
Bourne, Lucy, 270, 271.
Bouton, Nathaniel, 6.
Bowditch, Dr. Nathaniel, 33.
Brackett, Adino N., 77, 78.
Brackett, W. M., 202.
Bracy, C. F., 317.
Brass plate placed on Mt. Washington, 84.
Brazer, John, 83.
Bremer, Fredrika, her visit to the White Mountains, 148, 149.
Bretton Woods, xxviii, 63, 140, 191, 337, 343, 344.
Brewster, Edwin Tenney, 206.
Bridge, W. F., 102.
Bridle path, Crawford, made, 77. *See* Crawford Path.
Bridle path, Fabyan, made, 78. *See also* Fabyan Path.
Briggs, Fire Warden, 282, 283.
British Embassy at Intervale, 372.
"Briton's Woods." *See* Bretton Woods.
Brooks, Chapin C., 307–09.
Brooks, Rev. Frederick, 136.
Brooks, Luke, 101.
Brooks, Phillips, his connection with the White Mountains, 127, 133–37; on Mount Washington, 248.
Brooks, William G., 134.
Brown, George Loring, at West Campton, 66; at West Ossipee, 179; at Jackson and Jefferson Highlands, 195; his most noted White Mountain picture, 195.
Brown, George T., 168.
Brown, H. B., 203.
Browne, George Waldo, 175.
Bryant, William Cullen, his connection with the Mountains, 186–88; impressions of, quoted, 187–88.
Bryce, Ambassador James, 372.
Buckler, Reginald H., 284.

INDEX

Bucknam, Edward, 57.
Burnham, Denison R., 173.
Burnham, Senator Henry E., 391.
Burns, Major, 60.
Burt, Frank H., his chronology, xiii; his *Mount Washington*, xiii; his *Among the White Mountains*, cited, 55; editor of *Among the Clouds*, 252; lays out path from snow arch to Summit, 347.
Burt, Henry M., 252.
Burt, Joseph, 61.
Butterwort Flume, 213.

Cabot, Sebastian, map, 18.
Camden, Patrick, 369.
Camp, Ethan Allen Crawford's, destroyed, 98.
Campbell, friend of Chocorua, 11, 12.
Campbell and Whittier, 239.
Campton, grant and settlement, 65, 66; Whittier at, 178; Fieldses at, 178, 183; Lucy Larcom at, 183; artists at, 66, 203.
Campton Village, 66.
Cannon, Speaker Joseph G., 248, 394.
Cannon, Mount, 102, 104.
Carriage road on Mount Washington, 234–36; 243.
Carrigain, Mount, 18; Guyot ascends, 217; ascent by Vose and Morse, 348; by White Mountain Club, 348, 349.
Carrigain, Philip, map, xxxii, 18; secretary of state, xxxii, 19; ascends Mount Washington, 78; Mount Lafayette on his map, 106.
Carroll, 63.
Carter Dome, 302, 353.
Carter Notch Hut, 352, 353.
Cartland, Gertrude W., 181.
Cartland, Joseph, 181.
Cascade Camp, 355.
Casilear, J. W., 196, 197, 199.
Casola, 103.
Castellated Ridge, 356.
Caswell, Captain Nathan, 57.
Caswell, Apthorp, 57.

Cavis, C. H. V., 232, 235.
Center Sandwich, 68.
Central Vermont Railroad, 223.
Century Club, 199.
Chamberlain, Allen, 400.
Champlain, Samuel de, 19.
Champney, Benjamin, at West Ossipee, 179; life and work at North Conway, 195–99.
Chandler, Benjamin, 271, 272.
Chandler, Moses, 255.
Chandler Ridge, 272.
Charlestown, N.H., 54.
Chatauque, 159.
Cheney, Charles B., 317, 319.
Cherry Mountain, 26; slide, 304.
Child, Lydia Maria, *Chocorua's Curse*, 11, 12.
Chisholm's Guide-Book, xiii.
Chiswick. See Littleton, 61.
Chittenden, Alfred K., 388.
Choate, Jonathan, 68.
Choate, Rufus, 158.
Chocorua, chieftain, 4, 10; legend of, 11, 12; Longfellow's poem, 12, 186; other poems, 12.
Chocorua, mountain, 10, 67, 179; Whittier's opinion of, 180; Whittier's and Lucy Larcom's humorous poems on climbing, 181; Thomas Cole and, 191, 193; A. B. Durand, 195; John Williamson, 197; A. D. Shattuck, 198; J. W. Casilear, 199; Daniel Huntington, 201; William Hart, 203; in second geological survey, 210; Peak House, 255.
Chocorua, village, 68.
Chocorua Lake, 69.
Chocorua Pines, 403.
Christall hill or hills. See Crystal hill.
"Christus Judex," 103.
Church, F. E., 203.
Church's Falls, 203.
Civil War, 66, 68.
Clark, artist, 202.
Clay, Mrs. C. E., 255.
Clay, Mount, named, 37.
Clement, Daniel Q., 257.
Clement, Ezekiel A., 257.

INDEX

Clement, James, 256, 257, 312.
Cleveland, Grover, at Tamworth, 69.
Cliff House, 159.
"Climbs to the Clouds," 371, 372.
Clough, A. F., winter on Mount Moosilauke, 210, 311–14; winter on Mount Washington, 316, 318, 319.
Coast and Geodetic Survey, U.S., 250.
Cobb, J. O., 348.
Coffin, Ira, 168.
Cogswell, P. B., 318.
Coke, E. T., quoted, 81; his visit to the Mountains, 143–45.
Cold weather in June, 76.
Cole, Thomas, painting of death of Chocorua, 11, 193; at Jackson, 172; connection with Mountains, 190–93.
Colebrook, 70.
Coleridge, Lord Chief Justice, 248.
Colman, Samuel, 198.
Concord, State capital, 61; first railroad train, 222.
Concord. *See* Lisbon.
Concord Railroad, 222.
Concord and Montreal Railroad, 367.
Cone, Sergeant O. S. M., 326.
Connecticut, the, xxxi, 399.
Connecticut and Passumpsic Rivers Railroad, 223, 226.
Connecticut River Railroad, 226.
Conrad, Justus, on Woodstock, 63; on discovery of the Profile and the Flume, 102.
Conway, Henry Seymour, 50.
Conway, Indian remains, 3; Belknap's party at, 29; Bigelow's party at, 37; settled, 50; origin of name, 50; history, 50 *ff.*; hotels at, 159 *ff.*; and Portland and Ogdensburg Railroad, 227; Eastern Railroad reaches, 228; lumbering at, 378. *See also* North Conway.
Conway Corner, 159.
Cook, E. B., 356.
Cooper, Rev. Charles D., 134.

Cooper, J. M., 55.
Coös, Upper, 64; Rosebrook in, 70.
Coosucs, the, 2.
Copp, Benjamin, 59.
Copp, Joshua, 64.
Corcoran Gallery of Art, 199.
Courthouse, first, at Plymouth, 49.
"Cow Pasture," 232.
Cox, Edmund, 243.
Cram, Captain T. J., ascertains height of Mount Washington, 217.
Crandall, Governor, 9.
Crawford, Abel, lives in Nash and Sawyer's Location, 72; moves to Hart's Location, 72, 73; keeps inn there, 73, 158; acts as guide, 83, 84, 206; characterized, 84; makes first horseback ascent of Mount Washington, 84, 206; vigorous old age, 85; death, 85; and Samuel Willey, Jr., 91; effect of storm on his property, 97; portrait, 202.
Crawford, Ethan Allen, autobiography, xiv; on story of Nancy, 56; cares for grandfather and inherits latter's property, 75; physique, 75; burial place, 75; soldier, 76; instance of his strength, 76; Louisville, New York, 76; comes to grandfather's, 76, 77; house burned, 77, 157; first path, 77; guide, 77 *ff.*; builds shorter path, 78; stone cabins, 79, 229; tent, 229; enlarges house, 79, 157; again, 80, 157; annoyed by neighboring landlord, 80, 165; leaves Mountains and moves to Guildhall, 82, 163; returns to Mountains, 82, 166; dies, 83; age, 83; epitaph, 83; Willey disaster, 87; date of Willey House, 89; storm of August (1826), 92; searcher at Willey House, 95; effect of storm on his property, 98; guides Western travelers, 99; accounts of visitors, 107; Chancellor Kent, 107; and bo-

415

INDEX

tanist, 108; Hawthorne at his house, 115, 116; Emerson there, 119; Harriet Martineau and, 145; carries mail, 160; builds Notch House, 162; notice of painter, 190; makes provision for records of ascents, 357.
Crawford, E. A., 3d, 330, 375.
Crawford, Lucy Howe, her *History of the White Mountains*, xiii, 74; cares for Eleazar Rosebrook in his last illness, 75; burial place, 83.
Crawford, Stephen M., 376.
Crawford, Thomas J., makes bridle path, 77; keeps Notch House, 85, 162; builds road up Mount Willard, 85; guides Western travelers, 99, 100; names Mount Willard?, 113; builds first Crawford House, 162; and Nazro, 261; and Frederick Strickland, 268, 269.
Crawford, William H., 330.
Crawford family, in White Mountain history, 70; work in developing Mountain travel, 155, 156.
Crawford House, Beecher at, 131; first one built, 162; burned, 163; present one built, 163.
Crawford Notch, known to Indians, 25; made known to colonists, 25, 26; road, 25, 26, 27; turnpike, 27, 73; President Dwight, 34, 35; Colonel Whipple, 52; Rogers's Rangers, 54; Nancy, 55, 56; name, 75; Willey disaster, 85; turnpike destroyed and rebuilt, 97; Professor Silliman, 108, 109; Hawthorne, 115, 116; E. A. Kendall, 139; Henry Tudor, 141; E. T. Coke, 144; traffic through, 156; Thomas Cole, 191; Thomas Doughty, 194; Benjamin Champney, 197; H. B. Brown, 203; explorations, 213; railroad through, 227; State reserve, 401–03.
Crawford Notch Hermit, 263.
Crawford Notch Reserve, 401–03.

Crawford Path, built, 77; made bridle path, 77; shelter, 279, 354.
Cruft, Isaac S., 334.
Crystal Cascade Path, 347, 355.
Crystal hill or hills, xxv, 19, 20.
Cummings, G. E., 225.
Currier, Representative Frank D., 391, 393.
Curtis, William B., 275–79.
Cushman, Nathaniel, 62.
Cutler, Reverend Dr. Manasseh, first visit and results, 28, 31, 32; second visit, 33; motive, 154.
Cutler's River, 31.
Cutter, Louis F., 277.

Dalton, town, 57.
Dalton, Honorable Tristram, 57.
Dana, Professor J. D., 213.
Danas, the, 47.
Danforth, Rev. Samuel, *Almanac*, 20.
Darby Field, the, 283, 284.
Dartmouth (Jefferson), 29, 31, 52.
Dartmouth College, 105, 209, 211, 212, 213.
Dartmouth Outing Club, 305.
Davis, D. S., 230.
Davis, Jefferson, 232.
Davis, John C., 255.
Davis, Jonathan G., 355.
Davis, Nathaniel T. P., keeps Mount Crawford House, 73, 158; loses property, 137.
Davis Path, 346.
Dawson, George, 83.
Deer Park Hotel, 342.
Deluge tradition, 14.
Demerit, Eli, 62.
Demerit, John, 62.
Dennison, Noyes S., 77.
Devens, Charles, 248.
Devil's Den, on Mount Willard, described, 218; explored by Dartmouth men, 213, 219; by F. Leavitt, 219.
Dinsmore, Andrew, 255.
Dodge, Harriet D., 249.
Dodge, Captain John W., 249.
Dodge, Joseph A., 257.
Dog, the Willey, 92.

INDEX

Dolfinato, Nicolo del, map, 18.
Doughty, Thomas, 190, 194.
Douglass, William, quoted, xxvi.
Dover, N.H., Indian attack on, 9.
Dow, Colonel Stevens M., 257.
Downes, William Howe, ix.
Doyle, Private, 323, 324.
Drake, Samuel Adams, his *Heart of the White Mountains*, xii; quoted on name of Mountains, xxvi; on *Agiocochook*, xxix; on *Waumbekketmethna*, xxx; as to train-shed and Private Doyle's experiences, 322.
Dry River, 15, 22.
Duhring, Mrs., 232.
Dunstable (Nashua), 42, 43, 46.
Durand, A. B., at West Campton, 66, 203; at Jackson, 172; connection with White Mountains, 194, 195, 196.
Durand, John, 63.
Durand, town. *See* Randolph.
Durgin, Mr., proprietor of Sinclair House, 315.
Durgin, Mrs. Charles, 330.
Dwight, Theodore, Jr., on Crawford Notch road, 27; tour to Mountains, 110; notices of them, 110, 111; ascent of Mount Washington, 112.
Dwight, President Timothy (1752–1817), his *Travels in New England and New York*, xi; on visibility of Mount Washington, 19; his journeys to the White Mountains, 33, 34, 35; to Lake Winnepesaukee, 34; quoted as to Bethlehem, 61; on the character and achievements of Eleazar Rosebrook, 74; his name for Mount Lafayette, 106; motive for visiting Mountains, 154.

East Branch House, 158.
Eastern Railroad, 228.
Eastman, Amos, captured, 49.
Eastman, Daniel, 159.
Eastman, Lewis, 198.
Eastman, Mrs. M. E., 159.
Eastman, Moses, 161.

Eastman, Richard, 78.
Eastman, William, 68.
Eaton, J. F., 352.
Echo Lake, David Johnson's picture, 197; Sanford R. Gifford's picture, 198.
Edmands, Professor J. Rayner, searches for remains of Weiss, 275; King's Ravine Path, 346; builds camps and trails, 355; builds Valley Way, 356; opens Mount Pleasant Path, 356.
Edward VII, 195.
Eliot, John, and Passaconaway, 6, 8; and Wonnalancet, 9.
Ellis, George B., 194.
Ellis, George E., 36.
Ellis River, 31.
Emerson, Ralph Waldo, his connection with the White Mountains, 118–20; on Thoreau's injury, 124.
Emerton, J. H., scientific work, 218; on Mount Washington, 247.
Emery, ——, settler, 60.
Emmons, Charles G., 249.
English Jack, 263–66.
Estus, Timothy, 233.
Evans, Captain, builds road through Crawford Notch, 25; ascends Mount Washington twice, 25, 120; guides Belknap's party, 29, 31.
Evans, David, 40.
Evans, John, 40.
Evarts, William M., 248.
Everett, Edward, 158.

Fabyan, Abbott L., 338.
Fabyan, Horace, makes bridle path, 78; comes to White Mountains, 82, 163; repairs old Willey House and builds new one, 164; keeps Conway House, 164; keeps Mount Washington House, 164; his tin horn, 164; remodels hotel, 165; and Frederick Strickland, 269; hotel called after, 336.
Fabyan, White Mountains Railroad reaches, 225; Portland and

417

INDEX

Ogdensburg Railroad reaches, 227; Maine Central Railroad extended from, 228; connected with Base by turnpike, 238, 241.
Fabyan House, 336, 337; Mount Washington fire discovered at, 362.
Fabyan Path, 78, 356.
Fairfield. *See* Woodstock.
Fall of a Thousand Streams, 121.
Fassett, F. H., 339.
Faunce, Sewall E., 273, 274.
Faxon, Edward, 247.
Fay, Professor Charles E., 349.
Fenollosa, W. S., 346.
Ferrin's Pond, 101.
Field, Darby, and Crystal Hills, xxv; nationality of, 20; residence of, 20; explores Mountains, 20; ascends Mount Washington, 20, 21; account of riches found, 22.
Field, General Martin, 103.
Field meetings of Appalachian Mountain Club, 351.
Field Museum of Natural History, 239.
Fields, Annie, 66, 178.
Fields, James T., 66, 175, 178.
Fires, 47, 77, 157, 163, 165, 171, 172, 173, 174, 181, 336, 338, 339, 340, 360–64, 369, 370.
Fisher, Dr. Joshua, 28, 30.
Flint, William F., 214.
Flume, the, Justus Conrad on discovery of, 102; discovery of, 105; Harry Hibbard describes, 105, 106; Harriet Martineau visits, 146; boulder carried away, 303.
Flume House, Hon. Amelia Matilda Murray at, 151; early history, 167; burned, 168; present one erected, 168, 341.
Forest fires, 381–83.
Foster, Daniel, 50, 52.
Foster, John, map, 18.
Fox, Charles James, poem on Chocorua, 12; poetry, 175.
Fox, Daniel, 60.
Fox family, Campton, 66.

Franconia, settlement and history, 58.
"Franconia Mountain Notch," poem, 105.
Franconia Notch, road destroyed in 1826, 97; road building, 101; earliest printed description, 106; Hawthorne, 115; Thoreau, 122; Parkman, 126; Starr King, 130; E. T. Coke, 145; Harriet Martineau, 146; Sir Charles Lyell, 148; Fredrika Bremer, 148; Bryant, 187; Thomas Cole, 191–92; hotels, 166–69, 341–42; National Forest purchases in, 399.
Franconia Range, shelter, 354; path, 356; forests acquired, 397, 399.
Frankenstein, G. N., 38; pictures, 203.
Frankenstein Cliff, 15, 38, 203.
Frankenstein Trestle, 38, 227.
Franklin, Mount, named, 78.
Freeman, Colonel Orville E., 240.
Freeman, Mrs. Orville E., 330.
French, Mr., landlord of Fabyan House, 337.
Fresh Air Club, 276, 279.
Frothingham, Richard, quoted, 128, 129, 130.
Frye, Caleb, 255.
Frye, Chaplain Jonathan, 46.
Frye, General Joseph, 39, 51.
Frye, Joseph, Jr., 40.
Frye, Nathaniel, 40.
Frye, Nathaniel (fl. 1848), 255.
Fryeburg, Maine, Indian remains, 3; Indian village, 3; early history, 39 ff.; fire, 47; and Conway, 51, 52; settlers flee to, 65; Whittier, 178; Lovewell's Fight commemorated, 186.

Gallinger, Senator Jacob H., 390, 391, 396.
Garfield, Mount, lake, 212; path, 356; named, 356; fire, 382.
Gate of the Notch, 35, 89, 263, 372.
Gay, Sir Isaac Newton, 262.
Gay, W. A., 66, 198, 203.

INDEX

Geary, artist, 202.
Geological Survey of New Hampshire, first, 204–08; second, 208–14.
Geological Survey, U.S., 396, 397.
Geology, xxiii, 147, 204–15.
"Geology of New Hampshire, The," 214.
Gerry, S. L., 66, 202, 203.
"Giant of the Hills," 75.
Giant's Grave, tradition connected with, 14; first hotel at, 73; burned, 77; second, 77, 79, 80; echo at, 164; leveled, 336.
Gibb, J. L., 162, 163, 167.
Gibson, W. Hamilton, his illustrations, xii.
Gifford, Charles Alling, 343.
Gifford, Sandford R., 198, 200, 201.
Gile, Dr., of Hanover, 281.
Gile, R. T., 374.
Gilead, Maine, Indian raid, 65.
Gilman, Samuel, Jr., 67.
Glen, the, hotels in, 170–71, 338–40.
Glen Boulder Trail, 356.
Glen Ellis Falls, 30, 357, 404.
Glen Ellis House, 172.
Glen House, first one built, 170; J. M. Thompson, proprietor, 171; Millikens, 171, 338; Dr. Ball at, 287, 300, 301; era of prosperity, 338; burned, 338, 339; second one opened, 339; completed, 340; burned, 340; stables, 340; present house, 340; "Josh Billings" at first house, 341; Mount Washington fire discovered at, 363; salute at opening of new Summit House, 369.
Glines, Israel, 53.
Glines, John, 53.
Goffe, Colonel, 52.
Gookin, General, 8.
Gordon trail, 345.
Gorges, Thomas, 22, 120.
Gorham, Maine, 25.
Gorham, N.H., 65; Starr King at, 130; hotels at, 169, 170; railroad reaches, 221; present Boston and Maine railroad, 226.

Grand Pierre, Émile, 217.
Grand Trunk Railway, 221.
Grant, S. Hastings, 217.
Grant, General Ulysses S., visits Mount Washington, 242; coach ride, 243; Twin Mountain House, 335.
Gray, Asa, memoir of Oakes, 37; accompanies Professor Tuckerman, 121; and Honorable Amelia Matilda Murray, 150.
Gray, Francis C., 36.
Gray's Inn, 172, 173.
Great Carbuncle, legend of, 15, 116.
Great Gulf, crossed by Dr. Robbins, 108; path into, 347.
"Great Stone Face, The," 103, 116, 117, 149.
Greeley, Deacon, of Boston, 199.
Greeley, Horace, 232.
Greene, Benjamin D., 108.
Greenleaf, Abbie Burnham (Mrs. C. H.), 169, 173.
Greenleaf, Colonel C. H., 166, 168.
Griffith, George Bancroft, 175.
Griggs, artist, 66, 203.
Groveton, railroad reaches, 225.
Guernsey, Mrs. Jessie, 105.
Guernsey farm, 106.
Guildhall, Vermont, Rosebrooks at, 72; birthplace of Ethan Allen Crawford, 75; Crawford lives at, 82.
Gunthwaite. *See* Lisbon.
Guyot, Arnold, explores the Mountains, 216, 217.
Guyot, Mount, 217.
Gyles, John, quoted, xxix.

Hadley, Philip, 257.
Hale, Edward Everett, member of first geological survey, 207; at house on Mount Washington, 207, 230; Appalachian Mountain Club, 351; and national forest, 388.
Halfway House, on carriage road, 235, 243, 244.
Hall, Dr. A. B., 286.
Hall, Dr. Edward Hagaman, 17.

419

INDEX

Hall, Joseph S., in Tuckerman's Ravine, 121; builds first Summit House, 230; contractor on carriage road, 236; and Dr. Ball, 298, 299, 301.
Hall, Judge Obed, inn, 93, 158; characterized, 158.
Hanover, 35, 209, 316.
Harding, Chester, 202.
"Hark Hill," 65.
Harkness, Harry S., 371.
Harriman, Governor, 208, 384.
Harriman, Mr., settler, 60.
Hart, Warren W., on Darby Field, 20; reopens Davis Path, 346.
Hart, William, 203.
Hart's Location, 73, 76.
Hartshorn, Lucius, 305–07.
Hartshorn, Mrs. Lucius, 231.
Harvard College, 39.
Harvey, James C., 277.
Hatch, George W., engraving, 11, 193.
Havell, F. J., 194.
Haverhill, N.H., 71.
Haverhill and Franconia Iron Works, The, 59.
Hawthorne, Nathaniel, his *Great Carbuncle*, 15; *Ambitious Guest*, 86; *Great Stone Face*, 103; his relation to the White Mountains, 113 ff.; his visits, 114, 115, 117; death, 114, 118, 174; on the early inns, 157.
Hayes, Mount, 134.
Hayes, President Rutherford B., 248.
Haystack, Great, 106.
Haystack Lake, 212.
Hazard, Ebenezer, 28, 30.
Heard, Mr., 28.
Hearne, Sergeant M. L., 326, 327.
Henry, Professor Joseph, 310.
Hermit Lake, 121, 354.
Hermit of the White Mountains, 263.
Hibbard, Harry, poet, 105.
Higginson, Colonel Thomas Wentworth, 258.
Hill, Henry, 89, 158.
Hill, Thomas, painter, 200.

Hill, Rev. Dr. Thomas, president of Harvard College, 212.
Hill, W. P., 164.
Hilliard, W. M., 372.
Hitchcock, Charles H., on permanency of the Profile, 105; as to name of Mounts Webster and Willard, 113; appointed State Geologist, 208; conducts second geological survey, 209–14; on Devil's Den, 219; and winter occupation of Mount Washington, 310 ff.
Hitchcock, President Edward, 208.
Hitchcock, E., Jr., 211.
Hitchcock, Colonel John R., hotel proprietor, 170; lessee of old Tip-Top and Summit Houses, 232; house on Mount Moriah, 255; and winter occupation of Mount Washington, 311, 314.
Hitchcock Flume, 213.
Hoar, Senator George F., 390.
Hobart, Captain James, 48.
Hoit, A. G., 202.
Hoit, Benjamin, 66.
Holden, L. L. ("Ranger"), 318, 358.
Holland, Bert, 372.
Holland, Samuel, map, 18, 60.
Holmes, Christopher, 65.
Holyoke, Mount, 144.
Hooker, General Joseph, 248.
Horne, Superintendent John, 362, 363.
Hotels, first at "Giant's Grave," built, 73, 157; burned, 77, 157; second, 77, 79, 80; early, 154–74; later, 331–44.
House that Jack Built, 263.
Howard, Governor Henry, 332, 334.
Howells, William Dean, 47, 184.
Hubbard, ——, collegian, 28.
Hubbard, Oliver P., M.D., 214.
Hubbard, R. W., 198.
Hubbard, William, his *History of New England*, xxv; *Indian Wars*, 6, 18.
Hudson River School of artists, 189, 190, 194, 199.

INDEX

Humboldt, Alexander von, quoted, x.
Hunter, legend of, and church of St. Francis, 54.
Hunter, Harry W., 272, 273.
Huntington, Daniel, 201.
Huntington, J. H., assistant on second geological survey, 209–13; winter on Mount Moosilauke, 210, 311–14; "Scenery of Coös County," 214; winter on Mount Washington, 316 ff.; his winter ascents, 316, 318, 319, 330; ascends by Davis Path, 346.
Huntington's Ravine, 317.
Hutchinson, Thomas, 58.

Indian Island, 3.
Indian remains, 1, 2, 3, 48, 52, 64.
Indians of the White Mountain region, 1, 2; their fear of the mountain summits, 13, 21; accompany Darby Field, 20, 21; Col. Whipple's adventure with, 53; Mrs. Rosebrook's adventure with, 72.
Ingelow, Jean, 183.
Inness, George, at West Ossipee, 179, 200; at North Conway, 200.
Intervale, Whittier at, 181; junction point, 228; British Embassy at, 372; forest reservation meeting, 388.
Iron Mountain House, 171.
Iron works in Franconia, 58, 59; in Tamworth, 68.
Irving, Washington, visits White Mountains, 142, 143.
Island Pond, Vermont, 220, 221.
Israel's River, 53, 54.

Jackman, Richard, 68.
Jackman, Royal C., 373.
Jackson, 29, 31; settlement, 59; becomes a summer resort, 171; hotels at, 171–73; artists at, 171, 202; first winter meeting of Appalachian Mountain Club, 351.

Jackson, Dr. Charles T., and first Geological Survey of New Hampshire, 205–07, 208.
Jackson, Mount, named, 37.
Jackson-Carter Notch Path, 355.
Jackson Falls House, 171.
Jacob's Ladder, 241, 244.
James, Professor William, 69.
Jefferson, 29, 35; settlement and history, 52 ff.
Jefferson, Mount, named, 78; Phillips Brooks, 135; Edward Everett Hale, 207; Dr. Ball, 295, 297.
Jefferson, President Thomas, 101.
Jefferson Highlands, 195, 375, 376.
Jefferson Notch Road, 374–76.
Jenkins, an English trader, murdered, 6.
Jenks, Edward Augustus, 175.
Jewell, Sergeant W. S., 326.
Jillson, Stephen, 63.
Jilly, Paul, 60.
John Anderson Memorial Road, 373, 374.
John's River, 53.
Johnson, David, 197.
Jordan, Governor Chester B., 376.
Joseph Story Fay Reservation, 403.
Josselyn, John, *New England's Rarities Discovered*, xxvi, xxvii; *Account of Two Voyages to New England*, 14; explores Mountains, 23; description, 23, 24.

Kan Ran Vugarty, xxxi.
Kancamagus, Indian sachem, 9, 10.
Kearsarge, Mount, 186, 210; houses on, 254, 255.
Kearsarge House, built, 160.
Kearsarge Tavern, 159, 160, 196, 197, 198.
Keenan, John M., 279–84.
Keenan, Lawrence J., 283.
Kellogg, Stanley T., 372.
Kendall, Edward Augustus, his *Travels*, xxvii, 139; his discussion of the name White Moun-

INDEX

tains, xxvii, xxviii; quoted as to Willey House, 89; his tour of the Mountains, 139; on place names, 140.
Kennebec, river, 19.
Kensett, J. F., 196, 197, 199.
Kent, Chancellor James, 107.
Kent, Judge William, 107.
Key, D. M., 248.
Kilburn, Benjamin W., 318, 327, 328, 329.
Kilkenny, 382.
Kimball, H. A., 316–18.
King, Reverend Thomas Starr, his *The White Hills*, xi; quoted as to Indian legend, 3; Lovewell's Pond, 47; stature of Ethan Allen Crawford, 75; Mount Monadnock, 120; Professor Tuckerman, 121; his connection with the White Mountains, 127, 128–31; his book published, 130; Richard Frothingham on the book, 130; at West Ossipee, 179; and Dr. Ball, 286.
King Philip's War, 5, 9.
King's Ravine, 130; path, 346.
Kinsman, Mount, 213.
Knight, Captain Artemas, 58.
Knight's Tavern, 166.

Lafayette, Mount, named, 106; early ascents, 106; Thoreau ascends, 124; railroad charter, 238; house on, 255; fire, 382.
Lafayette House, Harriet Martineau at, 146; Fredrika Bremer at, 149; J. L. Gibb, 162; built, 167; acquired by Richard Taft, 168.
Lakeman, Dr. Mary R., 330.
Lakes of the Clouds Hut, 353, 354.
Lancaster, N.H., settlement, 56, 57; railroad reaches, 225.
Landslides, 92, 94, 100, 302–04.
Lane, George W., 236.
Langdon, Reverend Samuel, 63.
Lanman, Charles, 166.
Larcom, Lucy, at Campton, 66; at Center Sandwich, 68; and Whittier, 176; assists Whittier, 181, 182; Whittier befriends, 182; her connection with the White Mountains, 183–85; on Mount Washington, 247.
Latrobe, Charles Joseph, visit to White Mountains, 141–43.
Laurentian Mountains, xxix.
Lead plate, left on Mount Washington, 31.
Leavitt, F., 219.
Leavitt, John T. G., 337.
Lebanon, N.H., 223.
Ledge, the, on east side of Mount Washington, 235; Dr. Ball at, 288, 289, 299.
Lesley, Professor J. P., 214.
Lever, Representative Asbury F., 393.
Levett, Christopher, his *Voyage into New England*, xxv; his mention of the Mountains, xxv; sees Passaconaway, 5; voyage to New England, 19; quoted, 19.
Lewis, Samuel, map, xxiv.
Libby, E., & Sons Company, 363.
Lightfoot, chauffeur, 283, 284.
Lindsey, John, 337.
Line, Sergeant William, 328, 329.
Lisbon, iron ore, 58; granted and settled, 61, 62; discovery of gold in, 62; Ammonoosuc gold field, 209, 210.
Little, Reverend Daniel, 27, 28.
Little, Henry, 108.
Little, Colonel Moses, 57.
Little, William, his *History of Warren*, quoted from, 6; published, 64; landlord of Prospect House, 257; and winter occupation of Mount Moosilauke, 311.
Littleton, settlement, 57; railroad reaches, 223, 224.
Lloyd Hills, 60.
Log Cabin, the, 355.
Lok, Michael, map, 18.
Lonesome Lake, 102.
Longfellow, Henry W., poem on Chocorua, 12, 186; poems on battle of Lovewell's Pond, 46, 185, 186; in White Mountains, 114; association with Mountains, 185–86.

INDEX

"Lord's Hill," 60.
Lost River, 372, 373.
Lovewell, Captain John, his expeditions against the Indians, 43; battle at Lovewell's Pond, 44, 45; death, 45.
Lovewell's Pond, battle, 42, 44–46; ballad, 46; Daniel Webster, 47; Whittier, 178; Longfellow's poems, 185, 186.
Low, A. A., 194.
Lowe, Charles E., searches for remains of Weiss, 275; builds Lowe's Path, 345, 346.
Lowe's King's Ravine Path, 346.
Lowe's Path, 345, 346; Appalachian Mountain Club, 355.
Lower Bartlett, 159.
Lumbering, 378–79.
Lyell, Sir Charles, his visit to the White Mountains, 146–48.
Lyon, John E., Boston, Concord, and Montreal Railroad, 224; second Summit House, 246; Moosilauke Mountain Road Company, 257.

McClellan, General George B., 102, 248.
McMillan, Colonel Andrew, 159.
McMillan House, 159.
McNeill, William Gibbs, 222.
McNorton, James, 63.
Macomber, General David O., 235, 314.
Mad River, 185.
Madison, Mount, named, 78; Phillips Brooks on, 135; Osgood Path, 347; huts, 351, 352; register placed, 358.
Madison Hut, built, 351, 352; enlarged, 352; second hut, 352.
Maine Central Railroad, 227, 228.
Man at the Pool, 261.
Maplewood Farm, 334.
Maplewood Hotel, 334.
Maps, 18–19, 208, 209, 210, 214, 367.
March, Colonel, 41.
Marsh, David G., 257.
Marsh, Sylvester, his services, 237; conceives idea of mountain railway, 237; invents mechanism, 237; applies for a charter, 238; begins construction, 238; designs first locomotive, 239; later life, 241; quoted as to Rigi railway, 242; gives permission for use of train shed in winter, 314; and Fabyan House, 336.
Martin, Homer, 201.
Martineau, Harriet, her visit to the White Mountains, 145–46; as to building of Lafayette House, 167.
Mason, Mrs. Ellen McRoberts, 50, 159, 227, 255.
Massachusetts, and Passaconaway, 6, 8; bounty for Indian scalps, 12, 41, 42; punitive measures against Indians, 41; and White Mountain Reserve, 390.
Massachusetts Historical Society, Collections, xxx, 28.
Mayne, Edward, Robert, and Thomas, 59.
Mayne, Sir William, 59.
Maynesborough. See Berlin.
Medford (dog), 325, 328.
Mellen, Grenville, 84, 158.
Memphremagog, Lake, 54.
Mercator, Gerhard, map, 18.
Merrill, C. H., 335, 375.
Merrill, G. S., 202.
Merrill, John, 261, 262.
Merrill, Jonathan, 310.
Merrill's Mountain House, 257.
Merrimac, the, xxxi, 2.
Metropolitan Museum of Art, 201.
Milliken, Charles R., 338.
Milliken, Weston F. 338.
Mills, John, 64.
Mitchell, James E., 263.
Model of White Mountain region, 212.
Monadnock (Colebrook), 71.
Monadnock, Mount, and Emerson, 120.
Monroe, Mount, named, 78.
Montalban Ridge, 276, 346, 398, 399.

INDEX

Monument at Willey site, rock, 86; board, 89, 95; Rosebrook, 73; Crawford, 83.

Moody, Josiah, 60.

Moose Hillock or Moosehillock. *See* Moosilauke.

Moosilauke, Mount, as viewpoint, 64; E. A. Kendall on name, 140; Lucy Larcom, 184; first climbed, 255; Tip-Top House, 256, 258; account of ascent by Captain Partridge, 256; winter occupation of, 311–14; forests acquired, 397.

Moosilauke Mountain Road Company, 257.

Morey, George W., 138.

Moriah, Mount, 255.

Morris, Honorable Corbyn, 58.

Morristown. *See* Franconia.

Morse, G. F., 348.

Motor cycle, 372.

Moulton, Jonathan, 68.

Mounds, Indian, 3.

Mount Clinton Road, 375.

Mount Crawford House, built, 73, 88, 89; later history, 158.

Mount Lafayette House, north of Profile House, 169.

Mount Lafayette House, south of Profile House, 168, 169.

Mount Madison House, 170.

Mount Pleasant House, 337, 338.

Mount Pleasant Path, 356.

Mount Washington Carriage Road, 234–36; accident on, 243.

Mount Washington Hotel (Bretton Woods), 343–44, 376.

Mount Washington Hotel Company (Fabyan House), 336.

Mount Washington House (at Fabyan), Horace Fabyan keeps, 164; remodeled, 165; burned, 163, 165, 336; stables destroyed, 336.

Mount Washington Railway, John E. Lyon and, 224; history, 237–42; empty train wrecked, 244; slide-boards, 244–46.

Mount Washington River, 15, 22.

Mount Washington Road Company, 235.

Mount Washington Summit Road Company, 236.

Mount Whittier. *See* West Ossipee.

Mountain Coliseum, 121.

Mountain View House (Whitefield), 342.

Mularvey, Michael, 318, 319.

Murphy, D. C., 326.

Murray, Honorable Amelia Matilda, her visit to the White Mountains, 150–52.

Musgrove, Eugene R., his anthology, 175; on Whittier as poet of the Mountains, 176.

Myer, General A. B., 315.

Myers, J. D., contractor on carriage road, 235; and Bourne party, 270; and Dr. Ball, 288, 289, 299.

Nails, machine-made, first, 69.

Nancy, story of, 55, 56; Mount, 55; her surname, 55.

Nancy's Bridge, 55.

Nancy's Brook, 55.

Nash, Timothy, discovers Crawford Notch, 26.

Nash and Sawyer's Location, 26, 70.

Nashua and Lowell Railroad, 222.

Nashua and Worcester Railroad, 222.

National Forest, 388–401.

National Forest Reservation Commission, composition, 396; action in 1914, 398; approves further appropriations, 401.

Nazro, John Coffin, 259–61.

Nelson, S. A., raises fund for winter occupation of Mount Washington, 315; a member of party, 316; stay on Mountain, 318, 320.

New Hampshire, separate colony, 42; poets, 175; first geological survey, 204–08; second, 208–14; railroads, 222–28; lumbering and other wood industries, 378–80; forest fire protection, 382, 383; ownership of forests, 384; and national forest, 388–

INDEX

89; Crawford Notch purchase, 401–03.
New Hampshire Forestry Commission, 403.
New Hampshire Forests, Society for the Protection of, acquires Lost River tract, 373; work for fire protection, 383; advocates forest reservation, 387, 388; 400; Crawford Notch Reserve, 401; its reservations, 403.
New Hampshire Iron Factory Company, 58.
New Madbury, 59.
New River, 32.
New York Historical Society Gallery, 193.
New York Public Library Galleries, 194, 199, 201.
Newell, L. B., 318.
"Newspaper train" on Mount Washington Railway, 245.
Nichols, Rev. Dr. Harry P., visitor to Mount Washington, 247; ascent on June 30, 1900, 276; at opening of present Summit House, 369; accompanies Ambassador Bryce, 372.
Nickerson, David, 96.
North Conway, settled, 52; Durand at, 194; Champney and, 195–99; various artists at, 196 ff.; Portland and Ogdensburg Railroad reaches, 227; coaching parades, 245; first field meeting of Appalachian Mountain Club, 351.
North Stratford, 228.
North Woodstock, railroad reaches, 226; 342.
Northern Peaks, named, 78; Phillips Brooks, 134; Edward Everett Hale, 207; first paths, 345; first camp, 346; Madison Hut, 351; private camps, 355; forests, 397, 398.
Northern Railroad of New Hampshire, 223.
Northumberland, 71.
Norumbega, 18.
Norwich, and Worcester Railroad, 222.

Notch House (near Gate of Notch), 85, 122, 126, 129; origin, 161; built, 162; Thomas J. Crawford keeps, 162; repaired and burned, 163.
Notch House (Willey House). *See* Willey House.
Notch Mountain, 113.
Nowell, William G., Lowe's Path, 345; builds first camp, 346; Log Cabin, 355; trail to Castellated Ridge, 356; puts A. M. C. register on Mount Adams, 358.
Noyes, Nathaniel, 231.
Number Four (fort), 54.
Nuttall, Thomas, 108.
Nutter, Mr., of Lancaster, 319.

Oakes, William, his *Scenery of the White Mountains*, xi, 38; Cutler's collection, 32; botanical explorations, 37, 38; memoir, 37; collects plants, 108; Mount Webster, 113; Sir Charles Lyell, 147; Flume House, 167.
Oakes Gulf, 38.
Observatory, first, 233, 234; second, 250, 251.
"Old Man of the Mountain." *See* Profile.
"Old Man of the Mountain," railroad engine, 224.
Ordway, Alfred, 197.
Ormsbee, Allan, 275–79.
Osgood, Benjamin, innkeeper, 159.
Osgood, Benjamin F., Bierstadt, 202; winter ascent of Mount Washington, 306–07; builds paths, 347; places a roll for records on Mount Adams, 358.
Osgood, Samuel, 40.
Osgood Path, 347, 348.
Osgoods, the, 47.
Ossipee, town, Indian remains, 3.
Ossipee Pond or Lake, 44, 69.
Ossipee Range, 68, 129, 182.
Ossipees, Indian sub-tribe, 2.
Oxford Hotel, at Fryeburg, burned, 47.

Packard, Alpheus S., 214.
Packard, Winthrop, 218.

425

INDEX

Page, David, 40.
Page, Captain David, 57.
Page, Jeremiah, 67.
Page, John, 64.
Page, Governor John, 204, 205.
Page, Samuel B., 257.
Paine, Ralph D., quoted, 406–07.
Parker, Herschel C., 277.
Parker, Walter, 277.
Parker, Lieutenant Zachariah, 48.
Parkman, Francis, in White Mountains, 124–27; exploit at Willey slide, 127; on preservation of forests, 386.
Parsons, Colonel Charles, 230.
Parsons, Thomas, W., 87.
Partridge, Captain Alden, 256.
Pascataquack, 20.
Passaconaway, chieftain, 4–8.
Passaconaway, mountain, 67, 210.
Patch, Mrs. Daniel, 256.
Patch, Joseph, 64.
Path, first up Mount Washington, 77; second, 78.
"Patriarch of the Mountains," 73, 84.
Paugus, Indian sachem, 45.
Pawtucket Falls, 6.
Peak House (Mount Chocorua), 255.
Peaked Hill. *See* Agassiz, Mount.
Pearson, Samuel A., 77.
Peary, Lieutenant (now Admiral) R. E., 248.
Peck, Dr. W. D., 33, 37.
Peek, W. H., 356.
Peeling. *See* Woodstock.
Pegwagget. *See* Pequawket.
Pemigewasset House, 118, 173, 174.
Pemigewasset River, 48, 387.
Pemigewassets, the, retire to Canada, 49; home, 64.
Pendexter, ——, moves into Willey House, 100.
Pendexter, Honorable John, 158.
Pendexter Mansion, 158.
"Pennacook," quoted, 223.
Pennacooks, the, 2, 4, 5, 9, 10.
Pequawket, Indian village, 3, 40, 42, 43.

Pequawket, Mount, 254. *See* Kearsarge, Mount.
Pequawket House, 159.
Pequawkets, the, 2, 11, 12, 41.
Perch Camp, 355.
Perkins, Nathan R., 230, 231.
Philbrick, David, 68.
Photography on Mount Washington, 327, 328.
Pickard, Samuel T., 180, 182.
Pickering, Dr. Charles, 38.
Pickering, E. C., on Mount Washington, 247; founder and first president of Appalachian Mountain Club, 349.
Pickering, W. H., 247; on Davis Path, 346.
Picket Hill. *See* Agassiz, Mount.
Pierce, Franklin, 117, 118, 158.
Pigwackets. *See* Pequawkets.
Pingree, David, 260.
Pinkham, Captain Joseph, 59.
Pinkham Notch, 59.
Piscataqua, river, 5, 20.
Pitman Hall, 159.
Plato, a colored man, 65.
Playfair, Sir Lyon, 248.
Pleasant, Mount, named, 78; slides on, 100.
Plummer, Joseph, 161.
Plymouth, President Dwight, 34; settled, 48; history, 49, 50; hotels at, 173, 174; railroad reaches, 224.
"Plymouth buck gloves," 50.
Pone, artist, 203.
Pool, the, Man at, 261.
Poole, Fanny Runnells, 175.
Poor, Peter, 65.
Portland, Maine, 19, 34, 47; the Atlantic and St. Lawrence Railroad, 220, 221; connected with Montreal by rail, 221; Portland and Ogdensburg Railroad, 227.
Portland and Ogdensburg Railroad, 227, 228; effect on travel, 331; completed to Fabyan, 336.
Portsmouth, N.H., 17.
Potter, Chandler E., his *History of Manchester*, quoted from, 7, 9, 10.

INDEX

Potter, Bishop Henry C., 136.
Pourtalès, Count de, 142.
Pratt, Henry Cheeves, 191, 194.
Prescott, John, 67.
Presidential Range, xxiii, xxix; chief peak named, 32, 33; other peaks named, 78; traversed by Dr. Robbins, 108; casualties on, 267–84; Dr. Ball, 284–301; paths on 345–56; forests acquired, 397, 398, 399.
Prime, Dr. William C., on the discovery of the Profile, 101, 102; his camp at Lonesome Lake, 102; description of the Profile, 104; on Richard Taft, 167; and Mount Lafayette House, 169; on Mount Washington, 247.
Prince of Wales (Edward VII), 195.
Procter, George C., 318.
Proctor, Edna Dean, uses Agiochook, xxx; her poetry, 175.
Profile, Mount, 104.
Profile, the, discovery of, 101, 102; existence made known, 103; Dr. Prime describes, 104; measurements of, 105, 213; Professor C. H. Hitchcock on its permanency, 105; Hawthorne's story, 116; E. T. Coke on, 145; Fredrika Bremer on, 149; Hon. Amelia Matilda Murray, 151; Thomas Cole on, 192; David Johnson's picture, 197; S. L. Gerry's picture, 202.
Profile and Franconia Notch Railroad, 225.
Profile House, Hon. Amelia Matilda Murray at, 151; built and opened, 168; enlarged, 168; first cottage at, 168; railroad to, 225; General Grant at, 243; character of hotel, 341; torn down, 342; New Profile House built and opened, 342.
Profile Lake, 101, 104, 151.
Prospect House. *See* Tip-Top House on Mount Moosilauke.
Pursh, Frederick, "Flora of North America," 33.
Putnam, G. F., 257.

Quebec Junction, 228.
Quinebequy, 19.

Railway, up Mount Washington, 237–42; scenic, 366.
Randolph, settlement, 63; railroad, 226.
"Ranger." *See* Holden, L. L.
Ranney, Mrs. V. G., poem on Chocorua, 12.
Raymond, Major Curtis B., 347.
Raymond Path, 347.
Records of ascent, 31, 37, 84; history of provision for, 357–58.
Red Hill (in Moultonborough), President Dwight ascends, 34; Professor Silliman, 108; Thoreau, 123; Starr King, 129; Harriet Martineau, 145; Hon. Amelia Matilda Murray, 151; location and view, 151.
Reservations, Appalachian Mountain Club, 357; 403–04.
Revolutionary War, 53, 57, 63, 66, 67; Rosebrook in, 71, 72.
Riant, John, 62.
Ribero, map, 18.
Rich, John P., 235, 236.
Richards, Reverend Charles A. L., 133, 136, 137.
Richards, T. Addison, at West Campton, 66, 203.
Richards, Rev. Dr. W. R., 247.
Ricker, engineer on Mount Washington carriage road, 235.
Ricker, Mrs. L. J., 160.
Riggenbach, Nicholas, 242.
Rigi railway in Switzerland, 242.
Rindge, Captain, 65.
Ripley, Henry Wheelock, 130.
Riverside Cottage, 184.
Road through Crawford Notch, 25, 26, 27, 87.
Robbins, Dr. J. W., 108.
Rogers, Henry D., 214.
Rogers, Nathaniel Peabody, 177, 178.
Rogers, Major Robert, quoted, xxvi; attack on St. Francis and return journey, 53, 54.
Rogers, William B., 214.

INDEX

Rogers, Dr., of Lancaster, 319.
Romero, Señor, 248.
Rosebrook, Eleazar, settles in Nash and Sawyer's Location, 70, 72; Colebrook, 70; incidents of life there, 71; in Revolutionary army, 71, 72; builds first inn, 73, 157; life, undertakings, and death, 73; epitaph, 73; President Dwight on, 74; burial place, 75; inn, 88; President Dwight at his house, 34, 35; Dr. Shattuk, 35.
Rosebrook, Hannah, character and courage, 71; Northumberland, 71; adventure with Indians, 72; death, 73; burial place, 75.
Rosebrook, Lucius M., 230.
Rosebrook, William, 89.
Rosebrook, the guide, xxviii.
Rosebrook, ———, builds White Mountain House, 166.
Rosebrook family, 70, 166.
Rosebrook House, 166.
Roth, Professor Edward, 103.
Rumney, 65.
Russell's Riverside Cottage, 184.
Rutledge, Edward, 217.

Saco, the, source, xxxi, 20, 140; Great Carbuncle, 15, 16, 399.
Saco, town, 40.
Saco Pond, 44.
Sagadahoc, truce of, 9.
St. Francis, Indian town in Canada, 9, 11, 46; attacked by Rogers's Rangers, 53, 54.
St. Lawrence and Atlantic Railroad, 221.
Sandoz, Ernest, 217.
Sandwich, North, 183, 184.
Sandwich, town, settlement and history, 67; Lucy Larcom, 183.
Sandwich Addition, 67.
Sandwich Dome, 67.
Sandwich Range, 10, 66, 68.
Sanford, 40.
Sargent, Professor Charles Sprague, 386.
Sawyer, Benjamin, partner of Nash, 26.

Schoolcraft, Henry Rowe, as to name Agiocochook, xxix; as to Waumbek, xxxi.
Scott, Representative Charles F., 394.
Scott Bill, 394–95.
Scott's Mills, 228.
Scudder, Horace E., 69.
Scudder, Samuel H., scientific work, 218; first editor of Appalachia, 218, 359.
Searle, Jesse, 58.
Seward, William H., 232.
Shapleigh, Frank H., 202.
Shattuck, A. D., 198.
Shattuck, Dr. George, quoted on Crawford Notch turnpike, 27; explores White Mountains, 35.
Shaw, Chief Justice Lemuel, 36.
Shelburne, settlement, 65; Indian raid, 65; lumbering, 378.
Shelters on the Mountains, 351–55.
Shepard, Forrest, 106.
Signal Service, U.S., 250; 322–26.
Signal station, built, 250, 322.
Sigourney, Mrs. L. H., 86.
Silliman, Professor Benjamin, 103, 106; describes and explores the Crawford Notch, 108, 109; ascends Mount Washington, 109; Willey Slide, 109, 127.
Silver Cascade, 35, 194.
Silver image of St. Francis, 54.
Sinclair, John G., 161.
Sinclair, Richard, 67.
Sinclair House, General Grant at, 243; development, 332.
Singrawack, 53.
Slade, Daniel D., accompanies Parkman, 126; quoted, 127.
Slide-board, 244–46; 369.
Slides. See Landslides.
Slosson, Annie Trumbull, scientific work, 218; and Mount Lafayette House, 169; on Mount Washington, 247; her attachment to Summit House, 361.
Smillie, James, 197.
Smith, James, 169.

INDEX

Smith, Nathaniel, first settler in Fryeburg, 40.
Smith, Sergeant Theodore, 316, 318, 325.
Smith, Honorable Thomas J., 257.
Snow, Nathaniel, 60.
Snow arch in Tuckerman's Ravine, men dine in, 235; Sewall E. Faunce, 273, 274; party of Appalachians, 274.
Snyder Brook paths, 355.
Society for the Protection of New Hampshire Forests. *See* New Hampshire Forests, Society for the Protection of.
Sokokis, the, 2, 3.
Soltaire, 86.
Sparhawk, Mr., 106.
Spaulding, John H., his *Historical Relics of the White Mountains*, xiii; quoted, 13, 56; on Devil's Den, 219; in management of Tip-Top House, 231; and carriage road, 235; on Nazro, 259, 260; winter ascent of Mount Washington, 307-09.
Spaulding, Mary B. (Mrs. Lucius Hartshorn), 231.
Spaulding, Samuel Fitch, 231.
Spencer, Hobart, 66.
Spencer, Jared, 65.
Spencer, Joseph, 66.
Spooner, Thomas Jefferson, 161.
"Spotted fever," 76.
Sprague, Isaac, 38.
Stag and Hounds, the, 66, 185.
Stage office on Mount Washington, 249.
Stalbird, Granny, 56.
Stanley, F. E., 372.
Stanley, F. O., 371.
Stanley, Oscar, 304.
Stanley Slide, 304.
Starbird, Granny, 56.
Stark, John, captured by Indians, 49.
Stark, William, escapes from Indians, 49; grantee of Bartlett, 60.
Starr King, Mount, 130.
Start, Edwin A., 390.

Stearns, E. S., *History of Plymouth*, 50.
Stevens, Alice Bartlett, 243.
Stevens, William, 326.
Stickney, Joseph, Mount Pleasant House, 338; builds Mount Washington Hotel, 343.
Stillé, Professor C. J., 136.
Stillings Path, 345.
Stinson, David, killed, 49.
Stinson Lake, 49.
Stockbridge, Helen E., compiler of bibliography, xiv.
Stockwell, Emmons, 57.
Stone, B. G., 197.
Stone cabins on Mount Washington, 79, 229.
Storm of August, 1826, 91 *ff.*
Story, Judge Joseph, 172.
"Story of Jack," 263, 264.
Strickland, Frederick, 268, 269.
Strong, Rev. George Augustus, 133, 136, 137.
Stuart, Charles J., 77, 78.
Stuart, R. L., 194.
Stuart, Mrs. R. L., 201.
Sugar Hill, 61, 342.
Sullivan County Railroad, 226.
Summit House, first one built, 230; used as an employees' dormitory, 231; taken down, 231, 251; second, built and opened, 246, 247; cost, etc., 247; enlarged and improved, 249; storm of June 30, 1900, 276; Appalachian Mountain Club field meetings, 276, 351; cornerstone for new one laid, 366; large one planned, 366; present one built and opened, 367-69.
Summit House on Mount Moosilauke. *See* Tip-Top House.
Sumner, Charles, and Fredrika Bremer, 149; on Mount Washington, 232.
Sunset Hill House, 342.
Surprise, Mount, 134.
Survey for scenic railway and Summit House, 366.
Suydam, James A., 200.
Swain, Darius, 256.

INDEX

Sweetser, M. F., preparer of Chisholm's Guide-Book, xiii; his Handbook (Osgood's or Ticknor's *White Mountains*), xiii; historical material in latter, xiii; on St. Aspinquid, 5; opinion of Mount Chocorua, 10; his narration of the Chocorua legend, 10–11; corrects error as to Cutler's River, 32; on name of Conway, 50; as to house on Mount Kearsarge, 255; on Professor Huntington, 317; on leveling of Giant's Grave, 336; on "Josh Billings," 341.

Swindell, Jim, 55.

"Switzerland of America," origin of application to White Mountains, xxxii.

Taft, Richard, 167, 168.
Taft, President William Howard, 395.
Talbot, F. A., 242.
Tamworth, 11, 68, 69.
Tamworth Iron Works, 68.
Taylor family, Campton, 66.
Tent on Mount Washington, 229.
Thaxter, Celia, 175.
"Things as They Are," same as "Summer Tours," 111.
Thompson, Eben, 318.
Thompson, Dr. Ebenezer, 62.
Thompson, Rev. Frederick, his reissue of Willey's *Incidents*, xiv, 200.
Thompson, George, 177.
Thompson, J. M., buys first Glen House, 171; drowned, 171, 302, 338; body found, 202; first person to drive up Mount Washington, 236; and Dr. Ball, 287, 288, 296, 300; bridle path, 171, 347.
Thompson, Samuel W., tavern at North Conway, 159; carries the mail, 160; builds Kearsarge House, 160; present hotel completed, 161; Champney and other artists and, 196.

Thoreau, Henry D., visits to White Mountains, 122–24; injured in Tuckerman's Ravine, 124.

Thorn Mountain House, 172.
Thornton, 66.
Ticknor, William Davis, 117.
Tip-Top House, the old, opened, 231; upper story added, 232; used by employees, 233; office of *Among the Clouds*, 233, 252; disused, 233; used again as hotel, 233, 365; escapes fire of 1908, 364; burned, 369–71.
Tip-Top House (so-called) on Mount Washington in 1840, 207, 229, 230.
Tip-Top House on Mount Moosilauke, 256, 257, 258.
Token, The, an annual, 11.
Torrey, Bradford, natural history, 218; on Mount Washington, 247.
Torrey, Herbert, 217.
Tower, Ambrose, 272.
Train sheds on Mount Washington, 249, 322.
Trinity Height, 259.
Tripyramid, Mount, 303.
Trollope, Anthony, his visit to the White Mountains, 152–53; opinion of the scenery, etc., 153.
Trollope, Mrs. Frances, 141.
Trudeau, Thomas, 375.
True, Mr., settler, 65.
Trumbull, Dr. J. Hammond, on meaning of Agiocochook, xxx.
Tucker, Nathaniel, 36.
Tuckerman, Professor Edward, 32, 33; explores the White Mountains, 120; his botanical work, 121; his tastes, 121.
Tuckerman's Ravine, 22, 31; name, etc., 120; Thoreau in, 123; paths, 347.
Tudor, Henry, tour of White Mountains, 140, 141.
Tug-of-War Hill, 372.
Turner, Honorable George H., 281, 282.
Turner family, Bethlehem, 161.

INDEX

Turnpike, tenth New Hampshire, 27, 73, 87; partly destroyed, 97.
Turnpike from Fabyan's to the Base, begun, 238; completed, 241.
Tweed, Professor Benjamin F., 129.
Twin Mountain House, Beecher at, 132, 133; history, 334, 335.
Twin Mountain Range, Mount Guyot, 217; trail, 356; fire, 382.
Twin Mountain Trail, 356.
Tyler, Mr., proprietor of Profile House, 168.
Tyng, Colonel, 42, 46.

Upham, Warren, 214.
Upper Bartlett, 60, 158.

Valley Way, 356.
Vermont Central Railroad, 223.
Vermont Valley Railroad, 226.
Verrazano, sees White Mountains, 17.
Vials or Viles, John Alfred, 263.
Vines, Richard, 22, 120.
Viseu, bishop of, map, 18.
Vose, George L., on second geological survey, 209, 210; ascent of Mount Carrigain, 348.

Wadsworth Athenæum, 193.
Wahwa, 45.
Walker, Donald, 304.
Ward, Julius H., his *The White Mountains*, xii; "White Mountain Forests in Peril," 386, 387.
Warren, Jonas, 60.
Warren, Admiral Sir Peter, 64.
Warren, town, settlement, 64; summer boarders, 257.
Washington, Mount, Passaconaway legend, 4; visibility of, 19; ascended by Darby Field, 20, 21; by Josselyn, 23; by a ranging company, 24; by Captain Evans (twice), 25; by Belknap's party, 30; height estimated by Dr. Cutler, 32; receives its name, 32, 33; Dr. Cutler ascends again, 33; height as computed by Dr. Bowditch, 33; ascended by Dr. Shattuk, 35; by Dr. Jacob Bigelow and party, 36; height computed by Dr. Bigelow's party, 36; first path, 77; bridle path, 77; Ethan Allen Crawford guides people, 77 ff.; ascended by Adino N. Brackett, John W. Weeks, Philip Carrigain, and others, 77, 78; height computed by Brackett and others, 78; shorter path built, 78; the Misses Austin ascend, 79; first shelters built, 79, 229; first horseback ascent, 84, 85; Grenville Mellen ascends, 84; Western travelers' experience during storm of August, 1826, 99, 100; Professor Silliman ascends, 109; Hawthorne ascends, 115; Professor Tuckerman and, 121; Thoreau ascends, 122, 123; Parkman ascends, 126; Starr King ascends, 129; Phillips Brooks at, 136; Latrobe and Irving, 142; E. T. Coke, 144; Anthony Trollope, 152; J. M. Thompson's path, 171; Lucy Larcom, 183, 184; Bryant, 187; Edward Everett Hale, 207, 230; President Hitchcock, 208; height measured by Guyot, 217; ascertained by Captain T. J. Cram, 217; railroad reaches Base, 225; E. A. Crawford's tent, 229; hotels on, 230–33; first and second visits of Colonel Charles Parsons, 230; carriage road, 234–36; height measured by Engineers Cavis and Ricker, 235; railway, 237–42; President Grant visits, 242; fatal accident on carriage road, 243; empty train wrecked, 244; use of slide-boards, 244–46; building of second Summit House, 246, 247; notables on, 232, 247, 248; post-office established, 249; stage office built, 249; signal station built, 250; second observatory, 250; *Among the*

INDEX

Clouds office, 251; old Summit House taken down, 251; *Among the Clouds*, 251–53; Captain Alden Partridge, 256; Trinity Height, 259; J. C. Nazro, 259–61; casualties, 267 *ff*.; Dr. Ball, 287 *ff*.; winter ascents, 305–09, 327–30; winter occupation, 309–21; U.S. Signal Service, 322–26; low temperatures recorded, 319; velocity of wind, 320, 322, 323; train-shed blown down, 322; William Stevens dies on, 326; Sergeant Cone injured, 326; winter ascents by women, 330; Stillings Path, 345; Gordon Path, 345; Davis Path, 346; Tuckerman's Ravine Path, 347; records of ascents, 357; great fire, 360–64; cornerstone of a new Summit House laid, 366; plans for scenic railway and large Summit House, 366; present Summit House, 367–69; "Climbs to the Clouds," 371, 372; Ambassador Bryce at, 372; acquired for National Forest, 397, 398.
Washington House (Conway), 159.
Waterville, 210.
Watson, L. M., 356.
Waumbek, the name, xxxi.
Waumbek Hotel, railroad to, 226; history, 342.
Waumbekketmethna, xxx.
Webster, Daniel, teaches at Fryeburg, 47; plea at Plymouth, 49–50; visits Ethan Allen Crawford's and ascends Mount Washington, 112; name given to mountain, 113; Great Stone Face, 116; at Mount Crawford House, 158; at Jackson, 172.
Webster, Colonel David, 173.
Webster, John, 68.
Webster, Colonel William, 173.
Webster Tavern at Plymouth, 173.
Weed, Mr., makes augers, 69.
Weed, Orlando, 67.
Weeks, John W., the explorer, 77, 78.

Weeks, Representative (now Senator) John W., 393.
Weeks Bill and Act, 394–95, 396, 399, 400, 401.
Weiss, Ewald, 274, 275.
Wells River, Vt., 223, 224.
Wentworth, Governor Benning, 26, 50, 51, 60, 67.
Wentworth, General M. C., 172.
Wentworth, Mark H., 52.
Wentworth, Mount, 106.
Wentworth, Sir Thomas, 63.
Wentworth, ——, porter for Thoreau, 123.
Wentworth Hall, 172.
West Campton, 66, 185, 194, 203.
West Ossipee (now Mount Whittier), 179, 182.
West Thornton, mound, 3, 66.
Wheeler, Amos, 60, 161.
Wheeler, Vice-President William A., 248.
Wheelwright, Reverend John, 5.
Whipple, Colonel Joseph, 29, 52, 53, 55, 56.
Whistler, George Washington, 222.
Whitcher, Chase, 255.
Whitcomb, Francis, 101.
White, Franklin, 307–09.
White, Colonel John H., 166.
White Hills, use of the name, xxiii. See White Mountains.
White Mountain Club, 348, 349.
White Mountain Echo, 253, 254.
White Mountain House, 81, 83; history of, 165, 166, 336.
White Mountain National Forest, 388–401, 403.
White Mountain Notch. See Crawford Notch.
White Mountain School of artists, 189.
White Mountain Station House (Gorham), 169.
White Mountains, literature of, ix *ff*.; extent and character of the region, xxiii; physical geography and geology, xxiii; their name and its origin, xxiii, xxiv; first appearance of name in print, xxv–xxvi; Indian names,

INDEX

xxix–xxxi; as a river source, xxxi; as a summer playground, xxxi; dearth of historical interest, xxxii; Indian legend and history, 1 ff.; Indian legend of their origin, 13; early explorers, 17 ff.; maps, 18, 19; explored by Darby Field, 20; by Thomas Gorges and Richard Vines, 22; by John Josselyn, 23; by two parties of men, 24; by Captain Evans, 25; Belknap's party, 27 ff.; Dr. Cutler again, Dr. Peck and Dr. Bowditch, 33; visited by Reverend Dr. Timothy Dwight, 33, 34, 35; by Dr. George Shattuk, 35; by Dr. Jacob Bigelow and others, 35, 36; by Dr. Boott, 36, 37; by Oakes, 37; first settlements, 39 ff.; first hotel in, built, 73; various persons explore or visit, 101 ff.; Hawthorne in, 115; Emerson in, 118–20; Professor Tuckerman explores, 120–21; Thoreau in, 122–24; Francis Parkman visits, 124–27; Henry Ward Beecher in, 127, 131–33; Phillips Brooks in, 127, 133–37; T. Starr King in, 127, 128–31; Hosea Ballou, 2d, in, 128; early foreign visitors, 139 ff.; Washington Irving in, 142, 143; early hotels and beginnings of region as summer resort, 154 ff.; poets in, 175–88; Whittier, 176–82; Lucy Larcom, 183–85; Longfellow, 185–86; Bryant, 186–88; scenery described by Bryant, 187–88; painters in, 188–203; importance in American art, 190; Thomas Cole, 190–93; Henry Cheeves Pratt, 191, 194; Thomas Doughty, 194; Champney and other artists in, 195 ff.; later scientific explorations of, 204 ff.; first geological survey, 204–08; second geological survey, 208–14; early geological explorers, 214; Agassiz, 215–16; Guyot, 216, 217; railroads to and in, 220–28; John E. Lyon and, 224; General Grant, 242, 243; noteworthy "characters" of, 259–66; casualties, 267–84; Dr. Ball, 284–301; landslides, 302–04; later hotels, 331–44; early trails in, 345–48; White Mountain Club, 348–49; work of Appalachian Mountain Club in, 350–57, 358–59; Mount Washington fire, 360–64; lumber industry in, 378–79, 383–87; other wood industries, 379–80; forest fires, 381–83; history of National Forest Reserve, 388–401; recent changes in travel and business, 405–09; use as a winter resort, 408–09.

White Mountains Railroad, 224, 225, 336.

White River Junction, Vt., 223.

Whiteface, Mount, 67, 210.

Whitefield, 60, 342.

Whitefield and Jefferson Railroad, 226.

Whiting, Leonard, 62.

Whitney, Josiah Dwight, 206.

Whittier, John G., uses Agiocochook, xxx; accepts Hawthorne's "The Great Stone Face," 117; the poet of the White Hills, 176–82; friendship with Lucy Larcom, 182, 183.

Whittier, Mount, 182.

Wild River Valley, 382, 397.

Wilde, Hamilton, 198.

Wilder, Joseph, 63.

Willard, Frances E., 356.

Willard, Joseph, 113.

Willard, Mount, carriage road, 85; named, 113; Hon. Amelia Matilda Murray, 151; Anthony Trollope, 153; explorations on, 213; Guyot, 217.

Willard, Sidney, 113.

Willey, Benjamin G., his *Incidents in White Mountain History*, xiv; quoted, 13, 40, 53, 83; on the Willey disaster, 85, 87; on building of Willey House, 89; death, 90; on Frederick Strickland, 268.

433

INDEX

Willey, George F., 86.
Willey, Captain Samuel, 60, 90.
Willey, Samuel, Jr., 85; moves into Willey House, 90; thinks of removal, 90; body found, 96.
Willey, Mrs. Samuel, Jr., 90, 96.
Willey, Selden C., 178, 183.
Willey Brook Bridge, 227.
Willey Disaster, 85 ff.; 109, 110, 141.
Willey family, 70.
Willey Hotel, built, 164; burned, 343.
Willey House, built, 89, 157; repaired, 89; burned, 89; Ethan Allen Crawford runs it, 89; Samuel Willey, Jr., moves into, 90; Pendexter moves into, 100; 110, 111; engraving of, 111; repaired by Horace Fabyan, 164; Thomas Cole at, 191; burned, 343.
Willey Slide, occurs, 92; Professor Silliman, 109, 127; Parkman climbs, 127; Sir Charles Lyell examines, 147; Thomas Hill's painting, 200.
Williams, artist, 203.
Williams, M. B., 206.

Williamson, John, 197.
Willis, N. P., 194, 196.
Wilson, Edward L., *Mount Washington in Winter*, 305; on Mount Washington in winter, 319, 327, 328.
Wilson, General John, 77.
Wind velocity on Mount Washington, 320, 322, 323.
"Wine Hills" map, 18.
Winthrop, Governor John, *Journal*, xxv, 20; account of Darby Field's expeditions, 20, 21; account of Gorges and Vines's exploration, 22.
Wireless telegraphy between huts, 354.
Wonnalancet, Indian sachem, 9.
Wood, William, his *New England's Prospect*, quoted from, 8.
Woodbridge, F., 318.
Woodbury, Captain Lot, 161.
Wood-pulp industry, 379, 380.
Woodstock, mound, 3; granted and settled, 62, 63.
Wyman, Ensign Seth, 46.

Yale College, 34.

Zealand Valley, 381, 385, 399.

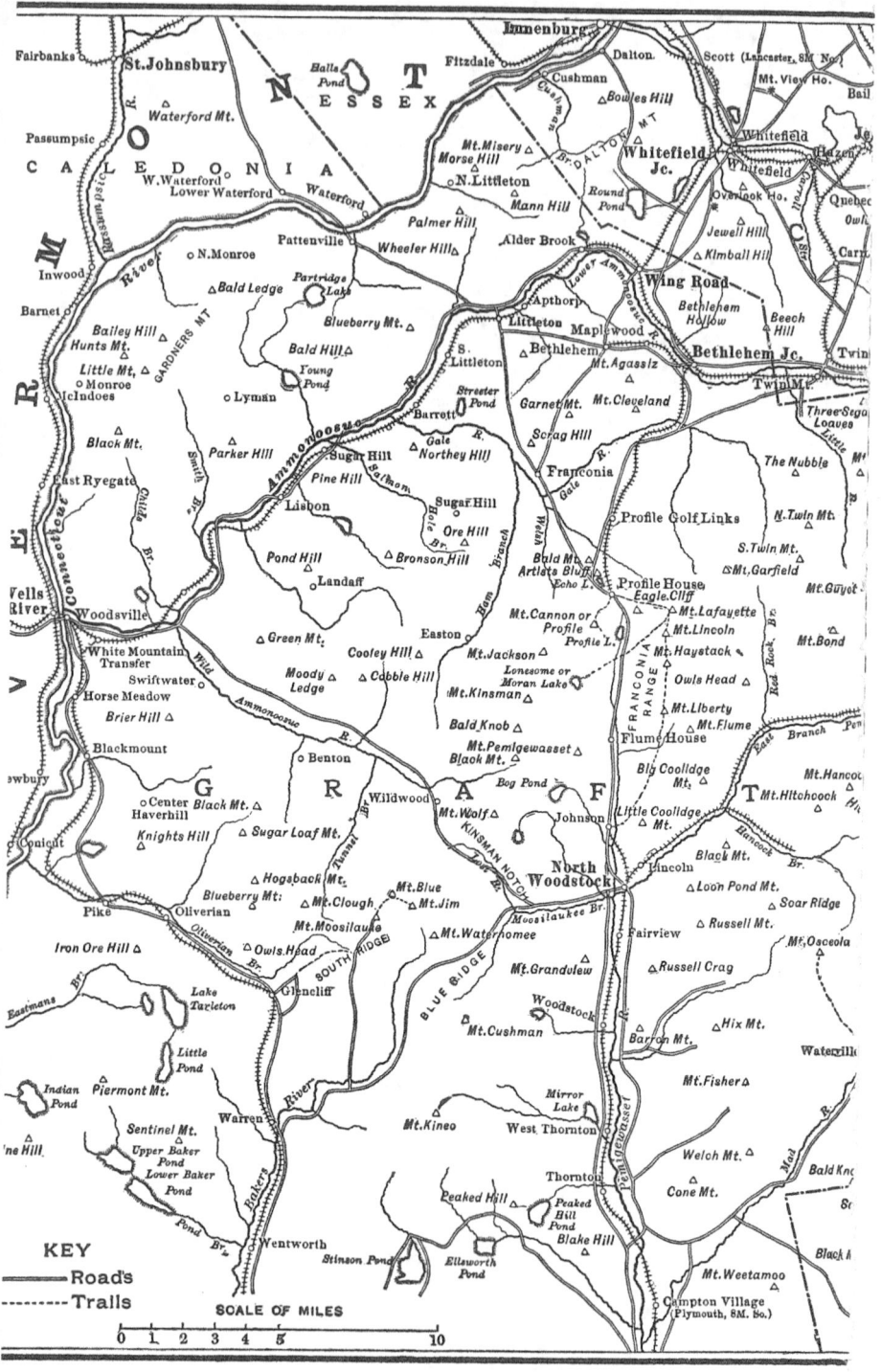

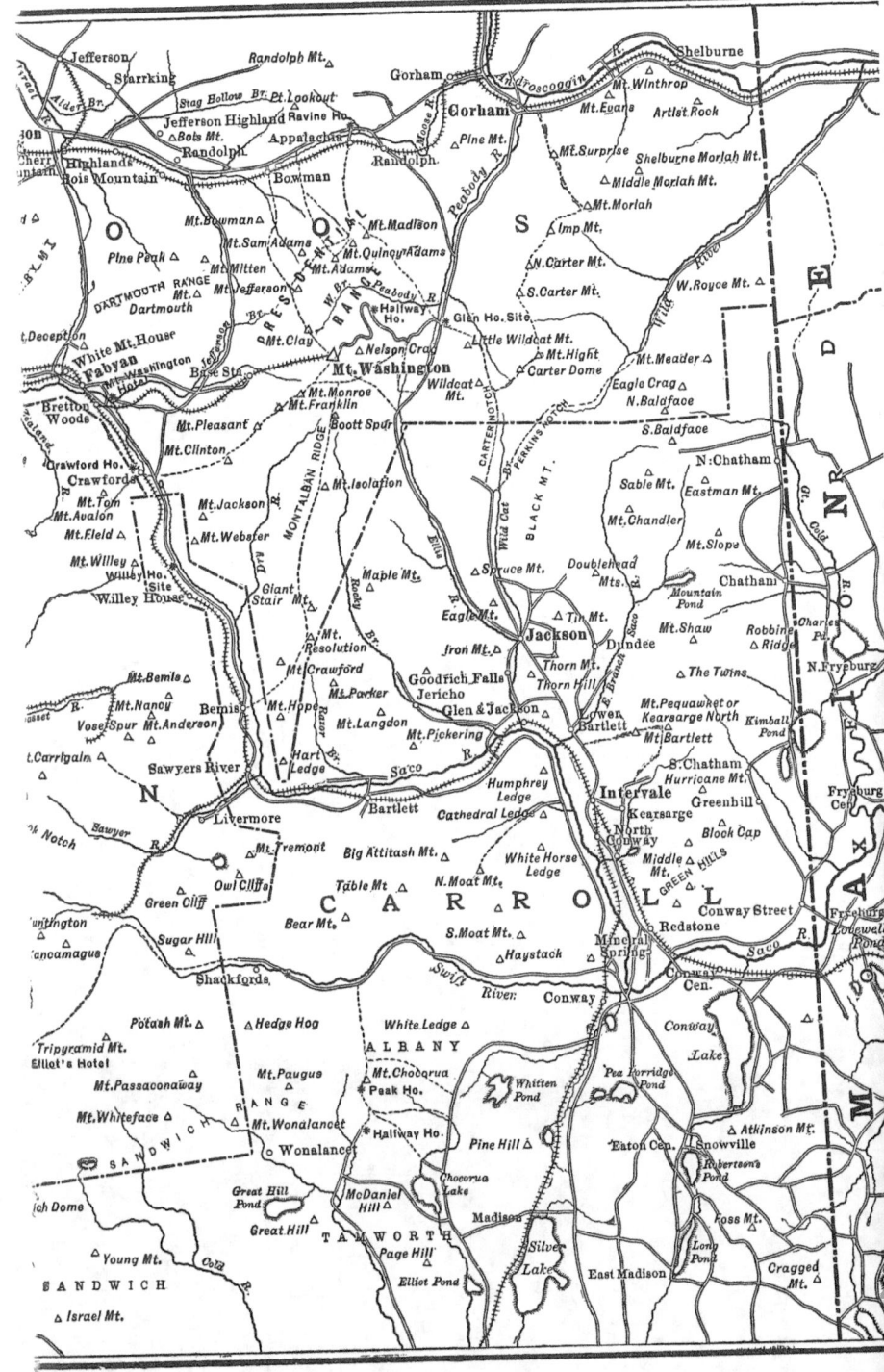

www.ingramcontent.com/pod-product-compliance
Lightning Source LLC
Chambersburg PA
CBHW060909300426
44112CB00011B/1401